# THE PASTOR

## ALSO BY EUGENE PETERSON

### FROM HARPERONE

*Answering God: The Psalms as Tools of Prayer*
*Leap Over a Wall: Earthy Spirituality for Everyday Christians*
*Living the Message: Daily Help for Living the God-Centered Life*
*Praying with the Psalms: A Year of Daily Prayers and Reflections on the Words of David*
*Reversed Thunder: The Revelation of John and the Praying Imagination*
*A Year with Jesus: Daily Readings and Meditations*

### OTHER WORKS

*Christ Plays in Ten Thousand Places: A Conversation in Spiritual Theology*
*The Christmas Troll*
*The Contemplative Pastor: Returning to the Art of Spiritual Direction*
*Eat This Book: A Conversation in the Art of Spiritual Reading*
*First and Second Samuel*
*Five Smooth Stones for Pastoral Work*
*Holy Luck*
*In a Word (with Anneke Kaai)*
*The Jesus Way: A Conversation on the Ways that Jesus Is the Way*
*Like Dew Your Youth: Growing Up with Your Teenager*
*Living the Resurrection*
*A Long Obedience in the Same Direction: Discipleship in an Instant Society*
*The Message: The Bible in Contemporary Language*
*Practice Resurrection: A Conversation on Growing Up in Christ*
*Run with the Horses: A Quest for Life at Its Best*
*Subversive Spirituality*
*Take and Read: Spiritual Reading: An Annotated List*
*Tell It Slant: A Conversation on the Language of Jesus in His Stories and Prayers*
*Traveling Light: Modern Meditations on St. Paul's Letter of Freedom*
*Under the Unpredictable Plant: An Exploration in Vocational Holiness*
*The Unnecessary Pastor (with Marva Dawn)*
*Where Your Treasure Is: Psalms That Summon You from Self to Community*
*The Wisdom of Each Other: A Conversation Between Spiritual Friends*
*Working the Angles: The Shape of Pastoral Integrity*

# THE PASTOR

## A MEMOIR

### EUGENE H. PETERSON

HarperOne
*An Imprint of HarperCollinsPublishers*

HarperOne

Published in association with the literary agency of Alive Communications, Inc., 7680 Goddard St., Suite 200, Colorado Springs, CO 80920. www.alivecommunications.com.

FIRST HARPERCOLLINS PAPERBACK EDITION PUBLISHED IN 2012

Library of Congress Cataloging-in-Publication Data
  Peterson, Eugene H.
    The pastor : a memoir / Eugene H. Peterson. — 1st ed.
      p.  cm.
    ISBN 978–0–06–198821–9
    1. Peterson, Eugene H. 2. Christ Our King (Church : Bel Air, Md.)—Biography.
3. Presbyterian Church (U.S.A.)—Clergy—Biography. I. Title.
BX9225.P466A3  2011
285'.1092—dc22
[B]                                                                                2010023007

        18   19   LSC (H)   10   9

*For Jan*

To insure the greatest efficiency in the dart,
the harpooners of this world
must start to their feet from out of idleness,
and not from out of toil.

—*Herman Melville*

# CONTENTS

# CONTENTS

# CONTENTS

# INTRODUCTION
## *Pastor Pete*

P astor Pete! Pastor Pete! It's Pastor Pete!" The chorus of exclamations came from the mouths of half a dozen children, their faces pressed to the glass of our living-room window. These voices—excited and clamorous—entered my gut with a feeling of poignant loss. I knew that I would never hear myself addressed that way again—*"Pastor."*

Jan and I had left our Maryland congregation a year previous to the children's chorus and had returned for a few days to complete arrangements to sell our house and move our belongings to another city across the continent. There I would be addressed as "Professor." Together we had been pastor to this congregation for nearly thirty years. We had said our good-byes, many of them heart-wrenching. We didn't think we could handle any more emotion. Nobody knew we were back. We were trying to get in and out of town as inconspicuously as possible.

But we were discovered by the children. They were out trick-or-treating while we were at work in our living room getting ready for the arrival of the moving van in the morning. We had forgotten it was Halloween and had left our drapes open as we made our preparations. Masked and costumed, their noses pressed against the glass, they were unrecognizable as the children I had baptized, children of parents I had married, children whose grandparents I had buried over a span of three decades. But they recognized me: "*Pastor . . . Pastor Pete.*"

**I** have no idea who started it, but many years before some of the young people in the congregation had begun calling me Pastor Pete. The usage soon filtered down to the children. Nobody had ever called me Pastor before. But as the years went on, I became accustomed to it and found that I rather liked it. Pastor.

Ours was an informal congregation, and, except for the children and youth, most of the people in it were older than I and addressed me by my given name, Eugene. Which was just fine by me. Somewhere along the way while growing up I developed a rather severe case of anticlericalism. I had little liking for professionalism in matters of religion. If I detected even a whiff of pomposity, I walked away. But *Pastor*, unlike *Reverend* or *Doctor* or *Minister*, especially when used by the youth and children, wasn't tainted with professionalism, at least to my ear. *Pastor* sounded more relational than functional, more affectionate than authoritarian.

**T**his book is the story of my formation as a pastor and how the vocation of pastor formed me. I had never planned to be a pastor, never was aware of any inclination to be a pastor, never "knew what I was going to be when I grew up." And then—at the time it seemed to arrive abruptly—there it was: Pastor.

I can't imagine now *not* being a pastor. I was a pastor long before I knew I was a pastor; I just never had a name for it. Once the name arrived, all kinds of things, seemingly random experiences and memories, gradually began to take a form that was congruent with who I was becoming, like finding a glove that fit my hand perfectly—a *calling*, a fusion of all the pieces of my life, a vocation: Pastor.

But it took a while.

I grew up in a Christian family and embraced the way of Jesus at an early age. *Christian* was a term that seemed as natural to me as my own name. Pastors were part of the landscape but never a significant part of it. In the small-town Montana world in which I was reared, they always seemed marginal to the actual business of living. The one pastor I respected in my growing-up years arrived too late to overcome the accumulation of indifference that in effect placed pastors on the margins of my life. I didn't take them seriously.

I took scripture seriously. I took Jesus seriously. I took church seriously. I took prayer seriously. But not pastors. For the most part, pastors seemed tangential to all that. In our congregation we had preachers and reverends, brothers and sisters, deeper-life teachers and evangelists, missionaries and revivalists and faith healers. But no "pastors." By the time I entered adolescence, putting together fragments of overheard conversations among the adults, I concluded that "pastors" basically came to kill elk with their Winchester 30.06 rifles and catch rainbow trout on dry flies. They came and went regularly from our church. Two years was the usual tenure—three at most. They arrived and left like migrating geese. Some headed north to Canada in the spring where the conditions for adventure were congenial, others south to Mexico in the fall for the winter warmth and solace of sun and sand. Nearly everything of what they talked, preached, and taught had happened someplace else. And it was always glamorous—remarkable miracles and visions. And conversions. As an adolescent, I envied the people who could tell stories of their dramatic conversions from lives of drink and drugs and assorted debaucheries. They were so much more *interesting*. I grew up in a church culture that made an art form of Damascus Road stories. Whenever I heard the stories—and I heard them frequently—I felt so ordinary, so left out. But that didn't last long. After a while all the stories started sounding alike and took on a patina of banality.

They were good storytellers and accomplished publicists for the gospel. But they weren't pastors. Mostly I liked them. But I never respected them. Outside of the morning our family spent with them each Sunday, none—there was one significant exception—seemed particularly interested in God. And I was beginning to get interested in God. But it never occurred to me to become a pastor.

As my world widened, nothing that I observed and experienced in pastors caused me to rethink my adolescent assessment. If anything, it confirmed it: being a pastor is not serious work. Within congregations the work of pastor seemed like a grab bag of religious miscellany. From among outsiders, the general attitude I picked up on was, at best, condescension, at worst, outright disrepute.

Later as a young adult, still attending church most Sundays, I found my way into a more congenial, at least to me, church culture. It wasn't as emotionally interesting as the one I had grown up in. I missed the melodrama. There was considerably less spontaneity and a much deeper sense of responsibility. Instead of emotional pleas for special offerings, supported by desperate stories of suffering and need, these churches had carefully prepared budgets to which people pledged their annual support. Spontaneity was elbowed to the sidelines by responsibility. The men and women in these pulpits were called doctor, head of staff, and minister. There was considerably less vagrancy. But still nothing that I would later identify as pastor.

I came across a poem by Denise Levertov in which she uses the phrase "every step an arrival." She was giving an account of her development as a poet. I recognized in her phrase a metaphor for my own formation as a pastor: every step along the way—becoming the pastor I didn't know I was becoming and the person I now am, an essential component that was silently and slowly being integrated into a coherent life and vocation—an arrival.

There is also this to be said. North American culture does not offer congenial conditions in which to live vocationally as a pastor. Men and women who are pastors in America today find that they have entered into a way of life that is in ruins. The vocation of pastor has been replaced by the strategies of religious entrepreneurs with business plans. Any kind of continuity with pastors in times past is virtually nonexistent. We are a generation that feels as if it is having to start out from scratch to figure out a way to represent and nurture this richly nuanced and all-involving life of Christ in a country that "knew not Joseph."

I love being an American. I love this place in which I have been placed—it's language, its history, its energy. But I don't love "the American way," its culture and values. I don't love the rampant consumerism that treats God as a product to be marketed. I don't love the dehumanizing ways that turn men, women, and children into impersonal roles and causes and statistics. I don't love the competitive spirit that treats others as rivals and even as enemies. The cultural conditions in which I am immersed require, at least for me, a kind of fierce vigilance to guard my vocation from these cultural pollutants so dangerously toxic to persons who want to follow Jesus in the way that he is Jesus. I wanted my life, both my personal and working life, to be shaped by God and the scriptures and prayer.

In the process of realizing my vocational identity as pastor, I couldn't help observing that there was a great deal of confusion and dissatisfaction all around me with pastoral identity. Many pastors, disappointed or disillusioned with their congregations, defect after a few years and find more congenial work. And many congregations, disappointed or disillusioned with their pastors, dismiss them and look for pastors more to their liking. In the fifty years that I have lived the vocation of pastor, these defections and dismissals have reached epidemic proportions in every branch and form of church.

I wonder if at the root of the defection is a cultural assumption that all leaders are people who "get things done," and "make things happen." That is certainly true of the primary leadership models that seep into our awareness from the culture—politicians, businessmen, advertisers, publicists, celebrities, and athletes. But while being a pastor certainly has some of these components, the pervasive element in our two-thousand-year pastoral tradition is not someone who "gets things done" but rather the person placed in the community to pay attention and call attention to "what is going on right now" between men and women, with one another and with God—this kingdom of God that is primarily local, relentlessly personal, and prayerful "without ceasing."

I want to give witness to this way of understanding *pastor*, a way that can't be measured or counted, and often isn't even noticed. *I* didn't notice for a long time. I would like to provide dignity to this essentially modest and often obscure way of life in the kingdom of God.

Along the way, I want to insist that there is no blueprint on file for becoming a pastor. In becoming one, I have found that it is a most context-specific way of life: the pastor's emotional life, family life, experience in the faith, and aptitudes worked out in an actual congregation in the neighborhood in which she or he lives—*these* people just as they are, in *this* place. No copying. No trying to be successful. The ways in which the vocation of pastor is conceived, develops, and comes to birth is unique to each pastor.

The only modifier I can think of that might be useful in honoring the ambiguity and mystery involved in the working life of the pastor is "maybe." Anne Tyler a few years ago wrote a novel with the title *Saint Maybe*. How about *Pastor Maybe?* That would serve both as a disclaimer to expertise (that if we could just copy the right model, we would have it down) and a ready reminder of the unavoidable ambiguity involved in this vocation. *Pastor Maybe*: given the loss of cultural and ecclesiastical consensus on how to live this life, none of us is sure of what we are doing much of the time, only *maybe*.

*Witness*, I think, is the right word. A witness is never the center but only the person who points to or names what is going on at the center—in this case, the action and revelation of God in all the operations of Father, Son, and Holy Spirit. I have neither authority nor inclination to tell anyone else how to do this. Those of us who enter into this way of life, this vocation, this calling, face formidable difficulties both inside and outside congregations—idolatrous expectations from insiders, a consignment to irrelevancy by outsiders. So: in light of the widespread misapprehensions thrown into this melting-pot postmodern culture that is North America, there may be a place for honest reporting from the field. A society as thoroughly secularized as ours hardly knows what to do with a life that develops out of a call from God and is lived out within the conditions of God's revelation. But a witness might be useful.

**W**illiam Faulkner was once asked how he went about writing a book. His answer: "It's like building a chicken coop in a high wind. You grab any board or shingle flying by or loose on the ground and nail it down fast." Like becoming a pastor.

# PART I

## TOPO AND KAIROS

I am a pastor. My work has to do with God and souls—immense mysteries that no one has ever seen at any time. But I carry out this work in conditions—place and time—that I see and measure wherever I find myself, whatever time it is. There is no avoiding the conditions. I want to be mindful of the conditions. I want to be as mindful of the conditions as I am of the holy mysteries.

Place. But not just any place, not just a location marked on a road map, but on a *topo*, a topographic map—with named mountains and rivers, identified wildflowers and forests, elevation above sea level and annual rainfall. I do all my work on this ground. I do not levitate. "Surely the LORD is in *this* place, and I did not know it." Get to know *this* place.

Time. But not just time in general, abstracted to a geometric grid on a calendar or numbers on a clock face, but what the Greeks named *kairos*, pregnancy time, being present to the Presence. I never know what is coming next; "Watch therefore."

I don't want to end up a bureaucrat in the time-management business for God or a librarian cataloguing timeless truths. Salvation is kicking in the womb of creation right now, any time now. Pay attention. Be ready: "The time [kairos] is fulfilled . . ." Repent. Believe.

Staying alert to these place and time conditions—this *topo*, this *kairos*—of my life as pastor, turned out to be more demanding than I thought it would be. But Montana gave a grounding for taking in the terrain and texture of the topo. And John of Patmos showed up in New York City at the right time; the city was a midwife to assist in the birthing, at my come-to-term pregnancy, my kairos, as pastor.

# 1

## MONTANA

### *Sacred Ground and Stories*

I live on the edge of what's left of a massive glacier that began melting ten thousand years ago. The glacier was four thousand feet thick when the meltdown began. It is now a mountain lake, named after an Indian tribe, the Flatheads.

Our Montana home is built on a low cliff of Precambrian rock overlooking this lake. A path curves down fifty feet or so to a boat dock where we launch our canoe and kayaks, swim in the summer, and skate in the winter. Seven miles across the lake to the east, the Mission Range of the Rocky Mountains begins its gradual rise, which in thirty miles spears the horizon with ten-thousand-foot alpine peaks on which a few remnants of the last glacial age stubbornly maintain a precarious existence.

My father bought the lakeshore property in 1946. The War had ended. His meat market was prospering. He wanted to mark this new beginning of peace and prosperity by building a cabin. I helped him. Mostly I carried boards.

We began building in the spring of 1948. I was sixteen. Two or three days a week, I walked after school to his market, picked up a list of supplies he had prepared, drove his red GMC half-ton truck to the O'Neil Lumber Yard, and loaded up. Then I drove across town to our home and picked up my mother, who would have a picnic supper prepared. My ten-year-old sister and four-year-old brother completed the work crew. Then back to the market to get my father and drive the fourteen miles to our building site. When it became too dark to work, we would build a fire on the lakeshore and eat. By October the cabin was built, complete with an outhouse. My father boasted to his friends that we even had running water: "Eugene runs down to the lake with a bucket, and runs back up the hill with the water." My mother named it Koinonia House.

None of us knew it at the time, but it wasn't long before we all recognized that it had become sacred ground, a place of hospitality and healing. My parents were generous people. It wasn't long before people who had been displaced or fallen on hard times were living there. Missionaries suffering from fatigue and illness recovered their health. A fifty-year-old stonemason, the wind knocked out of him by the death of his wife from cancer, started breathing again. After he left, we discovered he had built us a fireplace. An out-of-work bachelor lived there one winter, cut lodgepole pines, and made us a fence. Year in, year out, like so many autumn leaves, stories accumulated: stories of recuperation, of healing, of restored faith, of renewed hope.

A hundred years before we arrived, several Indian tribes—Kootenai, Salish, Kalispell, Flathead—had set up camps in this area. There is some evidence, left behind by early trappers in this valley, that a meadow two hundred yards or so back in the hills west of our cabin had been a medicine site for the Kootenais, a place of visions and healings.

A number of legends out of the Christian Middle Ages preserve stories of sacred sites where, for instance, the Holy Grail had been kept or the ark of the covenant had been buried and still retained holy energies—holy ground, ground soaked in the sacred where conditions were propitious for cultivating the presence of God. I don't know what to make of these stories, but in my adolescence I sometimes wondered if something like that could be going on in this place. I sometimes wonder still.

What I do know is that for sixty-five years now this place has provided a protected space and time to become who I am. It has been a centering and deepening place of prayer and meditation, reflection and understanding, conversation and reading. Here I savored experiences and meetings, making them my own, attentive as they arranged themselves within me, becoming me, and I all the while becoming, without my knowing it, a pastor.

A year or two after the completion of the cabin—I was about seventeen—I began intentionally coming to what I had already started thinking of as sacred ground for parts of a day, sometimes for overnight, seeking out the solitary, embracing the quiet, listening, listening, listening. Father, Son, Holy Spirit. I was not always alone. In those early years my parents and siblings were often present. Later, while in college, I would bring friends here on Christmas and spring breaks. And since marriage, my wife and three children and six grandchildren share the pilgrimage as we come and go from this place, this holy place.

I have often had occasion while walking these hills or kayaking this lake to reflect on how important *place* is in living the Christian faith. As I let the biblical revelation form my imagination, geography—this specifically Montana, Flathead Valley geography—became as important in orienting me in "the land of the living" as theology and the Bible did. I was becoming aware that every detail in the life of salvation that I was becoming familiar with in the scriptures took shape in named places that, with a good map, I can still locate: Ur and Haran, Bethel and Peniel, Sinai and Shiloh, Anathoth and Jerusalem, Nazareth and Bethlehem, Bethany and Emmaus. I was also learning that every detail in my life of salvation was taking place on and in a named place: Stanwood and Kalispell to begin with, later extended to include Seattle and New York City, White Plains and Baltimore, Bel Air and Pittsburgh, Vancouver and Lakeside. Soil and stone, latitude and longitude, lakes and mountains, towns and cities keep a life of faith grounded, rooted, in *place*. But wherever I went, I always ended up here. This was the geography of my imagination: the sighting of a pygmy owl in feathered silence pouncing on a field mouse on Blacktail Mountain, the emergence through spring snow of the first avalanche lilies in Jack's Meadow, surprising a grizzly bear, the iconic beast of these mountains, on the Garden Wall trail. Holy ground, sacred space.

I grew up in a church environment that tended to be dismissive of "this world" in favor of "spiritual things." By buying this lakefront property and building this cabin, my father provided me and, as it turned out, many others, with a rooting and grounding, a sense of *thisness* and *hereness,* for the faith that was maturing in me. He provided a shrine, a sacred place where "on earth as it is in heaven" could be prayed and practiced. I wouldn't have been able to articulate all this at the time, but in retrospect I recognize that a strong conviction was forming within me that the life of faith cannot be lived in general or by abstractions. All the great realities that we can't touch or see take form on ground that we *can* touch and see.

Several years later I came across a book by the Scottish pastor, George Adam Smith: *The Historical Geography of the Holy Land.* He had spent several months on horseback and mule crisscrossing Palestine in the late nineteenth century, describing what seemed to me, from his detailed reporting, every square foot of that land. His vivid writing put my feet on the ground where Abraham walked, the fields on which David did battle, the garden in which Jesus prayed. There were large, fold-out maps that I studied in detail. I lived in Smith's book. I think I must have spent as many months reading and rereading what he wrote as he did writing it. After those few months my imagination was furnished with a formidable geographical bulwark against disembodied truths, heaven disconnected from earth. It became every bit as significant to me as any text on theology I was to read. That book confirmed for me the emerging perceptions of "on earth as it is in heaven," a ladder, so to speak. With Jacob, I knelt on this holy ground, confessing with him that "God was in this place, but I knew it not."

This place and home on the shore of what's left of the glacier have provided the very conditions that North American culture has failed to provide, conditions in which I have been able to realize and live into the many dimensions that go into forming the vocation of pastor. If I need an adjective to identify the conditions, I think *sacred* would do just fine: *sacred* space—uncrowded and quiet; *sacred* canopy—the big sky "telling the glory of God"; *sacred* ground—

rocks and hills, mountains and meadows marked by the footsteps of my grand-parents and parents, my children and grandchildren, praying and climbing, strolling and wandering—sojourners all—on our way to what the writer of Hebrews names "a better country."

I was acquiring a sacred imagination strong enough to reject and resist the relentlessly secularized and ghettoized one-dimensional caricature that as-signed American pastors to jobs in a workplace that markets religion. When I looked around me and observed churches in competition with one another for their share in the religious market, hiring pastors to provide religious goods and services for a culture of God consumers, I wanted nothing to do with it. I couldn't see that either God or place—holy God, sacred place—was a signifi-cant consideration in forming a pastoral identity in America.

But all the while, this mountain lake, these *sacred* waters that brought to-gether all the elements of sacred place and sky, was doing its work in me:

> *Huge cloud fists assault*
> *The blue exposed bare midriff of sky;*
> *The firmament doubles up in pain.*
> *Lightnings rip and thunders shout,*
> *Mother nature's children quarrel.*
> *And then, as suddenly as it began,*
> *It's over. Noah's heirs, perceptions*
> *Cleansed, look out on a disarmed world*
> *At ease and ozone fragrant. Still waters.*
> *What barometric shift*
> *Rearranged these ferocities*
> *Into a peace-pulsating rainbow*
> *Sign? My enemy turns his other*
> *Cheek; I drop my guard. A mirror*
> *Lake reflects the filtered colors;*
> *Breeze-stirred pine trees quietly sing.*

I start with place: this two acres of holy ground perched high and dry on the edge of what's left of the melted glacier. Place gathers stories, relationships, memories. This two acres of sacred landscape in the mountains of Montana has provided the material conditions for preserving a continuity of story in the course of living in eighteen residences located variously in five states and two countries. It has provided a stable location in space and time to give prayerful, meditative, discerning attention to the ways in which my life is being written into the comprehensive salvation story. It is the holy ground from which choke-cherry blossoms scent the spring air and giant ponderosa pines keep sentinel watch in the forest. It opens out on an immense glacier-cut horizon against which the invisibilities of Father, Son, and Holy Spirit form a believing imagi-nation where the "inside is larger than the outside."

This is where the bulk of the formative work in my pastoral vocation either began, was clarified, or came to a fullness. Schools were useful as background but were never the main thing. Teachers and professors were significant but not at the center. Friends and books made their mark but only as voices in a larger conversation. This place is the holy ground—my Midian burning bush, my Horeb cave, my Patmos island—that has kept me grounded and to which I have repeatedly returned. I have lived sixty years of my adult life in cities and suburbs in other places, but most of those years I returned for at least a month, sometimes more, once for twelve months—an entire sabbatical year—to clar-ify and deepen my pastoral vocation on this sacred ground. And even when I was not here physically, the internalized space grounded me. And it is from this place that I am now writing my witness.

# 2

## NEW YORK

### *Pastor John of Patmos*

After a long period of gestation, the actual birthing of my pastoral vocation took place over a three-year period from 1959 to 1962 in and around New York City. The birthing center was at the intersection of two jobs, one as assistant professor at the New York City seminary from which I had graduated two years earlier, the second as associate pastor at a Presbyterian congregation in White Plains, just north of the city.

The seminary that trained me had a single focus, defined as a total immersion in the English Bible, the biblical revelation in our mother tongue. This immersion was not just individual but corporate, incarnated in students and professors who lived and prayed, studied and conversed in a twelve-story building on East Forty-ninth Street. It was a small school of seventy or so students that I realize now in retrospect formed a unique minority ethos. Daily life at the seminary comprised common prayer in the chapel, common meals in the refectory, common play in the requisite volleyball game on the roof after lunch each day. Classroom lectures and library reading were held together in this intricate relational network of common life. All of this took place on a quiet side street bordering the maelstrom of noisy, jostling, harried, secular, cutthroat, competitive New York City.

I had only the vaguest of ideas of why I was there and certainly nothing that I would recognize as a pastoral vocation. I didn't know it at the time, but what I absorbed in my subconscious, which eventually surfaced years later, was a developing conviction that the most effective strategy for change, for revolution—at least on the large scale that the kingdom of God involves—comes from a minority working from the margins. I could not have articulated it then, but my seminary experience later germinated into the embrace of a vocational identity as necessarily minority, that a minority people working from the margins has the best chance of being a community capable of penetrating the noncommunity, the mob, the depersonalized, function-defined crowd that is the sociological norm of America.

I had no idea then of how my years of study and community at the seminary would be worked out vocationally. The only real surprise academically was that in the process of a thorough saturation in the English Bible, I discovered a taste for Greek and Hebrew. When I graduated—the year was 1957—I was as vocationally vague as when I had arrived three years earlier. One of my professors took care of that by sending me off to Johns Hopkins University in Baltimore to do graduate study in Semitic languages with his old professor, William Albright, with the suggestion that I might return and teach with him in the field of Old Testament.

I did return, bringing Jan with me. We met and were married during the years in Baltimore. And I did teach. My assigned courses were Greek and Hebrew. The seminary was paying me what they could get by with, but it wasn't enough for us to get by with. So I added another job, this one as the associate pastor in the Presbyterian Church in White Plains, fully expecting it to be temporary. I thought of it as something of an off-the-cuff job. I did it for the money and only for the money, for I had no intention at the time of being a pastor. I assumed, in a rather desultory way, that I would be a professor. The church, a thirty-minute commute by train from the seminary, provided us with housing. Two days a week, Tuesday and Thursday, I was in the seminary classroom at 235 East Forty-ninth Street, teaching students Greek declensions and Hebrew syntax. Four days a week I worked out of an eighteenth-century stone church building at 39 North Broadway in White Plains. Monday was set apart as Sabbath. There I spent my time in prayer, conversation, and companionship with saints and sinners as they followed Jesus, many of them by fits and starts, as together we picked our way through the wasteland of American culture.

But the most significant thing at the time was that Jan and I were learning how to be married. We had been married the previous year while still in Baltimore, but the conditions there had been such that we hardly had time to be married. We lived in a dark basement apartment with sewage problems. Jan was plunged into her first year of teaching a crowded classroom of thirty-nine first graders from a rapidly changing inner-city neighborhood of mostly single-parent families. I walked with her to the streetcar at seven o'clock each morning. She returned in the late afternoon exhausted. Supper conversation was laced with a detailed narrative of her eight hours of tyranny at the hands of Brucie, Henry, Melissa and the other gang members. About three months into the school year I had occasion to drive to her school and pick her up. We were going Christmas shopping. I was waiting for Jan outside the classroom door when the bell rang. The door opened and the children poured out. I wasn't prepared for what I saw. I was expecting hulking Huns with switchblades and Amazonian warrior women, but here were all these little kids running and laughing, free from their classroom cage. These tykes? Terrorizing my wife? It turned out to be a long year.

Meanwhile I was doing doctoral work in Semitic languages—the most exhilarating intellectual world I had ever lived in but also the most demanding. At the same time I had taken a job at a large church to administer its educational programs. What I didn't know was that the man who would be supervising me was a tyrant. Not quite like the gang that tyrannized Jan every day but every bit as abusive.

A year of that life in Baltimore was all either one of us could take. We loved being married but didn't have much of either time or energy to explore this new way of life. We completed our commitments to the school and church as well as we were able and made our way to New York and the seminary. I taught my languages in a classroom; I worked as a pastor in a congregation where we were provided with generous housing on the ground floor of a spacious Victorian house with a wraparound porch and a large fireplace. Other members of the church staff occupied the second and third floors.

We had a three-year honeymoon. Jan had the space and time to create a place of welcoming hospitality. Our first child arrived: Jan became a mother and I became a father. We became a family. A friend pointed out to me that when God called Abraham and Sarah to be our ancestors in the faith, the definitive act was to make them parents. We entered into the practice of what we had promised and been promised—all the intricacies of love and forgiveness, of grace and humility. We didn't know how much we didn't know. We had a lot to learn. Me especially. Being married was far more demanding than mastering the Semitic languages of Akkadian, Syriac, and Ugaritic. We didn't know it was going to be this difficult—and this good.

In this new country of marriage I worked the two jobs, side by side, for most of three years: two days a week an assistant professor in a classroom, four days a week an associate pastor in a congregation. And all week, every week, marriage—realizing, detail by detail, the many dimensions involved in becoming "one flesh."

During those three years, our vocations, pastor and pastor's wife, gradually clarified and became integrated. When they finally came into focus, I realized that I was not, in my bones, a professor at all. I was a pastor. This came as a total surprise to me for I had never seriously entertained the life of pastor as a vocation. It was no less a surprise to Jan. Many years before we met, she had prayed for a vocation as a pastor's wife but had set it aside in order to marry me. For my part I now set aside my plans to be a professor-to-be in order to be married to her as a pastor.

When we left Baltimore, I had completed all my doctoral academic work but had not yet written my dissertation. And my professor, Dr. Albright, retired. He arranged for me to write the dissertation under the supervision of his friend Dr. Brevard Childs at Yale. I visited Professor Childs in New Haven, an easy drive from White Plains. We got on well together and arrangements were made, complete with a generous stipend. I was set. Except that by this time I was not at all sure about the professor business and I was becoming more certain of the pastor route, but that was not yet set in stone. Saying no to the Ph.D. would effectively shut the door to being a professor. Jan and I knew it was a big decision. All my friends advised against it. We talked it over from every angle. Certainty eluded us. And then our prayers for discernment cleared the air. I wrote a letter to Professor Childs and dropped it in the corner mailbox. Indecision evaporated in that act. I have never since, even for a moment, regretted that decision.

It was the conjunction of classroom, congregation, and marriage that did it, set off a chain reaction that produced *pastor* and *pastor's wife*. The world of the classroom, the world of congregation, and the world of marriage interacted at a level below consciousness. Interaction is too tame a word. The conjunction was *catalytic*. They were no longer three distinct worlds. A fourth world came into being. One and one and one did not equal three. It was more like they equaled five—a teaching assignment plus a church job plus marriage added up to a pastoral vocation. Not all at once. The gestation took most of three years. But at some point along the way the waters broke and there we were—pastor and pastor's wife. Pastor's wife became as vocational for Jan as pastor did for me.

Here is a rough sketch of how it happened. In addition to teaching the biblical languages at the seminary, I was also pressed into service as a kind of faculty utility infielder, each semester picking up a course vacated by a professor on sabbatical. One of those courses was the book of Revelation. As I taught, I began to recognize early embryonic outlines of my pastoral vocation that had been taking form a few years earlier when I was a student taking this same course. A few weeks into teaching the course, I began imagining myself in the apocalyptic world of the Revelation and identifying myself with John of Patmos as a pastor. John, doing his work on the prison island of Patmos, was exiled from the seven congregations that he served as a pastor. Remarkably, he was undeterred by the exile conditions, doing his Lord's Day work with them all the same, worshipping his and their Lord Jesus.

Until that time the term *pastor* had never set up any resonance in me—it was a flat word without depth. But now I was attempting to teach what John saw and wrote to his people and doing it in the exact pagan New York City conditions that mirrored the Roman culture in which John saw and wrote. John's pastoral identity worked itself into my imagination. I realized that John's vocation as pastor was not confined to those seven sermons addressed to his miniscule congregations, but got expressed in the urgency and sovereignty and beauty and drama that pervaded the entire book. The sermons, yes, but also the dragon and the throne, the horsemen and the trumpets, the whore and the bride, the lake of fire and the foursquare gem-emblazoned city—the entire work of salvation taking place on that very Lord's Day. And embedded, of all places, in the massive, arrogant, bullying Roman Empire. Meanwhile, on alternate days in the White Plains congregation I was getting a firsthand feel for what it meant to be a pastor on the ground.

Virginia, for instance. She was a shy worshipper easily overlooked. She showed up in my study one day visibly terrified. Shaking, she told me that her husband, Nick, was being threatened by the shylocks—if he didn't come up with five thousand dollars before the week was out, they would shatter his knees. Nick was a compulsive gambler, betting mostly on the horses. The shylocks who financed gambling addictions were merciless. She didn't know where to turn. After listening to her stories, the tangled web of criminal intimidation and deception, the shylocks and their victims, I knew I was in over my head. I was able to put her in touch with a retired Brooklyn cop who wasn't intimidated. I don't know if I was much help to her. But she was a help to me. She was in church each Sunday, but no longer overlooked. Her presence in the sanctuary was proof against any superficial assessment of people in the congregation as complacent shoppers for a comfortable pew. I was pastor to people who were in the lion's den, to men and women facing wild beasts in the Colosseum.

I began to think of John of Patmos as the patron saint of pastors. I began to imagine myself into that intersecting work and world of Patmos and White Plains and New York.

During that time I became aware of something else: the contrast between being a professor in a classroom and a pastor in a congregation. Professors and pastors have always held important leadership positions in the Christian world, but for me professors unquestionably topped the hierarchy. Pastors were shadowy, undefined figures in the background. And now I was a professor, a bona fide player in the minor leagues of academia but on my way, I assumed, to the big leagues. I loved the teaching; I loved the dynamics of the classroom; I loved getting it right, the truth of the scriptures—Isaiah and the Psalms, Matthew and Paul—the sense of being given responsibility for bringing the learning of the great teachers in our tradition—Origin and Augustine, Luther and Calvin—into the lives of these students. And I loved the mental and spiritual energy that was almost palpable as men and women participated and understood what it meant to be part of this great community of scripture-taught, scripture-formed Christians.

As I spent these weeks in the company of John of Patmos, with alternate days in the congregation, I was beginning to feel that the classroom was too easy. The room was too small and orderly to do justice to the largeness of the subject matter—the extravagance of the beauty, the exuberance of the language. Too much was excluded from the classroom—too much life, too much of the world, too much of the students, the complexities of relationships, the intricacy of emotions. The classroom was too tidy. I missed the texture of the weather, the smell of cooking, the jostle of shoulders and elbows on a crowded sidewalk.

In the congregation, by contrast, everything was going on at once, random, unscheduled, accompanied too much of the time by undisciplined and trivializing small talk. Babies born squalling, people dying neglected, and in between the parenthesis of birth and death, lifetimes of ambiguity: adolescents making an unholy mess of growing up and their parents muddling through as guilty bystanders. Also, of course, heroic holiness, stunningly beautiful prayers, sacrificial love surfacing from the tangled emotions in a difficult family, a song in the night, glimpses of glory, the sullen betrayal of a bored spouse quietly redeemed from years of self-imprisoned self-worship by forgiveness and grace: Father, Son, and Holy Ghost. And all of this mixed together. In this world, sin was not a word defined in a lexicon. Salvation was not a reference traced down in a concordance. Every act of sin and every event of salvation involved a personal name in a grammar of imperatives and promises in a messy community of friends and neighbors, parents and grandparents, none of whom fit a stereotype.

The only hour of the week that had any predictable, uninterrupted order to it was Sunday morning, when the story of creation and covenant was told and the prayers of confession and praise were said and sung. I was learning that for a pastor, the rest of the week was spent getting that story and those prayers heard and prayed in the personal and unique particulars of these people. I had just spent an hour of worship with them but now was mixing it up with them in a world of dragons and whores, blood flowing as high as a horse's bridle, and the news headlines trumpeting catastrophic disasters.

It took me by surprise to find myself preferring those four days spent in the congregation under the aegis of Pastor John of Patmos to the two days I was teaching about him in the classroom. There is something wonderfully satisfying about the clean definitions and precise explanations in a lecture hall. Chalkboards and PowerPoint presentations are not tolerant of ambiguities. I was finding myself vocationally at home in the mysteries of worship and baptism and Eucharist in my Ephesus-Smyrna-Pergamum-Thyatira-Sardis-Philadelphia-Laodicea congregation. I was finding congenial company rubbing shoulders with the four horsemen, the trumpeting angels, Michael and the beast with ten horns and seven heads, the 144,000, the supper of the Lamb, and the river of life bright as crystal.

It took a while to reorder our imaginations along the lines of John of Patmos, but in three years it was done: we were pastor and pastor's wife. Pastor's *wife*, not pastor's helper. Pastor's wife was as vocational for Jan as pastor was for me, a holy calling, holy orders. We didn't yet know the details of what we would be doing and how. But we knew who we were. Our vocational identities were different, but not competing. Jan's identity was not as defined by role and tasks as mine and did not carry with it social recognition, but month after month the conviction deepened—"this is who I am."

We were ready. We received a call to organize a new congregation near Baltimore. We spent the next twenty-nine years in that place, living into our emerging (and merging) identities ("every step an arrival") in an American suburb that was as marginal to the culture and politics of America as the congregations of John of Patmos were marginal to the culture and politics of Rome.

# PART II
## "INTENTLY HAPHAZARD"

In a poem, the same poem I mentioned earlier, Denise Levertov describes a dog going "intently haphazard." I can see that dog. I used to own that dog, going from bush to fire hydrant to tree, sniffing his way along, pausing momentarily to add his scent to what he had just come across, "intently haphazard." There is obviously no lack of intention in the dog's behavior, but if you could have asked him what his intention was and he could have answered, he wouldn't have been able to tell you where he was headed—just one scent after another. Seemingly haphazard. But not without purpose. A doggy instinct for what he wouldn't be able to name keeps him true to who he is, a dog. At the end of the day it is all absorbed in his canine psyche.

Something like that is the way *pastor* feels to me. Pastor: not something added on to or imposed on who I am; it was there all along. But it was not linear—no straight-line development. Seemingly unconnected, *haphazard* events and people turned out to be organic to who I am. In retrospect the *intent* comes as no surprise.

The topographical map of my developing pastoral vocation begins on the sacred ground of Montana, touches down at my university in Seattle, my seminary in New York City, graduate school in Baltimore, gathering stories along the way, with an eventual arrival at a corn field in Maryland, the building site for a new Christian congregation.

# 3

## MY MOTHER'S SONGS AND STORIES

en months after my parents married, my mother gave birth to me. She was twenty years old. In my early memories of her, memories confirmed by photographs, she was strikingly attractive. Her auburn hair was luxuriously long, never cut during my childhood years. This was for religious, not cosmetic, reasons. She was a little over five feet tall with a well-proportioned body. She had a passion for life and Jesus and was zealous to share it.

When I was three, maybe four, years old, she began taking me with her on Sunday evenings to hold religious meetings in small, out-of-the-way settlements of miners and lumberjacks scattered around our valley in the northern Rocky Mountains. We met in one-room schoolhouses and grange halls. There were six or seven locations to which we would go—Kila and Ferndale, Olney and Marion, Hungry Horse and Coram—making a circuit every couple of months. We did it all year long, summer and winter.

My father during these years was working long and hard hours as a butcher, cobbling together a meat-cutting business. He only shows up marginally in these early memories. I think it is possible that he didn't even know where we were those Sunday nights. It couldn't have been easy to start a small business in those Depression years. He was the son of immigrant Swedish parents who had left Sweden because of hard times. Now times were hard in America. While many in our valley were living in Civilian Conservation Corps camps and doing make-work for the Work Projects Administration (WPA), he was determined "to be my own boss," and he was—barely. The only thing worse than "working for the government" (FDR's WPA) was to be unemployed. He had no patience with someone who didn't work, even if there were no jobs to be had. It didn't stop him. He would work for himself. It was slow going, but in ten years his business was flourishing.

What I wasn't to learn for a number of years was that my father routinely extended his impatience to the pastors in our congregation. Not many of our pastors escaped his behind-their-backs dismissal: "He's never done a day's work in his life."

All this time, while my father was working those long and hard hours, determined to put bread on the table and meat in the pot, laying foundations that would undergird my eventual vocation as a pastor, my mother, without knowing what she was doing, was developing an imagination in me for being a pastor.

I have no idea how this young woman with a small child as her chaperone managed to gather a congregation of working men from those logging and mining camps to sing gospel songs, listen to gospel stories, and let themselves be prayed for on those Sunday nights in the thick of the Depression.

My mother had a plain contralto singing voice, a folksinger voice that years later I recognized in Joan Baez. She accompanied herself with either accordion or guitar. She led her rustic congregations in country gospel songs, religious folk ballads, and old hymns—"Life Is Like a Mountain Railroad," "Great Speckled Bird," "Old-Time Religion," and "When the Roll Is Called up Yonder." The lumberjacks and miners in their clomping hobnail boots, bib overalls, and flannel shirts sang along. As they sang the sentimental old songs, they wept, honking into their red bandannas, wiping their tears without embarrassment. Not genteel congregations these, the twenty-five or thirty men sitting on backless benches (I never remember a woman among them), meeting those Sunday nights. Occasionally one of them would spit tobacco juice out an open window. Sometimes they would miss. It was the first time I had seen that particular athletic feat performed.

Then she would preach. She was a wonderful storyteller, telling stories out of scripture and out of life. She elaborated and embellished the stories. Later in life when I was reading the Bible for myself, I was frequently surprised by glaring omissions in the text. The Holy Spirit left out some of the best parts. Occasionally she would slip into an incantatory style that I have heard since only in African American churches, catching a phrase at its crest, riding it like a surfer gathering momentum, and then receding into a quiet hush.

My favorite story from those years was Samuel's anointing of David to be king. The story began in my mother's telling of it with Samuel, an old man with his beard down to his knees. He was a thick, stocky man, built like a fire hydrant, who from a distance looked like a fountain, white hair pouring from his head.

There was an unhurried air about him, leisurely even. The kind of relaxed leisureliness that flows from a person who knows what he's about, who knows where he's going and what he's doing. No need for hurry if you're confident in who you are.

Samuel was headed for Bethlehem, a small town nearly identical with the one we lived in, surrounded by forested hills that were ominous with wild beasts. Three boys, out searching in the fields for Canaanite arrowheads—arrowheads were all the rage that year, and every boy in Bethlehem had his treasured collection—spotted him and ran back to town to report what they had seen. The news spread rapidly: God's prophet was approaching the village! Legendary Samuel. Fierce and famous Samuel. Fear gripped every heart. What had they done wrong? Who had sinned? Samuel wasn't known for his casual, drop-in visits. His enormous reputation didn't rest on a lifetime of accumulated small talk. What terrible misdoing in Bethlehem that required prophetic visitation had reached the ears of Samuel?

But the anxiety soon gave way to anticipation. Samuel let them know that he had come to lead them in festive worship, gather them in celebration before God. Word got around. The mood shifted from guilt to gaiety in no time. A heifer was killed and a barbecue pit prepared. Before long the entire village was caught up in something that resembled what I knew as the county fair that arrived the first week in August and was the high point of every summer for me.

As she told the story, my mother didn't herself introduce carnival rides and kewpie dolls, cotton candy and the aroma of hot dogs into Iron Age Bethlehem, but she did nothing to interfere with my imagination. I filled in all the details required to make me fully at home in the story: calf-roping, bull-riding, the greased pig, a Ferris wheel, all my friends with their 4-H animals, cowgirls and cowboys from miles around resplendent in sequined shirts and shining boots.

As it turned out, there was more to Samuel's visit than a villagewide celebration as the people of God. A local farmer named Jesse and his eight sons were singled out for attention. Why Samuel was interested in Jesse and his sons wasn't made clear to the villagers, and very likely the general festivities in which everyone was caught up distracted people from noticing the prophet's interest in the Jesse family, which is exactly what they were intended to do. But *I* knew why Samuel was interested. The storyteller had confided in me; I had insider information: Samuel was out looking for a replacement for King Saul.

Having located Jesse and his sons, Samuel proceeded to interview and examine each of them. I pictured this as taking place at the grandstand in the fairgrounds with Samuel, severe and venerable, out in the middle of the field at the judge's stand. Jesse brought his sons before Samuel one at a time, like prize farm animals on halters. The grandstand was packed with spectators.

Eliab, the eldest son and a swaggering bully, was the first. His mountainous size and rough-hewn looks commanded attention. Samuel was impressed. Who could *not* be impressed? Hulking and brutish Eliab was used to getting his own way by sheer force of muscle. He had a black mop of hair that he never bothered to brush. His nose wandered down his face looking, until it was almost too late, for a good place to stop. He dressed in bib overalls and wore hobnailed boots. He never changed his socks. It mattered little whether people liked or disliked what they saw—Eliab *dominated*. Clearly, here was a man who could get things done. Samuel, like everyone else in the community, was taken in by his appearance. But soon Samuel's God-trained prophetic eye penetrated the surface appearance to Eliab's interior. There he didn't see much to write home about. No king material within.

Abinadab, the next, was an intellectual snob. A tall, stringy beanpole, he stood before Samuel with sneering arrogance. He was the only brother who had been to college. He used big words, showing off his prestigious learning every chance he got. He had squinty eyes behind thick Coke-bottle glasses. Samuel dismissed him with a gesture.

Shammah, also called Shimea, was third. Shammah was a mincing little sophisticate in Calvin Klein jeans and alligator cowboy boots. He hated living in backwater Bethlehem. He could hardly get across the street without getting cow flop on his boots. Mingling with all these common people, with their vulgar games and coarse entertainment, was torture for him. He didn't know what Samuel was up to, but it looked as if it could be a ticket to a finer life—a life of culture and taste. But Samuel dismissed him with a shake of his head.

After the third son, the Bible quits naming. It was years before I knew that, for my mother named them all. It didn't matter that the names departed substantially from Semitic sounds; they served her purpose and my imagination well enough. Ole was the fourth, then Gump, Klug, and finally Chugger. Proudly presented by Jesse, each stood before Samuel. As each in turn was rejected, tension built up—*this* son, certainly, would be chosen. Yet none was chosen.

The show was over. Jesse was pathetic in his disappointment. The seven sons were humiliated. The grandstand and bleacher crowds were starting to get restless, feeling gypped, some of them demanding their money back. They had paid a good price, after all, to see Samuel in his prophetic appearance. And the performance had started off well enough as he got everyone's attention, skillfully building to a climax. And now this . . . this, *nothing*.

Samuel was bewildered. Had he missed a key element in God's message? Was he losing his prophetic edge? Did he have the right town? "This *is* Bethlehem, isn't it?" Did he have the right family? "You *are* Jesse, aren't you?"

Well—there must be another son.

As it turned out, and as the whole world now knows, there was another son—David. But he enters the story unnamed, dismissively referred to by his

father as "the baby brother"—in Hebrew, *haqqaton*, the youngest, in effect
saying: "Well, there's the baby brother, but he's out tending the sheep." If you
are the youngest of eight brothers, you're probably never going to be thought of
as other than the kid brother. *Haqqaton* carries undertones of insignificance,
of not counting for very much—certainly not a prime candidate for prestigious
work. The family runt.

His father's condescending opinion of him (shared presumably by his brothers) is confirmed by the job to which he's assigned—"tending the sheep." The
least demanding of all jobs on the farm, the place where he could do the least
damage. Babysitting for a neighbor or sacking groceries at the supermarket
would be equivalent jobs in our economy.

Because David was out of the way and mostly ignored as he tended the
sheep, nobody had thought to bring him to Bethlehem that day. Yet it was
David who was chosen. Chosen and anointed. Chosen not for what anybody
saw in him—not his father, his brothers, not even Samuel—but because of
what God saw in him. And then anointed as king by God through Samuel to
live to God's glory.

As so often happens in things like this, the dissonance between what was
done and what people expected was so great that it's unlikely anyone in Bethlehem "saw" the anointing. In looking back, they would have remembered that
David had showed up late as usual. But those memories would have faded fast.
It wouldn't have been long before the seven brothers were dominating the town
again with their pushiness and David was out with his sheep, out of sight and
out of mind.

But I didn't forget. Throughout my childhood, in my mother's telling of the
story, I became David. I was always David. I'm *still* David.

In the wonderful Montana winter nights of wind and cold, the rooms we met
in were heated by barrel stoves. On lucky nights I would be permitted to tend
the fire, inserting stove wood in the barrels, trying to maintain a room temperature roughly equivalent to the blaze kindled by my mother's songs and stories.

Leaving those grange halls and schoolhouses, we would sometimes get stuck
in snowdrifts. The men would rally to our rescue, pushing or pulling us out of
ditches or drifts, yelling curses—and then apologizing in confused embarrass-

ment. I heard the best preaching of my lifetime those nights—and the most colorful cursing.

Was she fearless or only naive, this genteel, beautiful woman out in the country those Sunday nights among those rough, all-male, female-starved congregations with a small boy as escort? I don't think it was naïveté. It was passion and the love that casts out fear.

I loved it. It was high adventure for me. Especially in winter, when there was an edge of danger in the driving and an aura of huddled coziness in the bare halls heated by barrel stoves. I loved the stories. I loved the songs. I loved being in the company of those rough-hewn men who seemed to have just stepped out of a Norwegian folk tale. I loved being with my passionate mother, who was having such a good time telling lumberjacks and miners about God.

This went on until I was six. It stopped because my mother gave birth to my sister and there was now a baby to tend to. But when my sister was old enough to join us, it was not resumed. Later, when I was a teenager, I asked her why she never started up the Sunday-night meetings again. She told me that a man, having learned of what she had been doing, confronted her after Sunday-morning worship in our church with an open Bible and read to her: "Let a woman learn in silence with all submissiveness. I permit no woman to teach or to have authority over men; she is to keep silent." She kept silent.

I will never know, nor did she then, what took place in the lives of those lumberjacks and miners, but by the time she was intimidated into silence, she had achieved something formative and lasting in me, an artesian spring of song and story.

A great deal of scholarly attention has been given to the power of liturgy in forming identity and the shaping effect of narrative in our understanding of ourselves and the world around us. The *way* we learn something is more influential than the something that we learn. No content comes into our lives free-floating: it is always embedded in a form of some kind. For the basic and integrative realties of God and faith, the forms must also be basic and integrative. If they are not, the truths themselves will be peripheral and unassimilated. It was with a kind of glad surprise that I realized that long before the academicians got hold of this and wrote their books, I had been enrolled in a school of song and story, God songs and God stories, said and sung by my God-passionate mother. Virtually everything I received in those impressionable years of my childhood had arrived in the containers of song and story, carried by a singer and storyteller mother—everything about God, but also about being human, growing up to adulthood, becoming a pastor.

In another year or so I entered the workforce of my father's butcher shop, and he took his part in contributing to my formation.

# 4

# MY FATHER'S BUTCHER SHOP

My father was a butcher. His meat market, within walking distance of our home, was just off of Main Street in Kalispell, our small Montana town. By the time I was five years old, I was permitted to walk by myself the five or six blocks from home to his market and work for him. Work at that time of my life consisted in accompanying him across the street to the Silver Star Café. He would have a cup of coffee with the cook, Phil, and take down the order for the next day's supply of hamburger, steaks, pork chops, sausage, and liver. The waitress always brought me a donut and glass of milk.

My father wore a white butcher's apron, even when he went across the street to the café. I wore one too. My mother made it out of flour sacks, identical to my father's, except for its size. She made me a new apron every year to match my growth. When I put on my apron in the butcher shop, I entered the adult world. And sitting on the counter stool in the café, being served alongside my father, was confirmation.

By this time I knew the story of the boy Samuel who had been "lent to the Lord" by his parents to live and work in the temple at Shiloh with Eli the priest. His parents, Elkanah and Hannah, visited him at Shiloh every year. His mother made him a priest's robe to wear, an ephod, as he assisted Eli. Every year as he added inches to his height, she would make him a new robe to fit his newly acquired stature. I knew exactly what that robe, that ephod, looked like—didn't I wear it every time I worked with my father? Didn't I get a new one every time I had grown another inch or two? I might have been the only person in our town who knew what an ephod actually looked like.

Shiloh couldn't have been that much different from my father's meat market. The three-year-old bull that was slaughtered at Samuel's dedication at Shiloh would become the hamburgers and sirloin steaks at my father's market and provided continuity between the shrine and the meat market.

I had no idea, of course, that I was acquiring a biblical imagination, finding myself in the biblical story, identifying myself as a priest.

As years went on, I graduated from the "work" of putting away the donut and milk that accompanied a business transaction to the beginner's work of grinding hamburger and slicing liver. One of Dad's butchers would pick me up and stand me on an upended orange crate before the big, red Hobart meat grinder, and I in my linen ephod would push chunks of beef into its maw. The day I was trusted with a knife and taught to respect it and keep it sharp, I knew adulthood was just around the corner. I was started out on liver (it's hard to mess up when slicing liver), but in a few years I was participating in the entire range of meat-cutting operations.

"That knife has a will of its own," old Eddie Nordcrist, one of my dad's butchers, used to say to me. "Get to know your knife." If I cut myself, he would blame me not for carelessness but for ignorance—I didn't "know" my knife.

I also learned that a beef carcass has a will of its own—it is not just an inert mass of meat and gristle and bone but has character and joints, texture and grain. Carving a quarter of beef into roasts and steaks was not a matter of imposing my knife-fortified will on dumb matter but respectfully and reverently entering into the reality of the material.

"Hackers" was my father's contemptuous label for butchers who ignorantly imposed their wills on the meat. They didn't take into account the subtle differences between pork and beef. They used knives and cleavers inappropriately and didn't keep them sharp. They were bullies forcing their wills on slabs of bacon and hindquarters of beef. The results were unattractive and uneconomical. They commonly left a mess behind that the rest of us had to clean up.

Not so much by words but by example, I internalized a respect for the material at hand. The material can be a pork loin, or a mahogany plank, or a lump of clay, or the will of God, or a soul, but when the work is done well, there is a kind of submission of will to the conditions at hand, a cultivation of what I would later learn to call humility. It is a noticeable feature in all skilled workers—woodworkers, potters, poets, pray-ers, and pastors. I learned it in the butcher shop.

Years later I acquired the phrase "negative capability" and recognized that it was something very much like submission to the material, the humility, that I had had so much practice in on the butcher block. The poet John Keats coined the term to refer to this quality in the worker. He was impressed by William Shakespeare's work in creating such a variety of characters in his plays, none of which seemed to be a projection of Shakespeare's ego. Each had an independent life of his or her own. Keats wrote, "A poet has no identity . . . he is continually . . . filling some other Body." He believed that the only way real creative will matured was in a person who was not hell-bent on imposing his or her will on another person or thing but "was capable of being in uncertainties, mysteries, doubts, without any irritable searching after fact and reason." Interesting: Shakespeare, the poet from whom we know the most about other people, is the poet about whom we know next to nothing.

All the while my imagination kept working on the priest theme with the slaughter of bulls and heifers, goats and sheep. We didn't offer turtledoves, but we made up for it with turkeys. All our sacrificed animals, cut up and wrapped and paid for, would be prayed over (I assumed that everybody prayed over meals), then consumed in our customers' homes.

Ours was a mostly storytelling church, but one year we had a pastor who specialized in the tabernacle, the temple, and the whole Hebrew sacrificial system. He took on the book of Leviticus as his text and preached three months of sermons on it. I was immediately interested. I was an insider to exactly this sort of world: I grew up experiencing the sights and sounds of animals killed and offered up. I had spent a lot of time by now in our local slaughterhouse and often helped with the slaughter.

But after a couple Sundays of Leviticus I lost interest in what our pastor was up to. This man knew nothing about killing animals. And though we never butchered goats, the rich sensuality of Hebrew worship was reproduced daily in our workplace. It never occurred to me that the world of worship was tidy and sedate. Our pastor had it all figured out on paper, but I knew it wasn't like that at all. I couldn't help but wonder how much he knew about sin and forgiveness. He certainly knew nothing about animal sacrifices. Sacrifice was messy: blood sloshing on the floor, gutting the creatures and gathering up the entrails in buckets, skinning the animals, salting down the hides. And in the summertime, the flies—flies everywhere.

My father had four meat cutters working for him. My favorite was Herb Thiel. He had a flat, expressionless face disfigured by a bad eye, milky and sunken. He didn't wear an eye patch. His face looked like a tombstone, with that dead eye engraved on it, so everyone called him Tombstone. Mostly we got the meat we sold in our market from the local slaughterhouse, but occasionally we would buy directly from a farmer in the valley. When we did that, Tombstone would go to the farm, kill the heifer or pig, dress it out, and bring it back to our shop. The other meat cutters sometimes called him the Killer. I loved to go out with him on those jobs. He never talked. But I didn't mind that—there was something rakish about being in the company of a man sometimes called Tombstone and other times the Killer.

On one of these occasions we were out to get a yearling calf. When we arrived, the calf was already confined to a loading chute to facilitate our work. The farmer had a large family. When we got out of the truck, the children were all over us, begging Tombstone not to kill the animal. It was a 4-H calf and had become a pet of the farm kids. Some of the kids were crying. All of them were upset. Emotional anarchy. In a low voice Tombstone said to me, "I'll fix 'em." He took his Remington .22 and shot the calf between the eyes. As it slumped to the ground, Tombstone took his knife from its scabbard and slit the calf's throat to bleed it. As the blood poured from the cut, Tombstone knelt down, let the blood run into his cupped hands and pretended to drink it, the blood dripping from that flat, one-eyed face. The kids ran in horror to the farmhouse fifty feet away. We could see them watching us from between the curtains. We completed our work without interference. Tombstone wiped the blood from his mouth and chin, and we returned to the butcher shop.

That butcher shop was my introduction to the world of congregation, which in a few years would be my workplace as a pastor. The people who came into our shop were not just customers. Something else defined them. It always seemed more like a congregation than a store. My father in his priestly robe greeted each person by name and knew many of their stories. And many of them knew me, in my priest's robe, by name. I always knew there was more going on than a commercial transaction. My father had an easy smile and was always gracious, especially with the occasional disagreeable ones: Alicia Conrad, who was always fussy about the leanness of the bacon; Gus Anderson, who made my dad trim off any excess fat from a steak before weighing it. Everyone felt welcome. He gave people dignity by the tone and manner of his greetings.

Two blocks away on a side street there was a brothel. There was always a good bit of talk on the street of the whores and the cathouse and the red-light district that was a blight on the street. But not in our place: when these women entered our premises, they were treated with the dignity of their Christian names. I remember three of them: Mary, Grace, Veronica. When they left with their purchases, there was no gossipy moralism trailing in their wake. They were in a safe place. Sometimes the women would telephone their order and ask for a delivery. I was always the delivery boy. When I brought the packages, they always knew my name and treated me the way they themselves had been treated in the butcher shop, not as a customer, which I would guess is how most of the people who came up the stairs to their rooms were treated, but as a named person.

Oddly, the one person who seemed out of place in our market was a pastor we had for a couple of years. He wasn't a regular customer, but when an evangelist or missionary would come to town, that pastor always paid us a call. He would get my father off to the side, put his arm across his shoulders, and say in the same "spiritual" voice that he always used when he prayed, "Brother Don, the Lord has laid it on my heart that this poor servant of God hasn't been eating all that well lately and would be greatly blessed with one of your fine steaks." My dad, ever generous, always gave him two. I never heard my father complain, but I could see the other meat cutters wink and exchange knowing looks, and I was embarrassed for my pastor who seemed so out of place in this holy place of work.

I am quite sure now that the way I as a pastor came to understand congregation had its beginnings in the "congregational" atmosphere of our butcher shop. Congregation is composed of people, who, upon entering a church, leave behind what people on the street name or call them. A church can never be reduced to a place where goods and services are exchanged. It must never be a place where a person is labeled. It can never be a place where gossip is perpetuated. Before anything else, it is a place where a person is named and greeted, whether implicitly or explicitly, in Jesus's name. A place where dignity is conferred.

I first learned that under my father's priesthood in his butcher shop.

I had learned much in my father's butcher shop that gave bone and muscle to my pastoral identity. I also learned something about work that could have destroyed it, something that I had to unlearn, with considerable difficulty as it turned out, twenty years later. It had to do with work, out-of-control work, work as a kind of pain killer which could well have caused a malignant cancer.

The focal point of the unlearning was Saturday, the climax of our workweek. The unlearning happened like this.

When I was thirty years old, I was assigned the task of developing a new congregation in Maryland. I was still in the early days of having acquired a pastoral identity. But I was full of anticipation, energized by the challenge of working out my pastoral salvation in fear and trembling with a new congregation. I had never done this before. I was learning on the job, but I felt honored to be entrusted with the task. In those first months as I realized how daunting the work that faced my wife, Jan, and me was, the adrenaline receded and the fear and trembling that Paul had recommended when dealing with a holy God and a holy salvation was replaced by a very unholy anxiety. I anesthetized the anxiety with work, long hours of it. I worked out of fear of failing. I worked when there was no work to do, worked even harder when there was no work to do. Spinning my wheels. Grinding my gears.

After a couple years of this, I knew the work wasn't working. One day, in a kind of prayerful reverie, wondering how I had gotten off on the wrong foot so badly, I remembered Prettyfeather, and as I remembered, the details of what I knew of her arranged themselves into a story.

Remembering Prettyfeather started a process of unlearning a way of working that destroys life. This story became the text by which I unlearned what I had learned only too well in those formative years in the butcher shop. Here's the story.

Prettyfeather placed two buffalo-head nickels on the countertop for her Holy Saturday purchase: smoked ham hocks; two for a nickel. In the descending hierarchy of Holy Saturday foods, ham hocks were at the bottom.

Large hickory-smoked hams held center position in the displays in my father's butcher shop. Colorful cardboard cutouts provided by salesmen from the meat-packing companies of Armour, Hormel, and Silverbow all showed variations on a theme: a father at an Easter Sunday dinner table carving a ham, surrounded by an approving wife and expectant children.

Off to the side of these displays were stacks of the smaller and cheaper "picnic" hams (a picnic ham is not, properly speaking, a ham at all, but the shoulder of the pig). There were no company-supplied pictures or even brand names on them. On Holy Saturday, customers crowded into our store, responding to the sale signs painted on the plateglass windows fronting the street and sorting themselves into upper and lower socioeconomic strata: the affluent bought honey-cured, hickory-smoked hams; the less-than-affluent bought unadjectived "picnics."

Prettyfeather was the only person I ever remember who bought ham hocks—gristly on the inside and leathery on the outside, but *smoked* and therefore emanating the aroma of a feast—on Holy Saturday. She was the only Indian I knew by name although I grew up in Indian country. Every Saturday she came into our store to make a small purchase: pickled pig's feet, chitlins, blood sausage, headcheese, pork liver.

She was always by herself. She wore moccasins and was wrapped in a blanket, even in the warmest weather. The coins she used for her purchases were in a leather pouch that hung like a goiter at her neck. Her face was the color and texture of the moccasins on her feet.

"Indian" was a near-mythological word for me, full of nobility and filled out with stories of the hunt and sacred ceremony. Somehow it never occurred to me that this Indian squaw who came into our store every Saturday and bought barely edible meats belonged to that nobility.

While she made her purchases from us and did whatever other shopping she did on these Saturdays in town, her husband and seven or eight other Indian braves sat on apple boxes in the alley behind the Pastime Bar and passed around a jug of Thunderbird wine. Several jugs, actually. As I made my back-door deliveries of steaks and hamburger to the restaurants along Main Street, I passed up and down the alley several times each Saturday and watched the empty jugs accumulate. Late in the evening, Bennie Odegaard, son of one of the bar owners and a little older than I, would pull the braves into his dad's pickup truck and drive them out south of town to their encampment along the Stillwater River and dump them out.

I don't know how Prettyfeather got back to that small cluster of tar-paper shacks and tepees. She walked, I guess. Carrying her small purchases. On Holy Saturday she carried four ham hocks.

I had never heard of any Saturday designated as holy. It was simply Saturday. If, once a year, precision was required, Holy Saturday was "the Saturday before Easter." It was one of the heaviest workdays of the year. Beginning early in the morning, I carried the great, fragrant hams shipped from Armour in Spokane, Hormel in Missoula, and Silverbow in Butte, and arranged them symmetrically in pyramids.

I grew up in a religious home that believed devoutly in the saving benefits of the death of Jesus and the glorious life of resurrection. But between these two polar events of the faith, we worked a long and lucrative day. Holiness was put on hold till Sunday. Saturday was for working hard and making money. It was a day when the evidence of hard work and its consequence—money—became publicly apparent.

The evidence was especially clear on that particular Saturday, when we sold hundreds of hams to deserving Christians, and four ham hocks to an Indian squaw and her pickup load of drunks.

I would have been very surprised, and somewhat unbelieving, to have known that in the very town in which I worked furiously all those *unholy* Saturdays, there were people besides the Indians who were not working at all, not spending, but remembering the despair of a world disappointed in its grandest hopes, entering into the emptiness of death by deliberately emptying the self of illusion and indulgence and self-importance. Keeping vigil for Easter. Waiting for the dawn.

And some of them listening to this ancient Holy Saturday sermon from a preacher now unknown:

*Something strange is happening on earth today—a great silence, and still-ness. The whole earth keeps silence because the King is asleep. The earth trembled and is still because God has fallen asleep in the flesh and he has raised up all who have slept ever since the world began. God has died in the flesh and hell trembles with fear.*

*He has gone to search for our first parent, as for a lost sheep. Greatly desiring to visit those who live in darkness and in the shadow of death, he has gone to free from sorrow the captive Adam and Eve, he who is both God and the son of Eve. The Lord approached them bearing the cross, the weapon that had won him the victory. At the sight of him, Adam, the first man he had created, struck his breast in terror and cried out to everyone: "My Lord be with you all." Christ answered him: "And with your spirit." He took him by the hand and raised him up, saying "Awake, O sleeper and rise from the dead, and Christ will give you light."*

(The reading for Holy Saturday in *The Liturgy of the Hours*)

As it turned out, I interpreted the meaning of the world and the people around me far more in terms of the hard working on Saturday than anything said or sung on Friday and Sunday. Whatever was told me in those years (and I have no doubt that I heard truth), what I absorbed in my bones was a litur-gical rhythm in which the week reached its climax in a human workday, the results of which were enjoyed on Sunday, and especially on Easter Resurrection Sunday.

Those assumptions provided the grid for a social interpretation of the world around me: Saturday was the day for hard work, or for displaying its results; namely, money. If someone appeared neither working nor spending on Satur-day, there was something wrong, catastrophically wrong. The Indians attempting a hungover Easter feast on ham hocks were the most prominent example of something wrong.

It was a view of life shaped by "the Gospel According to America." The rewards were obvious, and I enjoyed them. Hard work pays off. I learned much in those years in my father's butcher shop, yet there was one large omission that set all other truth dangerously at risk: the omission of holy rest. The refusal to be silent. The obsessive avoidance of emptiness.

It was far more than ignorance on Holy Saturday; it was weekly arrogance. Not only was the Good Friday Crucifixion bridged to the Easter Resurrection by this day furious with energy and lucrative with reward, but all the gospel truths were likewise set as either introductions or conclusions to the human action that displayed our prowess and our virtue every week of the year. God was background to our business. Every gospel truth was maintained intact, and all the human energy was wholly admirable, but the rhythms were off. Desolation—and with it companionship with the desolate, ranging from first-century Semites to twentieth-century Indians—was all but wiped from consciousness.

As the story formed in my prayer, this most poignant irony became embedded in my memory: those seven or eight Indians, with the Thunderbird empties lying around, drunk in the alley behind the Pastime Bar on Saturday afternoon, while we Scandinavian Christians worked diligently late into the night, oblivious to the holiness of the day. The Indians were in despair, *religious* despair, something very much like the Holy Saturday despair narrated in the Gospels. Their way of life had come to nothing, the only buffalo left to them was engraved on nickels, a couple of which one of their squaws had paid out that morning for four bony ham hocks. The early sacredness of their lives was a wasteland; and they, godforsaken as they supposed, drugged their despair with Thunderbird and buried their dead visions and dreams in the alley behind the Pastime, ignorant of the God at work beneath their emptiness.

People talk about steep learning curves. I was embarked on a steep *unlearning* curve. It didn't happen overnight, but it happened. Prettyfeather gave me the story that provided a text for the extensive unlearning before me, the unlearning that was necessary to clear the ground for learning that God at work—not I—was the center of the way I was going to be living for the rest of my life.

Inappropriate, anxiety-driven, fear-driven work would only interfere with and distract from what God was already doing. My "work" assignment was to pay more attention to what God does than what I do, and then to find, and guide others to find, the daily, weekly, yearly rhythms that would get this awareness into our bones. Holy Saturday for a start. And then Sabbath keeping. Staying in touch with people in despair, knowing them by name, and waiting for resurrection.

# 5

## GARRISON JOHNS

I grew up in a Christian home with good parents. I was told the story of Jesus and instructed in the Jesus way. I was loved and treated well. Childhood in my memory was a fair approximation of the garden of Eden—a good and wonderful life.

But there was also the neighborhood. Our modest home was on a gravel road on the edge of town, three or four blocks beyond where the sidewalks ended. It was a neighborhood with plenty of playmates, none of whom went to church. But their unbaptized condition never seemed to make any difference in that preschool life of games (kick-the-can, hide-and-seek, follow-the-leader, softball) and imagination (pretending to be explorers like Lewis and Clark and Indians like Chief Joseph and Sacagawea). There were trees to climb and a creek to swim in. A meadow in which cows grazed bordered our backyard. We used the dried cow flop for bases in our ball games.

And then I went off to school and discovered what the Gospel of John named "the world"—those people who do not regard God with either reverence or obedience. This knowledge entered my life in the person of Garrison Johns, the school bully. He lived in a log house a couple hundred yards beyond where I lived, the yard littered with rusted-out pickups and cars. I was in that house only once. It was a cold winter day, and his mother, a beautiful willowy woman as I remember, invited me and the Mitchell twins in to warm us up with a bowl of moose-meat chili that was simmering on the back of the wood stove. Struggling through deep snow, we were taking a shortcut home through her backyard. We must have looked half frozen—we *were* half frozen—and she had compassion on us. But Garrison wasn't there.

I had never seen Garrison close up, only at a distance. He wore a red flannel shirt, summer and winter, and walked with something of a swagger that I admired and tried to imitate. Being a year older than I and living just far enough away, he was beyond the orbit of my neighborhood games and friendships. I knew of his reputation for meanness, but the memory of his mother's kindness tempered my apprehension. I wasn't prepared for what was to come.

About the third day after entering first grade, Garrison discovered me and took me on as his project for the year. He gave me a working knowledge of what twenty-five years later Richard Niebuhr would give me a more sophisticated understanding of—the tension between *Christ* and *Culture*. I had been taught in Sunday school not to fight and so had never learned to use my fists. I had been prepared for the wider world of neighborhood and school by memorizing "Bless those who persecute you" and "Turn the other cheek." I don't know how Garrison Johns knew that about me—some sixth sense that bullies have, I suppose—but he picked me for his sport. Most afternoons after school he would catch me and beat me up. He also found out that I was a Christian and taunted me with "Jesus sissy."

I tried finding alternate ways home by making detours through alleys, but he stalked me and always found me. I arrived home most afternoons bruised and humiliated. My mother told me that this had always been the way of Christians in the world and that I had better get used to it. I was also supposed to pray for him. The Bible verses that I had memorized ("Bless . . ." and "Turn . . .") began to get tiresome.

I loved going to school—I was learning a lot, finding new friends, adoring my teacher. The classroom was a wonderful place. But after the dismissal bell each day I had to face Garrison Johns and get my daily beating that I was supposed to assimilate as my blessing.

March came. I remember that it was March by the weather. The winter snow was melting, but there were still patches of it here and there. The days were getting longer—I was no longer walking home in the late afternoon dark. And then something unexpected happened. I was with my neighborhood friends on this day, seven or eight of them, when Garrison caught up with us and started in on me, jabbing and taunting, working himself up to the main event. He had an audience, and that helped. He always did better with an audience.

That's when it happened. Totally uncalculated. Totally out of character. Something snapped within me. For just a moment the Bible verses disappeared from my consciousness and I grabbed Garrison. To my surprise, and his, I realized that I was stronger than he was. I wrestled him to the ground, sat on his chest, and pinned his arms to the ground with my knees. I couldn't believe it—he was helpless under me. At my mercy. It was too good to be true. I hit him in the face with my fists. It felt good, and I hit him again—blood spurted from his nose, a lovely crimson on the snow. By this time all the other children were cheering, egging me on. "Black his eyes!" "Bust his teeth!" A torrent of biblical invective poured from them, although nothing compared with what I would, later in life, read in the Psalms.

I said to Garrison, "Say 'Uncle.'" He wouldn't say it. I hit him again. More blood. More cheering. Now my audience was bringing the best out of *me*. And then my Christian training reasserted itself. I said, "Say, 'I believe in Jesus Christ as my Lord and Savior.'" He wouldn't say it. I hit him again. More blood. I tried again, "Say 'I believe in Jesus Christ as my Lord and Savior.'"

And he said it. Garrison Johns was my first Christian convert.

Garrison Johns was my introduction into the world, the "world that is not my home." He was also my introduction to how effortlessly that same "world" could get into me, making itself perfectly at home under cover of my Christian language and "righteous" emotions.

That happened seventy years ago. I have since moved back and taken up residence once more in this Montana valley in which I grew up, was beaten up by Garrison Johns almost daily for seven months, and on that March afternoon in 1938 bloodied his nose and obtained his Christian confession. When we are in town and drive down Fourth Street West I take some pleasure in pointing out to Jan the site of the "conversion." One day, returning home after having passed by the holy site, Jan said, "I wonder what ever came of Garrison Johns?"

I opened the telephone book and found his name listed with an address that located him about ten miles away. Should I call him up? Would he remember? Is he still a bully? Did the ill-gotten Christian confession "take"? Would a meeting result in a personal preview of Armageddon in which I would end up on the losing side? I didn't call. Jan accused me of procrastinating until the Last Judgment.

# 6

# THE TREELESS
# CHRISTMAS OF 1939

When I was seven years old, there was no Christmas tree in our home. It turned out to be a memorable event. Unlike many of our neighbors, we always kept Christ in Christmas. At the same time, like all of our neighbors, we had and decorated a tree on Christmas. But the Christmas of 1939 we didn't.

My mother, an intense woman capable of fierce convictions, was reading the prophecy of Jeremiah and came upon words she had never noticed before:

> Thus says the Lord:
> "Learn not the way of the nations,
> nor be dismayed at the signs of the heavens
> because the nations are dismayed at them,
> for the customs of the peoples are false.
> A tree from the forest is cut down,

*and worked with an axe by the hands of a craftsman.*
*Men deck it with silver and gold;*
*    they fasten it with hammer and nails so that it cannot move."*

There was no doubt in her mind that the Holy Spirit, through the prophet Jeremiah, had targeted our American Christmas in this passage. Every detail fit our practice.

A couple weeks before every Christmas, on a Sunday afternoon, my father would get the ax and check its edge. Being a butcher, he was used to working with sharp tools and did not tolerate dull edges. When I heard the whetstone applied to the ax, I knew that the time was near. Bundled into our Model A Ford pickup, my parents and baby sister and I set out to find our tree.

I rode in the open truck bed with our springer spaniel, Brownie, and held the ax. It was a bouncy ride of ten miles to Lake Blaine, just south of where the Swan Range took its precipitous rise from the valley floor. There had been a major forest fire in this region some years before, so the trees were young—the right size to fit into our living room. I always got to pick the tree; it was a ritual I stretched out as long as parental patience would accommodate.

My father then took over, swinging the ax. Four or five brisk cuts, and the green-needled spire was horizontal in the snow: *A tree from the forest is cut down.*

He then squared the base of the trunk so it would be easy to mount when we got it back home: *Worked with an ax by the hands of a craftsman.* My father was deft with the ax—the wood chips from the whittling released the fragrance of resin into the winter air.

When we arrived home, I climbed into the attic and handed down the box of decorations. We had multicolored lights on our tree and lots of tinsel: *Men deck it with silver and gold.* Across the street my best friends had strings of monotonous blue lights. I felt sorry for them, stuck with a monochrome Christmas.

My father took slats from packing boxes that our sausage and lunch meats were shipped in—there was always a pile of these boxes in the alley behind our butcher shop—and cut them into four eighteen-inch supports and nailed them to the tree trunk: *They fasten it with hammer and nails so that it cannot move.*

By now it was late afternoon and dark. Our Douglas fir—it was always a Douglas fir for us, no other evergreen was a Christmas tree—was secure and steady in front of our living room window.

When we were done, I ran out onto the gravel road (the paving on Fourth Street West fell short by about four hundred yards of reaching our house) and looked at it from outside, the way passersby would see it, the framed picture of our Christmas ritual adventure into and out of the woods. I imagined strangers looking at it and wishing they could be inside with us, part of the ax/Model-A-pickup/Lake Blaine/tree-cutting/tree-mounting/tree-decorating liturgy that I loved so much.

And I would look across the street at the tree with blue lights where the Mitchell twins, Alva and Alan, lived—so cold and monotonous. They never went to church, and at times like this it showed. I couldn't help feeling privileged and superior, but also a little sorry for them: Christian pride modified by Christian compassion.

Then, in the winter of 1939, we didn't have a tree: *For the customs of the peoples are false.* It wasn't just the tree that was gone; the richly nuanced ritual was abolished. A noun, "tree," was deleted from December, but along with it its adjective "Christmas." Or so I felt.

And it was all because Jeremiah had preached his Christmas-tree sermon. Because Jeremiah had looked through his prophetic telescope, his Spirit-magnified vision reaching across 12,000 miles and 2,600 years, seeing in detailed focus what we did every December and denouncing it as idolatry. And it was because my mother cared far more about scripture than the culture.

I was embarrassed—humiliated was more like it—humiliated as only seven-year-olds can be humiliated. Abased. Mortified. I was terrified of what my friends in the neighborhood would think. They would think we were too poor to have a tree. They would think I was being punished for some unspeakable sin, and so deprived of a tree. They would think we didn't care about one another and didn't have any fun in our house. They would feel sorry for us. They would feel superior to us.

As a regular ritual in our neighborhood, we went to one another's houses, looked at the presents under the trees, and wondered what treasures they contained. Every house was so different—I marveled at the odd ways people arranged their furniture. I was uneasy with the vaguely repellent odors in houses where the parents smoked and drank beer. At Garrison Johns's at the end of our street, there was a big pot of moose-meat chili simmering on the back of the wood stove for most of the winter. It was easily the best-smelling house in the neighborhood.

But that year I kept my friends out of our house. I was ashamed to have them come in and see the bare, treeless room. I was terrified of the questions they might ask. I made up excuses to keep them out. I lied: "My sister has a contagious disease." "My mother is really mad, and I can't bring anybody in." But the fact of *no-Christmas-tree* could not be hidden. After all, it was always in our front window.

Alva and Alan, the twins who never went to church, asked the most questions, sensing something wrong, an edge of taunting now in their voices. I made excuses: "My dad is too busy right now; we're planning on getting a tree next week." And so on.

I was mostly terrified that they would discover the real reason we didn't have a tree: that God had commanded it (at least that's what we thought at the time)—a religious reason! But religion was the one thing that made us better than our neighbors; and now, if they were to find out our secret, it would make us worse.

My mother read Jeremiah to me and my little sister that year and talked about Jesus. She opened the Bible to the story of the Nativity and placed it on the table where the Christmas tree always stood. I never told her how I felt or what I knew everyone in the neighborhood was saying. I carried my humiliation secretly, as children often do.

It is odd when I think back on it now, but we never went to church on Christmas Day. Every detail in our lives was permeated with an awareness of God. There was a rigorous determination to let scripture and Christ shape not only our worship but the way we wore our clothes, shape not only our morals but our manner of speech. Going to church was the act on which the week pivoted. But, for some reason, there was no churchgoing on Christmas Day.

We had a Christmas pageant at church the Sunday before Christmas. On Christmas Eve we exchanged presents; on Christmas Day we had dinner at our house with a lot of relatives, plus any people in the neighborhood who didn't have a family—bachelors, widows, runaways.

Christmas dinner was full of Norwegian talk. It was the only day of the year in which I heard Norwegian spoken. My uncles and aunts reminisced over their Norway Christmases and savored the sounds of their cradle tongue. The Christmas menu was always the same: *lutefisk*, cod fish with all the nutrients leached out of it by weeks of baptism in barrels of brine, and *lefsa*, an unleavened pliable flat bread with the texture (and taste) of a chamois cloth.

There was a stout but unsuccessful attempt to restore flavor by providing bowls of melted butter, cellars of salt, hillocks of sugar. It was a meal I never learned to like, but I loved the festivities, the laughter, the fun, the banter.

The primary source of the banter was my favorite uncle, Uncle Ernie. He was the best storyteller and always seemed to have the most fun. He also posed as an atheist (I think it was a pose), but he did come to the Christmas pageant, which I thought seriously compromised his atheism. On the Christmas that we had no tree, he surpassed himself in banter.

He was the first to remark on the absence of the tree: "Evelyn," he roared at my mother, "where the hell is the Christmas tree? How the hell are we going to have a Norwegian Christmas without a tree?" (He was also the only person I ever heard use profanity in our home, which set him apart in my child mind on a sort of craggy eminence.) My mother's reply, a nice fusion of prayer and indignation, was a match to his raillery: "No tree this year, brother. Just Jesus. We are not celebrating a Norwegian Christmas this year; we are celebrating a Christian Christmas." Then she got out Jeremiah and read it to him. He was astonished. He had no idea that anything that contemporary could come out of an old-fashioned Bible. Stunned by her impertinent piety, he muttered through a mouth full of lutefisk "damn, damn, damn" all through dinner.

Next year the tree was back.

The entire ritual was back in place without explanation. Our gray and rust Model A was replaced by a red Dodge half-ton pickup, but that was the only change. I never learned what authority preempted Jeremiah in the matter of the Christmas tree. Years later my mother occasionally said, "Eugene, do you remember that silliness about the Christmas tree when you were seven years old?" I didn't want to remember. And we didn't discuss it.

But now I do remember. And I want to discuss it. It doesn't seem at all silly now. My mother died thirty-one years ago, and so I am not going to find out the details that interest me now—the turns and twists of pilgrimage during those years when she was so passionate in pursuit of a holy life; her determination to preserve our family's practice of the Christian faith free from the secularizing contamination of a trivializing culture. She may have been wise—I am sure she was—in restoring the tree to our Christmas celebrations, but I am quite sure that it was not silliness that banned it that single year.

The feelings I had that Christmas when I was seven years old may have been the most authentically Christmas feelings I have ever had, or will have: the experience of humiliation, of being misunderstood, of being an outsider. Mary was pregnant out of wedlock. Joseph was an apparent cuckold. Jesus was born in poverty—everything involved in God becoming flesh was counter to the culture. God had commanded a strange word—the people in the story were aware, deeply and awesomely aware, that the event they were living was shaped by the presence and power of the Holy Spirit and at the same time vehemently counter to the culture.

They certainly experienced considerable embarrassment and inconvenience—did they also clumsily lie to their friends and make excuses at the same time they persisted in faith? All the joy and celebration and gift receiving in the gospel nativity story took place in a context of incomprehension and absurdity. My first inkling of that absurdity entered my life in the Christmas of 1939.

My mother's "No tree this year, brother, just Jesus" accompanied by my uncle's "damn, damn, damn" lay dormant in me for years, but in time it developed into practiced pastoral discernments—Jesus without tinsel—as I daily face the seductions of culture-religion.

# 7

## UNCLE SVEN

My grandfather brought his wife, Juditta, and nine children—six sons and three daughters—from Norway by ship in the early 1900s. Jim Hill's Great Northern Railroad had found a way across the Rocky Mountains of Montana a few miles south of the Canadian border in 1893, and new towns were springing up left and right. Andre Hoiland learned of the new town of Kalispell, named for an Indian tribe, that was being built in a valley on the west side of the Rocky Mountains that began in Canada and stretched to Mexico. He came for the work it promised. He was a cement worker and soon was employed laying out and pouring sidewalks.

Two more daughters were born, the last being my mother, Evelyn, born in 1910. Her mother, Juditta, died when she was five. The older siblings took over raising her and her sister.

My mother was a colorful but not always accurate storyteller. I have no outside source for any details of her family life, except for a newspaper clipping of her brother, Sven. He was her favorite. He was twenty years older than she and lavished her with attention. He would throw her in the air and twirl her in a dance. He took her riding on his horse and told her stories of Norway and the trolls in the Jotunheimen Mountains. He was charismatic, adventurous, always laughing, always playful. And he was the town's milkman. He ran alongside his horse-drawn milk wagon, grabbed the bottles of milk, and placed them on the porches of his customers, then ran back to the wagon for a fresh supply. He never rode the wagon, always on the run, laughing and greeting the neighbors. Everybody loved him. His cheer was contagious.

A newspaper clipping from our local paper, *The Daily Inter Lake,* gives a different portrait of her favorite brother. It is the report of Sven's murder by his wife, Myrtle. The murder trial was a sensation in our small town. It played to a packed courtroom for a week.

On the stand, Myrtle told Judge T. A. Thompson and the jury that on the night of the shooting, her husband, Sven, came to her room in the Bienz Hotel, drunk and sullen. He undressed, slid his revolver under the pillow, and crawled into bed. Soon they were arguing. Then he beat her. Moments later Myrtle grabbed the gun, struggled against her husband, then shot. Twice. Then twice more. Plainclothes officer Harry Ponaford was called to the scene. He found Mrs. Hoiland "standing there clothed only in her nightgown." She told Ponaford: "He wanted me to do something I wouldn't do for any man, and I shot him." At the trial it emerged that Hoiland had demanded she go out on the street and solicit. They had been married six weeks.

During the weeklong trial there was more. From the instant they met, Sven Hoiland had begun siphoning off whatever money Myrtle had, which included the sizable proceeds from selling her homestead. Once, in Shelby, she found him in a hotel room with another woman. The day of the wedding, he disappeared midafternoon, and she didn't see him again until four the next morning when he came in drunk, carrying a gun, and beat her. As the testimony accumulated, there were more stories of violence and drunkenness. He told her repeatedly that he'd "tame her as he had tamed lots of other women." After every beating he promised never to do it again. Not pretty stuff. Before Myrtle took the stand, Judge Thompson warned that some of the testimony "won't be congenial to the finer senses . . . if there are any women present who'd like to leave, now would be the time." The courtroom was jammed. Nobody left except one twenty-year-old girl, escorted out by the bailiff.

All week the prosecution endeavored to show that the killing was premeditated. Friday morning the jury returned the verdict: "The defendant has committed justifiable homicide and by this verdict is acquitted." The packed courtroom exploded into cheers. When she returned to the jail to get her things, the prisoners gave her a rousing cheer. Everybody in town, including the prisoners, felt safer with Sven dead.

The *Inter Lake* reported the verdict in the Saturday paper, November 17, 1917.

The next day Myrtle went to see Sven's parents. His mother, Juditta, asked her if he had said anything before he died, and she said, "Yes, he cursed." Pressed to give the exact words, Myrtle said, "Oh, God." Juditta interpreted the words not as a curse but as a prayer. Sven was rehabilitated, at least for her, with a death-bed repentance. He shares a grave plot with his mother in the Conrad Cemetery, where my parents and infant sister have since been buried. His half of the flat bronze grave marker says, *b. 1893, d. 1917.*

As far as the town and the family were concerned, Myrtle disappeared into anonymity.

My mother was seven years old when her brother was murdered. She knew, of course, about the murder and something at least of the scandalous circumstances surrounding it. But what she remembered when she talked to me about him was her laughing, fun-loving brother playfully tossing her high in the air, catching her, and twirling her in a dance, running alongside his milk-wagon chariot, brightening the streets of Kalispell with his high spirits.

The contradictions in Sven, the affectionate and playful big brother set alongside the abusive and violent husband, worked themselves into my adolescent imagination. Did one cancel the other? Was there any way to get the playful brother and the abusive husband into the same story?

In my high-school yearbook all the seniors were asked what they anticipated becoming in the next five years. My answer was "writer—a novelist." The novel I already had in mind to write was "Sven: Son, Brother, Husband." I had the sketch of a plot forming. I would portray Sven much as my mother experienced him, youthful and exuberant, spirited and charming. But interspersed with that, I was plotting circumstances that would account for his murder.

It would go like this: In the eyes of the whole town he was as my mother spoke of him. His milk wagon and dashing exuberance delighted everyone. But a morning or two a week his horse could be seen waiting patiently in front of some house or other on his delivery route. If asked about it, Sven would say that he was "having a cup of coffee." It would turn out later that these homes were occupied by wives whose husbands were traveling salesmen, gone much of the time, or young widows bored with their unsexed lives. There were also occasional police reports of thefts from homes where the occupants were away for a few days—money or a brooch or a gun. Myrtle would sometimes find money in a pocket when she was doing the laundry and wondered where it came from. Sven always had a plausible explanation. Then an acquaintance remarked to Myrtle on the frequency with which Sven had "coffee" at her next-door neighbor's.

By this time Myrtle had already begun to have suspicions. One early morning while it was still dark, she followed his milk wagon, prepared for what she expected she might find. She found the horse and wagon waiting patiently at curbside. She waited for the "coffee" to be brewed and served and then entered the house, found Sven "having coffee," and shot him dead. She then walked three blocks down the street to his parents' home, told them what she had done, reported his last words, went to the police station, placed the Colt 45 on the counter, and gave herself up.

Nothing ever came of the novel. But the effort to accommodate the ambiguities of the moral and spiritual life did. I had no idea as I was plotting this novel that I was developing a pastoral imagination adequate for entering into the complexities of good and evil, sin and salvation, that make up much of the daily life of a congregation. When I finally did become a pastor, I was surprised at how thoroughly Sven had inoculated me against "one answer" systems of spiritual care: "For every complex problem there is an answer that is clear, simple and wrong" is the warning posted by H. L. Mencken.

Thanks to Sven, I was being prepared to understand a congregation as a gathering of people that requires a context as large as the Bible itself if we are to deal with the ambiguities of life in the actual circumstances in which people live them. If the life of David that comprised prayer and adultery and murder could be written and told as a gospel story, no one in my congregation would be written off. For me, my congregation would become a work-in-progress—a novel in which everyone and everything is connected in a salvation story in which Jesus has the last word. No reductions to stereotype: not my grandmother's desperate reduction of her son to a death-bed repentance, not my mother's affectionate reduction of her brother to a fun-loving, devil-may-care naïf, not the jury's legal reduction of Sven to a drunken wife abuser, not the detached reduction by a psychiatrist of Sven to a narcissistic sociopath.

# 8

# THE CARNEGIE

The Carnegie was the public library in our town, a square redbrick building, roofed by a rotunda. In the entrance area there was a mountain goat, "the beast the color of winter," on display in a glass case, mounted climbing a rock face. I loved that goat, a wild and dramatic welcome ushering me into the world of books. Entering the library, I never passed that goat without stopping and admiring it for a couple minutes.

From an early age I loved learning but never cared much for school. The Carnegie was my school of choice. Schools were okay—I made friends and played games. But the Carnegie was where I found myself in a place of uninterrupted learning. I could lose myself there and indulge my curiosity in that magnificent world of books. I started early, soon after I could read. By the time I was in the seventh grade, I was riding my bike after school to the Carnegie and spending Saturday mornings there discovering novels and poems, captured by writers who led me into the way of words, the world of imagination.

One Saturday morning I pulled off the shelf a book with the title *A Critique of Practical Reason*. It was by a writer I had never heard of before, Immanuel Kant. Deep in the stacks, I sat on the floor to read. It was the first book of philosophy I had ever held in my hand. I read nonstop for a couple hours, fascinated, intrigued. I am sure now that I didn't understand a thing I was reading, but I knew I was onto something that I wanted to know more about. Later, in the same section, I found Will Durant's *Story of Philosophy* in which I understood maybe a third of what he wrote and picked up a smattering of what Kant was about.

But it didn't take me long to realize that as far as philosophy was concerned I had dived into the deep end of the pool—belly flopped was more like it—and was just splashing around, not getting anywhere. So I gave up on it for the time being. But something penetrated my psyche on those Saturday mornings in the philosophy stacks at the Carnegie that germinated into a concentration in philosophy when I arrived at my university.

Meanwhile, for the next few years the novelists took over. My first enthusiasm was James Fenimore Cooper. I devoured the entire corpus. Then the Montana novels of A. B. Guthrie Jr. By the time I graduated from high school, Charles Dickens and Leo Tolstoy were bosom companions. At that time I was sure I would be a novelist. Then the novelists were supplemented by Henry Thoreau and John Muir, who gave me eyes to see and ears to hear what was going on as I hiked in the hills and along the streams in our mountain valley.

The Carnegie supplied me with a faculty of great teachers. As I marched along the prescribed school itinerary from grade to grade, I acquired the rudiments of getting on in the world but my *education* took place in the Carnegie. That is where I learned to love learning for its own sake. The Carnegie is where I sat under the tutelage of Emily Dickinson. The Carnegie is where Melville and Hawthorne gave me the ballast of an imagination adequate to keep me steady in a culture that is naive regarding sin and evil.

I was twenty-four years old with diplomas from high school, university, and seminary before I finally set foot in a school that rivaled the Carnegie. I entered the Johns Hopkins University to do graduate work in Semitic studies and found myself in a world of learning that I never knew existed. My letter of acceptance was a postcard on which Professor William Albright had scribbled

one line: "Glad to welcome you—look forward to meeting you in September."
I had been accepted on the strength of a recommendation by my seminary
Hebrew professor.

That postcard set the tone for a way of schooling I had never experienced:
informal and personal. I didn't know that there was a place of learning that
was able to function with so little institutional structure. No pretension. No
hierarchy. No required courses. No grades. And no exams except for the final
doctoral exams. And, of course, the formidable dissertation. Students who were
serious about *learning*. There was a kind of relaxed camaraderie that suffused
the place. Semitic studies was a small department, maybe sixteen students and
two professors.

The centerpiece of the department, the world-famous William Foxwell Albright, had dominated the field of biblical archaeology and Semitic studies for
thirty years. It was the first time I had been in the working presence of a world-
class intellect. It was not so much that his knowledge was so wide ranging
and integrative, but that being with and around him I experienced his mind
in action—he was constantly thinking, reformulating, pushing the boundaries of ancient history, noticing the ways the several Semitic languages worked
comparatively.

He entered the classroom one morning telling us that he had awakened
having solved the meaning of Moriah while he slept. Both the meaning and
location of Mount Moriah, where Abraham had bound Isaac for sacrifice,
had always eluded scholars. Professor Albright went to the chalkboard and
soon had it filled with words from Ugaritic, Arabic, Assyrian, Aramaic, and,
of course, Hebrew. He continued, excited and intense, for twenty minutes, at
which point Prescott Williams, an older student who had already spent four
years with him, interrupted, "But Dr. Albright, what about this and this and
this [he was making reference to items of grammar and etymology that I knew
nothing about]. Do you think that holds up?" The Professor stopped, stepped
back, and stared at the chalkboard for twenty seconds. And then he said, "Mr.
Williams is right—forget everything I have said."

It was an act of humility that I would soon learn was characteristic of Dr.
Albright. Everyone in that room knew he was capable of dismissing Williams
and bluffing his way and none of us would have known he was bluffing. We

all knew he knew everything. But he knew he didn't know everything and let us know he didn't.

The world of the intellect came alive for me in those years in his presence. Knowledge wasn't just storing up information in a mental warehouse. It was the disciplined practice of thinking, imagining, formulating, testing for the truth. And teaching wasn't just getting information or data into students' minds. There was something deeply dialogical involved, as words sparked into meaning and started truth fires that blazed with comprehension.

Every week, listening to Professor Albright lecture, sitting with him in his study with five other students reading the Hebrew Bible, drinking coffee with older students in the commons, getting a feel for the immense world of the mind, the aesthetics of the intellect, I began to inhabit a world I never knew existed, a world of learning *embodied,* vibrant with energy. This was the Carnegie *plus.*

I confess I was bewildered much of the time. The famous Dr. Albright was surpassingly brilliant, but he couldn't comprehend the depths of ignorance in his students. But an interesting culture of learning had developed around him. The older students took us younger ones in tow and tutored us informally. For me it was Charles Fensham. He took my hand and became my Virgil. Dr. Albright showed me intelligence at work. Charles interpreted and explained that arcane intelligence in a language I could understand.

Charles was a professor of Old Testament from the University of Stellenbosch in South Africa. He was already the recipient of two Ph.D.s and would pick up a third under Dr. Albright that single year—it took everybody else three or four years. We lived a few doors apart in the graduate-student dormitory and became good friends. He patiently untangled and sorted out the stream-of-consciousness commentary that left me bewildered in the lectures and seminars. Sample: in that day's lecture in Egyptian history, Dr. Albright kept using the term *hypocoristicon*. I had never heard the word. I went to my dictionary and couldn't find it. I went to Charles and he laughed, "It's just a fancy term for a nickname—the old man is very fond of it and uses it every chance he gets."

But after two months away from his family, Charles became severely lonely. He had left his wife, Yvonne, his five-year-old daughter, Marianthe, and three-year-old son, Charlsie, behind in Stellenbosch and missed them terribly. He called his wife and booked her and the children passage on a ship. She was scheduled to arrive in New York City in three weeks at a pier on the Hudson River. He made arrangements to meet her. I had worked the previous summer for the YMCA, meeting foreign students arriving by airplane and ship and helping them make airline or train connections to the college or university that was their destination. I knew the city well and routines at Kennedy Airport and the Hudson River piers. I offered to go with Charles to get his wife and family when they arrived. We borrowed a station wagon from another student and were there at the pier when his family arrived. That developed into a quite wonderful friendship for the next six months—picnics and visits to the zoo, strolling the Inner Harbor. I became their guide to all things American; in turn, they immersed me in the stories of the ugly politics and extravagant beauties of South Africa. And always in the background Charles was navigating me through the labyrinthine world of Semitic grammar and ancient Assyrian and Egyptian culture. This was the world I expected to inhabit for the rest of my life.

# 9

## COUSIN ABRAHAM

It was a tradition in the athletic culture of my high school to prepare for basketball games played in Butte by visiting Henry's Plumbing on Second Street West. Butte was a mining town boasting the largest open-pit copper mine on earth. It was notorious for its ruthless and corrupt robber barons in their mansions and the thugs and gangs on the streets.

I was initiated into the mythic mayhem of Butte violence by being taken with a few of my teammates to Henry's in anticipation of my first game in Butte. Henry got us ready to deal with the brutality that we were sure to encounter by outfitting us with what he called "fist pipes." He cut a piece of pipe to a length of four inches, threaded both ends, filled the pipe with sand, and then capped the ends. When walking the streets of Butte, we were to keep this fist pipe enclosed in our grip. When assaulted by one of the Butte toughs, we would slug him with our weighted fist, and he wouldn't know what hit him. Henry had grown up in Butte. He knew what he was talking about. As he cut and threaded the pipe, he regaled us with Butte stories of street violence. He charged us two dollars for the weapon.

In the athletic subculture of our school, Henry was a legend. We called his fist pipes "Henrys." In the days approaching a road trip to Butte, "Do you have your Henry?" was part of the checklist. There were two high schools in Butte, one Catholic and the other public, so our team made the trip twice a year. Over the course of the two years I was on the team, we walked those menacing sidewalks four times, our concealed weapons at the ready, and never once had occasion to use them. A huge disappointment.

I had a more personal connection with Butte violence in Abraham Vereide. Abraham was my mother's favorite cousin. He was twenty years older than my mother. He had some of the charisma of her brother Sven, but he put his to far better use. A friend who keeps track of these kinds of things tells me that I am Abraham's first cousin, once removed.

Abraham arrived in Butte forty-two years before I showed up with my Henry. I was prepared for the violence. He wasn't. He arrived in America from Norway in 1905 at the age of nineteen. He heard that there was work in Butte and took the train across the country to get his start. Because of a few missed connections, compounded with difficulties with the English language, it took him fifteen days to get across the country. He got a job as a section hand. But he received a rough welcome—he was beaten up and robbed of his first three paychecks.

Eventually he received a friendlier welcome three hundred miles north of Butte in Kalispell. There he met Mattie, a Norwegian girl from Wisconsin. He proposed to her on a hill overlooking Flathead Lake, just a few miles north of where I now live. Abraham and Mattie were married in Kalispell in 1910, the year my mother was born in that same town.

Abraham's new father-in-law was a Methodist pastor. Under his influence Abraham himself became a pastor. In a few years he was a pastor with a congregation in Seattle.

After the death of his wife, my maternal grandfather moved to Seattle where there were family ties from Norway. Mother by this time was a teenager. The Norwegian network of cousins brought my mother and her cousin together. As she grew up, he took an interest in her. My mother admired her cousin extravagantly. As I grew up, her stories of her cousin Abraham significantly shaped my pastoral and moral imagination.

I grew up in a fiercely guarded sectarian church. Nobody outside the walls of the congregation of Spirit-filled souls we worshipped with on Sundays was considered "Christian." Abraham was the pioneer in my circle of immigrant ancestors who broke out of that tightly knit, self-defined sect that was hostile to any form of the faith that dressed or used language that betrayed "worldliness."

Through my mother's stories I learned a lot about cousin Abraham. The doors of Abraham's church opened out on neighborhoods of Scandinavian immigrants, "strangers in a strange land," marginalized and exploited. The windows and doors of this church didn't enclose; they opened out. Abraham's sense of congregation expanded greatly. He set about preparing these newcomers for a dual citizenship, American citizens and citizens of heaven. He was bold and energetic. He recruited the mayor of Seattle and leading business leaders as allies in developing a social conscience for bringing these immigrants into a full participation in the "welfare of the city." He started what he called Breakfast Groups. They were soon meeting all over Seattle.

Sometimes Abraham would bring his young cousin, my mother, and her boyfriend (later to be my father) to a Breakfast Group. She wasn't used to this—Democrats and Republicans, Lutherans and Methodists, Roman Catholics and Greek Orthodox, Jews and even an occasional Chinese Buddhist, Presbyterians and Pentecostals, churched and unchurched, sitting down together for a weekly breakfast of bacon and eggs, waffles and yogurt. And then this Norwegian pastor unobtrusively slipping the word "God" into that pot of mulligan stew, with the quiet invitation, "Let us pray."

"And do you know what, Eugene?"—this is now my mother speaking— "After a few times of seeing Abraham in action in those Breakfast Groups, that sectarian stranglehold on my throat loosened, and I found myself breathing freely."

My mother's stories of Abraham did the same for me, set me free from the claustrophobic confinement of sectarianism, opening wide windows and doors to wherever the wind of the Spirit is blowing.

Eventually in 1953 the Breakfast Groups found expression in his formation of an annual President's Prayer Breakfast in Washington D.C. It was during the Eisenhower administration. Billy Graham was the speaker. Three years later every state had a Governor's Prayer Breakfast. In 2007, I was invited to address the Governor's Prayer Breakfast in Montana and claimed my heritage as Abraham Vereide's first cousin, once removed.

I first met Abraham personally in 1960, when he was nearly eighty. I had driven to Washington D.C. to attend the President's Prayer Breakfast. I introduced myself to him. "Evelyn's son? How good of you to come and meet me."

A year later he came to our home in White Plains, New York, where my wife and I were then living, had lunch with us, and reminisced about my mother as a teenager in Seattle, his rude initiation to life in Butte, his marriage in Kalispell, and his first assignment as a newly ordained Methodist minister: "I was an itinerant circuit rider in and around Great Falls where the Great Plains begin to stretch out east from the Rocky Mountains. I had a horse under me, a rifle in its scabbard, a Bible tucked under my belt, in a sanctuary of Norwegian-like mountains."

I loved hearing his stories, loved swapping memories of our Butte connection, loved hearing about my mother and father as young people newly in love in Seattle. But the enduring pastoral legacy I received from Abraham was my rescue from the stifling sectarianism in which I had been raised.

# 10

## MENNONITE PUNCH

I grew up in a Pentecostal culture that was quite wonderful in many ways. The music, a mix of country and folk with all the old standards worked in, was full of energy and emotion. A remarkable number of people in our small congregation were surprisingly accomplished musicians: my aunt on the piano, my good friend on the violin, his father on the flute, my dad with his tenor saxophone, and my mother with her accordion. A strikingly statuesque young woman played her large bass fiddle with dramatic flair, slapping and spinning it. An elderly man who had spent his life as a logger, his fingers still agile, picked his banjo. I played the cornet. There were always impromptu trios and quartets. The preachers were great storytellers. A succession of missionaries on furlough entertained us through each year with heartbreaking stories out of Africa and Brazil. I was never bored. I loved it.

But pastors were in short supply. These preachers were great at the big picture and the great challenges ahead, but they didn't have any time for ordinary people devoid of drama.

I liked the preachers. They were never dull. Most of them were larger than life. As I entered adolescence, I began to get the feeling that God, except for the time they talked about him on Sunday, was not high on their agenda. They were pretty full of themselves. And by this time I was getting interested in God.

Brother Herman, for instance. (All our preachers were either "brother" or, occasionally, "sister.") He was *much* larger than life. And he was never larger than on one Saturday afternoon at a Mennonite wedding. There was a Mennonite community ten miles or so east of our town, nestled against the mountains. One of the young men from our church courted and proposed marriage to one of their girls. The wedding date was set, and all the young people from our congregation were invited to the wedding. Our preacher, Brother Herman, was invited by the bride's pastor to share in the marriage service. It was late spring. I remember that the lilacs and apple trees were in blossom. The wedding and reception took place on the family farm. A Mennonite feast was spread. After the wedding ceremony we all fell to at the tables of fried chicken and potato salad, coleslaw and deviled eggs. And punch.

Brother Herman remarked on how good the punch was and kept going back for refills. He kept saying that it was the best punch he had ever had, *Mennonite* punch, and to be sure and give him the recipe.

Meanwhile, the rumor was circulating among the younger set that one of the Mennonite kids had spiked the punch with vodka. We could hardly contain ourselves, watching to see when the effects would take hold, for one of the subtexts in virtually every one of Brother Herman's sermons was "Liquor has never passed my lips." We heard it every Sunday. Now we had a ringside seat, watching it happen, watching Mennonite punch in considerable quantities pass his lips. It took about forty minutes for the vodka to make its presence felt. Brother Herman spent the rest of the afternoon under an apple tree, but not quietly—his loud snoring announcing the cancellation of his proud years of teetotalling.

Twenty-seven years later I was speaking at a gathering of Mennonite pastors in Indiana and told that story by way of introducing my first encounter with Mennonites. After my lecture, one of the pastors came up to me and said, "I was at that wedding. I was the kid who spiked the punch."

# 11

## HOLY LAND

I memorized Psalm 108 sixty years ago. It was the job that did it. It was a summer job, working for the town of Kalispell, the town in which I had grown up and was now getting ready to leave. High-school graduation was behind me, and university ahead. In three months I would board the Great Northern Railroad and head out for Seattle.

A single sentence got me started: "I will awake the dawn." My job for the town that summer was in the Department of Street Maintenance. When the town was platted and laid out, all the residential streets were lined with Norway maples, with an occasional cottonwood thrown in. As U.S. Highway 93 entered the town limits from the south, it became Main Street, bisecting the town. A wide grassy boulevard divided Main Street down the middle. After four city blocks, the boulevard expanded into a park at the center of which was the county courthouse. The road split into one-way streets, north and south, that curved around the park, and then came together again, still divided by the boulevard for another four blocks, at which point asphalt and cement replaced the grass. The Norway maples gave way to Wheeler's Jewelry and the Conrad Bank, the Woolworth five-and-dime and Montgomery Ward, the Jordan Café, and Stockman's Saloon.

It made for a welcoming entrance to our town, and I was always proud of it. Unlike many western towns that have the appearance of being as unplanned as a teenage pregnancy, our wide streets, ample boulevards, and generous plantings of trees showed every sign of being the result of a thoughtful and affectionate courtship between the first settlers and the land.

My job that summer was watering those grassy, tree-studded boulevards. My workday began in the middle of the night. I started at eleven o'clock so that the bulk of my work would be done while there was a minimum of traffic. With the help of an alarm clock, I would get out of bed and be out on the street, watering the grass and trees. After six hours of working in the dark, I would begin anticipating the arrival of daylight. Some nights dragged on endlessly—would the sun ever come up? "Come on, you old lazy bones sun! Wake up!"

On one of those slow-arriving mornings, a sentence in the psalm came to mind: "I will awake the dawn!" My mind expanded exponentially. The mindless, repetitive work left plenty of room for the free play of my imagination. From the modest responsibility of keeping the grass a welcoming green through a mostly rainless summer, I found myself responsible for praying the sun up and over the mountains.

The wake-up call expanded into a workplace reflection on the entire psalm that occupied those summer nights and dawns. I had begun using the psalm for whimsical amusement, but as scripture so often does, it soon took over, and I found *it* using *me*. It wove a kind of valedictory meditation through those summer days of transition from the familiar streets on which I had grown up to the world beyond—to a university campus to begin with, then to whatever places and kinds of work that would come after that.

Three wake-up phrases bunched together at the psalm's opening: "Awake my soul" . . . "Awake, O harp and lyre" . . . and "I will awake the dawn." Was I awake? Truly awake? I had my eyes open; I was going through the motions of my work. But was I *God*-awake? Was my *soul* awake? If I was really awake, I would be doing more than watering that grass, I would be thanking and praising and singing. That's what wide-awake people do:

> *I will give thanks to thee, O Lord, among the peoples*
> *I will sing praises to thee among the nations.*
> *For thy steadfast love is great above the heavens,*
> *Thy faithfulness reaches to the clouds.*

I felt like I had those summer nights all to myself. It was my first extended immersion in silence and solitude. The whole town asleep and I alone awake, alive and alert to the movements of the summer constellations, *steadfast love* and *faithfulness* resonating through the phases of the moon, rising on the incense of the fragrant night air. There is something about getting up and going out in the middle of the night that gives you an edge on the rest of the world.

The monks know what they are doing when they get up at two in the morning to pray Lauds, the first office of the day. All summer long I kept vigil, took lessons in being a monk, present to hear the first birdsong, catch the first hint of light coming up from behind the Swan Range of the Rocky Mountains.

I never became a monk, but I got a feel for it that summer.

Wakefulness is the first thing. All the great spiritual teachers tell us that. *Awake my soul.*

But that kind of thing is just a little too good to last, and it didn't last long on the late night streets of Kalispell.

I watered my grassy boulevards with a fire hose. I had thirty yards of hose wrapped around a reel that was attached to a huge wooden cart. I would attach the end of the hose to a fire hydrant, unreel it to its full length, then play the sprinkling nozzle back and forth across the grass. Whenever I was watering the median strip or the boulevard on the opposite side of the street from the hydrant, my hose would be exposed in the street. I had a little sandwich-board sign that I propped in the middle of the road a hundred yards or so in either direction from where I was working, warning vehicles to slow down. When they read my sign and heeded it, I had plenty of time to get my hose out of the road and let them go through.

But not everyone honored my sign. Mostly it was the truckers who ignored it. They would roar into my silence, and I would dive to the curbside for safety, leaving my hose behind. Then they would hit it—those huge steel juggernauts, logging trucks and eighteen-wheelers—and the hose would spring leaks in three or four places. It was an old hose, donated to the town from the fire department when it was no longer fit for the serious work of firefighting. It couldn't stand much abuse. I would run to the fire hydrant, turn off the water, and spend the next hour or so repairing the leaks.

This didn't happen every night. Several nights would pass without incident. Then it would happen again. I would be meditating, relaxed and attentive in the stillness, at ease in the rhythms of my work, awake to God, praying

> *Be exalted, O God, above the heavens,*
> *Let thy glory be over all the earth,*

and then without warning one of these apocalyptic machines would be upon me, and my prayer would shift gears to

> *That thy beloved may be delivered,*
> *Give help by thy right hand, and answer me!*

**I** never got used to the intrusions. The night always seemed so large with God; my work always felt so fitting, so appropriate, so congenial. For it wasn't long into the summer that I was feeling quite proprietary about those streets and grassy boulevards. My mother had been born in this town only fifteen years after it had been established. My immigrant grandfather, who died before I was born, had laid out the first cement sidewalks. The homes of my several aunts and uncles were safe houses through my growing-up years. There was hardly a street corner that was not signposted by the memory of a fistfight . . . or an infatuation. This was *my* town, and I had this wonderful summer of nights to touch and smell and tend it. My appreciation was deepened by the sense of my approaching departure.

As the summer unfolded, Psalm 108 continued to guide me in praying my experience of this place. One night about halfway through the summer—it was early July—I noticed that halfway through the psalm the subject changed from *me* to *God*. The first half of the psalm is all I and me: "*My* heart is ready, O God *my* heart is ready . . . awake *my* soul . . . *I* will awake the dawn . . . answer *me*." "I" and "me," nine times. I loved that. I was given a grammar in which I could express myself in my surroundings with a vocabulary tailor-made to my experience. I'm sure that is why I liked it so much. I was an eighteen-year-old adolescent, full of myself, full of my town. I loved saying "I" and "me." I still do.

Then, abruptly, without a transition, God is speaking:

> *God has promised in his sanctuary,*
> *"With exultation I will divide up Shechem,*
> *and portion out the Vale of Succoth.*
> *Gilead is mine; Manasseh is mine;*
> *Ephraim is my helmet;*
> *Judah my scepter.*
> *Moab is my washbasin;*
> *upon Edom I cast my shoe;*
> *over Philistia I shout in triumph."*

This is "Promised Land" language: *I will divide up . . . I will portion out.* When Israel entered the land promised to them by God, the tribes assembled at Shechem, the geographical center, and each was assigned its portion, its God-promised place. Life always occurs in place. It is never an abstraction, never a generality. Place: Sinai, Galilee, Bethany. Place: Kalispell, Kila, Creston, Somers, Bigfork. Holy lands, holy places.

As the grass was soaking up the water, I was soaking up the place, relishing it not simply as my place but God's place.

Poets characteristically love place names. But whoever it was that laid out my town was not a poet. The landscaping of parks and trees was generous, but all the streets and avenues were numbered: 1, 2, 3, 4 . . . The only street in the core town that had a name was Main Street and there is precious little poetry in that, especially after Sinclair Lewis had finished with it.

So I took it upon myself to christen the streets with names worthy of their significance in my life. I didn't go so far as to cross out the numbered street signs and spray paint them with proper names, but I *said* them night after night: Shechem, Succoth, Gilead, Manasseh, Ephraim, Judah . . . and Shiloh, Beersheba, Shunem, Cana, Chorazin, Gaza, Jezreel, Ziklag, Gezer. I had learned to walk and talk, played, gone to school, made friends, sinned and repented, read and prayed and loved, on holy ground. This land had been portioned out by God, not primarily for farming and mining and logging, but for living out all the complexities of eternal life on this earth—salvation life. A holy land requires proper names to evoke its character. Numbers don't do it. The naming became a whimsical exercise in sanctifying the ground I had grown up on, The Holy Land.

There are nine place names in the list of holy places that God divided up and portioned out, but I didn't find much personal use for the last three. Moab, Edom, and Philistia were enemies, and I didn't have a very strong sense of enemy in those days. The closest thing to an enemy for me was a rival school's athletes in the next valley.

Except for those trucks, those bully trucks hurtling out of the darkness and puncturing my fire hose. I would yell out after them, "Moabite! Edomite! Philistine!" They never heard me, of course, but there was considerable satisfaction in having access to some biblically sanctioned invective. I grew up in a family and church in which there were strong taboos against using cuss words, but now I had a suitable vocabulary for venting my anger.

Of the three names, Edomite, with support from Psalm 137 and the obscure prophet Obadiah, eventually rose to the top as my invective of choice. If someone crossed me, irritated me, made life difficult for me, I had a word for him: "Edomite." I would mutter under my breath, "Damn Edomite! . . . good-for-nothing Edomite! . . . Edomite scum!"

When I left home for college after that summer's work, I left a holy land. The streets and trails, the hills and mountains, the rivers and lakes—all were holy ground, the valley that I had grown up in was sacred space. It still is. But it wasn't until years later that Edomite got rescued from the waste can of cuss words and got rehabilitated as prayer. I had been a pastor for fourteen or fifteen years and quite fluent in my use of biblical cuss words before I noticed how

Psalm 108 used Edomite not as profanity but as prayer. I had been so delighted that I had a word I could use to curse people I didn't like or who didn't like me that I had completely missed the way the psalmist used the word.

By then, as a pastor, I had extensive experience with Edomites. Edomites, with their noisy agendas for running the kingdom of God on their own terms, continued to take me by surprise, much as those truckers did, invading my practice of the presence of God, disrupting my work to the glory of God in my congregation. It is not just pastors who get surprised, but it is easy for pastors to harbor the presumption that when we are wronged or ignored or dismissed, God himself is being blasphemed. Biblically sanctioned cussing—damned Edomites!—seems quite in order.

The noticing took place gradually, but eventually it forced me to remove Edom from my vocabulary of invective and install it in my vocabulary of petition.

Here is how Edom ends up in the prayer:

> *Who will bring me to the fortified city?*
> *Who will lead me to Edom?*
> *Hast thou not rejected us, O God?*
> *Thou dost not go forth, O God, with our armies,*
> *O grant us help against the foe,*
> *for vain is the help of man!*
> *With God we shall do valiantly;*
> *it is he who will tread down our foes.*

I have a long way to go before I assimilate this final movement of the prayer and live it from the core of my being, especially my vocational being. But at least I now know the lay of the land: Edom is not the enemy that I curse or shake my fist at or avoid or dismiss. Edom is the enemy whom I, with God's grace and help, am led to visit and embrace.

Edom starts out as a negative. For years now I have been living in a place and doing work where I am learning to pray *for* instead of *against* Edom. Not very well much of the time—the sense of outrage and invective continues to linger, and all I can come up with many times is a prayer that God will tread down *my* foes. But I keep at it, praying to the God who in Jesus is teaching me to love my enemies, my dear Edomites, praying that God will *lead me to Edom*. When I started praying this prayer fifty-eight years ago, I didn't know this is where I would end up. Prayer often involves us in what the sociologists call "unintended consequences."

So what do I do with Edom? I ask God to bring me to Edom. And God does. Over and over and over again. The person, the task, the threat, the frustration, the circumstance to which my first impulse is to curse—"damn Edomite!"—becomes, through the patient praying of Psalm 108, an occasion for recycling my swords into plowshares.

# 12

## AUGUSTINE NJOKUOBI
## AND ELIJAH ODAJARA

In my last year of university I became good friends with two students from Nigeria with unpronounceable last names, Augustine Njokuobi and Elijah Odajara. They had been sent on scholarship from their Christian high school in Lagos City with the intent that they would return and teach in the school. They had also been instructed to recruit someone to teach English literature. I didn't know it at the time, but they had decided that I was the one. They told me stories about Nigeria, the storied tribal culture, and the school they were going to return to, an outpost of the kingdom of God in Africa. Eventually they got around to the business of recruitment. Nigeria needed me. Their high school needed me. Africa was seething with opportunities for serving Christ. They could arrange for an appointment to their high-school faculty.

It seemed like an answer to prayer. In four months I would be graduating, and I had no idea what I would do. I would have a diploma in philosophy and literature, but what kind of job did that qualify me for? I had never really thought about it. My university years had consisted in enjoying my friends, studying my books, being active in student activities, and competing in track-and-field athletics. I had not really thought beyond that. I had a vague idea of becoming a professor of philosophy and literature, but I knew that would require more schooling, and I had made no plans for it and no money. Who would hire me, and for what, when I showed them my degree in philosophy and a handful of gold medals I had accumulated in running the mile in various track meets in the Northwest? And one more thing: I was engaged to be married that summer. Was this an act of providence or not?

We talked about it, Augustine and Elijah and I. It didn't take long for the lure of exotic Africa, the prospect of immersing myself in a new culture, having a respectable job (the school would provide travel expenses and a salary), a couple honeymoon years in a world of wonders, and taking my place in an outpost of the kingdom of God—all of that and more seemed to require a grateful Yes. I said yes. Letters were exchanged, my dean wrote a recommendation; within a month I had received a letter of invitation, a two-year appointment to the faculty of the Christian high school in Lagos City.

Meanwhile things hadn't been going well with my fiancée. She called off the engagement. The termination of that romance at the same time put an end to my romance with Nigeria. The thought of going to Nigeria by myself drained all the appeal out of Africa. I told Augustine and Elijah. They were devastated. I wrote to Lagos City and resigned the position that I had not even begun. The day following graduation I packed my car and set out for Montana, a ten-hour drive, ten hours of reorienting myself to my now nonfuture. I already knew what I would be doing for the summer. I had earlier agreed to work for my father in his butcher shop and save money as I got ready for whatever was to come.

But what? The only thing I could come up with was to be a pastor. I had never considered being a pastor. For me, being a pastor was what you did when you couldn't do anything else, one step up the ladder from being unemployed. Right now I couldn't think that there might be "anything else." I was not exactly qualified to be a pastor, but in the church culture in which I grew up it didn't take much to qualify. Three years at a Bible school was standard. With my university degree I was probably already overqualified. It seemed better than nothing.

I talked it over with my parents. The next morning I called the person in charge of church appointments in our denomination in Montana. I had never met him, but he knew my parents. I asked him if there were any churches looking for a pastor. "Not right now, Eugene. But we have been hoping to start a new church in Townsend or in Fort Benton. You'd be welcome to give it a try." Both small towns were across the mountains at the beginning of the prairies. I had never been to either town. I arbitrarily chose Townsend and told him I would start in September. "Do you have any counsel or direction for me?" He didn't. "The Lord will teach you what you need to know."

So in September I drove across MacDonald Pass and the Continental Divide, an extravaganza of glacial-cut peaks and alpine meadows, and descended into the flat, featureless plains of Townsend to begin my life as a pastor. The topography of the five-hour drive was a metaphor.

I arrived at noon on Friday faced with two tasks: find a job; find a place to live. I went to a butcher shop and got a job as a meat cutter—I would start work on Monday. I then drove through the town looking for a place to live. I spotted a sign in a house window: Apartment for Rent. It was a basement apartment, and I took it. So far things were easy. The next day I went through the town, knocking on doors, introducing myself: "Hello. I'm Eugene Peterson, and I've been asked by my denomination to come here to start an Assembly of God Church. Can I talk to you about it?" Things were no longer easy. Over the next six hours I knocked on every door in town. I never got inside a single house. Everyone in town was either a Methodist or a Mormon. And apparently they all went to church.

I was out of houses but kept walking. I left the town and found a trail along the Missouri River. The sun was setting over the soaring peaks of the Rockies fifty miles to the west in a blaze of glory, and I was down here dragging my feet across this colorless flatland without a compass. Fort Benton, which also "needed a church," was on this same Missouri River about a four-hour drive northeast. Maybe I should just get in my car and try it. Maybe I had picked the wrong place. It was getting dark. I came to a diner, got a hamburger and a slice of apple pie, then went to my apartment and unrolled my sleeping bag.

But I didn't sleep. I wrestled with an angel all night, praying, asking questions, going over the ground of the last four months. When the sun came up, I knew I was in the wrong place at the wrong time doing the wrong thing. I was not a pastor.

On the drive home across the mountains I considered my options. I could work as a butcher with my father—all along he had wanted to make me a partner in his business. I could join the army—the Korean War was on. Or I could go to seminary. I had never considered seminary before—graduate study in philosophy, yes, but not seminary. In the church culture in which I was raised seminary was out of the question. But I couldn't get seminary out of my mind—a shift from philosophy to theology wouldn't be that difficult. I could be a professor in theology. When I arrived home at about three o'clock that Sunday, my mother met me as I drove up and asked, "What are you doing here?"

I told her, "I'm not going to Townsend."

"So, what are you going to do?"

"What would you think of my going to seminary?"

"I always thought you would go to seminary." *That* was a surprise—I just assumed that she harbored the hostile suspicion pervasive in my sectarian church culture that all seminaries were cemeteries.

There was a seminary in New York City that a friend I greatly respected had attended. And two professors at my university were graduates. A few telephone calls the next day made the way clear for admission. I didn't unpack my car. Within a week I was enrolled as a student in the Biblical Seminary in New York at 235 East Forty-ninth Street. (The name has since been changed to New York Theological Seminary.)

It had been quite a six months. From Augustine and Elijah's planting of the dream of Africa, to the devastation of rejection that woke me from the dream, to the attempt to become a pastor for all the wrong reasons, to an unlikely and unplanned enrollment in a New York City seminary. All steps on my way to becoming a pastor. But talk about *haphazard*.

# 13
## SEMINARY

A few days after arriving at the seminary, I found myself sitting in a classroom led by a professor, Robert Traina, who over the next three years would profoundly change the Bible for me, and me along with it, in ways that gave shape to everything I have been doing for the rest of my life. This is not an exaggeration.

I grew up in a Christian home and was familiar from an early age with the Bible. I read it daily, memorized it, and on entering adolescence argued with my friends over it. But quite frankly, I wasn't really fond of it. I knew it was important, knew it was God's word. To tell the truth, I was bored with it. More often than not it was a field of contention, providing material for truths that were contested by warring factions. Or it was reduced to rules and principles that promised to keep me out of moral potholes. Or, and this was worst of all, it was flattened into clichés and slogans and sentimental godtalk intended to inspire and motivate.

It took only three or four weeks in Professor Traina's classroom to become aware of a seismic change beginning to take place within me regarding the Bible. Until now, I and all the people I associated with had treated the Bible as something to be *used*—used as a textbook with information about God, used as a handbook to lead people to salvation, used as a weapon to defeat the devil and all his angels, used as an antidepressant. Now, incrementally week by week, semester by semester, my reading of the Bible was becoming a conversation. I was no longer reading words—I was listening to voices. I was observing how these words worked in association with all the other words on the page. And I was learning to listen carefully to these voices, these writers who were, well, *writers*. Skilled writers, poets, and storytellers who were artists of language. Isaiah and David were poets. Matthew and Luke were masters of the art of narrative. Words were not just words; words were holy.

The experience was not merely academic. The passion and patience that permeated that classroom instilled in me an inductive imagination: fiercely attentive to everything that is there and only what is there, alert to relationships both literary and personal, habitually aware of context—the entire world of creation and salvation that is being revealed in this Bible. And always accompanied by the insistence that I do this firsthand, not first filtered through the hearsay of others or the findings of experts. His faculty colleagues shared the work, but it was Professor Traina's intensity and comprehensiveness that penetrated my mind and spirit in a way that shaped everything I would do and am still doing as a pastor, professor, and writer. And not just my vocational life but also my personal life, my marriage and family, my friends and community and church. The inductive imagination developed into a biblical imagination.

But I'm getting ahead of myself. Meanwhile, I had learned that all the students were required to do field work in a church. I told the dean that I wasn't going to be a pastor. Didn't that qualify me for an exemption from the requirement? He was polite but firm: the requirement had nothing to do with vocational training; for a few hours every week it would keep my feet on ordinary ground, using ordinary language with ordinary people. "Unrelieved intellectual work, especially *theological* intellectual work, can shrivel your soul."

I thought I was going to have to teach a Sunday-school class or run a youth group. Neither prospect gave me any pleasure. I never did like Sunday school, and I had never been in a youth group. But I was lucky in my assignment. I became coach of the basketball team at Madison Avenue Presbyterian Church on East Seventy-third Street. I could work in a church without going to church.

But I went to Sunday worship the first week of my employment to get a feel for the lay of the land. I didn't know any Presbyterians and knew next to nothing about what they were up to. The preacher was George Arthur Buttrick. He had a reputation of being one of the great preachers in America, but it was two or three months before I learned that. But that first Sunday I knew he was good, very good, and went every Sunday after that. He introduced me to a way of preaching I didn't know existed. A quiet and careful, ruminative and thoughtful exposition of the scriptures, without ostentation, without calling attention to himself. He used language precisely, accurately—a poet in the pulpit. In the year of Sundays that I listened to him preach, I don't think I heard a single cliché pass his lips.

I had grown up on preaching that was a mixture of cheerleading and entertainment with a lot of scripture verses thrown in at random. I was rarely bored, but I was also aware that it was pretty thin soup.

Madison Avenue Presbyterian had a history of inviting several seminarians each year to work on the church staff and offered us a modest stipend for showing up. After every Sunday-evening worship and another sermon, Dr. Buttrick invited the seminarians—there were seven or eight of us—to his penthouse manse on Fifth Avenue overlooking Central Park. He removed his coat and shoes, put on a pair of worn slippers, sat on the floor with his back against a wall, filled his pipe and lit it (he was the first pastor I had ever observed smoking a pipe), and then gathered us into a freewheeling conversation for the next hour. We asked him questions, and he asked us questions. There was no agenda. We talked about preaching and prayer and worship but not in the abstract. He kept our conversation local and immediate and personal in a way that I later learned to identify as pastoral. He shied away from "big" truths. On one of these evenings he was asked by one of the students something about preaching. Something on the order of "What is the most important thing you do in preparing to preach each Sunday?" I think we were all surprised by the answer, at least I was. His answer: "For two hours every Tuesday and Thursday afternoon, I walk through the neighborhood and make home visits. There is no way that I can preach the gospel to these people if I don't know how they are living, what they are thinking and talking about. Preaching is proclamation, God's word revealed in Jesus, but only when it gets embedded in conversation, in a listening ear and responding tongue, does it become gospel."

I happened to know something about this "neighborhood" that was part of this pastor's sermon preparation. Most of my basketball players lived in this neighborhood of apartment houses and brownstones. This was not the affluent or prestigious part of the city that provided a goodly number of worshippers each Sunday. This was the neighborhood, east of Madison Avenue toward the East River, of middle- or lower-class working people. I later learned that Dr. Buttrick didn't drive a car. Whether he had never learned to drive or simply chose not to, I never knew. What I did know is that when he was working on his sermon, he did not select the rich or influential to listen to, but the people within walking distance in the neighborhood—a detail that later entered my pastoral imagination.

These Sunday evenings with this prominent preacher sitting on the floor in his slippers and smoking his pipe, was my introduction into the "backroom" of a pastor's life, what went on when the pastor was not in the pulpit, not in the public eye. There was far more to this life of pastor than I had ever had access to.

I was given a seminary assignment to write a profile of a contemporary American religious leader. I chose Harry Emerson Fosdick. In the world in which I grew up, Fosdick was the enemy—the incarnation of unbelieving liberalism that was eroding the foundations of the Christian faith in Christian America. And a Presbyterian no less. In the 1920s the fundamentalist/liberal lines were drawn as battle lines. Fosdick was targeted as the Antichrist by many of the evangelists who came through our town in my youth. As the religious wars heated up, Fosdick was forced out of his Presbyterian pulpit in New York City.

But I had just read a book by Fosdick, *The Meaning of Prayer*. It was the best book on prayer I had ever read. Could the Antichrist have written this? That was hard to believe. I was curious. This paper would give me an opportunity to find out what was behind, or not behind, all the vicious invective that surrounded the name Fosdick in my memory.

I was telling a friend about my choice of someone to write about, and he said, "Why don't you call him up. I just read a review of his autobiography. He lives on Long Island. Call him up."

"I can't call him up. He's famous. And I'm nobody. And besides, I'm not sure I want to meet him in person. One of my pastors always called him Beelzebub. I am not really interested in sitting down and talking with the devil."

My friend, Jim, responded by picking up the telephone directory, looking up the number of Harry Emerson Fosdick, and dialing the number. He handed the receiver to me. Two rings and a voice, "Hello, this is Harry Fosdick."

Now what do I do? I stammered a bit and said, "You don't know me, but I'm a seminary student and writing a paper on you. My name is Eugene Peterson. Could I meet with you and talk about it?"

"Certainly, Mr. Peterson. I'd be glad to. I come into Riverside Church every Thursday for a few hours. Could you meet me next Thursday at two o'clock? Come to my study. Somebody there will guide you."

That evening I read the autobiography and learned that the man I was going to meet was seventy-eight years old. I also learned that it was very unlikely that the man was going to remotely resemble Beelzebub. By this time I was looking forward to the meeting. The next Thursday I took the subway to Riverside Church and was directed to the elevator and the floor of Dr. Fosdick's study.

As I stepped out of the elevator, an elderly man with rosy cheeks approached me with quick steps and a welcoming smile, extended his hand, and said, "Hello, Mr. Peterson, I'm Harry."

He soon put me at my ease. I told him why I was there, that I had read his book on prayer and was completely taken aback. "This book couldn't have been written by the man I had heard about when growing up." I omitted the part about Beelzebub.

He laughed and gave me this in response: "A seminarian at Southern Baptist Seminary, which as you know is very conservative, is writing a doctoral dissertation on me and asked me to write out a statement of my belief, which I did. He showed it to his theology professor, who brought it to class the next day. He told the class, 'I was just given this letter, a statement of personal belief, written by one of the well-known religious leaders in America. I want you to guess who wrote it.'

"The class responded, naming all the well-known evangelical and conservative theologians, preachers, and evangelists they could think of. Billy Graham was most frequently named. When they had exhausted the possibilities, the professor said, 'This was written by Harry Emerson Fosdick.' Stunned silence. And then a young man on the front row blurted out, 'I don't care if his name is Harry Emerson Fosdick—he's still a Christian!'"

Now we both laughed. We continued in companionable conversation for another thirty minutes. Another name crossed off my "enemy list." By the time the subway had returned me to midtown Manhattan, my Christian and church world had expanded exponentially.

I entered seminary with little, if any, interest in theology. In my experience theology was too contaminated with polemics and apologetics to take any pleasure in it. It always left me with a sour taste. The grand and soaring realities of God and the Holy Spirit, scripture and Creation, salvation and a holy life always seemed to get ground down into contentious, mean-spirited arguments: predestination and free will, grace and works, Calvinism and Arminianism, liberal and conservative, supra- and infra-lapsarianism. At my university I had avoided all this by taking refuge in a philosophy major that gave me room and companions for cultivating wonder and exploring meaning. When I arrived in seminary, I continued to keep my distance from theology by plunging into the biblical languages and the English Bible.

And then I met Karl Barth. But not in the seminary. I was introduced to Barth by one of the young men on the basketball team I was coaching. Jordan was a graduate student in English literature at Columbia University and about my age. He was Jewish but not an observant Jew. All he had observed from his parents was their indifference to any and all religion. He had started coming to the church because of the basketball team and in the process became a Christian. It was a new world to him, and he loved talking about every latest book discovery. After our Saturday ball games we often had long conversations over coffee—conversations about God, Jesus, and this Christian life that was opening into a world of wonders.

He introduced me to Karl Barth on a Saturday evening while we were showering after winning a close game. "Eugene, you've got to read this book. I just found it in a used bookstore. You would love this." While we toweled ourselves dry and dressed, he described what he had been reading in Barth's *Epistle to the Romans.*

Jordan's excitement excited me. The first thing Monday morning I checked out a copy of the book from the library. I've been reading Barth ever since. He became the theologian I never had, a theologian who got me interested in God as God, not just talk about God. Franz Kafka in a letter wrote, "If the book we are reading does not wake us, as with a fist hammering on our skull, why then do we read it? . . . A book must be like an ice-axe to break the sea frozen inside us." This first book of Barth's that I read was "like an ice-axe."

What I had heard and read of theology up until this point was *about* God. God and the things of God as if they were topics for discussion, things to be figured out; there was no juice in them. What a contrast to the poetry of Whitman, the novels of Melville, the journalism of Chesterton. But there was juice and plenty of it in Barth. I couldn't get enough of him.

In reading Barth, I realized that for most of my life the people I had been living with and who had taught me had been primarily interested in getting the truth of the gospel and the Bible right, explaining it and defending it. (My parents were blessed exceptions to all this.) Barth didn't have much interest in that. He was a witness (a favorite word of his). He was calling attention to the *lived* quality of the Christian life, the narrative of the Bible, the good news of the gospel. *Listening* to God as God reveals himself in Christ and the Bible and preaching. Not taking the Christian life into a laboratory and dissecting it to figure out what makes it tick, but entering into God's action of creation and salvation that is going on all around us and all the time and *participating* in it. Barth wasn't indifferent to "getting it right," but his passion was in "getting it lived."

I later learned that Barth wrote *Romans* while he was pastor of a village church in Safenwil, Switzerland. He was pastor of that little Reformed church (the Swiss equivalent of Presbyterian) for ten years. He kept writing what he started in that book for another forty-seven years. His witness has kept me more interested in and attentive to what God is doing than anything I do or can think of doing.

Each year for three years, without requesting it, I had been assigned to a Presbyterian church for my seminary field work. I gradually became accustomed to what, previous to seminary, had been a church word I could not have defined. I was welcomed; I was affirmed; I almost *felt* like a Presbyterian. Then I made it official. I became a Presbyterian. Not only the word "Presbyterian" began to take on texture, but "pastor" was gathering associations that felt personal and congenial.

Bill McAlpin, the pastor I was working with at the time in that final seminary year, asked me into his study one Sunday after worship. "Eugene, I'd like to see you ordained into our Presbyterian ministry. I know that you don't expect to be a pastor. I know that you anticipate graduate school and becoming a professor, but I think this would be a good thing. You need a church in which you have responsibility to your peers and affirm an established theological tradition. Professors as well as pastors need a support system to which they are accountable. Professional ministry, whether as professor or pastor, is no place for lone wolves—there are too many pressures, too many seductions."

I took his counsel and prepared for the ordination examinations. I was examined and approved at a meeting at First Presbyterian Church. It was in the same sanctuary from which Harry Emerson Fosdick had been dismissed, a casualty in the theological war that had ravaged the church thirty years before. I hoped that the Presbyterians would treat me better than they did him. And they did.

The seminary was a good place for me to be. I found myself in a congenial company of professors and classmates, sharing a common faith. The seminary provided me with a secure community of friendship, prayer, and learning during those years when I was still in formation, not sure of what was ahead. What I had no way of knowing at the time is how significant "Presbyterian" and "pastor"—extracurricular seminary courses that don't appear on my graduation transcript—would soon become.

But there was one more stop along the way—doctoral studies at Johns Hopkins University in Baltimore.

# 14

JAN

I had no idea that in nine months I would marry the young woman who was leading the singing on that November Sunday evening. It was a gathering of young adults, most of them university students, in a Presbyterian church in Baltimore. I had seen her the previous evening when I was the one leading the singing at an area meeting of university students at Johns Hopkins Hospital. I had noticed her seated in a second-row aisle seat in the large amphitheater lecture room. In a room of two hundred or so young people, she was the only one I did notice. I anticipated meeting and talking to her after the meeting. But I was too late; by the time I got to where she had been seated, she was gone.

Here she was again. I wasn't going to let her get away this time.

I was at this gathering reluctantly. I had planned to attend an evening performance of Handel's *Messiah* by the Baltimore Symphony and Chorus. But my friend Dr. Charles Fensham from South Africa, a fellow student at Johns Hopkins University in Semitic studies, had been invited to speak to the students on apartheid and didn't know the way to the church. We went together by streetcar.

When we arrived, even though I liked Charles very much, I can still remember feeling that I would have rather been at the symphony. A discussion of apartheid seemed like a plodding replacement for the soaring music of the *Messiah*. But that feeling of regret was quickly dissipated in the chorus of untuned voices conducted by my future wife.

She didn't get away. I kept her in my peripheral vision while I made a pretence of attention to apartheid. We rather shyly exchanged names. I was more aggressive, though, in arranging with a friend for a return ride for Charles to the university, and then, with another friend, a ride home for myself and Jan (I now knew her name). That gave us another twenty minutes of conversation without the distractions of apartheid.

Back at the graduate student dorm at the university, I told my roommate, Bob, about meeting Jan. Bob was a graduate student in geology. He was preparing for a lucrative career in the oil business. I was studying Semitic languages, preparing to be a scholar and professor in comparative penury. We couldn't have been more different in our fields of study, our goals in life, and even our temperaments. The biggest difference had to do with God: Bob was an atheist; I was a Christian. But it was worse than that. He not only didn't believe in God; he didn't like Christians. It was worse even than that—he held Christians in contempt. There was something about the Christian way of life that deeply violated his sense of order and reality.

By this time Bob and I had lived together for nearly three months and had discovered that we liked each other, got along well. He had a Jeep station wagon, and I kept him company on weekends, walking the rivers and exploring the Piedmont. Somehow he managed to make an exception for me while maintaining his generalized contempt for Christians. Between us the contempt softened into a kind of teasing banter.

When I announced to Bob that Sunday night that I had met Jan, he was immediately on my side. "What does she look like?"

"Brunette, about five four. Slim, attractive. Two eyes, two ears, a mouth, all of them in the right places. A soft Southern voice. A kind of quiet welcoming simplicity. You'd like her."

"Let's call her up."

But I hadn't gotten her telephone number. I didn't even know her last name.

"You Christians! You are so stupid. You meet an attractive woman and you walk off without arranging for any way to see or talk to her again. How do you even manage to propagate your species? I've never encountered such idiocy."

So I called up a friend, John, at the church, described Jan to him, and asked for her last name. He conferred with his wife. They couldn't come up with anyone.

"Sorry."

Stumped, I sat on the edge of my bed, rummaging through the bulletin and newsletter I had picked up earlier at the church. I read, "Vincent and Janice Stubbs are leaving for the missionary convention in Urbana next week." Just an hour ago she had told me that herself.

I said, "Bob, I know her name—Stubbs. Her family name is Stubbs."

He grabbed my arm and pulled me up from the bed. "Come with me, I'll show you how to handle this."

He led me across the street to a drug store, handed the cashier a ten-dollar bill, and said, "Give me a roll of dimes" (this was in 1957 when telephone calls were ten cents).

He gave me the dimes, handed me a telephone book, pushed me into the phone booth, and said, "Start calling."

I started calling.

There were sixty-six Stubbs in Baltimore. I began with the first listing. "Hello, can I speak with Jan?"

"Who?" And I hung up.

Then I dropped down to the last listing: "Hello, can I speak with Jan?"

"Who?" I hung up.

Back and forth, top to bottom, bottom to top. On the sixth call—her father's name was Vincent—the voice said, "She's next door. Can I ask who is calling?"

"My name is Eugene, and I'm calling from a phone booth. I'll call her back."

But I never did call her back. The next day, John, the friend I had called earlier, got in touch with me and said, "Anne and I figured out who that girl was you were asking about. She is coming to dinner on Friday night. Will you come and join us?"

I did join them. Thanks to the bold initiative of atheist Bob and the Christian hospitality of John and Anne, I didn't need to call her back. It had already cost me sixty cents.

Bob continued to take an interest in his sixty-cent investment in our lives. He arranged for excursions to museums and bird refuges, Saturday picnics and public lectures. Sometimes one of his several girl friends would join us. He had never known a Christian before, and he was curious, like coming upon a rock formation that was new to him and using his geologist's hammer to figure out how it got there. He never got over his astonishment over how Christians managed to get along in the world without knowing anything about the world. He took considerable pride in being able to do for Jan and me what God couldn't, or at least didn't, do for us. And Jan and I were in grateful awe of the surprising way in which God's providence was able to weave Bob's atheism into our deepening affection for each other.

But a serious problem surfaced quite early. From her early adolescence Jan had wanted to be a pastor's wife. And from an early age I had wanted nothing to do with pastors. For Jan, "pastor's wife" was not just being married to a pastor; it was far more vocational than that, a way of life. It meant participation in an intricate web of hospitality, living at the intersection of human need and God's grace, inhabiting a community where men and women who didn't fit were welcomed, where neglected children were noticed, where the stories of Jesus were told, and people who had no stories found that they did have stories, stories that were part of the Jesus story. Being a pastor's wife would place her strategically yet unobtrusively at a heavily trafficked intersection between heaven and earth.

Years later a Carmelite nun, a good friend by that time, was visiting in our home. She had entered the convent when she was eighteen, having wanted to be a nun from an early age. Jan told her of her early desire to be a pastor's wife. Sister Genevieve said, "If I had been raised Protestant, that's probably what I would have wanted. And if you had been Catholic, you probably would have aspired to being a nun. It was our respective ways of entering holy orders."

"Holy orders." Jan had never heard those words used for what she had entered into. But the words seemed accurate. She thanked our friend for blessing her, for including her in a vowed life of eucharistic hospitality. The term clarified what she had aspired to and then named what she had experienced—a sacred vocation, holy orders, pastor's wife.

Meanwhile, "pastor" held no such associations for me. The most influential and admired adults in my life had been laypersons, whether Christian or non-Christian, or even, like Bob, atheist. I had always been part of a worshipping Christian community and liked it, liked the people, liked being a part. But I hadn't been fortunate in my pastors. I didn't like the condescending way they treated me, didn't like the Holy Joe tones in which they preached and prayed, didn't like the clichés that infected their use of language. Religion, as they represented it, lacked juice. It is curious to me now, as I reflect on it, that my sense of the Christian life itself was never dulled or discredited by them. Pastors, with a single exception, just seemed to inhabit another form of life altogether, one that held no attractions for me.

And so as Jan and I were getting to know each other, and liking what we were getting to know, this business of pastor loomed large. Pastor as in pastor's *wife*, seemed nonnegotiable to Jan. And pastor as a vocation for me seemed like being put in charge of one of those old-fashioned elevators, spending all day with people in their ups and downs but with no view.

During these early months of getting acquainted and falling in love, I was at the same time immersed in a world of studies that was more strenuous and exhilarating than anything I knew existed. I was studying with the world's premier scholar in the field of Semitic languages and biblical archaeology and history, William Foxwell Albright. I was in the company of Jews and Jesuits, Presbyterians and Episcopalians—the brightest company of men and women I had ever been invited into. And there was no question that this was the world I wanted to work in. I would be a professor, a scholar, a writer.

But by this time I also wanted to marry Jan—who wanted to be a pastor's wife. Something was going to have to give. I was intoxicated with the life of the mind, the world of wonders opened up by these ancient languages—Akkadian and Aramaic, Ugaritic and Hebrew, Syriac and Arabic—happy with the prospect of a life spent in learning and helping others to learn the many-layered and richly textured world of Abraham and Moses, David and Isaiah, Jesus and Paul, that continued to work its way into our understanding and practice of the

Christian faith. Jan was poised on the cusp of a world of relationships, anticipating learning the names and stories of the men and women, the children and elderly, who were out there in the world, just waiting to be met in conversations and meals, people to love and enjoy, people to sing and pray with.

I was going to write books for people I would never meet. She was going to cook meals for family and friends, and for strangers who would be strangers no longer.

But the longer we were together, the vocational divide between us didn't seem so formidable. I had never met anyone who was so naturally and spontaneously relational, with a simplicity of spirit, limpid and uncomplicated. Those years of graduate study could have marked the beginning of a slow withdrawal from a relational life into a world of books. She rescued me from that. I was in love with books and language and the life of learning. I never knew that there was so much adrenaline in it. But I was also in love with Jan, the accessibility of her emotions, her immediacy to present things and people, her delight in the *hereness* and *nowness* of life. I had never met anyone quite like her and knew that I wanted to marry her. Reading and writing books didn't seem a very attractive prospect without Jan.

What I didn't know was that when we did marry, something had already been going on in me at some deep level, as yet undetected, that would soon disqualify me from the life of learning that I anticipated. In not quite three years, she was what she had always hoped to be—a pastor's wife.

# PART III

## SHEKINAH

We were on a two-week August vacation in New England. Driving through a small Vermont town, we approached a picture-book Congregational church, complete with four white pillars on the porch and a steeple with a bell. Jan and our infant son were asleep in the backseat. Karen, three years old, was sitting beside me.

"Oh, Karen," I said, "look at that lovely church."

She said, "Where—I don't see any church."

I slowed down and pointed it out.

"Well, it doesn't look like a church."

At the time of this conversation I had been a pastor for eighteen months. I had been assigned by my denomination to organize and develop a new congregation twenty miles northeast of Baltimore. We didn't have a "church that looked like a church." The church was our basement. During the week, at least on rainy days, our children rode their tricycles and built forts out of cardboard boxes in the church. We dried diapers on lines stretched between pulpit and lectern. On Sundays Jan and I set up folding chairs for the hundred or so people who came together and worshipped God.

That basement was the only church Karen had any memory of being in. *Of course* that colonial New England church didn't look like a church.

The neighborhood subdivision where I was entrusted to develop the new congregation was named Colonial Acres. Given the geography and history of the place, it was an appropriate name.

A committee of six men and women had been working with an architect and me for several months to design a church that expressed the way we intended to live in this place and worship God in this place. When the church members saw the proposed design, some of them commented, "It doesn't look like a church." They expected a porch with white pillars and a steeple. This was, after all, colonial country. George Washington had marched his army through these valleys and along these rivers. But George and his soldiers were long gone, and this was a *church* we were building, not a historical museum.

On returning from vacation, and given the many stereotypes of what a church should look like that were circulating through the congregation as we worshipped in our basement, I told the congregation that story. Most were amused, as I had been. But one family—they had been worshipping, quite happily, I thought, for that year and a half in our basement church that didn't look like a church—were offended and never returned.

I told Karen's "It doesn't look like a church" story a couple weeks later to a friend, Paul Ivrey. Paul was a rabbi about my age who had been given the task of developing a new synagogue a few miles north of where I lived. His beard put him in a class with Isaiah. We had become friends. On hearing the story, he laughed and said, "It sounds like the Shekinah to me—do you know the story of the Shekinah?"

I had heard the word and knew it had something to do with the presence of God, but I knew no story.

Paul said, "Eugene, you need to know this story. It's an old rabbinic story. 'Shekinah' is a Hebrew word that refers to a collective vision that brings together dispersed fragments of divinity. It is usually understood as a light-disseminating presence, bringing an awareness of God to a time and place where God is not expected to be—a *place*. It's not a public spectacle but more like a selective showing at God's discretion to encourage or affirm, to reveal a reality of something that we do not yet have eyes to see. It is not a term found in the Bible but was frequently used in the mystical Judaism of the Middle Ages."

Paul, from behind his Isaianic beard, continued: "That's what it is, but here's the story. The story is set in Jerusalem at a time when Jews were returning from their Babylonian captivity. Babylon had destroyed Jerusalem and its magnificent Solomonic temple. Meanwhile the Persian king, Cyrus, had conquered Babylon and gave the Jews permission to return to their homeland. He also generously made provision for them to rebuild the destroyed temple. Hope was at high tide. The devastation and heartache of those long years of living in a pagan culture among foreign gods was over—they would be able to worship God again on their native soil, reenter the splendid sacred precincts, and begin again to serve God in the place redolent with storied memories.

"You know all that. But here's what you need to tell Karen and your congregation, especially that family that walked out on you. When the first people arrived they took one look at the restored temple and wept at what they saw. The Solomonic temple that for five hundred years had provided a glorious centering for their life as a people of God had been replaced by what looked to them like a tarpaper shack. The squalid replacement broke their hearts, and they wept. As they wept, a dazzling, light-resplendent presence descended, the Shekinah— God's personal presence—and filled that humble, modest, makeshift, sorry excuse for a temple with glory. They lifted their arms in praise. They were truly home. God was truly present. The Shekinah faded out. The glory stayed.

"People like you and me," Paul continued, "need that Shekinah story. And our congregations need it. Most of what we do in getting our congregations going doesn't look anything like what people expect it to." (Paul's congregation was worshipping in a three-car garage that didn't look at all like a synagogue.)

"And do you know something else, Eugene? You don't look like a pastor— you are way too young. It might help if you grew a beard. But tell Karen and your congregation the story of the Shekinah."

I did both.

It had taken a long time to come to realize that I was a pastor, the "intent" that all along had been working "haphazardly" in and through the stories that I lived, slowly and silently coalescing into *pastor* in the Pastor John of Patmos epiphany that I described earlier. It was a good feeling, this vocational clarity, a way of work that fit who I was. Not just a job so that I could make a living, but a way of living that was congruent with what I had spent all my life becoming. It had taken a long time. It felt like an arrival at an appointed destination. Likewise with Jan—pastor's wife.

We were ready for a congregation. But where?

Throughout the previous decade, the 1950s, there had been an unprecedented increase in church attendance in North America. New churches were being started all over the place. My Presbyterian denomination was particularly active. I had not consciously paid much attention to the nature of church until recently. I was a new Presbyterian. Why not get in on the ground floor in forming a congregation, experience firsthand all the details that went into making a local church a *church,* and at the same time find out just what was involved with being a pastor in the real-life conditions of church?

In an earlier conversation, Doug Bennett, an older pastor, asked me, "When are you going to launch out on your own? Don't you think you have been here as an apprentice long enough?" I said that I was ready and that I would really like to start a new congregation but didn't know how to go about it. He said that people in Baltimore whom he knew were looking for someone just like me. He went to a telephone, called the person responsible for starting new churches in Baltimore, and put me on the phone with him. A four-hour drive the next day put me in Baltimore. Two months later Jan and I and our daughter Karen moved into a new home a quarter of a mile from the cornfield that was the site of the proposed church.

# 15

## ZIKLAG

What happened next took some getting used to. A congregation. I was not only a pastor but pastor of a church. A congregation, a gathering of saints and sinners, was my workplace. This was where I went to work every day.

It had taken me a long time to arrive at the realization that *pastor* is who I am and, without being aware of it, always have been. But my realization of the nature of *congregation* as my primary workplace lagged behind my sense of pastoral identity. Why the lag time? Maybe because I hadn't had the long development in understanding congregation that I had had in becoming a pastor.

I had entered congregations. I had belonged to congregations. But church had never been my primary workplace. I had always gone to church but, to be quite honest, I had never been much interested in church as church. As a child, I vigorously disliked Sunday school. I was allergic to things "churchy." I was interested in God and prayer and scripture, but I pursued these interests in ways and settings that had little to do with what I understood as church.

And then I "outed" as a pastor. After those three years of apprenticeship as a pastor in White Plains, I found myself going to work every day in a *church*. I was not *just* pastor. I was pastor of a church, a congregation. Pastor was not an autonomous vocation. Pastor was not a vocation negotiated privately between me and God. There was a third party—congregation. As it turned out, the congregation and I didn't have much in common. It turned out that what I had signed up for required spending a term in church boot camp to get a basic orientation in the conditions I would be dealing with as pastor of a church.

What I wasn't prepared for was the low level of interest that the men and women in my congregation had in God and the scriptures, prayer and their souls. Not that they didn't believe and value these things; they just weren't very interested. I had assumed that it would be self-evident to a congregation that the vocation of pastor had primarily to do with God. And I had assumed that the primary reason that Christians became part of a congregation had to do with God. They would come to church because they were interested in God and the scriptures, prayer and their souls. And I would be the person expected to give guidance and encouragement to matters of God and scripture, prayer and their souls.

It didn't happen. I couldn't have been farther off the mark.

This lack of common cause resulted in what it seemed to me was a lot of religious clutter, much of what struck me as an accumulation of trivia. My imagination had been schooled in the company of Moses and David; my congregation kept emotional and mental company with television celebrities and star athletes. I was reading Karl Barth and John Calvin; they were reading Ann Landers and *People* magazine.

## THE ACTS OF THE CHRISTIANS AT CHRIST OUR KING CHURCH

Karen's "It doesn't look like a church" and Paul's story of the Shekinah came together to give me a text for discovering my workplace fundamentally as *God's* workplace. It set off a long process of reunderstanding church, and specifically my congregation, as God's way of being local and personally present to these people to whom I was pastor. My work consisted of being local and personally present to them in Jesus's name. I had a lot of sorting out to do.

I had more or less taken church for granted, thoughtlessly, a kind of blurred background to a way people lived, whether in or out of church. Now that it was my workplace, I had to pay careful attention to this place and these people—and with appreciation—alert to how God was present and how God was working. Now that church provided the place for my work, I had to attend to the expectations that my congregation brought to church and to me as their pastor. I soon learned that those expectations were more often than not distorted by romantic illusions, ambitious goals, consumer habits, competitive instincts. The congregation's expectations were not totally wrong. And my pre-pastor indifference was not a total waste. There was usually some piece or other of the one, holy, catholic, apostolic church embedded in my years of inattention and their culture-tainted expectations. But both were going to require considerable time in the refining fire to burn out the dross.

Which is to say, I didn't find my workplace—this congregation, this church—exactly congenial. An understatement—it was far from congenial.

On the other hand, other surprises, more welcome surprises, kept coming. Very often, disappointments in my congregation workplace, sometimes accompanied by gnashing of teeth, were replaced by a glimpse of the Shekinah. I was looking for the wrong thing and almost missed what was actually there.

One of the attractions for Jan and me in accepting the assignment to organize a new congregation was the prospect of forming a church of disciplined and committed Christians, focused and energetic. I think I had the image of a congregation of Green Berets for Jesus. No half-Christians, no almost-Christians, but the real thing.

I had imagined that when word got around that a new congregation was being formed, it would attract men and women who were willing to take risks, who were prepared to make sacrifices, who weren't interested in comfortable pews. I went through the neighborhoods, knocking on doors, introducing myself and asking if I could talk to them about this new church. More times than not I never made it through the door. It was slow going. I felt like a Fuller Brush salesman. After six weeks of what felt like the most demeaning work in which I had ever engaged, I wrote a letter to everyone who had expressed an interest, inviting them to worship with us in the basement of our home the next Sunday. Forty-six people showed up. None of them were Green Berets.

This was our embryo congregation. In three months there were a hundred of us, charter members, and christened as Christ Our King Presbyterian Church. This would be Jan's and my workplace for the next thirty years. And still no Green Berets.

Word did get around. People told their neighbors. Friends brought friends. As I was getting to know these men and women and children, I realized that nearly everything that I had imagined or expected in the formation of church was wrong. I had a lot of remedial learning ahead of me.

There is an account of David in the wilderness, running for his life from King Saul and eking out a bare existence, holed up in the cave of Adullam. He wasn't alone for long. He soon had a company of four hundred men gathered around him, a company that included "his brothers and all his father's house." Apparently there were a considerable number of others who didn't fit into Saul's kingdom either. Later the Philistine king, Achish, became David's protector and gave him the village of Ziklag as a base to work from. It became his "church," if you will, for his family and his soldiers. The congregation was made up of "every one who was in distress, and every one who was in debt and every one who was discontented"—the sociological profile of David's congregation: people whose lives were characterized by debt, distress, and discontent—a congregation of runaways and renegades. It isn't what I would call the cream of the crop of Israelite society. More like dregs from the barrel. Misfits all, it appears. The people who couldn't make it in regular society. Rejects. Losers. Dropouts.

Ziklag: for me this became the premier biblical site for realizing that when we get serious about the Christian life, we eventually end up in a place and among people decidedly uncongenial to what we expected. At least uncongenial to what *I* expected. That place and people is often called a church. It is hard to get over the disappointment that God, having made an exception in my case, didn't seem to call nice, accomplished, courteous, alert people to worship.

I was now well on my way to learning that congregation is a place of stories. The stories of Jesus, to be sure. But also the stories of men and women I had grown up with: Brother Herman and Tombstone and Henry, Mary and Vivian and Jane, Prettyfeather, my uncles Sven and Ernie. My cousin Abraham. And now the stories that I was hearing in my new neighborhood. It is never just my story; it is a community of stories. I learn my story in company with others. Each story affects and is affected by each of the others. Many of these others are distressed, in debt and discontent—or out of tune, angry, rude, or asleep. This complicates things enormously, but there's no getting around it. We're a congregation. We're looking for meaning to our lives. We catch a thread of the plot and begin to follow it, receiving the good news that God is gracious, receiving the sacraments of God's actions in our actual lives. And then we bump up against someone else's story that we don't even recognize as a story and are thrown off balance. Distracted, we stumble.

This is my workplace.

And every once in a while a shaft of blazing beauty seems to break out of nowhere and illuminates these companies. I see what my sin-dulled eyes had missed: Word of God–shaped, Holy Spirit–created lives of sacrificial humility, incredible courage, heroic virtue, holy praise, joyful suffering, constant prayer, persevering obedience—Shekinah. And sometimes I don't—Ziklag.

# 16

## CATACOMBS
## PRESBYTERIAN CHURCH

We worshipped underground for the first two and a half years. Our sanctuary was the basement of our home. Circumstance, not choice, dictated the place. In the local political atmosphere at the time, it was not permitted that public schools be used for religious purposes, and nothing else seemed available. So we chose the house with the largest basement. Our home was a suburban ranch house in a new housing subdivision on Saratoga Drive. We calculated that we would be able to seat 130 persons on folding chairs until we could construct a church that looked like a church.

Our home was two miles southeast of the small, historic, colonial village of Bel Air. At the center of the village there was a Presbyterian church, First Presbyterian, dating from just before the Civil War. It was constructed of stone with a bell tower for a spire, a "church that looked like a church." Third- and fourth-generation families and many of the town's leaders provided stability and leadership to the congregation. There was a fine pipe organ and an even finer organist to play it. The pastor, Richard Shreffler, the senior member of the clergy in town, known among his friends as His Holiness, greeted us with a warm welcome. And generosity—he encouraged the members of his congregation who lived in our neighborhood to join with us and help pioneer the new congregation. Thirty-one of them did.

Two months before our arrival, the Sparrow's Point Presbyterian Church, twenty miles south of us, had closed its doors for good. For a hundred years it had been a flourishing church in the neighborhood of the Bethlehem Steel Company, a giant industrial complex. The congregation was made up of steel workers and a few of Bethlehem's executives. For the previous twenty years the company had been gradually shutting down its operation. Finally it was down for good, and the congregation dispersed.

The elderly pastor of the church, Gus Mitchell, soldierly and stoical as he entered retirement, knowing that a new congregation was in the making a few miles north of him, offered us what was left of his church: a communion table, a baptismal font, three large pulpit chairs—all made of oak—and a set of communion ware complete with chalice, paten, and linen. I arrived in a borrowed pickup truck, an old International, to receive the gift. It was an emotional transaction for Gus, the pastor. As I realized what he was feeling, the loss of the symbols that had defined and centered his work for twenty-five years, it became a poignant moment also for me. I had not met him before. As it turned out, I would not see him again. He reminisced over his life with this congregation and welcomed me as I received what was left of it in the table and font and pulpit chairs. Conversation smoothed the transition. I thanked him for entrusting me with these holy things that would also define and center my work. He blessed me as I prepared to develop this new church. Another congregation donated an old pump organ, but failed to send along an organist to play it.

The exterior entrance to our sanctuary was down eight steps of a cement stairwell. The floor of the room was cement. The walls were cement blocks. There were six horizontal narrow exterior windows bordering the top of two of the walls at the outside ground level. After we had been worshipping in this bare, unadorned basement for about four months, Ruth, a vivacious sixteen-year-old, said to me as she was leaving after the benediction one Sunday, "I love worshipping in this place! I feel like one of the early Christians in the catacombs." Her enthusiasm was contagious. Some of her friends overheard her. The name caught on with the youth. For everyone under twenty we were Catacombs Presbyterian Church.

The austere basement sanctuary turned out to provide the perfect setting for reimagining church apart from the stereotypes that most Americans, including me, would bring to it. It also had a suitable name—Catacombs. The name never got placed on a sign or printed on our stationary, but it seemed to authenticate noble and sturdy beginnings that reached back to our early ancestors.

But apart from the stereotypes, what is church? Why "church"?

The short answer that I had come to embrace through the years of my pastoral formation and that I anticipated taking shape in our catacombs sanctuary is that the Holy Spirit forms church to be a colony of heaven in the country of death, the country that William Blake named, in his comprehensive reimagining of the spiritual life, "land of Ulro." Church is a core element in the strategy of the Holy Spirit for providing human witness and physical presence to the Jesus-inaugurated kingdom of God in this world. It is not that kingdom complete, but it is that kingdom.

It had taken me a long time, with considerable help from wise Christians, both dead and alive, to come to this understanding of church: a colony of heaven in the country of death, a strategy of the Holy Spirit for giving witness to the already-inaugurated kingdom of God.

My understanding of church as I grew up was of a badly constructed house that had been lived in by renters who didn't keep up with repairs, were sloppy housekeepers, and let crabgrass take over the lawn. It was the job of the pastor to do major repair work, renovate it from top to bottom, and clean out decades, maybe even centuries, of accumulated debris and make a fresh start.

I acquired this understanding from pastors who served the congregation I grew up in. They never lasted long in our small Montana town. It was not a way of life that appealed to me.

One of the memorable sermon texts on church, preached by every pastor I can remember, was from the Song of Songs: "You are beautiful as Tirzah, my love, comely as Jerusalem, terrible as an army with banners." The church was the beautiful Tirzah and the fierce army with banners. Those metaphors were filled with glorious imagery by my pastors. For at least thirty or forty minutes, our shabby fixer-upper church with its rotting front porch was transformed into something almost as good as the Second Coming itself.

Those sermons functioned like the picture on the front of a jigsaw-puzzle box. Faced with a thousand disconnected pieces spread out on the table, you keep that picture propped before you. You know that if you just stay with it long enough, all those pieces will finally fit together and make a beautiful picture. But my pastors never stayed with it long enough. Maybe they concluded that there had been some mistake in the packaging of the puzzle and many of the pieces had been accidentally left out. It became obvious to them that there were not enough pieces in the pews of our congregation to complete the picture of Tirzah and the army with banners, marching to make war against the devil and all his angels. My pastors always left after a couple of years for another congregation or some other employment. Obviously our church was too far gone in disrepair to spend any more time on it.

Later on in my young adulthood, I found that the romantic and crusader imagery that I had grown up with had changed. Sermons from the Song of Songs were no longer preached to eroticize or militarize the church. Bible texts were no longer sufficient for these things. Fresh imagery was now provided by American business. While I was growing up in my out-of-the-way small town, a new generation of pastors had reimagined church. Tirzah and the "terrible as an army with banners" had been scrapped and replaced with the imagery of an ecclesiastical business with a mission to market spirituality to consumers and make them happy.

For me, these were new terms for bringing the church's mandate into focus. The church was no longer conceived as something in need of repair but as a business opportunity that would cater to the consumer tastes of spiritually minded sinners both within and without congregations. It didn't take long for American pastors to find that this worked a lot more effectively as a strategy for whipping the church into shape than the centerfold Tirzah and terrible-as-an-army-with-banners sermons. Here were tried-and-true methods developed in the American business world that had an impressive track record of success.

As I was preparing myself to begin the work of developing a new congregation, I observed that pastors no longer preached fantasy sermons on what the church should be. They could actually do something about the shabby image the church had of itself. They could use advertising techniques to create an image of church as a place where Christians and their friends could mix with successful and glamorous people. Simple: remove pictures of the God of Gomorrah and Moriah and Golgotha from the walls of the churches and shift things around a bit to make the meeting places more consumer friendly. With God depersonalized and then repackaged as a principle or formula, people could shop at their convenience for whatever sounded or looked as if it would make their lives more interesting and satisfying on their terms. Marketing research quickly developed to show just what people wanted in terms of God and religion. As soon as pastors knew what it was, they could give it to them.

At the time that I took up my responsibilities for developing a new congregation, this understanding of church and pastor was widespread and vigorously promoted by virtually everyone who was supposed to know what they were talking about. I was watching both the church and my vocation as a pastor in it being relentlessly diminished and corrupted by being redefined in terms of running an ecclesiastical business. The ink on my ordination papers wasn't even dry before I was being told by experts, so-called, in the field of church that my main task was to run a church after the manner of my brother and sister Christians who run service stations, grocery stores, corporations, banks, hospitals, and financial services. Many of them wrote books and gave lectures on how to do it. I was astonished to learn in one of these best-selling books that the size of my church parking lot had far more to do with how things fared in my congregation than my choice of texts in preaching. I was being lied to and I knew it.

This is the Americanization of congregation. It means turning each congregation into a market for religious consumers, an ecclesiastical business run along the lines of advertising techniques, organizational flow charts, and energized by impressive motivational rhetoric. But this was worse. This pragmatic vocational embrace of American technology and consumerism that promised to rescue congregations from ineffective obscurity violated everything—scriptural, theological, experiential—that had formed my identity as a follower of Jesus and as a pastor. It struck me as far worse than the earlier erotic and crusader illusions of church. It was a blasphemous desecration of the way of life to which the church had ordained me—something on the order of a vocational abomination of desolation.

But for right now we were safe in the catacombs. The lies would have a hard time penetrating our cement bunker. There was nothing marketable about either the place where we were meeting or the people who were gathering there. Nobody came to the catacombs to add comfort or aesthetic quality or pizzazz to their lives. The childhood and adolescent illusions of church that I grew up with didn't survive very long as I was finding my way as a pastor in the church, worshipping and working for the most part with decidedly unglamorous and often desultory men and women. There were always a few exceptions but nothing that matched the lissome Tirzah or the terrible army or the newly franchised Church of What's Happening Now.

Vivacious Ruth's Catacombs Presbyterian Church was readily picked up by the younger set. It struck just the right note and provided precisely the right visual image for getting back to Square One. As we worshipped in our underground sanctuary, we were voluntarily setting aside both churchly and secular expectations and religious stereotypes of what church was and what pastors did.

There was another element embedded in our newly acquired catacombs identity that helped to provide me at least with imaginative distance from the Americanized consumer culture in which we were all living. I hadn't been in the neighborhood for very long before learning that many of my neighbors had excavated bomb shelters beneath or in the backyards of their homes. It was the era of Sputnik, and suburbia was preparing to survive a nuclear attack. Given the hysteria of fear that was permeating the times, I didn't say anything to anyone, but I wondered if people might notice that Catacombs Presbyterian was providing a very different kind of underground sanctuary, preparing us for the kingdom of God. I hoped someone might notice. Nobody did. Or if they did, nothing was said. Even so, the catacombs, like the bomb shelters scattered through the neighborhood, protected us from radiation fallout that was destroying the seed antibodies of leaven and salt and light among God's people and that was resulting in lethal cancerous growth throughout the body of Christ in America.

The catacombs gave us a kind of protected laboratory setting for going back to Square One in matters of church. Square One here meant the Acts of the Apostles. I would immerse myself and our church-in-formation in the story of the first church-in-formation. Acts would give us a text for cleansing our perceptions from the blurring and distorting American stereotypes.

I didn't know how long we would be worshipping underground. I didn't know how long it would take to gather a congregation that understood itself as a people of God—a *church*. I didn't know how long it would take to gather the financial resources to build a sanctuary. Several months? Several years? I had no way of knowing. (It ended up being two and a half years.) But I did know that this time in the catacombs was precious—a protected time and place to develop an understanding of what we were as a church apart from the competing and distracting stereotypes that many of us were carrying with us of "a church that looks like a church."

There were many things ahead of us. But "one thing was needful." Together, pastor and people, we needed a grounding in the nature of what we were about, what church was, what we were becoming as church. We were given the gift of doing it in an out-of-the-way place without a lot of kibitzers giving us advice and comparing us to others in the church business that they had observed or read about. We were not exactly keeping what we were doing a secret, but we were going to embrace the anonymity of our basement sanctuary for as long as it was given to us—a place set aside for the worship of God—and we would take as our text the story of church formation given to us in the Acts of the Apostles, the story of the formation and development of the first church.

For several weeks I had been getting acquainted with people in the community, most of them newly or recently arrived from all over the country—this was classic suburbia. Day after day I went from house to house, telling people what I was doing. Some of them expressed interest. Occasionally I was greeted with hostility. A woman on Ring Factory Road invited me in and when we were seated asked me, "Do you get paid for doing this?" I said that I did. Accusingly, she snapped, "Don't you know that is forbidden by the Bible? You are a tool of the devil."

That tipped me off that she was a member of a sect that I was familiar with, a sect that was convinced that all clergy were in league with the Antichrist. I feigned surprise that such a thing was in the Bible and asked where it was written. She had a Bible on the coffee table and fumbled to find the citation. After letting her fumble for a while, I asked her to let me see if I could find it. I did a little fumbling myself and then said, "Is this what you were looking for?" I read Jesus's words to his followers whom he was sending into the neighborhood to tell people about him: "Freely ye have received, freely give. Provide neither gold, nor silver, nor brass in your purses . . . neither shoes . . ."

She said, "That's it." I looked up, and then down at her feet. She was wearing an expensive looking pair of red shoes.

"Tell you what," I said. "I'll work for nothing, beginning right now, if you will get rid of those shoes and go barefoot."

She wasn't amused. I was disappointed that she got me out of the house before I had a chance to read the rest of what Jesus said on that occasion: "Whosoever shall not receive you, nor hear your words, when ye depart out of that house or city, shake off the dust of your feet." I felt a little gypped that I had to "shake off the dust" without an audience.

There were a few more instances when I shook the dust off my feet but none that compared with the satisfaction of leaving the house on Ring Factory and the lady with the red shoes. Mostly I was invited into homes to exchange stories. Some were lapsed Catholics, some enthusiastic charismatics, some lifelong Methodists, some veteran Presbyterians, a few burned-out Baptists. Before long I was meeting "the others," men and women who knew nothing about church and had never been interested in the Christian faith but were curious.

Obviously, the first thing we needed to do as we gathered to worship in our catacombs sanctuary was to establish a common ground. I couldn't take anything for granted. I didn't expect the woman with red shoes to show up, nor did she. So—the story of the Church at Square One. We gathered each Sunday for worship: "Let us worship God." By this time we were used to the conversational language of story with one another. It was time to introduce another story: the Church at Square One, the Acts of the Apostles.

Luke wrote two books: the story of Jesus (the Gospel) and the story of the church (the Acts). The story of Jesus is an account of Jesus revealing God to us, Jesus as God among us, Jesus telling us stories and doing things that make us insiders to God's salvation, Jesus inviting men and women to follow and trust-ingly participate with him in what he was calling the kingdom of God. Three other first-century writers—Matthew, Mark, and John—wrote this same Jesus story, with variations. But Luke went on to write a second book (he is the only Gospel writer to do this), telling the story of the church: the followers of Jesus who after his death, resurrection, and ascension became a community of Jesus. This community was called church. The term *church* occurs twenty-four times in Acts, more than in any other biblical book.

As we began a life of worship together as a church-in-formation, my intent was to ground whatever was going to develop among us in the next months and years into the story of the church-in-formation in Acts. I wanted to get our imaginations so saturated in Acts that we would be alert to noticing and participating in the church-in-formation that was us. Acts would be our text. We would listen to this text. We would hear God speak to us from this text. It didn't take us long to get the hang of what Luke is doing. He is rewriting the story of Jesus as it is now lived by the community of Jesus. It is the same story: the story of Catacombs Presbyterian in Maryland and the story of Jesus in Galilee and Jerusalem.

Our first service of worship in the catacombs was November 11, 1962. Forty-six worshippers were present. I preached my first sermon from Acts. I preached forty-six sermons from Acts over the next thirty months, most of them in the first year. (I was never aware of the repeated *forty-six* until just now while writ-ing this. I wonder if it means anything.) I wanted to drench the collective imagination of my congregation in the story of church as a reliving, a retelling of the story of Jesus.

I had been having conversations with my fledgling congregation for several weeks by now and realized that we—congregation and pastor—had very dif-ferent concepts of church. Most of us read the story of Jesus as the story of God doing for us what he wills for us: the story of Jesus, the story of God among us, revealing himself to us, calling us, saving us. But the moment Jesus ascends into heaven as told in Acts, the story shifts to church. It is common at this point to let Jesus slip into the background and proceed to understand the story of church as what we are doing for God. Doing for Jesus to be sure, doing in the name of Jesus certainly. But *we* are in charge. *We* are now making the decisions. *We* have Jesus's commands; *we* have Jesus's example. But now it is up to us: *we* take responsibility for the church. Or *we* don't.

The American stereotype of church. Salvation is God's business. It is what God does. And then he turns it over to us. Church is our business. It is what we do. God, having given himself to us in Jesus, now retires to the sidelines and we take over. Occasionally we call a time-out to consult with God. But basically, we are the action.

But that is not the way Acts tells the story.

I thought that my pastoral task at this point was to do my best to get my congregation to understand scripture, and for right now Acts, as a story. Not Acts as information about our church ancestors, not a record of the assent to truth required for membership, but a story that includes us, a story in which we are invited in as participants. The conditions were ideal. We were in an informal setting with people we were getting to know. It doesn't take long to get to know the names of forty-six people. And given welcoming and congenial conditions, it isn't long before the names expand into stories. As newcomers gradually arrived, they became incorporated into the naming and storytelling. Stereotypes began to fall away.

Calvin was a long-haul truck driver with an eighth-grade education and talked like it. He lived with his wife and kids in a trailer-park mobile home wallpapered with Elvis Presley posters. He obviously wouldn't fit in with our mostly white-collar, college-educated, suburban congregation. He had married June, a Presbyterian girl who hadn't been to church since childhood Sunday school. He had recently returned home from a trip and told June what had just happened to him. Driving through Tennessee, listening to the CB radios of other truckers on the road, he was suddenly violently repulsed by the obscenities and pornographic stories that were polluting his cab. He shut off his radio and prayed. "God, save me. Give me a clean life. I can't live like this any longer." He told June, "I think I'm a Christian. Let's go to church."

June had heard of our basement church from a neighbor and thought it might be just the place for her and Calvin together to make a fresh start. Calvin and June and their three children attended Catacombs Presbyterian the next

Sunday. Calvin didn't know that he didn't fit. And as people heard his story and he heard theirs, they didn't know that he didn't fit—common ground began to appear beneath their feet. Within a year he had been chosen by the congregation to serve as deacon.

You never knew who was going to show up at Catacombs Presbyterian. There were no entrance requirements and nothing in the catacomb itself to tell us what was going on there. But for those who entered and stayed (not everyone stayed; not everyone wanted to know and be known), something like a story developed, the story of church, the story of the Church at Square One.

There is this about a story: when we get caught up in a story, we don't know how it is going to end. Nor do we know who else is going to be part of the story. Nobody expected Calvin and June to show up. Nothing in a skillfully told story is predictable. But also, nothing is without meaning—every detail, every word, every name, every action is part of the story.

If we get acquainted with church in language that comes to us in the form of the story, we don't know exactly what is going to take place or who will be in it or how it will end. We can only trust or not trust the storyteller to be honest in the story he or she tells. If the story of the first church is told in the form of story, we are given encouragement to understand our new church also in the form of story. That means we can't know the details of how it will look, who will be in it, or how it will end. The only thing we know for sure is that it is the story of Jesus being retold with us being the ones listening, responding, following, believing, obeying—or not.

Knowing that helps enormously in reading Acts. And knowing that Acts is a story of the coming into being and development of church helped enormously in understanding and participating in what we were doing as Catacombs Presbyterian Church. We were developing a vocabulary—God, Jesus, Spirit—for noticing and discerning and participating in what we didn't see, the church that was coming into being among us.

Acts is not a manual with blueprints and a set of instructions on how to be a church. Acts is not a utopian fantasy on what a perfect church would look like. Acts is a detailed story of the ways in which the first church became a church. A story is not a script to be copied. A story develops a narrative sense in us so that we, alert to the story of Jesus, will be present and obedient and believing as we participate in the ways that the Holy Spirit is forming the Jesus life in us. The plot (Jesus) is the same. But the actual places and circumstances and names will be different and form a narrative that is unique to our time and place, circumstances and people.

Churches are not franchises to be reproduced as exactly as possible wherever and whenever—in Rome and Moscow and London and Baltimore—the only thing changed being the translation of the menu.

But if we don't acquire a narrative sense, a *story* sense, with the expectation that we are each one of us uniquely ourselves—participants in the unique place and time and weather of where we live and worship—we will always be looking somewhere else or to a different century for a model by which we can be an authentic and biblical church. The usefulness of Acts as a story, and not a prescription or admonition, is that it keeps us faithful to the plot, Jesus, and at the same time free to respond out of our own circumstances and obedience.

After a couple months, Calvin and June invited Jan and me for dinner in their trailer-park home with interior design by Elvis Presley. They wanted to talk about the story they were finding themselves in. The children all had a voice in the story. Calvin said that he had never read a book in his entire life, and he was now thirty-seven. But he was now halfway through the New Testament and was telling the Jesus stories to his children. I asked him where he came up with a Bible. He hesitated. It was a Gideon Bible. He had stolen it from a motel while on the road.

Calvin and June occasionally had questions. They would call or drop by. But there was no question in their minds about what they were doing—they were in a story in which God was speaking and acting.

What had set me off on this strategy—the church as story—in the weeks preceding our first gathering for worship in our catacombs sanctuary was the question, repeated with variations in virtually every conversation I would have those days, "When will you build this church?" or "What kind of church are you talking about?" or "Is this going to be a biblical (or Bible) church?" It was the same question Jesus was asked as he was getting his followers ready to be the first church: "Lord, is this the time when you will restore the kingdom to Israel?"

When is this going to happen? How long do we have to wait? When does construction begin?

Jesus's response was "It is not for you to know the times or periods that the Father has set by his own authority."

In other words, it's none of your business. Your question is irrelevant. That kind of information is of no use to you. It would probably confuse you, might discourage you, and would certainly distract you.

Was it the Spirit of God that directed me to begin with this text? It seemed so at the time, and circumstances confirmed it. I introduced Acts as the text for understanding and participating biblically in becoming a church, a congregation in the Maryland hills in AD 1962 in continuity with the church in the Judean city of Jerusalem in AD 33.

By this time my pastoral understanding of congregation had jelled: if we were to be formed as a church after the pattern of Acts, we absolutely had to absorb it into our imaginations as a story, not a manual, a story that gave us room to respect our church-in-formation in all its unique particularities. A story to enter, not a blueprint to follow. The stories in Acts unobtrusively began to meld with the stories we were telling one another in the catacombs. Stereotypes began to blur.

Delores was forty years old and single, living with her elderly parents, who had retired from farming. She held down a menial desk job with the telephone company. But that was only temporary work until she found her place in the musical world as a singer. She was a soprano with aspirations to the opera. Her parents had encouraged her, providing her with voice lessons ever since she was sixteen. She had heard about our new church from a fellow worker and got her parents to invite me to their home to get acquainted.

The farm buildings were kept up, and the fences in good repair. Only the milk cows were missing—the forty head of cattle that they had milked for fifty-two years. The green Maryland hills were bucolic. The parents let me know how much they admired me for taking on the daunting task of forming a new congregation and suggested that they might be interested in offering their lifelong experience of leadership in the church to help us out. "Life on a farm and in a congregation are a lot alike—we can help each other." I also learned that Delores was an accomplished singer. They began attending our Sunday services.

After a couple months the parents came to see me. They wanted to let me know that Delores was quite shy and didn't like to put herself forward but that if I asked her, she would be quite willing to sing a solo during our Sunday worship. I asked her. She came by after work the next week with some musical selections from which I could choose. We agreed on one that would fit into the order of worship that I had planned. It never occurred to me to ask her to rehearse it for me. I had it on her parents' authority, after all, that she was "accomplished."

Her debut on Sunday was excruciating. She belted out "His Eye Is on the Sparrow" with operatic zest but with all the higher notes flat. It was like fingernails scraping a chalkboard. I arranged to visit with her on Wednesday over lunch at a restaurant near her workplace. I wanted a chance to get acquainted with her apart from her parents. I wanted to find out if there might be an area of her life other than rehearsing for the opera in which I could find a foothold as her pastor. But music was her entire life—singing was God's gift to her, and she wanted to share the gift. The visit didn't work. But I wasn't ready to give up.

By now I suspected that finding a church for Delores to sing in was more her parents' ambition than Delores's. Playing for time so I could get to know her personally apart from the role of operatic diva she had been given by her parents, I asked her to sing a couple more times at two-month intervals. But that didn't work either. Within a year the family had given up on both me and the congregation. I later learned that a similar strategy for getting Delores a place to sing had failed in most of the churches in our county. But this is also part of the church as story. Not everyone wants to be in the story if she (or he) doesn't have a starring role.

I observed Ben with considerable interest in the first community-association meeting I attended in our new neighborhood. There were forty or fifty men and women in attendance. I had asked if I could make a brief announcement to the association about the church that I was organizing in this newly developed subdivision. They let me. I introduced myself and what I was hoping to do. Then the business of the meeting began. It turned out to be the most rancorous, uncivil, angry exchange of ideas, concerns, and problems that I would have thought possible among neighbors. These people hardly knew one another but already they didn't like one another.

Ben was the angriest of the lot. I thought at the time, *I've got my work cut out for me. If any group of people needs a church, this one does.* Ben, with his wife and teenage daughter, was in our basement church the next Sunday. He sat in my congregation every Sunday until his death, twenty-seven years later. He never spoke to me, only perfunctory nods. Never sang a hymn, never recited the Creed. Once when he was hospitalized, I visited him. I tried to make small talk but failed. As I was getting ready to leave, he said, "No praying. If you have to pray, do it in silence," the only words I ever remember his speaking to me. I wonder if he also prayed in silence. Maybe he was more in the story than he intended.

Francis was a recent college graduate from the Midwest who had moved to our community, employed to teach high-school biology. He had no social graces but made up for it by being exceptionally intelligent. Unlike Ben, he always spoke to me as he left worship. What he said was always a criticism of my sermon. Sometimes he corrected my grammar or pronunciation. Sometimes he argued with my interpretation of the text. Sometimes it had to do with failing to address a social or political condition that needed dealing with. But always something. It wouldn't have been so irritating if he had been ignorant or misinformed, but he was mostly right. And always rude. It was a relief to have him return to his parents' home near Chicago for the summer vacation. But he continued his harassment—it felt to me like harassment—by means of letters. He had taken me on as a cause. Two years later he moved back to the Midwest, and I thought he was out of my life. But he wasn't done with me. A sermon tape his friends sent him would set him off, or a book of mine he read. After three or four years, he lost interest. Concluding, I am sure, that I was incorrigibly unteachable.

And Oscar, a colonel retired from the army after a career in the military. He was a veteran of World War II and was always in attendance at worship. He also always went to sleep halfway through the first scripture reading. In the early days of the church I arranged with my elders that one of them would join me in leading worship each Sunday. Oscar was the first to do it. Early in the service, after the opening prayers and the first hymn, he was to lead the congregation in the antiphonal reading from the Psalter. When it was time for Oscar to lead, nothing happened. I looked over, and Oscar was sound asleep. So I stood up and did it myself. He continued to sleep through the service. After the benediction his wife spoke to me, "Don't you think Oscar can better serve the Lord in some other way than making him a poster child for 'he gives to his beloved sleep'?" I agreed. He told me later that through those war years he had developed the capacity to sleep under stress anywhere and in whatever circumstances. He was a translator of Russian and spent most of three years being driven in a jeep from place to place along the Eastern Front. Most Sundays he slept while I prayed and preached. But at least he was there. I had no idea that my sermons were that stressful.

Jan and I talked this over a lot in the catacombs—stories and the way stories work. Getting to know these men and women as participants in God's story, not as problems that we can fix. Letting them be themselves. Not trying to force them into the story. Americans are not used to taking stories seriously as a way to deepen our participation in the communities where we live and as a way to expand our participation in what God is doing. The language we are taught in our schools is language as information: naming and explaining. We are also taught language for getting things done: making things, solving problems, going to the moon.

Knowing things, knowing how to name the world, knowing how to read and write, knowing what is going on, is important. And making things, making bread, making money, making airplanes, is important.

But language as participation? Language as a means of relationship? Language that involves us with other people? Language that deepens our capacities for community? Language that forms Calvin and Delores and Ben and Francis and Oscar into a church?

The catacombs were serving us well. But not everyone entered the story, at least the part we were telling. Coffee following the benediction and an occasional potluck Sunday lunch or supper provided a congenial setting for practicing (they didn't know what we were practicing) listening to and telling one another stories.

But there was more to it than that. The reason that as a church-in-formation it is so important—more than important, *essential*—to absorb and distinguish the different ways that language is used is that the primary way language is used in church is in worship, and the language of worship is the language of participation. And the primary form for this language of participation is story: song and story, conversation and story, poetry and story. But, pervasively, story.

I thought if I could get this storytelling way of language going among us, I might be able to minimize, maybe even eliminate, the gulf between the language used by Luke telling the story of the church in Acts and the language we were using to tell our church-in-formation stories in the catacombs. And maybe, just maybe, this could prevent us from mindlessly disconnecting ourselves from Acts and going it on our own, dealing with the church impersonally and functionally. We were starting to get it. As we nurtured this participatory, narrative language, we were showing signs of recognizing Jesus, present in the Holy Spirit in Acts, speaking and acting in our stories in our catacombs church. In the same way that those first Christians became a church as they participated in the stories and prayers and deeds of Jesus in the "days of his flesh," we were dealing with one another in our worship of Jesus as the Holy Spirit was forming us into a church. Calvin, Delores, Ben, Francis, and Oscar were no better or worse than the 120 who were gathered together and about to become the church on the day of Pentecost.

Here is something, if you can believe it, new to me. Despite all my years of reading the Bible, I had never noticed the way Luke set the two birth stories, the birth of Jesus and the birth of church, in almost exact parallel: Luke 1–2, the story of the birth of Jesus, our Savior; Acts 1–2, the story of the birth of church, our salvation community.

None of us, beginning with me, had an imagination adequate to take this in. We thought we were forming a church. After all, we were getting to know one another. We were anticipating the work of organization, matters of finance and architecture. Someone had to set out the folding metal chairs on Sunday morning for worship. Fred lived only a block away and said he would take care of that. Energetically social Beatrice saw the need for coffee to be brewed and served following the benediction and volunteered to organize it. But we had no more sense of what was going on to form a church in our catacombs than any of us had when the embryos that were once us were being formed in our mothers' wombs. But we were learning.

We were learning that the Acts text set the entire church operation as the work of the Holy Spirit. We were also learning that folding chairs, the urn of coffee, and financial reports were included in the operation.

This "conceived by the Holy Spirit" way of understanding what was going on in our Maryland basement, this cement bunker, as parallel to what had gone on in Mary amounted to a totally new way of thinking about church. Some people call this a "paradigm shift." It meant shifting from one way of organizing our understanding of reality, making sense of it, to something totally different. It was like the shift that took place from Ptolemy, who told us that the sun goes around the earth, which it obviously does from our subjective point of view, to Galileo, who told us that the earth and our entire planetary system, goes around the sun, which no one would guess by looking, and which, of course, no one had guessed for many thousands of years by just looking. Comprehension was slow and incremental. I may have been the slowest to assimilate, in large part because I had been given responsibility to organize this congregation. I was being paid to do it. I needed to keep up my end of the bargain.

New Church Development (NCD), the umbrella organization under which I worked, had developed a thick loose-leaf notebook of guidelines and instructions on how to go about organizing and developing a congregation. It was always open on my desk. I studied it meticulously. The man who prepared it and gave it to me, Franklin—he was the first person I had talked to about the possibility of developing a new church—had never organized a church himself, but he had thought of everything. Except for that paradigm shift—the shift from understanding church as what we do to continue the work of Jesus in his absence to understanding church as the creation and continuing work of the Holy Spirit. The paradigm shift from understanding the church in terms of what we plan and accomplish and take responsibility for (the Ptolemy paradigm) to understanding church as what God plans and accomplishes and takes responsibility for (the Galileo paradigm). The Ptolemy paradigm is oriented around what we can observe and understand by naked-eye observation. The Galileo paradigm is oriented to a great deal that we cannot understand and account for by naked-eye observation.

Franklin's red three-ringed loose-leaf notebook, except for occasional asides, operated out of a Ptolemaic paradigm. *This* and *this* and *this* is how a church is formed. Ptolemy is a lot of help in day-by-day things—how to calculate sunrise and sunset, how to figure out a calendar, how to organize a committee, how to prepare a budget. But if we are going *cosmic* (read "kingdom of God"), we need a way of taking into account numerous invisibles—gamma rays and speed of light and gravitation (read Holy Spirit and Trinity and salvation). In those early months the red notebook, commonly referred to as NCB (New Church Bible), was referred to less and less as I and my embryonic congregation reoriented ourselves in the parallel birth-of-Jesus/birth-of-church stories in the Gospels and Acts.

How did God bring our Savior into our history? We have the story of what he could have done but didn't. God could have sent his son into the world to turn all the stones into bread and solve the hunger problem worldwide. He didn't do it. He could have sent Jesus on tour though Palestine, filling in turn the seven grand amphitheaters and hippodromes built by Herod and amazing everyone with supernatural circus performances, impressing the crowds with Super-God in action. He didn't do it. He could have set Jesus up to take over governing the world—no more war, no more injustice, no more crime. He didn't do it.

We also have the story of what he, in fact, did do. He gave us the miracle of Jesus, but a miracle in the form of a helpless infant born in poverty in a dangerous place with neither understanding nor support from the political, religious, or cultural surroundings. Jesus never left that world he had been born into, that world of vulnerability, marginality, and poverty.

And then the parallel question: how did he bring our salvation community into our history? (We were getting the hang of this by now.) Pretty much the same way he brought our Savior into the world—by a miracle, every bit as miraculous as the birth of Jesus, but also under the same conditions as the birth of Jesus. Celebrities were conspicuously absent. Governments were oblivious.

God gave us the miracle of congregation with the same sign he gave us the miracle of Jesus, by the descent of the dove. The Holy Spirit descended into the womb of Mary in the Galilean village of Nazareth. Thirty or so years later the same Holy Spirit descended into the collective womb of men and women, which included Mary, who had been followers of Jesus. The first conception gave us Jesus, the second conception gave us church.

It was a miracle that didn't look like a miracle—a miracle using the powerless, the vulnerable, the unimportant. Not so very different from any random congregation we might look up in the yellow pages of our telephone directories. When Paul described his first-generation new-church development in Corinth—"not many of you were wise by human standards, not many were powerful, not many of noble birth, but . . . the low and despised in the world"—he could have been writing about us.

Some people have a hard time believing that Jesus was conceived in the virgin womb of Mary. We were having a hard time believing that the church was being conceived in that catacomb womb which was us. But we stayed with the story. It would have been a lot easier to imagine a church formed from an elite group of talented men and women who hungered for the "beauty of holiness," congregations as stunning as the curvaceous Tirzah and as terrifying to the forces of evil as the army with banners. But then where would *we* be? We wouldn't have had a chance of being part of it.

The story had its way with us. It became more and more clear that when God forms a church, he starts with the nobodies. That's the way the Holy Spirit works. Those are the people he started with—Zechariah and Elizabeth, Mary and Joseph, Anna and Simeon—to bring our Savior into the world. Why would he change strategies in bringing the salvation community, church, this congregation into formation?

Luke is a careful storyteller. The longer we paid attention to the way Luke told the story of Jesus in the Gospel and paid attention to the way he told the story of the church in Acts, the better we were able to see ourselves in continuity with what was taking place right before us in the catacombs. Comprehension came slowly. Maybe more slowly for me than for the forty-six who started out with me on November 11, 1962. Those old romantic illusions of sweet Tirzah and the terrible army were hard to give up. And the deceptive rush of adrenaline and the ego satisfaction that would put me in control of a religious business were continually seductive. Spiritual consumerism, the sin "crouching at the door" that did Cain in, was always there. But Luke's storytelling had its way with all of us. We began to understand ourselves on Luke's terms. Emily Dickinson has a wonderful line in which she says that "the truth must dazzle gradually or every man go blind."

We were acquiring a church identity as the truth that dazzles gradually. We were learning how to submit ourselves to the Spirit's formation of congregation out of this mixed bag of humanity that was us—broken, hobbling, crippled, sexually abused and spiritually abused, emotionally unstable, passive and passive-aggressive, neurotic men and women. Chuck at fifty who has failed a dozen times and knows that he will never amount to anything. Mary who had been ignored and scorned and abused in a marriage in which she remained faithful. Phyllis living with children and a spouse deep in addictions. Lepers and blind and deaf-and-dumb sinners. Also fresh converts, excited to be in on this new life. Spirited young people, energetic and eager to be guided into a life of love and compassion, mission and evangelism. A few seasoned saints who know how to pray and listen and endure. And a considerable number of people who pretty much just showed up. I sometimes wonder why they bothered. There they are: the hot, the cold, and the lukewarm; Christians, half-Christians, almost-Christians; New Agers, angry ex-Catholics, sweet new converts. I didn't choose them. I didn't *get* to choose them.

The paradigm shift started taking place for me in my father's butcher shop and my mother's songs and stories. Those thirty months in the catacombs completed it. We didn't get a church formed to our expectations. But once we understood that the Holy Spirit brings church into being his way, not ours, we saw something very different, a Spirit-created community that forms Christ in *this* place—not in some rarefied "spiritual" sense—precious souls for whom Christ died. They are that, too, but it takes a while to see it, see the various parts of Christ's body here and now: a toe here, a finger there, sagging buttocks and breasts, skinned knees and elbows. Paul's metaphor of the church as members of Christ's body is not a mere metaphor. Metaphors have teeth. They keep us grounded to what is right before our eyes. At the same time they keep us connected to all those operations of the Trinity that we can't see.

Those months in the catacombs were exactly what we needed to free us from the lingering romantic, crusader, and consumer images of church that in various configurations all of us brought with us. We had been given sufficient time and a congenial place to have our imaginations cleansed of church-that-looks-like-a-church illusions and to have the Holy Spirit paradigm shift established. Not totally, of course. It would always be an ongoing work in progress. But without this substantial "cleansing" and "shift" that took place in the catacombs, we would not have been able to recognize and participate in the actual church that was being formed among us. Without that, the church that most of us expected and wanted would have become the enemy of the church we were being given.

# 17

## TUESDAYS

Sixteen of us—two priests, one rabbi, and thirteen Protestant pastors (six Presbyterians, a Lutheran, an Episcopalian, two Baptists, three Methodists)—sat on metal folding chairs arranged in a circle in Harford County's Department of Health Services, the same kind of chairs my congregation sat on in our basement sanctuary on Sundays. We did this every Tuesday for three hours over the course of two years (minus summers). Dr. Hank Hansen, a psychiatrist from Phipps Clinic, the psychiatric unit of Johns Hopkins Hospital, convened us.

Harford County, an area northwest of Baltimore in Maryland, is mapped on the coastal plain between the Chesapeake Bay and the gentle, rolling hills of the Piedmont that in thirty or so miles to the west begin a gradual rise to become the Appalachian Mountains. For two hundred years it had been a quiet place of dairy and horse farms, interspersed with forests of oak and beech, bounded on the north by the Mason-Dixon Line and the Susquehanna River.

The millennium preceding the naming and dividing of this land, it had been home to Indian tribes, whose way of life had been interrupted by the arrival of explorers and adventurers from Europe. The Europeans saw that "the land was good" and proceeded to steal it from the Indians and begin the settlements that eventually became the United States of America. A few years before I arrived, real-estate developers had been busy promoting the green hills and suburban privacies of our county as an alternative to the pollution, noise, congestion, and rising crime rate in the city.

The population was growing—the reason that I had been assigned here to develop another congregation—and with the influx of new people, mental-health needs had increased, exponentially as it turned out. It wasn't just that there were more people. Social conditions were changing. Just a few years earlier, the psychiatrist Rollo May had diagnosed our time as the "Age of Anxiety." The buffer of green hills and lush forests, small villages and family farms, soon failed as a defense against both the miasma of anxiety and the Egyptian plague of emotional and mental problems. By the time I arrived in October 1962, two military installations, Aberdeen Proving Ground and Edgewood Arsenal, were links to the war in Vietnam. People were coming unhinged at many levels: uprooted, loss of place and neighborhood, military families under special stress, civil rights and racial tensions, three major assassinations (John Kennedy, Martin Luther King Jr., and Robert Kennedy), the sexual revolution, the drug culture, young people in new schools finding themselves strangers for the first time in their lives. A lot of insecurity, a lot of stress.

The doctors at the Phipps Clinic in the city were facing a dramatic increase in the number of people coming from our county needing help, often, if and when they did come, too late. There was no infrastructure in our county adequate to respond to this unanticipated demand for emotional- and mental-health services. Who could have guessed we might need it? We were in a secure, green place of farms and historic villages with storied roots in our colonial past. People arriving thought they had left social and personal problems in the city, or wherever else they had come from. No one anticipated this. We had few counselors, a sprinkling of psychologists and psychiatrists.

Dr. Hank Hansen took the initiative. He envisaged using pastors as a first line of response to the burgeoning mental-health needs. He chose our county to try it out. The hospital administration authorized the program. The Phipps Psychiatric Clinic would donate Dr. Hansen's services to us every Tuesday morning. By letter he invited all the clergy in our county to meet with him. Sixteen of us showed up.

Dr. Hansen introduced himself and the program. He told us he thought that pastors were probably the most likely persons in the community to be in touch with people in mental and emotional crisis. And people who didn't have a pastor would most likely know someone who did.

He told us what he wanted to do: train us to provide a kind of front-line safety zone for intercepting mental-health needs. He would train us to evaluate and respond to the mental-health needs that were proliferating in our increasingly dislocated, uprooted, anxiety-stressed population. We would learn how to identify and deal with routine emotional difficulties, but even more important, how to discern psychotic breaks with reality, serious suicidal threats, and symptoms of potential violence and then arrange with the hospital or police for emergency referrals or interventions.

"Here's my plan: I'll meet with you each Tuesday morning for three hours. The first hour and a half I'll lecture; the second hour and a half we will do group therapy, working through one another the various things we might expect to face. We will do this for two years.

"Would you be interested?"

We were.

So began a two-year immersion in aspects of congregation that I knew next to nothing about: strategies of deception and denial, passive-aggressive neuroses, alcoholism and other addictions, anxiety and depression, family dynamics, sexual confusion. I learned a lot. It was heady stuff. Dr. Hansen was young—thirtyish, with high cheek bones, black hair, a ready smile, and a strong chin. Crisp and decisive. He lectured without notes, conversationally. The group-therapy session was an education in itself as I observed his skill in bringing out into the open the intricacies of emotional and body language, demonstrating the impact of relationships on communication as the sixteen of us dealt with one another.

The only other psychiatrist I had known was a member of the White Plains congregation where I had worked before I knew I was a pastor. Dr. James Wall was the chief psychiatrist in the Westchester County Hospital, just north of

New York City. He was a large and imposing man seated, along with his wife, in the front pew of our congregation each Sunday. Our church sanctuary in White Plains was imposing in itself, a stone gothic structure constructed on a battlefield of the Revolution of 1776 and dignified by a cemetery of the colonial dead. Dr. Wall worshipped with his eyes shut. I always assumed he was sleeping. And then one Sunday while I was preaching, he opened one eye and nodded his approval. I took it as the equivalent of an audible, affirming "Amen." Psychiatrists for me were the high priests of the medical profession. This was the first time one of them had noticed me, even though it had only been with one eye.

Later that summer my senior pastor was away on vacation and I was left in charge. The church had recently employed an Indonesian immigrant to help with the janitorial work, a young man in his early twenties with as yet very little English. He was apprehended molesting a nine-year-old boy in the men's restroom. Irate, the boy's parents came to me. I panicked—I was into something way over my head. The only person I could think of to ask for help was Dr. Wall.

Without hesitation he said, "Bring him to me," and gave me directions to his office at the hospital. We were there in fifteen minutes.

We were shown into his office by a receptionist. I was expecting something on the order of the holy of holies. He was, after all, a high priest. This was very ordinary. What followed was also ordinary.

He asked Dennis what had taken place. Dennis was matter-of-fact. Dr. Wall said, "Dennis, you remember very well. You have a good memory. Do you ever forget things?" Dennis nodded.

"This is something I want you to forget. Use your forgetter on this one."

And that was it.

That evening Dr. Wall stopped by the home of Dennis's parents and talked it over with them. I wasn't there. He let me know that he would check in with the parents monthly for the next year to see how things were going. And that was the end of the matter.

But not for me. For me it was the beginning of a discernment and clarification of relationship between pastor and psychiatrist, what we have in common and what we do that's different, a clarification and discernment that was about to accelerate in the two years of Tuesdays with Dr. Hansen.

———

**I** was a new pastor, only recently secure in my vocation as pastor, and still in the early days of realizing what my workplace, my congregation, consisted of and what was actually involved in going to work every day in this workplace. For a number of years I had assumed that I would be a professor, with students in a classroom. But then the Pastor John of Patmos epiphany in New York City catalyzed my identity as pastor. *Pastor* was my vocational home ground. Drawn into it by many previously unrecognized threads, I entered a life centered in sanctuary and congregation, contextualized by growing up on the sacred ground of Montana.

The two years of Tuesday mornings further clarified my new working life as pastor. I joined the group of sixteen out of a sense of community service. I, along with my clergy companions, was asked to help the mental-health professionals at this time of social and moral confusion and distress, and it seemed like a good thing to do. In the process I was introduced to the complex field of counseling and psychology.

The pastoral counseling movement in the American church had been in session thirty years or so at this time. Most seminaries were giving at least some training in dealing with the emotional needs of people. But not my seminary. I had only peripheral acquaintance with it and not much interest. I was intoxicated with the miracle and mystery of language—American English to begin with, but Hebrew and Greek not far behind. I was intrigued by the complexities involved in understanding all the operations of the Trinity and the many dimensions in which these operations entered human lives.

But people in particular—it seems odd to even say this now—I had pretty much taken for granted. I liked some of them and didn't like others. I tried to be polite to those I didn't like. I had my life to live and they had theirs. Those close to me, my wife and children in particular, I took delight in knowing in more and more detail, and if I came across details I didn't like, I brushed them aside, pretending that they didn't exist, or clumsily tried to eliminate them by rebuke or "good advice."

And now I was gathering a congregation to worship God. When the invitation came to join the Phipps Clinic project to prepare pastors to serve the community in the way Dr. Hansen would guide us, I didn't anticipate that it would have anything directly to do with understanding my work with the congregation. It was a time of social disruption when many of the landmarks, family and neighborhood security systems, were either eroding or falling apart. I thought I was just being helpful, doing good Samaritan work, on those Tuesday mornings. Maybe something like a payback for the good Samaritan work psychiatrist Dr. Wall had done to help me out as a pastor.

What happened, though, is that it became a major factor in understanding congregation and the nature of my work in it.

I was in the process of coming to terms with my congregation, just as they were: their less-than-developed emotional life, their lack of intellectual curiosity, their complacent acceptance of a world of consumption and diversion, their seemingly peripheral interest in God. I wasn't giving up on them. I didn't intend to leave them where I found them. By now I was prepared to enter a long process of growth in which they would discover for themselves the freshness of the Spirit giving vitality to the way they loved and worked and laughed and played. And I was finding areas of common ground that made us fellow pilgrims, comrades in arms in recognizing unexpected shards of beauty in worship and scripture and one another. I was learning to not impose my expectations of what I hoped for them but rather let them reveal to me, as they were able, who they were. I was becoming a pastor who wasn't in a hurry.

Meanwhile on these Tuesdays I was being given another way to give definition to congregation. In our Tuesday seminars I was given a vocabulary and imagination to understand the people in my congregation as problems. This was refreshing. Here was a way of giving clarity to this haphazard gathering of people with various, mostly undefined, aspirations to get in on something more than they were experiencing, something that had to do, maybe, with a vaguely imagined God. Defined as problems, my congregation gave me an agenda that I could do something about. Problems have names: anxiety, alcoholism, depression, narcissism, Oedipus complex, transference, countertransference. Once there was a name for the problem, you could do something about it. On Sundays, as I looked over my congregation, they often appeared as a gray assemblage of weakly motivated people hoping for something, as yet undefined, that might fill in the gaps in their jobs and their marriages. On Tuesdays I was being given an entirely different way to define my congregation—as problems. People with problems, men with baggage, women with neuroses. I was fascinated. The intricacy of emotional problems was intriguing. I listened with new ears and heard with heightened attention. If problems were the problem, problems could be fixed. I found that I was good at this. I had an aptitude for dealing with people in need. I liked helping them. I liked helping spouses understand and work on their marriages. I liked helping parents understand and guide their children. I liked helping people understand and forgive their parents. I was soon devouring the writings of Erik Erikson and Carl Jung, Bruno Bettelheim and Viktor Frankl.

Being a pastor put me amid people with needs: marital needs, family needs, identity needs. I was doing good work, work that gave me satisfaction, work that was recognized and praised by others as good work. I didn't know at the time how close I was to abandoning my haphazardly intended but finally achieved pastoral vocation. It was a time when pastors all over the country were abandoning their vocation to take up counseling. I could have ended up among them.

Those two years of Tuesdays were critically important for me. Besides orienting me in the details of the emotional, mental, and relational difficulties that bedevil people's lives, an orientation that I very much needed, it did something even more important—it clarified what I was not: I was not primarily dealing with people as problems. I was a pastor calling them to worship God. My parishioners had problems, of course—who doesn't? And I was always present to listen and understand and pray. But when and if a person in my pastoral care had a problem that made it difficult to function in a satisfactory way or that was life-threatening emotionally in marriage or work, the Tuesday seminar was providing me with the names and whereabouts of people who could help. By this time I had acquired appreciation, understanding, and deep respect for the psychiatrists and psychologists, the psychoanalysts and counselors, who were taking seriously and working skillfully with the problems that were being visited on my generation.

But this was not my work, at least not my primary work, not the work I had been called to do. Gradually this became clear to me in the Tuesday seminar. The people who made up my congregation had plenty of problems and more than enough inadequacies, but congregation is not *defined* by its collective problems. Congregation is a company of people who are defined by their creation in the image of God, living *souls*, whether they know it or not. They are not problems to be fixed, but mysteries to be honored and revered. Who else in the community other than the pastor has the assigned task of greeting men and women and welcoming them into a congregation in which they are known not by what is wrong with them, but by who they are, just as they are?

The call I, frightened and panicked, made to Dr. Wall that day I was in over my head with Dennis and his parents has been repeated in similar circumstances hundreds of times. What on my own I certainly would have bungled, he handled with intuitive dispatch made possible out of long years of experience and practice. In the disordered times in which we live, pastors can't get along without Dr. Wall and Dr. Hansen. But their work is not my work. Knowing they are there to do their work, I am free to do my work. And my work is not to fix people. It is to lead people in the worship of God and to lead them in living a holy life.

Tuesdays, besides helping me be a better good Samaritan in my community (a good thing), also introduced me to ways I could be useful to my congregation that would satisfy them without having to deal seriously with God or with themselves as children of God (a bad thing).

I can remember the moment that clarified this unique nature of congregation as over against the world of the therapeutic into which I was being introduced on Tuesdays. It was the chairs that did it, those gray, metal, folding chairs arranged in the Department of Health Services so that we were looking into one another's faces, carrying on conversations, with Dr. Hansen probing our relationships with one another in observations and questions. During the lecture part of our morning we were considering people, other people, as problems, dealing with them as problems, discussing ways to go about fixing the problems. In the therapy section of our morning *we* were the problems. Our avoidances, our defense tactics, our passivities, our body language—all under scrutiny. We didn't get by with much. And if we did, it wasn't for long. Our lives, our language, our relationships with one another, our habits of concealment, our silences that spoke louder than words, slowly, sometimes painfully, surfaced.

And then one morning I noticed the chairs. The chairs in which we were sitting were exactly the color and material and style of the chairs Frank arranged each Sunday in our basement sanctuary for our worship of God. On Sundays they were arranged in two sections set at right angles to each other in our L-shaped basement so that we could look into the faces of at least half of the congregation. All the chairs faced an open space occupied by a cross and pulpit, communion table and baptismal font. Same chairs, similar configuration as on Tuesdays, but a totally different focus. In therapy we were looking at one another, noticing what was obscured or held back, identifying problems that we could solve or fix. In worship we were all fairly accessible to one another but looking not *at* one another but beyond one another, cultivating a listening, responsive attention to what we could not see—God. The Celtic cross, communion table, baptismal font, and pulpit called us to attention before the God we could not see or figure out. Therapy, fixing problems, fixing people, was about us. Worship, becoming whole, opening our lives to what we could not control or understand, was about God.

I observed this without any sense that one was better or worse than the other. They were both necessary, both appropriate, given the work that was there to be done in each setting.

It was an epiphanic moment, seeing the chairs of Tuesday in contrast to the chairs of Sunday. In the Tuesday chairs I was learning to understand people in terms of their problems; in the Sunday chairs I was learning to understand people in terms of God's grace working in them. The epiphany was not in the observation itself, but in the realization that I was gradually becoming more interested in my congregation as problems to be fixed than as persons made in the image of God, capable of living, just as they were, to the glory of God.

The Morrison family put the epiphany into a story. For a couple years now, I had been calling people to worship God in our basement sanctuary, visiting the men and women of the congregation in their homes, getting to know their stories, giving up my romantic illusions of putting together a cadre of Christians who would showcase the gospel to the community. I thought that I had come to terms with the nature of a Christian congregation—not as an exceptional gathering of people who were eager to pursue a sacrificial life, following Jesus in the way of the cross, but something more like the way Paul described his

Corinthian congregation: "God chose what is foolish in the world to shame the wise; God chose what is weak in the world to shame the strong . . . things that are not, to reduce to nothing things that are."

This pretty much described the people I was working with. These were not just random drop-ins from the neighborhood as I had previously thought. These were men and women whom God *chose*. They were his *choice*. Not my choice by a long shot, but God's choice. This is what a "biblical" congregation looked like.

I was becoming comfortable with this and thought I was settling into the unspectacular work of keeping company with these people as together we were learning to believe in Jesus and practice the life of resurrection together.

The week preceding my epiphany with the chairs, Ann Morrison had come to see me, asking for help. I had been her pastor for about a year. She came with what I assumed to be a fairly minor family difficulty. Her son, Roger, had returned for the Christmas vacation from Brown University, where he was studying law. He had a reputation in the community for being very bright, a reputation that was later to prove accurate. But things weren't going well at home on this vacation. When he took a shower, he was careless with the shower curtains and inevitably left puddles of water on the floor. Every morning his father would erupt at breakfast, furious. Roger would politely apologize, but the next morning it was the same thing, only accelerated. Things were disintegrating. Ann, the mother, was caught in the middle, helpless to do anything. The vacation was turning into a first-class disaster.

Tuesday mornings had given me insights and perceptions for understanding what was going on between Bruce the father, Roger the son, and Ann the mother-in-the-middle. I met with them and was able to defuse the hostilities and provide a few days of truce until Roger returned to Brown. I had been useful. I was pleased with myself.

Until the moment of the chairs.

I suddenly realized that I was gradually becoming more interested in dealing with my congregation—the Morrison family was only one instance—as problems to be fixed than as members of the household of God to be led in the worship and service of God. For one thing it was much easier. The family dynamics and emotional difficulties could be isolated and defined and worked on. Christian growth was all-encompassing and could only be entered into as a mystery. In dealing with my parishioners as problems, I more or less knew what I was doing. In dealing with them as a pastor, I was involved in mysteries, mostly having to do with God, that were far beyond my understanding and control. No person shows up in worship without problems; pastoral care involves knowing how to respond appropriately to them. Nothing wrong with that. But what alarmed me was that I was slipping into the habit of identifying and dealing with my congregation as problems, reducing them to problems that I might be able to do something about or at least refer to someone who could help.

Incrementally, without noticing what I was doing, I had been shifting from being a pastor dealing with God in people's lives to treating them as persons dealing with problems in their lives. I was not being their pastor. I could have helped and still been their pastor. But by *reducing* them to problems to be fixed, I omitted the biggest thing of all in their lives, God and their souls, and the biggest thing in my life, my vocation as pastor. I began to assess what was going on. Unaware of what I was doing, I had been making a subtle shift in attitude toward the people to whom I was pastor—and I had been doing it for several months. I was trading in the complexities of spiritual growth in congregation for the reduced dimensions of addressing a problem that could be named and understood. I had been doing this quite a lot.

The Tuesday-Sunday comparison brought clarity to exactly what was unique in my workplace: my congregation. Would I trade my pastoral birthright for the mess of pottage that provided the immediate satisfaction of affirmation and discernable results? Or would I be willing to live in the ambiguities of congregation in which growth was mostly slow and mostly, at least for long stretches of time, invisible? Would I embrace the emotional gratification of solving a problem that could be diagnosed and dealt with head-on rather than give myself as a companion in searching out the sacred mysteries of salvation and holiness?

I had assumed that Tuesdays were a way to be of help to the community. And they were. The unintended consequence was that they helped me understand the vocational priority for me, a pastor, of Sunday—the uniqueness of congregation. I liked the Tuesday world in which I was being immersed, but maybe too much. I liked helping people. I liked the feeling of being important to them. But it was on Tuesdays that I realized in myself a latent messianic complex, which, given free reign, would have obscured the very nature of congregation by redefining it as a gathering of men and women whom I was in charge of helping with their problems. As it turned out, the Tuesday meetings developed muscle and sinew that clarified and strengthened the "hints and guesses" that had for twenty-five years been forming in bits and pieces the vocation of pastor that had so recently—it had been a long pregnancy!—come into renewed focus. The recovery of congregation, as *congregation*—defined by Sundays, not Tuesdays—turned out to be a big part of it.

The messianic virus, which can so easily decimate the pastoral vocation once it finds a host (me!), is hard to get rid of. As with the common cold, there doesn't seem to be any sure-cure or preventive medicines. The best you can do is try to stay healthy on a decent diet and plenty of exercise in worship with the people of God.

But by now I was well warned. I knew I had turned a corner when a year or so later I visited Marilyn in the hospital. Marilyn was in her midtwenties, married, and newly employed as a lawyer with an established firm in our county. And new in our congregation. I was still getting acquainted with her. She said that she was in the hospital for tests—she hadn't been feeling well, and the doctors were having difficulty diagnosing anything. In the visit from her physician earlier that morning, he had suggested that maybe something other than just the physical might be going on, maybe something emotional or mental. I was in the habit by this time of asking someone who gave me that opening, "Would you like to talk to me about it?" But I was now in the process of detoxing from my messianic mode. I said nothing. Later I felt guilty for not jumping in to help. Another month went by, and I visited again, this time in her home. She told me she had agreed that her physician might be right about her trouble being emotional. She had made an appointment with a psychiatrist. Feeling cautiously safe, I ventured "Is there anything you want me to do?" Marilyn hesitated. And then, shyly, "Yes. I've been thinking a lot about it. Would you teach me to pray?"

I had been pastor of my new congregation-in-formation for three years. It was the first time anyone had asked me to teach them to pray. Marilyn's shy request gave a fresh focus to the work and the workplace, a focus that I had come to believe was at the very center of my pastoral vocation.

Up until then I had concluded that prayer was not something for which there was much of a market. Wanting to serve my congregation on their terms, I kept my prayers to myself and did what I was asked. Marilyn's "Would you teach me to pray?" was a breakthrough. I reflected on the irony: the work that I was most equipped for, that I most wanted to do, what most pastors for most of our twenty centuries of working in congregations expected to do and did, was not expected of me. Until Marilyn asked.

An inner resolve began forming within me: I was not going to wait to be asked anymore. In the secularizing times in which I am living, God is not taken seriously. God is peripheral. God is nice (or maybe not so nice) but not at the center. When people want help with their parents or children or emotions, they do not ordinarily see themselves as wanting help with God. But if I am going to stay true to my vocation as a pastor, I can't let the "market" determine what I do. I will find ways to pray with and for people and teach them to pray, usually quietly and often subversively when they don't know I am doing it. But I'm not going to wait to be asked. I am a pastor.

# 18

## COMPANY OF PASTORS

With the two years of Tuesdays completed, I invited the other fifteen pastors to meet weekly in my study. We had gotten to know one another well, liked one another's company, and agreed that we would continue our Tuesday meetings. But from then on we would meet intentionally as *pastors*.

At about this time I visited a pastor friend in Baltimore, a friend I had learned to respect and admire and enjoy. We met for a couple of hours every month or six weeks. We were both young and finding our way as pastors, but Tom was a few years ahead of me. He was stimulating in conversation and we had a lot in common—not least of all, our inexperience.

Our congregations couldn't have been more different. His was located in an old, historic village that had been swallowed up by the city of Baltimore but had managed to maintain its local identity. Great oaks and giant elms gave character to the streets. All the houses had been built at least a hundred years ago. Every home held a story, and every street was marked by Civil War history.

His congregation had been in decline for a number of years. He had been called in to salvage this precious segment of Baltimore and Presbyterian heritage. In contrast, my church was still in blueprints and there were no homes, only houses. I envied Tom's workplace, thick with history. He envied my *tabula rasa*. We talked a lot about our respective congregations, looking for the continuities that linked the deep traditions of his old Presbyterian village with my complex of houses and newly posted street signs that directed the weekly arrival of moving vans into what was not yet even a neighborhood.

Recently he had been introducing me to the writings of Charles Williams. On this particular day it was *The Descent of the Dove: A Short History of the Holy Spirit in the Church*. The writings of Williams in a few more years were going to provide me with an imaginative framework that would give coherence to much of what I was discovering as a pastor working in a congregation. Tom was telling me that Williams's book leveled the playing ground between our two congregations, that the essential thing that was going on in his old-city congregation and my un-city congregation was not geography or demographics but the Holy Spirit. The work and presence of the invisible Spirit was the same in both congregations.

He told me that outsiders looking at his aging congregation counseled him to start preparing for a funeral. And outsiders looking at my infant congregation would soon be counseling me to arrange for diaper service. But if we could learn to submit our imaginations to Williams and his evocation of the Holy Spirit in all the details of our two-thousand-year history, we might be able to see what was *really* going on and enter into it, praying *Veni Creator Spiritus*, "come Creator Spirit." That was the only thing, aside from our friendship, that we had in common as pastors, but it was the biggest thing. The biggest thing in this case was invisible. It always is. Without interrupting the conversation—by this time the dialogue had become monologue—we walked across the street from his church to a diner for a cup of coffee.

Tom and the waitress exchanged greetings. He introduced me to her, "Vanessa." She was a slightly overweight forty-year-old trying, but unsuccessfully, to hide her fast-fading youth behind liberally applied makeup. Our coffee mugs were empty. As we were preparing to leave the diner, I went to the washroom. As I returned, Vanessa and Tom were engaged in what was obviously an intense conversation. I took a stool at the end of the counter and picked up a newspaper so as not to interrupt them. In a few minutes, Tom joined me and we walked out into the street.

Tom said, "Eugene, did you see us talking, the way *she* was talking—that intensity? I wish I could do that kind of thing all day long, every day. Every time I come in here and there are no customers, she wants to talk about prayer and her life."

"So, why don't you do it—have conversations like that?"

"Because I have to run this damn church."

The statement struck me hard. An immense irony. Tom had just spoken his passionate conviction of the Spirit-created conditions in which the church exists and then without transition called it "this damn church." Why did he find the diner a more hospitable venue for being a pastor than the church?

**I** reported this conversation to the Company of Pastors. This is what we were now calling ourselves, Company of Pastors. All of us knew what Tom was talking about and had expressed it ourselves in various ways. But maybe not as irreverently and succinctly as his "this damn church."

The two years of Tuesdays had been a good thing to do. We all agreed on that. We had learned a lot. We had developed skills and insights that were useful to both our congregations and the community. But the Tuesdays had also given us fresh eyes to see, in contrast to the psychotherapeutic world of mental health, what a unique workplace a congregation is. Sometimes it felt like "this damn church." But we had gradually begun to recognize something else, and it was beginning to seem like something *more*. We wanted to honor that more, to understand and treat our congregations not as a gathering of problems to be fixed but as souls being formed for salvation in a community of worship. Not men and women defined by what we could do for them but by what God was already doing for and in them. We wanted to develop facility in saying God and Jesus as prayer, *personal* prayer, not as an item of religious information.

We had been stimulated and attracted by the work world of mental health, but it had also introduced an element of dissonance. Compared to the diagnostic precision we experienced and envied in the lectures of Dr. Hansen, our work world of congregation more often than not felt like a mess, murky and disorderly. We would have loved to have the protective boundaries of hospital and consulting room to work within. But we didn't.

We also realized that we envied the authority that Dr. Hansen carried as a psychiatrist. We would have loved to experience that, but it didn't seem likely. People in general, even when they don't know exactly what a psychiatrist does in detail, assume that *he* knows. Pastors have no comparable identity recognition. Virtually nobody knows what we do—not our congregations, not the community, very often not the professors who taught us, not even (and this is the most unsettling) the bishops and executives and superintendents who provide overall direction and counsel to our work.

It wasn't always like this, but in the America of the twentieth and twenty-first centuries, "pastor" has become a catchall designation. We all now realized that in the course of our Tuesday seminars there had been a growing, but as yet unspoken, feeling that we were different from what Dr. Hansen recognized in us, namely, that being pastor was somehow or other unique. We were not adjunct pastors, getting our identity in relation to someone else's work we respected, as we had with psychiatry and community mental health those Tuesdays. We wanted to clarify for ourselves, even if not for others, what was unique about us as pastors. We were tired of letting people who were not pastors tell us what we should be doing or not doing as pastors. The sociologists and academics, the psychologists and business executives, the talk-show gurus and religious entrepreneurs had all had their say about us long enough.

We agreed that our Tuesday agenda as the Company of Pastors would be to recover, as best we could, what pastor-in-congregation meant personally and locally for each of us in our churches, synagogue, and county. After the dissolution of our Tuesday group, Paul decided to stay with us in the Company of Pastors—"We have more in common together than I would have guessed," he said.

If there was no social consensus either in the secular or ecclesial worlds on who we were vocationally and the conditions in which we did our work, we would form a consensus of our own. We would be self-defined as a Company of Pastors. We would cultivate our vocational identities as pastors and our responsibility for working in our people-of-God congregations.

Tom's "this damn church" kicked us off. We would no longer be shaped by what we were not. No longer treat our workplace as the enemy. Where would we start? We decided to start with the Christian Sunday and Jewish Sabbath.

When we became pastors, we had been given primary responsibilities for dealing with congregations that we called into the worship of God each week. Everyone knew what we did on the day of worship. But very few people knew what we did on weekdays. After we gave our benedictions, an identity chasm opened up. We were the same persons away from church and synagogue, but the continuity was not obvious to many, maybe most, in our congregations or community.

As we talked together, we realized that on weekdays we tended to fit into the expectations of our congregations. Each of us was the same pastor all week long, but it was difficult to maintain the high-definition identity given to us on Sabbath and Sunday. By Wednesday who we were and what we did had become blurred in a swirl of competing expectations, indifference, and incomprehension. By Friday we knew that we were working against the grain full-time. The orderly and respectful worshipping congregation had become "this damned church." We determined to cultivate a pastoral identity that could integrate our day of worship with our weekdays. As a Company of Pastors, we would help one another. That was our new agenda for the two hours we would meet on Tuesdays.

My church was at the geographical center of the county and so convenient to all as a gathering place. Every Tuesday we met in my study at noon. I prepared an urn of coffee and a kettle of hot water for tea. We each brought a bag lunch and ate together.

It didn't take long to find our center and to keep ourselves centered. Sunday or Sabbath, the day that defined the week, was center. On that day we were most visible. Everyone expected us to show up and lead worship. What they didn't expect was that it was the day that defined who we were and the way we worked the other six days. So our Tuesday agenda was set: think and pray into the meaning of Sunday (or Sabbath) with all its implications—not just the defining day of the week on the calendar but the day that shaped the entire week. In our conversation we would cultivate an imagination that shaped the ways we conducted our work through the week. Even if our congregations did not, we would let this biblical text be definitive not only for the hour of worship but also for the way we would conduct committee meetings, make small talk in the parking lot, visit the elderly, study scripture and theology, read novels, go to the hospital and pray with the sick, write letters.

We kept the structure simple. The sixteen of us took turns leading the study/discussion. We followed a common lectionary, but the leader was free to substitute another text if he or she preferred. The leader gave an exegetical orientation in the text, along with homiletical suggestions that then led into conversations on ways of being a pastor in sanctuary and homes and community through the week. If personal issues among us needed attention (death, divorce, conflict, illness, etc.), we would table the agenda and deal with them. But we agreed that this was not primarily a therapy group. Our agenda was our vocation as pastor in the actual conditions of our workplaces, our congregations.

When a new pastor moved into the area, one of us invited him or her to join us. They usually came. Some stayed. But often they didn't. When they realized we were not interested in debating doctrinal positions or moral "stands" or comparing church statistics, they lost interest.

Every June, before vacations began to interfere with the continuity of attendance, we drove a few miles into Pennsylvania to a retreat center for a day of silence, fasting, prayer, and the Eucharist.

Through the years the core identity and procedure maintained itself remarkably. Our Company of Pastors was like the woodsman in a Thomas Mann short story who at eighty-five years of age was still using the same axe. Sometimes the blade would wear out and he would replace it. Sometimes the helve would wear out and he would replace that. But it was always the same axe.

I hosted the Company. After twenty-six years I moved across the continent for other work, but the Company continued to meet. The Company is still meeting—it's been forty-two years now—with the same agenda and in the same place. I recently received a letter from one of the early participants, now retired but still attending. He said, in effect, "It's the same Company. The same axe."

We were a diverse group in most ways. In age we ranged from thirty-three (me, I was the youngest) to fifty-one-year-old Richard, our senior member, who had acquired the honorific "His Holiness." Three of our congregations were new-church developments still in the toddler stage at three and four years old. The oldest congregation got its start in an open-field revival meeting under the preaching of the English evangelist George Whitefield in the 1700s. The largest was St. Matthew's Roman Catholic with a thousand families. The rest had memberships of ninety to four hundred. Four of the congregations were in small towns, the rest out in the country surrounded by farms or in newly forming suburban settlements on ex-farms. Theologically we covered the spectrum, from Christian to Jew, from conservative to liberal, and nearly every shade in between.

This diversity did not divide us. This is a rare thing among pastors, maybe a rare thing in general. But it came from our common assumption of our common vocation—not temperaments, not politics, not theology, not reputation. We were pastors, a Company of Pastors. And we were pastors in a culture that "did not know Joseph." Our identity out of which we lived was unrecognized by virtually everybody, in and out of church.

Which also meant that we were lonely, and sometimes angry that we were lonely. A few years before we started meeting, Ralph Ellison wrote one of the great novels on being African-American in America, with the title *Invisible Man.* He provided a detailed and penetrating understanding of what it means to live in a society in which nobody even "sees" you, the actual you, the feeling, thinking, working you. If you are black, your skin color makes you, the real you, invisible. In prisons, solitary confinement is the cruelest punishment. In society, nonrecognition is comparable. Our vocation made us invisible. A pastor in America is the invisible man, the invisible woman.

Without quite knowing what we were doing, or even how we were doing it, we were acquiring a vocabulary and a corresponding imagination for seeing ourselves, seeing one another, for what we really were: *pastor.* We were recovering our vocation. And we were doing it in the company of colleagues who were neighbors (not looking for expert advice from nonpastors) and in the actual conditions of our workplace, our congregations (not going to the protected laboratory conditions of a retreat center or campus).

For several years, I had been on the lookout for writers who would give me direction and affirmation for who and what I had become and was becoming as a pastor. I wasn't coming up with much. I asked around for the names of the leaders in the field of pastoral theology. One name, a professor at one of our leading Presbyterian seminaries, came up frequently.

I learned that he was giving a seminar in a church in Philadelphia, a little over an hour away, and drove up to spend a morning in his company. He was absolutely brilliant. I was absolutely impressed. He appeared to know everything and fluently articulate the everything. There were about twenty pastors in the seminar. As we spent the morning talking about the life and work of pastor, I was totally awed by the clarity and probing insights he brought to the subject. For the first hour or so I was under his spell. And then I began feeling that something might not be quite right. What I was doing, working in a congregation characterized by interruptions, false starts, and unfinished work, seemed like a far cry from anything he was presenting. A fog worked its way into the room, obscuring the clarity of his words. I asked how we might extend the conversation after we left the seminar. What would he recommend? He recommended his books: "Stay in conversation with me through my books." I probed a little about his experience in all of this. He kept referring to his pioneering writings in the field. Others joined in. He was evasive. It turned out that he had been an associate pastor for one year in a town in Connecticut. It was clearly not a subject that he wanted to pursue.

When I returned home, I bought all his books—there were eight of them—and began reading. If he was the person who knew the most about pastoral theology in America, I wanted to be informed. After the second book and starting on the third, something didn't seem right. I looked in the index under the heading "prayer." Nothing. Not a single reference to prayer. I went through the indices of the other books. Still nothing. I still had a great deal to learn about the vocation of pastor, but I knew one thing for sure: the work of prayer was at the heart of everything. Personal conversation with God had to intersect with everything I thought or said, whether in the sanctuary or on the street corner. And here was a man who, I was told by many, was our leading pastoral theologian, writing eight of the most influential books on being a pastor in America in the twenty or so years preceding my becoming a pastor—and not a single reference to prayer.

I looked for references to congregation, the workplace of pastors. For church. For worship. For preaching. For scripture. These were subjects high on the interest level of the Company of Pastors. I remembered the reluctantly divulged item in Philadelphia of the famous professor's meager one year of experience in pastoral work. And this was my generation's leading authority on pastoral work? His brilliant works on pastoral theology obviously had little or no grounding in the pastor's workplace, "this damned church." I felt gypped.

I took the books to the landfill and dumped them. Pastoral theology without prayer and without congregation? Nobody in my neighborhood was going to read these books if I had any say in it.

The first area of consensus that developed in the Company of Pastors was that the vocation of *pastor* had to be understood *entirely* under the shaping influence of the biblical text. The Sunday text placed pastor and worshipping congregation in a living relationship with the people of God formed as a salvation community. This is who we are together, pastor and congregation. The preaching and teaching, the singing and praying, baptism and Eucharist. God's word in scripture, sermon, and sacrament formed us, pastor and congregation, as a community of the resurrection, the living Christ living in us.

The most obvious and congenial place to do that was in an act of worship in a sanctuary on Sunday, the day of resurrection. For the rabbi, of course, it was the commanded Sabbath. Christians have been doing that for two thousand years now. Through those two thousand years we have disagreed over many things, sometimes, to our shame, with violence. But we have always worshipped, pastor and congregation. The role and responsibility of both pastor and congregation to worship is relatively straightforward.

The one day of worship is followed by six days of work. It is on these workdays that both pastoral and congregational identity enters a fog of secularity.

We floundered. There didn't seem to be any clear vocational models of pastor in our scriptures. Our scriptures had prophets and priests and the wise, teachers and missionaries—but pastors? People like us assigned to congregations to know them in locale? And in barely concealed competition with other congregations? As much as it seemed there must be a way to join the first day with the following six, it was eluding us.

And then one Tuesday, as we were groping for a way to integrate our Sunday preaching with our week of congregational work, Paul surprised us with some information that was new to all of us. He told us of an old practice designed to maintain the continuities of public worship within the world of work. He wasn't sure just when or where the practice originated, but it was almost certainly post-Christian, after the destruction of the temple and the fall of Jerusalem.

There are five mandated annual acts of public worship in Judaism. *Passover* marks and celebrates the Exodus salvation from slavery. *Pentecost* centers the Sinai revelation of the law in a worship festival. *The Ninth of Ab* (a date in August on our calendars) is a fast to remember the destruction of Jerusalem and the Babylonian exile. *Tabernacles* provide a ritual to keep the forty years of God's providence in the wilderness alive. *Purim* sanctions a festival of revelry and gift-giving in celebrative response to the narrowly averted genocide in Persia.

Each of these five great acts of worship kept an essential aspect of what it meant to be the people of God alive in their common life, their unique identity as Jews when they weren't gathered for worship. These five acts of worship were the big events, the identity-forming events, that made them who they were: Jews. But what about between the times of worship, between the festivals? Festivals in one sense are easy—you have crowds of people in celebration mode to affirm you in who you are as God's people. But how about the "in-between"?

Paul had been part of our conversations those two years of Tuesdays and had stayed on with our Company of Pastors out of camaraderie and affection. As we now were trying to find our way in this new setting, he was there to give us exactly what we needed.

Paul told us something none of us had known: that at some point in those centuries of Jewish Dispersion, when the Jews were trying to keep their identity alive and fresh and sharp in towns and cities and villages all over the Middle East and Europe, somebody came up with the strategy of pairing a biblical book of "ordinary life" with each of the five great nation-defining events. Paul called it a pastoral innovation of genius. It just so happened that they had five books exactly suited for just that use. The five brief books were bound together in a single volume, in Hebrew named Megilloth ("little scrolls").

Paul had never known a Christian pastor or priest before he had joined us on our two years of Tuesdays. He didn't know what pastors did, and we didn't know what rabbis did. But we soon learned that day-by-day we did much the same things. He and we were all vocationally reaffirmed by the unexpected mutuality of our work.

On this particular Tuesday, it seemed that we had been down one dead-end alley after another, trying to make a direct connection between our Sunday text and our weekday work and finding ourselves instead mired in detours or cul-de-sacs. Paul got us out on a road that went someplace. He told us about the Jewish use of the five books. He desired, he said, for us to acquire a "rabbinic imagination," which he thought we might want to call a "pastoral imagination." In summary, this is what he told us.

*Passover*, the feast of the salvation accomplished at the Red Sea, was paired with the Song of Songs, the basic text on prayer for early Christians and Talmudic Jews. How do you take the life of salvation into your ordinary, daily lives? You pray. In salvation God makes himself personally present to us; in prayer we respond by making ourselves personally present to God. The Exodus salvation is an event in history; prayer cultivates the daily intimacy of salvation. Paul said, "You pastors do that, announce salvation in the sanctuary once a week. You pray with and for people every day of the week."

*Pentecost*, the feast of the revelation of the law on Sinai, is paired with Ruth, a story of four ordinary people in a lawless time when "every man did what was right in his own eyes." The story is a quiet, out-of-the-way contrast to the wild turbulence of those decades. The story of two widows, their mother-in-law, and a farmer is woven into the fabric of God's Sinai revelation through the ordinary actions of a common life. Paul told us, "You pastors do that. You listen to people every day of the week and help them recognize the stories they tell us are continuously being integrated into the large story told at Sinai."

*Ninth of Ab*, the fast of grieving the loss of city and temple and, it seemed, even God, is paired with Lamentations, the outpouring of desolation and loss, a plunge into the experience of suffering. Suffering is *there*, for everyone, and where the sufferer is, God is. Five poems of anguish bring suffering front and center. Paul said to us, "You pastors do that. You don't explain the suffering, you don't promise that 'everything will be better soon.' You don't blame them for their suffering. You face it with your people. You become a companion with them, patient in the suffering."

On *Tabernacles*, the years of wilderness wandering are reenacted by building booths (tabernacles) on rooftops and in backyards and then living in them for a week, giving thanks for a no-frills diet of quail, manna, and water—God's provisions that kept them alive for forty years. The assigned text for *Tabernacles* is Ecclesiastes. Providence, God's goodness and blessing that keeps us alive, is often confused with God's providing for us whatever we think we want or need. The religious market swarms with miracle-mongers and answer-makers, all of them claiming credentials authorized by God. Ecclesiastes forbids us to join that crowd—it is an exercise in nay-saying. What pastors do not do and say is important. Biblical religion is not getting what we want from God. As Paul told us, "You pastors do not do what people want from you or ask of you. Saying no is as important as saying yes."

On *Purim*, the deliverance from genocide in Persia is celebrated, *enjoyed*, in a festival of food and gift giving and laughter in the early spring. It continues to be the gayest of all the Jewish holidays. The book of Esther is the text. Salvation is not only individual, but corporate as well. Not only single souls are part of the pastor's concern, but also community—*souls-in-community*. The indisputable *fact* of community and the irrepressible *feast* of the community are interwoven in the story and the festival. Esther and *Purim*, the story and the feast, are two parts of the community of faith. Paul put it in perspective when he said, "You pastors are working, always remember, with a *God-formed* community—not fear-formed, not success-motivated, not needs-meeting. Let the story of Esther become the text for understanding your congregation."

Paul was obviously enjoying himself—a Jewish rabbi preaching to a congregation of Christian pastors.

There was considerable irony involved in this: a Jewish rabbi providing fifteen Christian pastors with a biblical-pastoral imagination that was designed to keep our week of pastoral work congruent with our first-day proclamation of God's work. He didn't do it by organizing our week into categories scheduled by time-management calculations. He gave us texts and stories that set everything we did on weekdays within the structure of what we preached on Sundays: prayer directing, storytelling, pain sharing, nay-saying, and community building. These are the ways that our Sunday worship and its biblical text are reconfigured in our congregational workplace between Sundays.

It took a while. But after several weeks of discussing, reimagining, and praying, with Paul keeping us oriented in this venerable rabbinic pastoral practice, we had gotten it translated into the context of our workplace: our congregations. We gradually realized that our pastoral identity was gathering dignity.

And then Paul left us. It was a reluctant leaving, and we missed him. He left his mark. What our Christian pastoral theologians failed to do, he did—gave us a biblical-pastoral imagination. The occasion of his leaving was that he had learned to drive a car. Paul had grown up in Brooklyn in a neighborhood where no one owned a car or needed to. When he and his wife and two children moved to our rural and suburban county, he had a car but he didn't know how to drive it. His wife, Shoshana, drove. She drove him the fifteen miles to our Tuesday meetings, to hospitals to visit the sick, and to Baltimore to meet with the rabbis who were supervising his development of a new synagogue. All the while she was also teaching him to drive. Each Sunday, the Sabbath services having been completed on Saturday, she would take him out on country roads so he could practice driving. Sundays were safer—there weren't as many cars on the road. He was a slow learner.

He was a brilliant exegete of the Hebrew Bible, a deeply intuitive pastor, surprisingly companionable in entering into a collegial and pastoral friendship with fifteen Christian pastors. But he had a difficult time acquiring the reflexes and coordination for negotiating city traffic, especially rush-hour traffic. But eventually Shoshana felt that she could trust him with their Toyota. The driving lessons had gone on for a little over three years, probably the longest driver education course ever given.

He was ready to join his rabbi colleagues in Baltimore. Maybe he thought that, although he didn't say this, he had completed his mission to the Company of Pastors. He planned to form a group of rabbis on the model of what we had been doing as pastors.

The unintended consequence of the continuation of the Tuesday meetings under our new banner as Company of Pastors and Paul's gift of the Megilloth as our text was a book. The longer we had been doing this, the more clarity had emerged in our vocation. We were finding a way to keep our Sunday worship organic with our weekday work. Every week details developed that seemed, well, *pastoral*. Weekday work was no longer a hodgepodge of disconnected acts. We began to realize the interior connections between our weekday work—the seemingly random and disconnected prayers, stories, pain, nay-saying, community—and Sunday. The weekly study and conversations and prayer matured into a coherent whole. I started writing what the Company was becoming. It was published in 1980 as *Five Smooth Stones for Pastoral Work*.

One Tuesday as we were getting ready to break up, one of our company announced that he was leaving his congregation for another, a church of a thousand members, three times the size of where he was. He described it as "more promising." I had lunch with Phillip later that week, and he told me that he felt his gifts were being wasted where he was, that he needed more of a challenge, more opportunity to "multiply his effectiveness" (his term). He had not been one of the original members of the Company, but he had been with us for seven years. He was thoroughly familiar with the particular ethos of pastor that had been developing among us.

The more he talked that day over our plate of breadsticks and bowls of vichyssoise, I realized that he had, despite the Company of Pastors, absorbed a concept of pastor that had far more to do with American values—competitive, impersonal, functional—than with what I had articulated as the consensus of our Company in *Five Smooth Stones*. That bothered me. It didn't bother me that he was changing congregations—there are many valid, urgent, and, yes, *biblical* reasons to change congregations. But Phillip's reasons seemed to be fueled by something more like adrenaline and ego and size. I made a few shy demurrals, but he wasn't listening. So the next week I wrote him a letter.

*Dear Phillip,*

*I've been thinking about our conversation last week and want to respond to what you anticipate in your new congregation. You mentioned its prominence in the town, a center, a kind of cathedral church that would be able to provide influence for the Christian message far beyond its walls. Did I hear you right?*

*I certainly understand the appeal and feel it myself frequently. But I am also suspicious of the appeal and believe that gratifying it is destructive both to the gospel and the pastoral vocation. It is the kind of thing America specializes in, and one of the consequences is that American religion and the pastoral vocation are in a shabby state.*

*It is also the kind of thing for which we have abundant documentation through twenty centuries now, of debilitating both congregation and pastor. In general terms it is the devil's temptation to Jesus to throw himself from the pinnacle of the temple. Every time the church's leaders depersonalize, even a little, the worshipping/loving community, the gospel is weakened. And size is the great depersonalizer. Kierkegaard's criticism is still cogent: "the more people, the less truth."*

*The only way the Christian life is brought to maturity is through intimacy, renunciation, and personal deepening. And the pastor is in a key position to nurture such maturity. It is true that these things can take place in the context of large congregations, but only by strenuously going against the grain. Largeness is an impediment, not a help.*

*Classically, there are three ways in which humans try to find transcendence—religious meaning, God meaning—apart from God as revealed in the cross of Jesus: through the ecstasy of alcohol and drugs, through the ecstasy of recreational sex, through the ecstasy of crowds. Church leaders frequently warn against the drugs and the sex, but, at least in America, almost never against the crowds. Probably because they get so much ego benefit from the crowds.*

*But a crowd destroys the spirit as thoroughly as excessive drink and depersonalized sex. It takes us out of ourselves, but not to God, only away from him. The religious hunger is rooted in the unsatisfactory nature of the self. We hunger to escape the dullness, the boredom, the tiresomeness of me. We can escape upward or downward. Drugs and depersonalized sex are a false transcendence downward. A crowd is an exercise in false transcendence upward, which is why all crowds are spiritually pretty much the same, whether at football games, political rallies, or church.*

*So why are we pastors so unsuspicious of crowds, so naive about the false transcendence that they engender? Why are we so knowledgeable*

*in the false transcendence of drink and sex and so unlearned in the false*
*transcendence of crowds? There are many spiritual masters in our tradition*
*who diagnose and warn, but they are little read today. I myself have never*
*written what I really feel on this subject, maybe because I am not entirely*
*sure of myself, there being so few pastors alive today who agree. Or maybe*
*it is because I don't want to risk wholesale repudiation by friends whom*
*I genuinely like and respect. But I really do feel that crowds are a worse*
*danger, far worse, than drink or sex, and pastors may be the only people on*
*the planet who are in a position to encourage an imagination that conceives*
*of congregation strategically not in terms of its size but as a congenial*
*setting for becoming mature in Christ in a community, not a crowd.*

*Your present congregation is close to ideal in size to employ your pastoral*
*vocation for forming Christian maturity. You talked about "multiplying*
*your influence." My apprehension is that your anticipated move will*
*diminish your vocation, not enhance it.*

*Can we talk more about this? I would welcome a continuing*
*conversation.*

*The peace of Christ,*
*Eugene*

That was the end of it. We never did have the conversation. He accepted
the call to the big church, and then another, and then another. I would get occasional reports on him from friends. All the reports seemed to document that
size was turning out to be a false transcendence in his life.

Meanwhile, the momentum of what was being termed *church growth* was
gathering. All of us in the Company agreed that it was misnamed. It was more
like church cancer—growth that was a deadly illness, the explosion of runaway
cells that attack the health and equilibrium of the body. A year or so later, another of our Company left us. We hadn't realized the rapid spread of the lust for
size that was spreading through the American church and was now penetrating
our own Company.

A new friend, recently called to a congregation in our community and a
newcomer to the Company of Pastors, was having lunch with Jan and me in
our home. He was delighted at having come upon a group of pastors who so

obviously liked one another and liked being pastors. He was not used to this. He had been a pastor for eighteen years and had more or less given up on finding companions among pastors. He asked us how this had happened for us. "How did you manage to find men and women who were more interested in being pastors than beating out the competition?" It was spring. The forsythia and dogwood were in bloom. The fragrance of lilacs was in the air. Spring in Maryland is all lightness and color. The multiple beauties of spring and the beauty of holiness that the Company had introduced into our lives gave texture to our conversation on the flowering of the pastoral vocation in our Maryland hills.

Gerard took his leave from our luncheon. Jan and I knew that he would become a good friend and ally in pastoral work.

The Company had been in existence now for twelve years and had become what we had so much needed, a place to form and nurture a pastoral identity that had theological and biblical integrity. We knew it was a rare thing. And we knew that none of us could have done it on our own. We needed one another. There was too much in American culture that was hostile to who we were. And too many pastors who had quit being pastors.

Gerard welcomed our welcome into the Company. His participation in the Company was an infusion of fresh energy into our conversations.

His readiness to become one of us was an affirmation of how critical such a commitment the Company had become for maintaining a pastoral vocation in the cultural conditions of our time. His enthusiasm and appreciation sharpened our sense of how much the weekly give-and-take each Tuesday had made it possible for us to develop incrementally through the years the pastoral identity we had been ordained to. He gave us fresh eyes that brought what we had become into appreciative focus. The two pastors who had left us for what they thought were greener pastures had been a disappointing reminder of the increasing degradation of the pastoral vocation, seeping into congregations all over the country like a massive oil spill. Gerard raised our spirits.

We might have been a minority among American pastors, but at least we were not alone. Gerard was confirmation that there were probably far more than seven thousand pastors in America who had "not bowed the knee to Baal."

———

After we had been meeting as the Company of Pastors for about twelve years, we were having our late spring retreat of silence and Eucharist. As we were preparing to leave, we were reminiscing about what we had been doing, how the Company had shaped us. A sense of blessing permeated the conversation.

I had been invited to speak to a gathering of pastors later in the summer and asked the group, "What is the most important thing that we have done with one another? What of our experience has been helpful? Anything stand out that I can tell them?"

Tony didn't hesitate: "To look at and understand my congregation as a holy congregation. That has revolutionized the way I have gone about my work. Treating my congregation with respect and dignity. I think 'holy' is the right word." Consensus was immediate.

I reported back on the pastors' conference when we reconvened in September. "I told them what you told me to say. But I'm sorry to report that they didn't buy it. Maybe this kind of pastoral imagination can only be achieved in 'prayer and fasting' among friends."

# 19

## WILLI OSSA

During these formational years I remembered another early ally in who we were becoming, Willi Ossa. He was an unlikely player in shaping who I became, for he despised pastors and hated the church. Willi Ossa was an artist, the first artist I had ever known personally.

In the small Montana town that I grew up in, I had never even seen an artist. The sectarian church in which I was raised was far too serious about keeping me separate from worldly contamination to waste time on artists. But beginning when I was twenty-two years old and a theological student in New York City, artists started entering my life in ways that profoundly shaped who I was in the process of becoming as a pastor in America. Willi Ossa was the first.

Willi gave me a way to understand the term *pastor* that was new to me, as a vocation in contrast to a job. Being a pastor is a vocation, not a job. But when I became a pastor, I soon learned that I was living in a culture that didn't know the difference between a vocation and a job. Artists were the first men and women who gave me a way to discern the difference.

My seminary professors had no idea what pastors were or did. Only one had ever been a pastor, and he was an adjunct. Many of my pastor friends and colleagues since my ordination have embraced the secularized job identity of pastor that is pervasive throughout American culture. They have been less than helpful.

I met Willi at West Park Presbyterian Church in New York City on West Eighty-sixth Street. The year was 1955. I had been employed by the church to supervise a group of young adults on Friday nights, about thirty of them. They were all from someplace else, most of them artists who had come, mostly from the South and Midwest, to the city in which they hoped they would find affirmation and opportunity as artists. Most of them were dancers and singers. Two were poets. There was one sculptor. All of them had menial jobs. Some were secretaries, some waiters and waitresses, one drove a taxi, another sold shoes at Brooks Brothers. But they were all serious artists. I didn't know how accomplished they were in their art, but I soon realized that whatever they had to do to pay the rent, none of them was defined by his or her job. They were artists, whether anyone else saw them as artists and regardless of whether anyone would ever pay them to be artists. Artist was not a job; it was a way of life, a vocation.

I don't remember much of what we did on those Friday evenings—they weren't markedly religious or spiritual as I recall, although sometimes they asked me to talk to them about something in the Bible or about God. Most had some church background, but none seemed particularly devout. The group was not intentionally formed for artists, and I have no idea how they happened to find one another in that church. But there they were. And me, the youngest and the only nonartist. When they just wanted to relax and have fun, we would square-dance. I grew up in square-dancing country, but I had never seen square dancing like this—these men and women were *dancers*, I mean *real* dancers.

Willi Ossa wasn't one of the group, but he was always there. Willi was the church janitor. But janitor was not who he was. Janitor was his job. He himself, Willi Ossa, was a painter, a serious painter. He painted mostly on canvas with oils. Something unspoken drew us together, and within a month or two we were friends.

Willi was German and had married the daughter of an officer in the occupying American army in postwar Germany. He and his wife, Mary, had come to New York a couple years before I met him. He lived in a third-floor walk-up apartment with Mary and their infant daughter, six blocks from the church where I worked. Willi was slight of build, a wiry, intense five foot eight. I always had the sense of seething energy in him, like a volcano about to erupt. Mary was about the same height but without the intensity. She seemed fragile, but there was a tough maternal attentiveness just beneath the surface. The nighttime janitorial job suited Willi because it left the days free for painting in natural light.

It wasn't long before they were inviting me for supper on Fridays before the evening meeting with the singles group. And then one Friday Willi said he would like to paint my portrait—why didn't I come, say, about four o'clock on Fridays and he would paint me for an hour or so. Then we would eat supper and walk over to the church together.

In the weeks of our getting acquainted, before the portrait painting began, I had learned that Willi had a severely negative opinion of the church. "Severely negative" is an understatement. It was outraged hostility. He had lived through the war and personally experienced at close quarters the capitulation of the German church to Hitler and the Nazis. His pastor had become a fervent Nazi. He had never heard of Dietrich Bonhoeffer or Martin Neimöller or Karl Barth of the Barmen Confession. All he knew was that the state church he had grown up in hated Jews and embraced Hitler as a prophet. The state-church Christians Willi had known were baptized and took communion and played Mozart all the while they led the nation into atrocities on a scale larger than anything the world had yet seen. He had watched as they turned his beloved Germany into a pagan war machine. He couldn't understand why I would have anything to do with church. He warned me of the evil and corrupting influence it would have on me. He told me that churches, all churches, reduced pastors to functionaries in a bureaucracy where labels took the place of faces and rules trumped relationships. He liked me. He didn't want his friend destroyed.

And then he began painting my portrait. He said he wanted to work in a form that was new to him. But he would never let me see what he was painting. There was always a cloth over the easel when I walked into his cluttered living-room studio. Every Friday I would sit with the afternoon sun on me, mostly silent, as he painted and Mary prepared a simple supper. Then we would walk the six blocks to the church.

One afternoon Mary came into the room, looked at the nearly finished portrait, and exclaimed *"Krank! Krank!"* I knew just enough German to hear "Sick! Sick!" In the rapid exchange of sharp words between them, I caught Willi's *"Nicht krank, aber keine Gnade"*—"He's not sick now, but that's the way he will look when the compassion is gone, when the mercy gets squeezed out of him."

A couple weeks later the portrait was complete and he let me see it. He had painted me in a black pulpit robe, seated with a red Bible on my lap, my hands folded over it. The face was gaunt and grim, the eyes flat and without expression. I asked him about Mary's *Krank*. He said that she was upset because he had painted me as a sick man. "And what did you answer her?" He said, "I told her that I was painting you as you would look in twenty years if you insisted on being a pastor." And then, "Eugene, the church is an evil place. No matter how good you are and how good your intentions, the church will suck the soul out of you. I'm your friend. Please, don't be a pastor."

His prophetic portrait entered my imagination and has never faded out. But I didn't follow his counsel. Eventually I did become a pastor. But I have also kept that portrait in a closet in my study for fifty-five years as a warning: Willi's prophecy of the desolation that he was convinced the church would visit on me if I became a pastor. I still pull it out occasionally and look at those vacant eyes, flat and empty. The face gaunt and unhealthy. Willi's artistic imagination created a portrait that was far more vivid than any verbal warning. The artist has eyes to connect the visible and the invisible and the skill to show complete what we in our inattentive distraction see only in bits and pieces.

I was with those artists and Willi Ossa on Friday evenings for two years. I had never been intimately involved in a community of people who lived vocationally while immersed in a society in which everyone else seemed to be living a job description. The artists seemed to me quite unself-conscious about their vocational identity. I never heard any one of them talk of being a "successful" artist. Their vocation didn't come from what anyone thought of them or paid them. Certainly they wanted to act and dance and sing on Broadway. And Willi would have loved to have had a showing of his paintings in one of the galleries on Madison Avenue. But their identity was vocational, a calling, not a job description.

It would be another five years before I became a pastor. But when I did, I knew that it was a vocation, not a job. I told my friends in the Company the story of Willi and my New York City artists. Most of us had stories to tell. We were honing our observational skills in discerning the difference between vocation and job. As we were seeing pastors left and right abandoning their vocations and taking jobs, we were determined to keep the distinction clear for ourselves. A job is an assignment to do work that can be quantified and evaluated. It is pretty easy to decide whether a job has been completed or not. It is pretty easy to tell whether a job is done well or badly.

But a vocation is not a job in that sense. I can be hired to do a job, paid a fair wage if I do it, dismissed if I don't. But I can't be hired to be a pastor, for my primary responsibility is not to the people I serve but to the God I serve. As it turns out, the people I serve would often prefer an idol who would do what they want done rather than do what God, revealed in Jesus, wants them to do. In our present culture the sharp distinction between a job and a vocation is considerably blurred. How do I, as a pastor, prevent myself from thinking of my work as a job that I get paid for, a job that is assigned to me by my denomination, a job that I am expected to do to the satisfaction of my congregation? How do I stay attentive to and listening to the call that got me started in this way of life—not a call to make the church attractive and useful in the American scene, not a call to help people feel good about themselves and have a good life, not a call to use my considerable gifts and fulfill myself, but a call like Abraham's "to set out for a place . . . not knowing where he was going," a call to deny myself and take up my cross and follow Jesus, a call like Jonah's to "go at once to Nineveh," a city he detested, a call like Paul's to "get up and enter the city and you will be told what to do"?

How do I keep the immediacy and authority of God's call in my ears when an entire culture, both secular and ecclesial, is giving me a job description? How do I keep the calling, the *vocation*, of pastor from being drowned out by job descriptions, gussied up in glossy challenges and visions and strategies, clamoring incessantly for my attention?

Our Company kept at it, asking the questions, alert for signs within ourselves of defection, telling stories of the people we knew or knew about who were living vocationally.

One day I brought out Willi's prophetic painting of me and hung it on the wall of my study, our meeting place. Sobering. After six weeks I put it back in the closet.

# 20

## BEZALEL

The day was overcast with a light drizzle of rain. I and Simon, the architect we had chosen to design and supervise the building of our church, were getting acquainted. We were the same age. The year before, he had returned to his hometown to open an architectural practice. And I was just eighteen months into being a pastor. He had never designed a church. And I had never been a pastor. It seemed a little risky—two newcomers to this church business pooling our inexperience. But we had both grown up in the church, Simon right there in that small town and I in a town of similar size in Montana.

We were having our conversation while strolling over the six acres of farm-land that had only recently been a cornfield and was now the site for building a new church. The land had been purchased by the Presbyterian Church four years earlier, anticipating population growth as the city of Baltimore spilled out over the surrounding beltway that contained it.

Simon had suggested the six acres as a good place to get acquainted. "Let's get a feel for that land together. For the next couple of years it is going to be common ground for us."

"So, Simon, what is it going to be like for you to build a church? Isn't it a little scary? You know, don't you . . . that you are going to have to please a lot of people? Wouldn't an office building be a lot safer when you are just getting started?"

"Maybe safer, Eugene, but not as interesting—or challenging. You know what First Presbyterian in town is like. I grew up in that church. It was built a hundred and fifty years ago—a fine piece of architecture to center and anchor a small town and farming community. When I was in high school and thinking I might like to be an architect, more times than not during the sermon I would sketch a church, both inside and out, a church that would fit the times I live in. I imagined and sketched hundreds of churches. Believe me, I'm no newcomer to this. Later while studying architecture, I learned that building a church is the most interesting task there is to set before an architect. It brings the best out of us—so many things working together, everything you see but at the same time, everything you don't see. But not many architects get to do this anymore. Especially today, when everything else has become so functional, church is still a work of art. I can't wait to get started. And how about you?"

The rain had picked up and there were no trees for refuge. We drove back into town for coffee in the shelter of a local diner.

"Unlike you, I didn't have that long, imaginative preparation going for me. But about three years ago several things converged for Jan and me, and the pastoral vocation became both clear and compelling. I realized that a lot of what I had been experiencing as I grew up were bits and pieces of a pastoral identity that had now come together—earlier I just didn't have a word for it. Now I do: pastor. When I was given the opportunity to organize and develop a new church here, the adrenaline kicked in. I'll tell you more of the story as we work together. But I hold an advantage over you. You have never built a church, and I've already been a pastor for eighteen months."

Our building committee, seven of us, had selected Simon to be our architect after a disappointing meeting with a consultant from a large architectural firm that specialized in churches. The consultant had been recommended to us by my denominational office that was responsible for supervising the organization and development of new churches.

Brisk. All business, he introduced himself and asked for our names and occupations. He learned that Ralph, our chairman, managed a farm equipment and feed store, Jeff sold asphalt to road builders, Harry was in charge of music for the public schools of the county, Ethel a homemaker, Andy recently retired from an insurance agency, and Miles owned a food-catering business.

He was crisp. "I see. Since none of you has experience in planning for church building, I'll start with the basics."

I told him that I had some building experience in carrying boards for my dad as he built our summer cabin when I was sixteen years old. He was not amused. He opened his briefcase and began pulling out building plans for us to consider.

"Here's a colonial. This is historic colonial country you are living in; I think this might suit the ambience of the culture here. And here is a kind of neogothic. It has a distinctive "church" look—it would probably attract people who don't know much about church but are looking for something solid and safe."

And then this: "I think you would be interested in considering this one. It's very popular right now—a multipurpose building, easily convertible from sanctuary to church suppers to community gatherings. Very functional. Given your circumstances, I would probably recommend this. Give me a call and let me know what you decide."

The man left. Mr. Consultant had been with us about half an hour; he had another appointment. He had not asked us a single question beyond getting our names and functions. He left knowing nothing about who we were or the way we understood church. Harry was irritated: "All he knows of church is in those half dozen building plans in his briefcase."

What he didn't know and didn't bother to find out was that we had been worshipping together for well over a year in this multipurpose house basement, the catacombs, in which our meeting with him had just taken place. What he didn't know and didn't bother to find out was that we were already a church, a church-in-formation.

What he didn't know and didn't bother to find out was that in Baltimore's

Enoch Pratt Library we had discovered several large folio volumes of churches damaged and rebuilt in Europe after World War II, complete with photographs and commentary. The seven of us had spent an afternoon in the library with these books spread out before us. Some of the best architects in Europe had been enlisted in that work.

One French architect categorized the forms in which churches took shape in the terms *cave, fortress,* and *tent.* The great cathedral churches of Europe were fortress churches. They dominated the landscape and provided a center and sanctuary, protection against the barbarians, a visual statement that *church* defined and ruled everything around it. The first three centuries of Christian churches were cave churches—unobtrusive house churches and catacombs. We had combined house and catacomb. Churches took the form of tents in a nomadic society, inexpensive and impermanent for a people on the move. The first biblical form of church architecture was a tent, the wilderness tabernacle. "People on the move" certainly described the suburbia where we were living. The French architect we had come across in the library was urging that in this postwar, post-Christendom society, Christians should be building tent churches, modest churches that don't overpower the neighborhood but, rather, enter it, becoming neighbors in the neighborhood. That seemed right to us.

And, finally, what our consultant didn't now and didn't bother to find out was that the seven of us had been taking field trips for the previous six weeks, visiting new churches that had been built in the previous ten years or so. (We got their locations from denominational offices.) Every Saturday we loaded up two vans and visited churches within fifty miles that included Baltimore and parts of Pennsylvania and Delaware. We usually managed to visit three, sometimes four, churches each Saturday. After six weeks and twenty churches we decided we had seen enough. Out of twenty church buildings, only two showed any evidence of artistic imagination or liturgical integrity—two "tent" churches.

The consultant was off to his next appointment. We were dispirited. Nobody said anything. We all felt Harry's irritation. We didn't need to take a vote on "what to decide." Ethel broke the silence, "Do you realize what has just happened? We have just been shown the building plans of all those churches we visited on our Saturday field trips—stereotypes of 'what looks like a church' along with a depressing number of 'multifunctional' nonchurches ranging from bland to ugly. And not a hint of what can give expression to who we are and are becoming. But we know it can be done. Remember? There were those two tent churches."

We agreed that we didn't have the energy for anything more. We quit for the night.

Alan, our denominational supervisor, was not happy with our decision to reject the "expert" (his term) counsel that he had provided for us. He warned us that we were being very foolish. He used the word "headstrong." He had been through this process dozens of times; we knew nothing. Which was not quite true. We were new at this, true, but already well on our way in discussing the nature of worship, the nature of congregation, and the part that architecture played in expressing and shaping our identity in this local neighborhood. Week after week we had been accumulating a sense of church. And we knew we were not a set of blueprints.

At our next meeting Ralph, our chairman, said that he had just learned of a young architect who had recently begun his practice in our town. He knew his parents. I was sent to talk to him. He had never designed a church but was very interested in what we were doing. He agreed to come and talk with us. A lot of questions were asked, back and forth. We liked one another. We asked Simon to be our architect. He asked for some time, that first he would like to worship with us to get a sense of who we were as a congregation. After he and his wife, Deborah, had worshipped with us for a few weeks, he was ready. Yes, he would like to be our architect.

At the same time that my pastoral identity was in formation, the congregation was discovering its unique identity. What does it mean to be a church of Jesus Christ in America? We had let Luke's storytelling in The Acts of the Apostles give us our text. We saturated our imaginations in the continuities between the conception, birth, and life of Jesus and the conception, birth, and life of the church. As we let Luke tell the story, it became clear that being the church meant that the Holy Spirit was conceiving the life of Jesus in us, much the same way the Holy Spirit had conceived the life of Jesus in Mary. We weren't trying to be a perfect or model or glamorous church. We were trying to get out of the way and pay attention to the way God worked in the early church and was working in us. We were getting it: worship was not so much what we did, but what we let God do in and for us. These months of worship in our catacombs sanctuary had made their mark on us: we were a people of God gathered to worship God. The single word, "worship," defined what we were about.

The congregational consensus emerged not so much by talking about it but by simply doing it: worship was our signature activity, the distinctive act that set us apart from all other social structures—schools, businesses, athletic teams, political parties, government agencies. It was not achieved through a Bible study or a discussion that pooled our various expectations and came up with something we could all live with. We simply met every Sunday and worshipped God. We sang together, prayed together, listened to scripture together, received the Sacrament together, baptized our children and converts, and went back to our homes ready to enter a week of work with the blessing of God on us. Our infant son, Eric, was the first child I baptized in our catacombs sanctuary. He did his part in making sure we wouldn't romantically sentimentalize the holy moment—the moment the baptismal water touched his head, he set up a loud wail.

The ordinariness of our lives and the circumstances of the catacombs cleared our minds of romantic and utopian illusions regarding church. We weren't a church that "looked like a church." No prayer groups, no Sunday school, no social groups—just worship. As our church matured, some of these ancillary activities were added, but not until our basic worship identity was well established.

And it was well established. The catacombs had served us very well as we found our formation as a worshipping congregation. But more and more people were arriving. Basic hospitality required that we make room for them—a *place* for worship, a *sanctuary* to preserve and cultivate our identity as a people of worship.

As pastor to these people in these circumstances, what was my part? I asked God for guidance, for wisdom. It didn't take long for clarity to come. Just as I had used Acts as the text for our being formed as a worshipping people of God, I would use Exodus as the text for building a place for welcoming others to worship with us.

———

The Exodus world was full of congregation-in-formation stories. Moses rescued as an infant from the river, his long years of formation as a pastor while tending sheep in Midian, years he didn't know he was being formed as a pastor, the voice from the burning bush, the ten plagues, the Red Sea deliverance, thunder and lightning from Sinai, the Ten Words.

Moses: leading his people out of Egypt into a life of free salvation and forming them into a congregation. Moses: developing a sense of community that was held together by the providence of God, a people understanding themselves in terms of the revelation and action of God. Moses: leading a people into an understanding and practice of being a people of God, a church. Moses: my mentor in forming a people-of-God congregation. Moses: building a sanctuary for worship in the wilderness.

I wanted to make the most of this unprecedented opportunity of being in on the ground floor, rethinking, reliving the basics—God's salvation, God's community, God's revelation, God's church, God's congregation, God's sanctuary—with variously informed and uninformed people. This was not only new territory for me but for everyone in my infant congregation. Not exactly wilderness as it had been for the people to whom Moses was pastor, for we all had running water in our homes and Safeway bread on our tables. But all of us were in a position to rethink and refresh our memories of just what being a people of God consisted of. The life and words of Moses as he led his congregation from Egyptian slavery through uncharted wilderness to Canaan freedom gave us common ground to work from. I wanted to take advantage of this once-in-a-lifetime opportunity to work through the ways in which we lived theology and ethics and worship.

As I was living into this Exodus story, finding ways to include my congregation in it—this text that I had so recently received as Holy Spirit given, an answer to prayer for pastoral guidance at this transitional time—I came across a name that I had never paid attention to before, Bezalel. I thought I knew this Exodus story inside and out. How had I missed Bezalel?

Every three of four weeks Simon and I got together and conducted an informal seminar on what we were doing. Sometimes we did it while walking on the site where we would be building our sanctuary. Our vocations merged. We began to discern common themes in our respective vocations—the perpetual interaction between visible and invisible, sound and silence, flesh and spirit, materiality and spirituality, order and chaos.

It was now April. The juices were running in our imaginations. We were again strolling on that empty cornfield that was filling up with hints and guesses of the Shekinah of our yet to be constructed sanctuary. Simon stopped, kicked up a piece of dirt, and said, "This is where we'll pitch our tent. I think this is just the right location." And then, as an afterthought, "too bad just the two of us are present for this groundbreaking."

A few moments later Simon said, "I've been thinking a lot about our Exodus text. I think I have found my name in it—Bezalel. Bezalel the architect of the tent of meeting. I'm Bezalel."

For Moses and his congregation all the basic stuff of salvation was packed into a story that covered about three months. But the three months in which the salvation had been accomplished and the revelation defined was just the beginning. A foundation was established, but after four hundred years of Egyptian slavery, this was a lot to take in. This was going to take a while. Forty years for a start: salvation, the God-shaped life, absorbed—*assimilated*—into their lives. The assimilation would take place through worship. Bezalel was the architect responsible for shaping the place of worship that would shape the worship of the people, that would in turn shape the way the people lived their common lives, their lives in common.

Later that day I wrote in my journal. "Wednesday, April 1963. This morning while a spring breeze played on the grass, Bezalel, architect of the wilderness tent, made his appearance in Simon, architect of Christ Our King Church: 'I'm Bezalel.'"

There are forty chapters in Exodus. I had never read, *really* read, past chapter thirty-four. Those first thirty-four chapters are where all the action is with Moses at the center of the action. At chapter thirty-five the action comes to a stop. The chapter opens with Moses talking about Sabbath keeping—what the people *don't* do, withdrawing from daily work in order to give God time and space to do God's work in *them*, God's congregation. The first thirty-four chapters narrate the defining actions of salvation and revelation. The final six chapters narrate the preparations for continuing worship that would assimilate that salvation and revelation into the fabric of their common life, week after week, month after month, year after year after year, for another twelve hundred years, at which time Jesus would bring it all to a new beginning. It is here, at chapter thirty-five, that the name Bezalel appears for the first time. Bezalel the architect. Bezalel the artist.

I had never noticed this transition before, the transition that moved the Hebrews from experiencing the salvation and revelation of God under the leadership of Moses to involving them in a lifetime of living in response and participation in that salvation and revelation under the forms of Bezalel's art and architecture.

The story of the Red Sea and Sinai with Moses playing a leading role defined the life of God's people. Telling and retelling that story in a place of worship would keep their identity alive and focused. Now with Bezalel playing the leading role, the account of planning, designing, and constructing a building for worship provided the structural form for rehearsing and practicing their identity in the materials and circumstances of their lives for as long as they lived.

Moses dominates the story in its inception and formation. Bezalel is the architect of its continuation and maturation. At chapter thirty-five, Moses steps aside and hands things over to Bezalel. Bezalel provides the people with the material means for worshipping through wilderness and Promised Land living, assimilating what had been given at the Red Sea and Sinai. For these final six chapters Bezalel is in charge. What he is in charge of is making provisions for worship, building a place of worship.

Simon noticed and took seriously what I had never seriously noticed before: Bezalel designing and supervising the building of the wilderness tabernacle, the portable sanctuary, the tent, in which the people of Israel worshipped God during their forty years of transition from Egyptian slavery to Promised Land Canaan, the approximate half century from 1250 to 1200 BC.

And now our church had its Bezalel. Simon and I had long conversations in which we discussed the formation of congregation. I immersed him in all the liturgy that I knew, the nature and ways of worship. From his side he taught me the aesthetics of space and the ways that color and light and material textures worked together, the "fit" of the structure with the landscape and the community that would surround and inhabit it. The conversations of that year, formed in the ambience of Bezalel and Moses in the wilderness and the congregation at worship in our catacombs sanctuary, developed into first blueprints and then a sanctuary on the six acres of empty Maryland farmland fronting Emmorton Road. It would become a place of worship and learning and community formation: simple and honest—a piece of art for worshipping God in the "beauty of holiness" in this suburban desert of secularism.

As those months of planning and decision making developed, we worked out in detail the ways that worship would keep us connected with our defining story and make adequate provision for its continuous development in the lives of the congregation.

I had never paid attention to a sanctuary as a piece of art, doing what art does—using the sensory (material, sound, texture) to give access to mystery, to the "behind the scenes" of our ordinary lives—to see, hear, touch, taste, and smell the vast world of beauty that inhabits, underlies, and permeates space and time, place and each person. The Holy.

Our priority as we prepared to go public with our congregation was coming into focus: provide a sanctuary for the worship of God, the central formative act for shaping the people of God as a people of *God*. Not just pilgrims on the way to the Holy Land. Not just a people defined by their place and circumstances in history.

Called to worship each week, we would repeatedly enter a place of awareness of the presence and word and action of God, keep alert and participating in that presence and word and action. It was not me, the pastor, telling them. We were realizing it together, in company with one another.

Back to Exodus. Bezalel goes to work. He designs and oversees the construction of the sanctuary, the tabernacle, also called the tent of meeting. Meticulous detail is given to everything that goes into a sanctuary where every detail of our lives is being integrated into responsive obedience and a life of salvation: weaving the curtains and the covering of the tent, with careful attention given to fabric, size, design, colors, and embroidery work, along with the hooks and clasps to connect them, tent poles ("frames") and rods to hold the curtains. Furniture to provide tangible and visual witness to what they are doing: the ark of the covenant, a table for offerings with plates and dishes, bowls and flagons. An elaborate lamp stand with six branches, all of gold. An altar of incense. Holy anointing oil. The altar of burnt offering. Vestments for the priests: robes and tunics, some of them trimmed with bells, a turban crown. A huge work crew. Building materials: acacia wood, skins, gold, silver, bronze, gemstones, cords, pegs.

Worship has to do with God, whom no one has ever seen: "Let us worship God" is our standard rubric. But worship has to do simultaneously with all the stuff that we see wherever we look: acacia wood, fabrics and skins, tent pegs and altars, tables and flagons. To say nothing of all the workers in textile, metal, and wood, weaving and carving, smelting and casting.

First salvation from Egypt, then worship in the wilderness. First the great events at the Red Sea and Sinai, then bringing every detail of our lives and all the stuff of our lives into the sanctuary where we are formed into lives of salvation, detail by detail, day by day.

Up until those months of dealing with Bezalel in the Sinai desert in 1200 BC and Bezalel (aka Simon) in the lush greenery of Maryland in 1963, I had considered worship as something that provided a setting for proclamation and teaching and singing, primarily verbal acts. The congregation thought of it that way too. But now we were plunged into revising virtually everything we had assumed about worship. We were understanding it as the formation of salvation detail by detail, day by day, in the bodies of men and women and babies, neighborhoods, homes, workplaces, through the "hopes and fears of all the years." The salvation "land of the living" was being created in our neighborhood.

Moses led people to salvation freedom; Bezalel paid scrupulous attention to the details of that freedom embodied in a holy life. Moses brought down the Ten Words from Sinai; Bezalel assembled them coherently in acts of offering and sacrifice. Moses and Bezalel.

Moses at the Red Sea and Sinai: the once-for-all events of salvation, the story that we keep telling one another to remember who God is and who we are.

Bezalel, aka Simon, and the Christ Our King sanctuary: the place of worship where a life of salvation identity is formed in time and place, in everyday-ness and in detail.

Moses the prophet formed my pastoral vocation kerygmatically.

Bezalel, aka Simon, formed my pastoral vocation liturgically.

Without Moses, worship would soon degenerate into aesthetics and enter-tainment.

Without Bezalel, aka Simon, salvation would blur into generalities of heav-enly bliss and fragment into isolated and individualized fits and starts.

Finally, all was ready. We had a groundbreaking. After worship we processed (not quite the right word—"meandered" was more like it—with the children racing and skipping) the quarter mile from our catacombs sanctuary to the site of our new tent sanctuary. Anticipating what was to come, we had chosen a name for our church, Christ Our King Presbyterian. Lucy purchased two hundred seven-inch red shovels and hand painted them to give to everyone there that day:

## CHRIST OUR KING GROUNDBREAKING
### JULY 12, 1964

The next day the Jeager Construction Company showed up with equipment and workmen to build the sanctuary that would give architectural expression to the life of worship that defined and expressed who we were as a people of God. Nine months later the sanctuary was complete.

We had our first service of worship in our new sanctuary on April 7, 1965. After the benediction most of the congregation lingered, talking and com-menting on what we had done. Ruthie, the girl who had two and a half years earlier named our basement sanctuary Catacombs Presbyterian, interrupted Simon as he was in conversation with a few others, excitedly grabbed his arm, and said, "I just realized what you did! You modeled the interior of the sanctu-ary on those praying hands of Dürer—you know, that famous woodcut. That is so cool. I think we ought to rename this place Church of the Praying Hands. That is so cool."

I was just a few steps away and overheard her. She was right. The abruptly steep, upward sweep of the roof automatically directed attention upward. Interiorly, the church was all steeple—or as Ruthie observed, praying hands. I said to her, "Not bad, Ruthie—you're getting pretty good at church christening. First Catacombs Presbyterian and now Praying Hands Presbyterian. I like that."

Our experience of worship in the catacombs had developed into decisions about the architecture of worship. Two and a half years of worshipping together underground provided the experience that would inform what we would continue when we opened our doors to the community and invited them to worship.

In the months that we had spent planning and thinking through the details of what was involved in our worship, and then building a sanctuary, it very soon became clear that what we were primarily concerned with was not what the church looked like but what went on within the church. The interior of the church was more significant than the exterior. And often, the feature of the sanctuary that was commented on was its spaciousness, roominess; a couple people mentioned "elbow room."

A most conspicuous witness to that spaciousness, at least to me, came from the children. A few months after our sanctuary was completed, we opened a preschool for four-year-old children. Most of those enrolled were from other churches or no church at all. Each Tuesday I would meet with them in the sanctuary to get acquainted and tell them a story. Their classroom was in a separate building, about twenty feet away. On their first Tuesday, the teachers lined them up in a straight line and prepared them for the solemn occasion—going to church! They were to be reverent and talk in a quiet voice. The procession from classroom to sanctuary was dignified. But the moment they entered the sanctuary, they broke ranks and ran. Some skipped. There was exuberance and laughter. There was something about the openness, the sun shining through the expanse of windows, the dramatic upward sweep of the ceiling, the palpable largesse of that sanctuary, that invited playfulness. It was like they had been let out of a cage and were breaking free. The two teachers did their best to restore a decorum of reverence without much success.

I had my banjo with me and sat down on the floor and began singing "Mr. Froggy went a courtin' and he did ride . . ." Soon they were gathered around and singing with me. We exchanged names. I told them a story. We did that every week through the school year.

Later that first day the teachers and I talked about what we had just experienced. Neither of them attended my congregation. They were embarrassed that they hadn't been able to control the children. I was surprised but pleased at the spontaneous sense of playfulness that they displayed. They explained to me that part of their responsibility was to develop a sense of proper social behavior. I told them that I respected that but that I hoped when people entered this place of worship, they would sense that they were being invited into something larger than they were used to. I was hoping that the way this sanctuary had been designed did not suggest socialization but *theologization* (I didn't use that word with them—I just now coined it), a sense of God in whose presence is fullness and joy. And maybe we had just been given a demonstration of the biblical phrase "and a little child shall lead them."

It was a good conversation. And a quiet confirmation that the architecture was doing its work.

A very different confirmation came a year or so later, not from four-year-old children but from a professor and his students. The Roman Catholic diocese of Baltimore had recently constructed a new cathedral church, The Cathedral of Mary Our Queen. I had a friend on the faculty of St. Mary's Seminary, just around the corner from the cathedral, who told a colleague, the professor of liturgics at the seminary, about our new sanctuary and suggested he come and see it.

Father Dominic telephoned and came out to visit. He had been the theological consultant to the architect of the new cathedral much as I had been to Simon, my Bezalel. We had a lot of common experience. But also a very different experience. He was in on the design and construction of a large fortress sanctuary. Under the circumstances, that was fitting. Baltimore is a largely Catholic city and has a strong historical rootage in Roman Catholicism from colonial times. I was in on the design and structure of a modest tent sanctuary in a suburb that had virtually no history or memory.

That initiated a practice that continued for several years. Each year Father Dominic brought his class of seminarians out to Christ Our King Church and used it as a case study in liturgical practice. These were the years of Vatican II. There was a lot of reform going on, much of it having to do with worship.

There were striking contrasts, the names for a start, the Cathedral of Mary Our Queen and Christ Our King Presbyterian. The church in the city was massive, dominating everything around it. Our church was modest, fitting into the neighborhood. But Father Dominic was mostly interested in observing how our two very different traditions had each skillfully employed architecture, attentive to every detail in order to reinforce an awareness and receptivity of a people of God to the presence and gifts of God.

And he never failed to comment on the sense of spacious simplicity in our sanctuary, using a line from a Narnia tale to describe Christ Our King Church, "Its inside is bigger than its outside."

Father Dominic was an astute observer and good teacher. His students were lively and appreciative. It was affirming to have someone notice and approve. Mary Our Queen and Christ Our King worked well together.

Earlier we had found a text that gave clarity to what we hoped would take place in our sanctuary. It was a sermon that Martin Luther preached at the dedication of a church in Torgau, Germany, in 1544. He asked the congregation that "nothing should take place therein than that our dear Lord should speak with us through his holy word, and we again speak with him through prayer and praise." We let Luther's words guide our discussion on our interior architecture by paying attention to what took place between the polarities of worship: the North Pole of our Lord speaking "with us through his holy word" and the South Pole of our speaking "with him through prayer and praise."

We wanted the architecture of our sanctuary to give as much sensory help as possible so that precisely that North/South polarity would be preserved, that from every angle the presence and Word of God would be honored, and that our words would be in response to God's Word.

**The North Pole of God's Word:** "That our dear Lord should speak with us through his holy word."

In our tradition (Presbyterian) the "holy word" is referred to as the "audible word" of scripture and sermon and the "visible word" of the biblical sacraments, baptism and the Lord's Supper. God speaks the same word to his people whether in word or sacrament. Our first decision was to place pulpit, baptismal font, and Lord's table emphatically in the large central space of the sanctuary, with the pews arranged around them to give visual prominence to the "holy word."

Earlier we had talked about using local building materials whenever possible. And wouldn't it be appropriate to use something distinctively local for the baptismal font, communion table, and pulpit? Ted and Isabel were retired farmers who had lived their entire lives in our county. They called our attention to an abandoned marble quarry twenty miles north of our building site—Maryland green marble would be about as local as we could get. Stone as a building material for font, table, and pulpit has a long tradition in the church. And what better way to show the continuity of "the holy word," audible and visible, than by using locally quarried Maryland green marble in the construction of font, table, and pulpit? It turned out that Ralph, our building chairperson, used to live near the quarry and knew the family who owned it. It was no longer a working quarry, but he thought there was still a warehouse of discarded marble slabs. He went to the family and inquired. He brought back in his pickup several pieces of what he thought might be usable marble. Bezalel, aka Simon, designed the font, table, and pulpit in a way that featured the marble.

The Maryland green marble surface of the font and table and the face of the pulpit anchored our sanctuary in the context of the local.

Baptismal Font. Baptism is the sacrament of entrance into the Christian church, marking the beginning of our life in Christ. The first thing a person meets on entering the sanctuary is the font—God's first word to us is that he accepts and forgives us. But baptism is also an act of congregational worship, shared by all of God's gathered people. We placed the font at the end of the short center aisle, which is at the same time the exact center of the church. It was a forceful sign to all who have been baptized that they have been received into Christ, are forgiven, and have passed "from death to life."

Lord's Table. Six feet beyond the font, still occupying the spacious center of the sanctuary, we placed the table from which we would serve Holy Communion, the sacrament of nurture for Christians. From the earliest days of the church the Lord's Supper has been the defining act of worship, the axis upon which all else turns. It is an open table, placed on the level with the congregation, inviting all who trust in Christ to receive the Christ who offers himself to us.

Pulpit. Another six feet in toward the southeast wall and elevated slightly (seven inches) is the pulpit. The Holy Spirit speaking in scripture determines and regulates the life of the church. The open Bible that is clearly visible on the pulpit desk is emphatic that it is scripture, read and preached, and not a human word, that is authoritative in worship. The slab of marble that is the face of the pulpit is quietly dramatic. The green marble has a wild chaotic grain reflecting the stormy, unruly rebellious precreation world that God's Genesis word ordered into a cosmos. Marcia had earlier designed a symbol for Christ Our King—the crown over the cross over the circle of the world, the crucified and risen Christ ruling the world as King. Loren fashioned the symbol out of burnished aluminum and fixed it on the marble face: the Word of God in scripture and sermon, a witness to Christ reconciling the disordered world into the order of salvation.

Things were falling into place. We had learned a lot and learned it well during those months in the catacombs.

**The South Pole of the Congregation's Words:** "And we again speak with him through prayer and praise."

A place of worship is a place for listening—listening to God speak. But it is also a place for answering, responding to what is spoken. God's words initiate a conversation. We come together as a congregation in worship to speak "through prayer and praise" with the God who speaks with us.

We arranged the seating to emphasize this communal, conversational dimension to the language used in worship. Our sanctuary measured sixty feet by sixty feet, a square. The pews were in four sections, arranged to face the central open space that held the baptismal font, communion table, and pulpit: two sections directly opposite, two sections on a diagonal separated by the center aisle. No one was seated more than thirty feet from the center grouping of font, table, and pulpit. And the faces of at least three-quarters of the congregation were visible from wherever you sat. We were participants in worship, visually accessible to one another, not spectators peering over the backs of heads.

By placing the pews around the matrix of font-pulpit-table, we were making a statement: we can't hear God's love being spoken to us without at the same time looking into the faces of our neighbors, whom God also loves and commands us to love. When we come to worship, we are not isolated individuals, but a family of God. We come to worship not just to see and hear, but to pray and praise God *with one another*. The aisles were wide, providing a sense of spacious hospitality.

Earlier when the church sanctuary was about two months away from completion, some of us were talking together after worship, and the subject of a chancel cross for the sanctuary was discussed. William, whose father had been a Presbyterian pastor, was of the opinion that if we had a cross, it ought to be a Celtic cross, the style of cross associated with the Presbyterian Church in Scotland. The distinguishing mark of the Celtic cross is a circle fixed behind the cross arms, representing the world for which Christ died. By juxtaposing Christ's cross and the world, it maintains the worshipper's attention simultaneously on the Christ who died for the world and the world for which Christ died—the word God spoke to us in Christ and the men and women who respond to the word in prayer and praise.

Robert entered the conversation: "I'd like to make that cross. I have some American black walnut timbers stored in a barn back in Ohio on the family farm. They would be just the thing." The next weekend he drove to Ohio, lashed the timbers on the roof of his station wagon, and brought them back. For the next two months he worked in his basement workshop, fashioning those timbers into a cross. By the time the sanctuary was complete, that cross was also finished and installed on the east wall, the chancel area, elevated above the congregation in full view of everyone. Eight feet tall with a three-and-a-half-foot crossbeam, it centered the attention of our listening, praying, and praising congregation on God's complete work for his people accomplished in the death and resurrection of Jesus. Another statement: if out of forgetfulness or inattention our worship doesn't take place *under* the cross of Jesus, worship almost inevitably becomes an exercise in wish fulfillment, and praise becomes self-congratulation—private needs and emotions given religious sanction. And notice the proportions: the cross is larger than the world—the action initiated in that cross is larger and more comprehensive than anything that is going on in the world.

Bezalel was not only an architect, a master builder: he was an artist. The piece of art that he is best known for is a sculpture, the ark of the covenant, placed in the tabernacle to center Israel's acts of worship. The tabernacle, a portable, moveable structure for worship, served Israel throughout their forty-year sojourn in the wilderness. After arriving at their destination, "the land flowing with milk and honey," it was pitched at Shiloh near the center of Canaan and became the fixed place of worship for Israel. Later it was placed within Solomon's temple in Jerusalem. When that temple was destroyed in 586 BC, the tabernacle and its centering ark were also destroyed.

The ark, placed at the heart of the wilderness tabernacle, was a visible focus for the worship of God. It was a rectangular coffinlike box, four feet two inches long and thirty inches wide and high, covered with gold. The center was designated the mercy seat. It was flanked by cherubim with outstretched wings. But the mercy seat was not a seat at all. It was empty space, a void, an emptiness framed by the angel wings that marked the presence of the enthroned God, Yahweh. Yahweh: "enthroned upon the cherubim." Yahweh, who revealed himself to Moses as Presence; Yahweh, who delivered his people from Egyptian slavery; Yahweh, who spoke in thunder from Sinai; Yahweh, who fed his people on quail and manna on their way through the wilderness to Canaan. Inside the ark, the coffinlike box, were the Ten Words carved into stone tablets.

The focus and function of the ark was the empty space marked off by the cherubim—nothing to see, nothing to hear, nothing to handle. But it was not mere emptiness, but rather an emptiness that is fullness, "the fullness of him who fills all in all": "I AM that I AM."

The core empty space at the center of the ark provided a way of attending to God as he revealed himself to Moses at the bush in Midian, a revelation that became history at the Red Sea and Sinai and tabernacle. When God spoke from the bush, Moses asked God to identify himself—"There are a lot of gods loose in the world; which one are you? Tell me your name." The voice answered in a three-word sentence (in Hebrew) *ehyeh asher ehyeh*. Moses had asked for a name; the answer he got was not a name. A name is a noun. It identifies, locates, objectifies. What Moses heard from the bush was a verb: "I AM . . . I AM just who I AM . . . I AM here . . . I AM present." The verb in Hebrew (*hayah*) is the basic verb for "to be" spoken in the first person, "I AM," and then repeated, "I AM." *I AM WHO I AM*. "I AM" doubled—most emphatically: I am present. I am Presence. The nonname "Name" is vocalized in English as *Yahweh*.

I thought a lot about this. But it wasn't just me. We talked a lot among us in the congregation throughout those months in the catacombs, gathering into our imaginations the interpenetration of visible and invisible. We had all taken a lot for granted in worship. Now we had both occasion and motivation to think through what we had been doing thoughtlessly, mindlessly as "the thing you do on Sundays." We kept reflecting on the immense significance of this empty space between the cherubim: we can only know God in relationship. We cannot see a relationship—it is what takes place between persons. We only know one another in relationship, in the between. We only know God in relationship, the Between. We can only be present to the Presence. The art of the ark repudiates all idolatries, all ideologies, all strategies. Most, in fact, of what goes for religion.

We cannot make an object of God: God is not a thing to be named. We cannot turn God into an idea: God is not a concept to be discussed. We cannot use God for making or doing: God is not a power to be harnessed.

Bezalel the artist. Bezalel sculpted the piece of art that centered Israel's worship of Yahweh. Every detail of the sculpture drew attention to an empty space—the space over the ark and between the cherubim, the invisible mercy seat on which was seated the invisible Yahweh. Yahweh cannot be seen or touched. We can only be in attentive presence, in prayer and submission, in adoration and obedience. Artists do that, use material and sound, color and form to see the invisible, listen to the silence, touch the interior.

Bezalel used his art as a sculptor to lead his people to worship God—to provide a way for his Israelites to attend to the saving action of God at the Red Sea in a way that prevented them from reducing God to a no-god idol they could take charge of and order around. Bezalel as a sculptor used his art to lead his people to worship God—to listen to the revealing Word of God at Sinai without reducing that Word to words of information or incantation. Most of what Bezalel's ark of the covenant called attention to was that empty silence at the mercy seat, framed by the wings of the two cherubim. A visibility that gave witness to invisibility.

Worship is an art, using the sensory to bring us into an awareness of and attentiveness to the mystery of God. Worship has to do with practicing a way of life that is immersed in the salvation and revelation of Yahweh. Bezalel led the people whom Moses had led out of Egypt into making and worshipping in a sanctuary, a place designed to keep them aware and responsive to a way of life in which all their senses were brought into lively participation in the stuff of creation and the energies of salvation. He designed a worship center, the ark of the covenant, in which all visibilities converged into an Invisibility: Yahweh—a presence, a relationship—who can only be worshipped and never used.

The ark of the covenant at the holy of holies center of the tent that centered Israel's worship marks God as present to us. Our task now is to be present to the one who is present to us. This sounds simple enough—and it is. But none of us find it much to our liking. We have a long history in wanting to make God into our image and use him for our purposes. The prophet Moses and the artist Bezalel, followed by a long succession of Hebrew prophets, did their best to free God's people from ideas, attitudes, and practices that prevent us from letting God be God for us on God's terms, not ours.

All of us were getting a crash course in architecture and art and worship. At our first Easter Sunday worship in our now completed sanctuary the story of the empty tomb was our text. After the benediction, three of our young college youth—Steve, Wanda, and Jim—were huddled in conversation on a back pew of the now empty church. I was returning to the pulpit to pick up my sermon notes. They called me over. Wanda said, "Pastor, we think we might be on to something. That empty tomb—could that be an echo of the empty mercy seat of the ark? That the two angels in 'dazzling clothes' who gave witness at the empty tomb of Jesus might be an allusion to the two cherubim marking the emptiness that is fullness at the ark?"

I had never thought of that before. I was intrigued and told them so. Forty-five years later I am still thinking about it. I keep noticing the multiple ways in which artists and their works of art keep taking us *inside* what we see and touch, taste and hear—enter the mystery. And that worship is the supreme art.

# 21

## EUCHARISTIC HOSPITALITY

Meanwhile as Simon and I were making plans for a place of worship that would support and deepen our identity as a worshipping congregation, a congregation with a distinctive identity as people who worshipped nothing less or other than *God,* Jan was in her element, making a neighborhood out of our nonneighborhood neighborhood.

It surprised us both when we moved into our home and began to hold services of Christian worship in our basement that our neighbors were not our neighbors. We weren't used to this. We were used to *neighborhood,* families living in houses next to one another who were, well, neighbors, not just "the people next door from Ohio." Jan grew up in Alabama, a Southern culture in which neighbors not only knew one another's names but the names of their uncles and aunts and cousins and grandparents along with the stories that went with them. I grew up in a small Western town where if you didn't know people personally you at least knew about them. There is little anonymity in a small town. This is not always a good thing. But it is probably preferable to this cultivated isolationism that we were experiencing in our suburban nonneighborhood.

She didn't have a strategy. She didn't have a "business plan," or a "vision statement." She just went about being what she always has been, a neighbor, a friend. She was a pastor's wife, but there was no job description that went with that identity. Our complementary vocations were different in that way. I had a role that was recognizable as pastor: I led worship and preached on Sunday, I visited the sick and distraught, I administered the affairs of the congregation, I prayed with and for people. I wrote books about getting the truth revealed in Jesus and the scriptures embodied in our ordinary days. She mingled in the neighborhood, got to know the mothers of the children our three children played with, had coffee with the alcoholic woman three doors down, picked up on the Georgia accent of another, and made common cause with her, having to live with "these Yankees."

If there is a single word that catches the relational complexity of who Jan is and what she does, it would be hospitality. But it is hospitality that goes far beyond making up beds and preparing meals. *In*hospitality is in the air these days. If hospitality is not to be secularized into "the hospitality industry" or privatized into "having the Smiths over for dinner," it requires intentionality, imagination, and context. In Jan's case, the context is a worshipping congregation. It is not Lone Ranger work.

We were facing this in a more personal and vocational way as we were starting out in this new congregation in the decade of the sixties. Jan, in particular, was noticing that inhospitality is epidemic in America. There are a lot of displaced persons in our American society. It is hard to be a woman in America today. It is hard to care for creation, its resources and its beauties, when we are immersed in a culture of consumption. It is hard to take time to be personal, leisurely, relational with another when there are so many impersonal time-saving technological shortcuts at hand. It is hard to cook a nutritious meal and gather children and spouse and friends around a table in conversation and blessing when there are so many easier and quicker ways to get fed. There is a lot of hate in the air and strangers who are suspicious of one another. There is a lot of rude, even rapacious, treatment of the creation—air and water, soil and forests—that is our home. The conditions are not propitious for hospitality. No wonder we have turned it over to hotels and restaurants and reduced it to what we do in our homes at our convenience.

Strong prophetic voices were in the air those days. Jan made sure we were there to hear them in person every time we had the chance. Martin Luther King Jr.: having grown up in Alabama, Jan was particularly sensitive to matters of race. Betty Friedan: in the company now of a lot of women who didn't want to do "women's work," Jan was listening to feminist voices with new ears. Wendell Berry: his novels and poems and essays deepened her already considerable commitments to growing food and caring for the actual ground, the place in creation where she was placed.

Hospitality had always been in her blood and bones. But until then, as she was working out the implications of it vocationally, she had not been aware of how inhospitable our society had become. She called my attention to organizations being formed to do something about it: fair housing, advocacy of racial equality, conservation efforts, war on hunger, women's rights, you name it, and began to contextualize these concerns in this congregation, this place of worship.

It is not difficult to account for the epidemic of inhospitality that we find ourselves facing. The increase of mobility with a consequent loss of place and tradition, the rapid proliferation of technology that replaces personal interrelations with machines and computers, the increasingly frenetic pace of life that leaves little margin for intimacy. But where do you start?

Jan planted a garden. There was very little landscaping on the half-acre lot on which we were living, and she wanted flowers. She asked me to dig up a plot of ground for a flower garden. I rented a Rototiller, and it was done. Bordering the back of our property line, our neighbor Mike, a lumbering, gruff hulk of a man who never smiled, had a huge garden. One day while Jan was working in her garden, he came over and introduced himself. When he learned that she was planting flowers, in mock and shocked disapproval, he said "I grow *food*." He offered to help Jan make the shift from what he considered the frivolous work of growing flowers to the serious cultivation of food. He also introduced her to something she had never heard of: *organic* gardening. Mike was a chemist, employed at the Edgewood Arsenal, a center for developing chemical warfare. He knew a lot about chemicals. And however they were being used in Vietnam at the time and on the manicured lawns in our neighborhood, Mike wasn't going to have anything to do with them in his garden. He taught Jan how to have a healthy, chemically free garden—organic. The garden grew in size and health year after year for the twenty-eight more years that we lived there. The children pitched in, worked the garden, weeded and picked potato bugs, harvested and canned. All of us learned a lot about nutrition and were soon eating a wide variety of vegetables including okra and kohlrabi.

One day after he had launched her into growing food, she looked out of her kitchen and saw him doing something in her garden. Later she went out to find out what it was. He had "planted" plastic flowers for her—an uncharacteristic touch of aesthetic tenderness.

Mike and his wife, Alma, were considerably older than we were and childless. Our children by this time were referring to Mike as farmer McGregor. One day Jan told him of his new name. He had never heard of farmer McGregor. Jan bought him a copy of the book *The Tale of Peter Rabbit*. Still unsmiling, he seemed to like being in the story.

Jan's garden was both a fact and a metaphor. In fact, it provided us with a focal practice for reflecting on the strategic importance of growing and preparing and serving food in a way that honored and gave dignity to the creation and connected us to the entire living creation, both human and material. As a metaphor, it spilled over into the congregation. Together we began to understand all meals, and everything that went into the making of meals, as Eucharistic. The Holy Eucharist is a meal—the body and blood of Jesus, prepared and served to God's people as they assemble at the Lord's table. The ultimate act of hospitality, the matrix of all hospitality. Everything and everyone is interconnected in an organic way: birds and fish, soil and air, black and white, gay and straight, rich and poor, male and female; and all the meals we eat at home—breakfast, lunch, supper—are derivative in some deep and powerful sense from the Lord's Supper.

When we realized that all meals have a Eucharistic shape, all the motifs of worship began to get worked into the meals we ate in common around our tables in our homes and beyond.

Is it possible to live in this increasingly inhospitable world in a hospitable way? Is it possible to do something focused and intentional about what is wrong in our society without turning the wrongdoers into the enemy? Gathering friends and family to the table for a meal is our most frequent act of hospitality. Coming to the table where Christ is the host is hospitality at its most complete, receiving the Christ and the entire creation and community of Christ in thanksgiving. When we leave that table, any table, we are blessed, predisposed to engage in a hospitable life.

Jan is a quiet person. Quiet but not timid. She planted a garden. Not an abstract cause. Local, relational, immediate, hands-in-the-soil act. She arranged for church suppers that made connections between local eating practices and the implications for world hunger. She was part of the local Fair Housing Committee working with Realtors and builders on behalf of minorities and the poor.

And she began listening more deeply and attentively to the women who didn't want to be defined by "women's work." Feminism was in the air. Many women in the congregation and neighborhood were trying to find an identity that wasn't imposed on them by marriage or what society was expecting of them. Jan was aware and interested in this. The details of her own vocation were getting filled in. She was now naming it, at least among ourselves, Eucharistic hospitality. She was acquiring an imagination to bring to these women who had not yet been given vocations.

This happened more and more frequently, women hungry for hospitable conversation, being listened to, not harangued, being understood, not enlisted in a cause. When they asked for advice, she demurred. "Why don't we just be friends, maybe meet regularly together, get to know one another, and feel free to talk about what we are learning or wondering about in this life of faith that Jesus has joined us in? Why don't we just agree to be faith friends?"

I don't think I have ever known anyone in whom the life of hospitality is so integrated in everything she is and does and is carried off without calling attention to who she is and what she is doing. It often took me by a kind of surprise that she wasn't self-conscious about what she was doing. This is just who she was. This is what she did when she didn't know what she was doing. But it seemed to me that she was becoming the hospitality center of both neighborhood and congregation.

Where did this come from? It didn't take us long to find that there had been years of preparation for it: her parents; like their daughter, neither was self-conscious about their faith or witness to Jesus. Their Christian faith had been thoroughly integrated into their lives. Her father was a Presbyterian elder; her mother played the piano for the Sunday school. Or maybe it was the other way around, their lives had been so thoroughly integrated into the Christian faith. There was something seamless about the way they lived that gave authenticity to who they were.

After we had been married for a few years, I began thinking of (and inwardly naming) her father as Atticus, the southern lawyer played by Gregory Peck in the movie *To Kill a Mockingbird*. He even looked like Gregory Peck—tall, a full head of silvery hair, handsome profile. There was an unassertive, quiet dignity about the way he went about life that I always associated with what I thought of as the quintessential southern gentleman. He was relaxed both in his body and place.

Not that the circumstances of his life had been at all easy. He entered the work force at the height of the Depression. He had to drop out of law school but managed to get a job with the U.S. Fidelity and Guaranty Company as an insurance adjuster and married Dorothy. After twenty-three years in Alabama they returned to Baltimore to the home office of the company. They brought Jan with them (her older brother and sister had left home by then). They lived in a modest row house facing Chinquapin Park with its oak trees and creek. In that house Jan's father and mother cared for his ninety-year-old father, raised two preschool grandchildren after the divorce of their parents, and cultivated azaleas and roses.

Those azaleas and roses were a witness to the way they lived—the cultivation of extraordinary beauty in very ordinary circumstances in which they practiced a welcoming hospitality to everyone in their family. When I was in their company, I experienced a kind of deep serenity in a way of life that seemed capable of absorbing whatever came into wholeness, naturalness. I thought of it as a kind of Wordsworthian gracious acceptance of whatever came their way, everything fitting without forcing, without questioning. I was still new in the Presbyterian way. Was I also experiencing something quintessentially Presbyterian?

That was the home I entered on a Thursday evening in February 1958 to ask for permission and a blessing to marry Jan. I rang the doorbell. Jan's father opened the door, surprised to see me. "Jan isn't here. She is at choir practice."

"Yes, I know she's not here. That is why I'm here."

"Well, come in and sit down." We sat side by side on the sofa. I didn't know how to do this. He made small talk. Then a silence. And then, "Tell me why you're here, Eugene."

"I . . . well . . . what I wanted to . . . I mean . . . well, I mean, it's this way, I . . ."

He put his hand on my shoulder and said, "Eugene, you don't have to go through with this. Let's have a cup of coffee."

He rescued me. An act of hospitality. I never did have to ask him. Over coffee we were able to have an easy conversation in which he gave both permission and blessing. No interrogation. No conditions. "Welcome to the family."

If Jan had to give a name to what she was doing, it would probably be something on the order of "hanging around this intersection between heaven and earth and seeing what there is to be done." But she would never have described it as "church work." She participated in the church's life and sang in the choir, but she wasn't much interested in women's circles and such. It never occurred to her to think of "pastor's wife" as "assistant pastor." Her vocation, while not as easily recognized by others or defined to others as mine, was nevertheless distinctive and not to be confused with any of the stereotypes that are still too common. She came across a sentence written by Alan Jones, dean of the Cathedral of San Francisco, copied it out and taped it on the inside of the door of her spice cabinet as her job description: "To live no tight, neat role is truly sacrificial, it is also truly creative because it leaves us open and free (dare we say) like God himself."

Twenty years or so after these hospitality instincts and skills in Jan had matured and been noticed, we had both of us been asked to speak to a group at

Laity Lodge in Texas. Her assignment was to give a talk on hospitality. After she made her presentation, someone asked, "Do you have any pearls of wisdom that you can give us for raising our children?"

Her answer: "Have a family meal every evening."

That seemed a little abrupt so she elaborated by telling of a women's retreat she had led a few years before. Her subject was, as it was here in Texas, hospitality. But she had decided to be as specific and down-to-earth as she could. No generalities, no big goals like taking in strangers or working in a soup kitchen for the homeless, but just zero in on one manageable task: gather the family for the evening meal. Every evening.

"I know that it might be difficult, but it should be possible to get everyone away from the TV in their rooms with their microwaved meal on a TV tray to eat together. A time to gather the events of the day into conversation, to enter into the mutuality of passing and receiving, of stories, potatoes, carrots, and pork chops. Share food and conversation with one another. Listen to one another. Receive a blessing."

She got uneasy when she received no response. Hoping for some interaction, she asked, "How many of you have an evening meal with your family?" There were thirty-eight women. Not one of them raised a hand.

"I came home and told Eugene. I was depressed for three weeks."

And then this to the person at Laity Lodge who had asked for a pearl: "There are no 'pearls' out there that you can use—no scripture verses to hand out, advice to guide, prayers to tap into. As we live and give witness to Jesus to our children and whoever else, we are handing out seeds, not pearls, and seeds need soil in which to germinate. A meal is soil just like that. It provides a daily relational context in which everything you say and don't say, feel or don't feel, God's Word and snatches of gossip, gets assimilated along with the food and becomes you, but not you by yourself—you and your words and acts embedded in acts of love and need, acceptance and doubt. Nothing is abstract or in general when you are eating a meal together. You realize, don't you, that Jesus didn't drop pearls around Galilee for people as clues to find their way to God or their neighbors. He ate meals with them. And you can do what Jesus did. Every evening take and receive the life of Jesus around your table."

———

When, in 1991, they heard that Jan and I would soon be leaving our congregation, Bill and Yolanda returned to see us and say their good-byes. They had been charter members of Christ Our King Church. Bill was an engineer. He had headed up our first capital-funds campaign that financed the building of our sanctuary. Yolanda had organized and taught our preschool. They had invested a lot in the church. Five years earlier they had retired and moved to a village on the New Jersey coast. Now we were talking in our living room. It had been the children's nursery when they had first worshipped with us in our basement. We reminisced about what we had done together for twenty-four years.

As they were getting ready to leave, Bill said, "Eugene, you were a pretty good pastor, but Jan—you were an absolutely incredible pastor's wife."

A nice tribute. Pastors' wives get used to being invisible, or taken for granted, or sidelined from considerations of appreciation. It was nice for Jan to hear. And I didn't mind coming in second.

# 22

## APPRECIATION AND FOOLERY

When I accepted the call to organize and develop this new church, the agreement was that the office of New Church Development (NCD) for the Presbyterian Church USA would pay my salary and the mortgage on the house that the church provided for three years, reducing the payment by a third each year. The institutional expectation was that we would be self-supporting at the end of the three years.

The three years was now completed. Christ Our King Presbyterian Church had been worshipping in our new sanctuary for six months. The membership was just under two hundred. Our finances were adequate to pay the mortgage on our home, the church building loan, and my salary.

One of my assigned duties as an organizing pastor was to provide a monthly report to the office of NCD of the Presbyterian Church located at 475 Riverside Drive in New York City. I was glad to do it. I owed the institution a lot. They had ordained me and trusted me with the daunting task of developing a congregation. They had spent a lot of money on me. They gave me access to a tradition in theology and polity that I found stabilizing and foundational. Writing those reports turned out to be a monthly exercise in appreciation.

The first page was statistical: the number of home visits I made, how many people attended worship each Sunday, a financial report on the weekly offerings, progress on building plans, committee activities. This was followed by several pages of personal and theological reflection on my pastoral work: what I understood of God's presence in the congregation, the ways in which worship and my preaching were being received, areas of inadequacy that were showing up in my ministry, strengths and skills that seemed to be emerging. I was encouraged to tell stories that would provide a feel for the texture of what was going on. After a year or so of doing this without any response from the NCD office, I started to wonder if my denominational superiors were reading past the first page of statistics. I thought I would test out my suspicion and have a little fun on the side.

So the next month, after compiling the statistical data, I slipped another sheet of paper into my typewriter and described as best I could what seemed to be a long slow slide into depression. I had difficulty sleeping, I couldn't pray. I was getting the work done at a maintenance level, but it was a robotic kind of thing with no spirit, no zest. Having feelings like this, I was seriously questioning whether I could keep this up, maybe even be a pastor at all. Could they recommend a counselor for me?

Getting no response, I upped the ante. The next month I developed a drinking problem that became evident one Sunday in the pulpit. Everybody was very understanding, but one of the elders had to complete the sermon. I felt that I was at the point where I needed treatment. How should I go about getting it? Were there any funds available?

Still no response. I got bolder. The next month I cooked up an affair. It started innocently enough as I was attempting to comfort a woman through an abusive marriage, but something happened along the way, and we ended up in bed together, only it wasn't bed but one of the church pews, where we were discovered when the ladies arranging flowers for Sunday worship walked in on us. I thought it was all over for my ministry at that point, but it turned out that in this community swingers are very much admired. The next day, Sunday, attendance doubled.

This reporting was turning into a gala event one day each month in our house. I would go to my study and write these extravagant fictions and then bring them out and read them to Jan. We would laugh and laugh, collaborating by embellishing details.

Next I reported some innovations I was making in the liturgy. This was the 1960s, an era of liturgical reform and experimentation. Our worship, I wrote to my NCD supervisors, was about as dull as it could get. I had read some scholarly guesses about a mushroom cult in Palestine in the first century in which Jesus might have been involved. I thought it was worth a try. I arranged with one of our college kids who was going to Mexico on spring break to purchase some psychedelic mushrooms (psilocybin?). When he returned with them, I introduced them at the next celebration of the Eucharist by having Jan bake them into the communion bread. It was the most terrific experience anybody had ever had in worship, absolutely dazzling. But I didn't want to do anything that was in violation of our church constitution and couldn't find anything in our Book of Order on this. Could they please advise me on whether I was permitted to proceed along these lines.

These report-writing days were getting to be a lot of fun. Month after month I sent the stories to the men and women who were overseeing the health of my spirituality and the integrity of my ministry. Never did I get a response.

At the end of three years I was released from their supervision. As pastor and congregation, we were now more or less on our own—organized, developed, and on our way. I got a letter from the NCD office under which I had worked, asking me to come to New York City for a debriefing and evaluation of their supervision of me through these three years. I took a train to the city and then the subway to their offices on Riverside Drive.

Two men and a woman met with me. After some introductory small talk they congratulated me on the work I had done and asked me for my comments on how things had gone over the three years. I told them that I appreciated their help. The checks arrived on time each month. I was treated courteously. But I did have one minor area of disappointment: they had never, it seemed, read past that first page of statistical reporting that I had sent in each month.

"Oh, but we did. We read those reports carefully; we take them very seriously."

"How can that be?" I said. "That time I asked for help with my drinking problem, and you didn't respond. That time I got involved in a sexual adventure, and you didn't intervene. That craziness I reported when I was using hallucinogens in the Eucharist, and you did nothing."

Their faces were blank, and then confused—followed by a splendid vaudeville slapstick of buck passing and excuse making. It was a wonderful moment. I replay the scene in my imagination a couple times a year, the way some people watch old Abbott and Costello movies.

When I confessed my foolery, they were not amused.

## A BADLANDS BEAUTY

What came next was a surprise. In my Company of Pastors, my newly formed pastoral identity had been tested and confirmed. In our Catacombs Presbyterian Church week after week after week, there had been the quiet euphoria of watching a congregation of what seemed (to me at least) an unlikely and unpromising group of people come into being as a people of God. And now a sanctuary, Christ Our King: a place of worship, architecturally shaped into the form of praying hands, spacious with an emptiness that invited us into fullness, a piece of art worthy of Bezalel that offered participation in the beauty of holiness. The scriptures had become autobiographical to me and my worshipping congregation as never before as we became aware of living together in continuity with the biblical narratives in Acts and Exodus. We had learned so much, not just book or classroom learning—we were becoming what we were learning: learning to pray by praying, learning to worship by worshipping, learning the scripture story by living out the story of salvation in Maryland.

We had planted the cross of Christ Our King on this Maryland hill and were claiming the territory for the kingdom of God. The dedication of the new sanctuary was celebrative. A lot had happened in three years. The exhilaration of our accomplishment was palpable.

———

The surprise was that a month or so after the dedication of our sanctuary attendance at worship began to drop off. Men and women who had been faithful in worship from the beginning disappeared for three or four Sundays at a stretch. Men and women who had plunged into the business of planning and organizing and inviting friends and neighbors were finding other enthusiasms. If someone didn't show up for a month or so at worship, I went to see him or her: "I've been missing you, anything wrong?"

"Oh no, pastor, nothing's wrong. We really did it, didn't we? Who would have thought that people like us could have done this, pulled a congregation together and built a church like this. We sure have put our mark on the neighborhood, haven't we? I've never been part of something this significant in my life. Thanks for getting me in on it."

I found I was listening to variations on this response almost daily.

Charles and Betty Graham hadn't worshipped with us for six weeks when I went to visit them. They were in their late forties. Their primary identity at the time I met them came through their son, who was the star football and basketball player in the high school. He kept their family name in the local newspaper headlines. But it wasn't long before their involvement in the development and worship of Christ Our King Church was competing with athletics for identity purposes. Charles held a middle-management position in the civil service at a nearby military training and testing grounds. Betty was active in several community-service organizations. With the exception of their son's name-grabbing headlines almost weekly on the sports page of the local newspaper, they were swallowed up in suburban anonymity—until they started worshipping in the catacombs each Sunday, their imaginations (and their faith?) activated by a fresh immersion in the church and worship narratives in Acts and Exodus.

Early in our conversation in their living room, Charles put it like this: "You know, pastor, I think I am as surprised as you are that I am not in church these Sundays. All my life I have attended church regularly. I don't think there have been more than fifteen or twenty Sundays in the last forty years that I have not been in church. I always liked being in church—there is something centering and stabilizing about it—a protected time to reflect and stay in touch with the way I was brought up. And then a few weeks ago on a whim that seemed totally spontaneous—I didn't really think about it—I said to Betty, 'I think I'll go fishing today.' She was as surprised as I was. It was a beautiful spring day. The wildflowers were in bloom, and the warbler migration was under way. I got my fly rod and fishing gear together, she packed a picnic lunch and put her watercolors and sketch pad in a tote bag. We drove to the Big Gunpowder River, and while you preached, I fished and Betty caught the emerging blood-root and round-lobed hepatica blossoms with her watercolors. It was a lovely three hours.

"When we got home we both were astonished that we felt like we always felt on Sundays—easy, calm, rested. We had abruptly, even though casually, interrupted a forty-year routine of Sunday worship and nothing happened. We didn't feel guilty. We didn't miss it. Lightning didn't strike us. Everything was just the way it had always been. We didn't intend to make a habit of it, but I guess we have.

"We aren't quitting the church. We still want you for our pastor. But don't expect us to be there every Sunday, at least while the fish are biting and the wildflowers are in bloom."

I went to Alan, my immediate supervisor in charge of new church development in our area. "Alan, what do I do now?" He had a ready answer: "Start another building program." I protested: "We don't need another building program. We need to mature as a congregation. We have had this great beginning. But it is only a beginning. We are now in a position to fill out the many dimensions of being a church in this neighborhood."

He insisted: "People need something tangible, something they can get their hands on, a challenge, a goal. Trust me. I've been through this before. It's the American way." In the weeks that followed I realized that he was probably right, at least about the "American" part of it. But something didn't seem right about his diagnosis. I felt an inner reluctance to embrace his counsel. This didn't sound like the voice of God to me.

The challenges and demands of forming a congregation and building a sanctuary had been very stimulating. I had loved doing this—encouraging, interpreting, developing a biblical imagination that was adequate for seeing Jesus in the faces of spouses and neighbors, a vocabulary for recognizing the presence of the Holy Spirit in the invisibilities of daily life. I had just assumed that when we had completed the demanding work of organizing and building, everyone would be energized to embrace our newly formed identity as the people of God, Christ's body, *church*—living together, grateful for what had been given to us and ready to invite and serve others out of who we had become. I expected that the church into which we had been formed as a worshipping community would shape us into men and women who were growing up in Christ, serving our children and spouses, neighbors and fellow workers in Jesus's name.

I was wrong.

As a kind of malaise seemed to spread through the congregation, I could also feel the adrenaline drain out of my blood stream.

How could I recapture the spirited purpose that had infused so much energy into the formation of our congregation, finding ourselves as part of something new, a fresh expression on Maryland soil of this magnificent story of salvation, following Jesus as if for the first time on the roads and sidewalks of this suburban wilderness?

I had no way of knowing it at the time, but I was entering into a time of my life that I later named the "badlands." And I had no way of knowing how long I would be there.

It was going to last six years.

# 23

## PILGRIMAGE

Jan and I now had three preschool-age children. While the church was being developed, we had only taken brief summer vacations, but now there seemed to be breathing space for something more substantial. We decided to drive to Montana for the month of August and visit and vacation with my parents at the family summer cabin. Jan's parents and sister lived nearby in Baltimore, and we had frequent meals and visits with them on birthdays and holidays. But we had been a long time away from our Montana family. This year seemed like a good time to get away and take our full month of vacation. It seemed like the right time to put some perspective on the intensities of these three years: gathering a congregation, worshipping in our basement while having two babies, building a sanctuary, and now, with the wind knocked out of us by this unexpected congregational apathy, pull back and talk it over. We would drive to Montana and see if we could recover our breath.

As August approached, we started getting ready for the trip. With three young children it required serious planning. The trip took us five days. We spent the nights in state parks in our backpacking tents. We fixed picnic lunches in town parks or roadside vistas along the way and cooked our suppers on a camp stove.

The first day was the most difficult. Driving north for a couple hours, we left the colorful Amish farms and turned west on the Pennsylvania Turnpike. Almost immediately our children started clamoring, "Are we there yet? . . . How much longer is this going to take . . . I'm bored. There's nothing to do . . ."

The first night we camped at the Indiana Dunes, the second at Loon Lake in Minnesota, the third in the Black Hills of South Dakota, the fourth at Three Forks in Montana. We arrived at our destination, the family cabin on Flathead Lake, late afternoon of the fifth day.

For the first two days of the trip, forested hills and fertile farms made up the landscape. The fourth and fifth days we drove through the Great Plains and into the Rocky Mountains. It was magnificent country all the way, except for a portion of the third day. On the third day we drove several hours through the Dakota Badlands, where nothing is green or growing. No trees, no water, no towns. The only sign of life was an occasional vulture cruising for carrion, but even that vulture was more like a reminder of death. The only visual interruptions to the tedium were huge signs telling us to be sure to stop at Wall Drug, an unlikely oasis in the middle of the Badlands: Wall Drug. The signs for Wall Drug begin appearing two hundred miles before you get there. Then suddenly, seemingly out of nowhere, a rambling, jerry-built structure spilling out with souvenirs and knickknacks. The store and its billboards rivaled the ugliness of the Badlands landscape. But at least they promised cool drinks and ice-cream cones. The children demanded that we stop.

And then we were on our way again. In a few hours we entered the pine-fragrant forests of the Black Hills. In a few more hours we sighted the Rocky Mountains and knew we were nearing the sacred ground where Jan and I hoped we could reestablish and clarify our pastoral vocation and workplace.

We did gain perspective on what we had been doing. We did begin to recover our breath. It was a beginning.

This family August vacation journey became a family tradition. It turned into something more like an annual pilgrimage to a holy place. We were soon

imagining ourselves in the company of the holy family with their donkey on
their annual Passover trip from Nazareth to Jerusalem. The only thing that
marred our biblically soaked imagination was our substitution of a green Ram-
bler station wagon for Joseph and Mary's donkey.

Each year the itinerary of camping sites was unvarying. The changing
landscape across the continent became etched into our memories. Arrival was
always welcoming: reunion with parents and grandparents and cousins, conversations and stories, hiking and backpacking in the mountains, swimming
and canoeing on the lake, reading and birding.

But there were also those few hours of the Badlands at the midpoint, coming
and going, of our annual pilgrimage. That first year the badlands presented
themselves to Jan and me (but not the children) as a metaphor for what we
were at that moment putting behind us for a month. The sudden, unexpected
transition from a green landscape of growth and fertility to a seemingly featureless aridity. A metaphor: Dakota Badlands—Maryland church. The color
had drained out of both vocation and congregation, and we didn't know what
to make of it. But as the pilgrimages were repeated year after year, the Badlands
metaphor incrementally developed unanticipated meanings. One year I wrote a
poem in which the phrase "a badlands beauty" unexpectedly appeared.

> *Flash floods of tears, torrents of them,*
> *Erode cruel canyons, exposing*
> *Long forgotten strata of life*
> *Laid down in the peaceful decades:*
> *A badlands beauty. The same sun*
> *That decorates each day with colors*
> *From arroyos and mesas, also shows*
> *Every old scar and cut of lament.*
> *Weeping washes the wounds clean*
> *And leaves them to heal, which always*
> *Takes an age or two. No pain*
> *Is ugly in past tense. Under*
> *The Mercy every hurt is a fossil*
> *Link in the great chain of becoming.*

*Pick and shovel prayers often*
*Turn them up in valleys of death.*

The sacred space of Montana furnished us with a context in which we re-
treated annually for a month from the daily disappointments, misunderstand-
ings, fatigue, and yes, failures that make up the life of congregation and pastor.
Those three years of organizing and developing had been quite glorious: gathering a congregation and building a sanctuary, discovering holiness in unlikely
people and tapping into springs of energy in souls that had been commodified,
"thingified," in the desert of suburbia.

I had just assumed that the energy would keep coming. Why wouldn't it?
Isn't that what pastors are supposed to do? Stoke the fires? Prime the pump?
Charge the batteries? Do the "American" thing? After only three years was I
already a failed pastor?

Every August 2,500 miles and a month provided substantial space and
time, space and sufficient quiet, to pay attention to the complexities involved
in living a mature life, of growing up in Christ.

This was a start. But there is more to the Badlands than, well, badlands.
There is a badlands beauty that can only be perceived in the Badlands.

Did I think that being a pastor in the workplace of a congregation was all
fertile farmland and rolling green hills, grand horizons and majestic mountains? I was a pastor in a place and with a people in an American culture and an
American church that seemed more like the Badlands and Wall Drug than the
continental kingdom of God fertility and horizon and peaks in which God's
throne is established and over which God reigns.

Annually on pilgrimage to the sacred ground of Montana, my vocation
was renewed in the company of my family. I was a pastor: I would stay with
these people for as long as necessary to acquire an imagination and develop a
faith to follow Christ right here, in this congregation, in this place, with this
family, in this workplace. Didn't I know by now that growth, any growth—but
especially character growth, spiritual growth, church growth, body-of-Christ
growth, *soul* growth—had periods of dormancy? Did I want to be a nonpastor
who by diversions and novelties and distractions—"challenges"—perpetuated
a kind of sub-Christian adolescence? I remembered a line from the English

novelist E. F. Forster: "Ecstasy doesn't last. But it can cut a channel for something lasting." The channel had been cut. Now what?

Up until this time in my life I had never had to deal with anything quite
like this. I lived from goal to goal. Schooling had been measured out one grade
after another, evaluated with report cards, periodic graduations, academic de-
grees, caps and gowns. Various ventures into the world of work had consisted of
job assignments and were rewarded with pay raises and promotions. Athletics,
which was very important to me, was fueled almost entirely by competition—
winning was the bottom line. Winning games (basketball) and winning races
(middle distances and mile) defined who I was throughout my adolescence.
Getting married and having children were socially recognized accomplish-
ments. I began my life as a pastor by being given goals to meet: gather a congregation, become self-sufficient financially, build a sanctuary. I was a competitor.
I had always been a competitor. Competition brought the best out of me. It is
what I did best. Competition had brought me a long way.

And now I was faced with engaging in a way of life, a vocation, in which
I had to learn to submit to conditions, enter into conditions, embrace conditions, in which my competitive skills and achievements were virtually worthless. Worse than worthless: actively destructive.

Following that first holy-land pilgrimage, I returned to my congregation
considerably chastened. I didn't know what I was going to do, but I did know
what I was not going to do: I was not going to start the new building program
that Alan had advised. I was not going to go looking for another congregation
that I could challenge with fresh goals. I was not going to surround myself with
cheerleaders and turn Sunday morning into a pep rally for Jesus.

Not that I wasn't tempted. I was told about churches that were looking for
a pastor. From a distance they looked pretty good. From their self-descriptions
they were obviously a lot more promising than the lethargic congregation I was
dealing with. I even talked to a couple of them. In the process I remembered
Willi Ossa and the artists on West Eighty-sixth Street in New York City, artists who knew they were artists regardless of affirmation or recognition. And I
remembered Willi's prophetic portrait of me, warning me against entering the
American competition to be a pastor who "gets things done" and who is "going
somewhere."

# 24

## HEATHER-SCENTED THEOLOGY

Ian, born in Wales, was twenty-five years my senior. He was pastor of an old, historic Presbyterian church in Baltimore. When he was young, his family had moved to Scotland, and he spent his early years as a pastor in the Highlands before immigrating to America. His accent preserved the soft burr of his cradle tongue. I knew he went to the Rocky Mountains in Montana every summer on holiday, the same range of mountains that extended three hundred miles north to the sacred ground I had grown up on and was now returning to each August. At area church meetings we would sometimes exchange Montana stories.

One summer night he was mugged while walking his dog. His assailant took his watch and then, just to let him know who was running the show, threw him to the ground and kicked him a couple of times in the ribs. When I saw him a few days later, he was bruised, sore, and still feeling the emotional effects of the violence. He told me that he was looking forward to leaving the next week for Montana, where he would vacation for a month near Yellowstone Park, far from the crime-ridden city. The high country there is pristine and exhilarating. There it is impossible to harbor a mean thought for more than ten seconds, let alone act in a mean way. The nearest criminal is at least a hundred miles away as the crow flies.

Six weeks later at a gathering of pastors and elders at Govans Presbyterian Church, he had his arm in a sling. We had both recently returned to Maryland from our holidays. I asked, "What happened?" He told me that he had been riding a horse on a mountain trail in the Bridger Range, and the horse had been spooked by a coyote. He was thrown into a rocky ravine and broke his arm. And then he said, "It is safer to walk on the streets of Baltimore at night than in the mountains of Montana in daylight. Those mountains are magnificent. But they have twenty different ways to kill you. Just like the church."

The conversation stuck in my memory. It was lonely in the badlands. I didn't know him very well but liked and trusted him. A couple weeks later I telephoned and asked if I could come and talk with him. We arranged for a Friday-morning appointment. It was his phrase "twenty different ways to kill you, just like the church" that I wanted to talk about with him.

I told him about the transition I found myself going through from the high-energy years of organizing, developing, and building Christ Our King Church and now into this slump, what felt like congregational passivity. I told him about my reflections on wanting to stay with these people but wondered if I had the emotional wherewithal to do it. They were reducing me to their level—flat and complacently self-satisfied in the wake of our achievement. I didn't seem capable of rousing anything approaching the enthusiasm of the last three years. And my supervisor's counsel, "start another building campaign," seemed cheap. I had a vague idea of what I wanted but didn't know if I even knew how to begin. I had been a competitor since getting out of diapers. I was addicted to adrenaline. And now I was realizing how my already well-honed competitive instincts were exacerbated by the competitive and consumerist church culture that surrounded me.

Was it realistic to think I could develop from a competitive pastor to something maybe more like a contemplative pastor—a pastor who was able to be with people without having an agenda for them, a pastor who was able to accept people just as they were and guide them gently and patiently into a mature life in Christ but not get in the way, let the Holy Spirit do the guiding?

He suggested, "Why don't you come into Baltimore and see me every couple of weeks or so, and we'll talk. I know it isn't easy for you. It isn't easy for me." Two years of biweekly conversations on Friday mornings were the result.

Ian's early years in the Scottish Highlands had shaped his imagination. The Rocky Mountains in the American West weren't the Highlands of his homeland, but there was that quality of fresh air and wildness that gave him a feeling of "home." Yet he missed the heather. I learned from him that a lot of Scots had immigrated a hundred years or so earlier and taken up sheepherding along the Rocky Mountain front. A lot of the names of people and names of places reminded him of Scotland. He also introduced me to a Montana novelist, Ivan Doig, who told the stories of many of these Scots who found themselves at home in this austere country. Jan and I are still reading those novels. And I learned that Ian was one of the early translators of Karl Barth into English. He insisted that Barth was a "pastor's theologian" without peer and that I should immerse myself in his writings. Which I did.

After a few weeks of our getting acquainted, Ian suggested that we begin our biweekly time in the prayer chapel adjoining the sanctuary. He sat on one side of the chapel, I sat on the other side, fifteen feet or so removed. We knelt in our respective pews. Out of his Scottish prayer book he read prayers aloud for twenty minutes. I prayed in silence. He never suggested I do otherwise. He was, it turned out, a fierce Barthian with little tolerance for a spirituality emotionally soaked in feelings.

After the twenty minutes of prayers he said, "Eugene, let's get a cup of coffee." We crossed the street to a neighborhood coffee shop and talked. We talked about Barth. He told me of his youthful bird-watching in the Scottish Highlands (he was an avid collector of birds' eggs) and the newspaper column on birding that he wrote for the local paper. We swapped stories of hiking in the mountains of Montana. And we talked together of the dangers of being a pastor in America, where the magnificent church, like the magnificent Rocky Mountains, "has twenty different ways to kill you."

The conversations came to an end when he was called to be the professor of preaching at Pittsburgh Theological Seminary. Several years later when he was retiring from his faculty appointment there, he called and asked if he could recommend me to become his successor. But by then, thanks to him, I was more than ever what I had been becoming for a long time—a contemplative pastor.

In these early years when I was becoming a pastor, I needed a pastor. Some deep and cultivated pastoral instinct in Ian responded: he became my pastor without making me a project, without giving me advice, without smothering me with his "concern." There wasn't a hint of condescension, not in his prayer, not in his conversation. I learned, without being aware that I was learning, of the immense freedom that comes in pastoral relationships that are structured by prayer and ritual and let everything else happen more or less spontaneously. The competitiveness didn't exactly leave me, but it developed a root system that didn't depend on artificial stimulants or chemical additives—like "start another building campaign."

# 25

## PRESBYCOSTAL

I grew up Pentecostal. As an adult, I became a Presbyterian. I made the transition effortlessly. At my New York City seminary I was assigned field-work as a student seminarian in Madison Avenue Presbyterian Church on East Seventy-third Street. I knew nothing about Presbyterians, but it didn't matter—my assignment was to coach the church's basketball team. And on Friday evenings I was responsible for the church's recreational program: swimming pool, pool tables, gymnasium. On Saturday nights my team played its scheduled game in the Church Basketball League in Manhattan. The young adults who made up the team were primarily from a nearby Czech and Hungarian neighborhood. They had learned to play on the street with an improvised backboard. And they were good. They could easily have beaten the college basketball team that I had played on. We won the church league that year. I don't know if praying with them before each game had anything to do with that.

As I mentioned earlier, on Sundays, morning and evening, I worshipped with the congregation and sat for a year under the preaching of the pastor, George Buttrick. I later learned that he was the premier preacher in New York City, some thought in the entire country. On Sunday evening after worship he invited the seminary interns (there were seven or eight of us) to his Fifth Avenue penthouse apartment overlooking Central Park for informal conversation on preaching and worship and the pastoral vocation. I had no interest in being a pastor at that time, but I liked him, liked his stories, liked his evident delight in his vocation.

And now ten years later I was not only a Presbyterian but, of all things, a Presbyterian pastor. The move from Pentecostal to Presbyterian didn't seem like a big thing at the time. It still doesn't. Certainly nothing that could be called a crisis. I was not aware that I was changing any part of what I believed, and certainly not how I lived. But was I still a Pentecostal?

I assumed I was. I hadn't renounced anything that I had grown up believing. I wasn't aware that my Christian identity had eroded in any way. But here I was parched and thirsty in this badlands. Christians, especially pastors, if they are walking "in the Spirit" and living obediently, aren't supposed to feel this way.

If I were to define what for me makes up the core Pentecostal identity, it is the lived conviction that everything, absolutely everything, in the scriptures is livable. Not just true, but livable. Not just an idea or a cause, but livable in real life. Everything that is revealed in Jesus and the scriptures, the gospel, is there to be lived by ordinary Christians in ordinary times. This is the supernatural core, a lived resurrection and Holy Spirit core, of the Christian life. What Karl Barth expressed dialectically as the "impossible possibility." I had always believed that. I believed it still. So what happened to the zest—the *Pentecostal* zest that had energized both me and the congregation through these developmental years as pastor of a congregation?

I entered into Presbyterianism as a competitor, coaching the Madison Avenue Presbyterian basketball team to the church-league championship. That same spirit of competition continued to serve me well in organizing and developing a new congregation. Now what? The two years of Friday prayers and conversation with Ian provided a context for moving from being a competitive pastor to being a contemplative pastor. A corresponding movement was taking place as the integration of Pentecostal and Presbyterian in me was now well under way.

Our August pilgrimages to the sacred ground of my formation in the Christian way—Montana—provided a leisurely and safe time and place in the company of my Pentecostal family to ask questions and pray my perceptions. Another "badlands beauty" that emerged in the maturation of my vocation.

I was not aware of choosing to be a Presbyterian. I didn't go over the options available to me, study them, interview representative men and women, assess the pros and cons, pray for discernment, and then apply for membership. The Presbyterians needed a coach for their basketball team. I knew how to do that and did it. But as the months added up to years, I kept being assigned to Presbyterian churches for seminary fieldwork. I was never self-consciously a Presbyterian. I am still not. But something was going on, incrementally, that formed an identity that vocationally fused Pentecostal and Presbyterian. Later I learned that there was a name for it: presbycostal.

What I needed, but didn't know that I needed, the Presbyterians offered me: the gift of a living tradition. I grew up in the West in a town that was only forty-three years old when I was born. Pentecostalism as a denomination was even younger than that. I was a child of the first generation of Pentecostalism in America. Growing up, I had almost no knowledge or awareness, maybe none, that anything of Christian significance had taken place between the Day of Pentecost in Jerusalem ten days after Jesus had ascended into heaven and the Azusa Street revival in Los Angeles in 1903 that marked the birth of Pentecostalism in America. My church history consisted of the names of half a dozen evangelists holding tent revivals in the Northwest. My family history was also thin—fragments of stories torn out of barely remembered diaries and letters of Norwegian and Swedish immigrations.

One of my favorite "church history" stories was of Jimmy McGinnis, an Irish immigrant, thick-necked, with a body like a brick privy. He became a Christian in a Seattle street mission, converted from a roughneck life of brawling and drinking to starting churches in frontier towns of Montana. He started a Pentecostal church in Missoula, a hundred miles south of the town I grew up in. I knew his son, Jerry. We played on rival high-school basketball teams. The legendary stories of Jimmy McGinnis were all variations on his pastoral visits to the local saloons on Saturday nights. He would enter the saloon, command all the men to get out on the street, where he would line them up against the saloon wall. If anyone objected, he would fight him into submission, drag him outside, and prop him against the wall alongside the rest of his congregation. Then he would preach, making Christians out of any who were still standing. While my Lutheran friends were learning about Martin Luther nailing his Ninety-five Theses to the Castle Church door in Wittenberg, defying Tetzel and the pope, I was listening to the latest story of Jimmy McGinnis pounding salvation into the drunks in Missoula.

As an adolescent, I much preferred Jimmy McGinnis—I knew his son— to Martin Luther, who had been dead five hundred years. As a Pentecostal, church history was a current event. I felt sorry for my Lutheran friends who had to dig out their stories from the cemeteries. But now as a Presbyterian adult, I was discovering that my Christian family tree had roots all over the world and through twenty centuries. Presbyterianism grafted me into immense continuities of prayer and worship, of saints and artists, of countries and continents. I began to relish the sense of stability, of continuity, of being on speaking terms with personal names that held stories that touched my own and extended it. There was texture and depth to be explored, intricacy and complexity. There was far more to learn and assimilate about the Christian way than the latest stories, wonderful as they were, of Jimmy McGinnis and his ilk.

Also I found that among the Presbyterians, I was meeting pastors who took seriously the vocation of pastor, persons who knew and valued and loved people in place and over time and seriously in Jesus's name. Madison Avenue's George Buttrick was the first. I started at the top. I had known men and even a few women, who were addressed as pastor. But they weren't pastors in this local and personal way. My adolescent impression was that they were never interested in the people in our congregation and certainly not in me. All their attention was either on "the furniture of heaven and the temperature of hell" or on dramatic healings and revivals in other cities or countries. *Pastor* was an interim position on their way to some more celebrated work or exotic location.

As I became at home in the environment of Presbyterianism, I realized that *pastor* was a term that carried a certain innate dignity, involved disciplines of learning, demanded attentiveness to the personal details of men and women in pain and doubt, required an understanding not only of what took place on the church premises but also in the workplace and household world of the church members. I observed pastors like Ian, who entered into their vocation as an all-inclusive way of life, not just taking on a religious job. This was new for me. I met pastors who were modest, not self-important, not prima donnas, not hungry for attention—pastors who were, well, just pastors. Pastors who actually liked being pastors. Not all of them, of course, but more often than not. I felt comfortable in the company of these pastors, and when I myself became one, I knew that I was with men and women I could trust.

I know many wonderful people in Pentecostalism but, in retrospect, not many pastors. There is a lot of energy in Pentecostalism, exuberance and praise and commitment—the *livability* in *real* life—firsthandedness, immediacy. I wasn't about to give up any of my Pentecostal identity—but I also realized that I could never be a pastor worth his salt if I couldn't integrate it into my Presbyterianism, a tradition that put me into a comprehensive speaking relation with all my brothers and sisters in all the forms that church takes across the country and through the centuries. I needed a context for developing patient attentiveness to the ways that holiness develops over a lifetime, which necessarily includes stretches of boredom and pain and suffering, what Dorothy Day named "the long loneliness." Pentecostalism and Presbyterianism were for me both irreplaceable gifts, polarities that made a continuum, not opposites in tension. In the badlands I was learning that being a pastor didn't put me on the fast track for encountering the most interesting people, the most promising leaders, the latest in innovations, and living on the cusp of the "breaking news."

# 26

## EMMAUS WALKS

One summer on our return trip from our annual Montana pilgrimage, refreshed in body and renewed in soul—we happened to be driving through the Badlands section of our itinerary just then—I said to Jan, "Why wait for August, why wait for Montana? What's wrong with September through July, what's wrong with Maryland?"

On the first days after our return, instead of plunging headlong into congregational affairs, we took some time to look around the neighborhood, this Maryland country. In my preoccupation with gathering a congregation under the auspices of "Our Father who art in heaven," I had virtually ignored the first half of the familiar phrase "*on earth* as it is in heaven" that is the transitional midpoint in our frequently prayed Lord's Prayer. This *Maryland* earth. This *local* earth on which we lived eleven months of the year. We found some Sierra Club maps to the hiking trails that, as it turned out, were all around us. We bought guidebooks for eastern birds, for tree and fern, for wildflower and seashell identification. We looked around us and discovered that we had been set down in a world of wonders: Assateague and Chincoteague, the Big and Little Gunpowder Rivers, beeches and sycamores, Chesapeake Bay and the Appalachian Trail, Gettysburg and Appomattox.

Our children were all in school by now. We decided that each Monday, after getting them ready and sending them off to get the school bus, we would familiarize ourselves with *this* earth, spend the day immersing ourselves in what we had for too long ignored. We returned in midafternoon in time to meet our children as they returned from school.

After doing this for several months, we drove north two hundred miles to be on a three-day retreat at Kirkridge Retreat Center in the Pennsylvania Pocono Mountains with Douglas Steere. Professor Steere, a Quaker, taught philosophy at Swarthmore College. We had never met him, although I had heard him lecture a couple of times. Both of us had read his books and deeply respected his prayerful and centered life. What we didn't know was that this was a silent retreat. We hadn't read the fine print: silence for three days. Silence in our rooms. Silence at meals. About twenty of us in silence for three days. For one hour in the morning and another in the afternoon each day Steere read a lecture to us in his quiet voice. We could sign up for a half-hour conversation with him if we wished.

In welcoming us to the retreat and orienting us to this three days of silence, he told us the story of a burly, gruff, heavily accented German Lutheran pastor he once knew who specialized in men's retreats. His procedure was to greet his retreatants and gather them into a meeting room with their luggage. He then directed them to open their suitcases. He examined each piece of luggage, confiscated their whiskey, and then sent them off for an hour, two by two, on trails through the woods on what he called E-Mouse walks, his German rendition of Emmaus.

And that, Professor Steere told us, is what he wanted us to do. He assured us that he wasn't going to confiscate our whiskey, but following his morning and afternoon lectures we would take an Emmaus walk. Otherwise, silence. Silence, he told us, was hugely undervalued in our American way of life as a way of being in communion with one another and with God. American Christians were conspicuously deficient. "Think of it as remedial silence." This would be three days for practicing silence. "These might be the quietest three days you will ever spend. Don't waste them."

Jan and I signed up together for our half-hour conversation with Professor Steere. We told him of this continuing badlands period in our lives and how interminable it seemed to be—wasn't there something to *do*? He warned us against shortcuts. He encouraged us to submit ourselves to the boredom, the refining fire of nonperformance, not to be in a hurry. "A lot is going on when you don't think anything is going on." We told him about our day off each Monday. "So—you're practicing Emmaus walks. Good."

He went on to suggest that we deepen our understanding of what we were already doing into an intentional Sabbath. A day off, he said, is "a bastard Sabbath." He affirmed our commitment to a day of not-doing, a day of not-working. "That's a start. You've gotten yourselves out of the way. Why not go all the way: keep the day as a Sabbath, embrace silence, embrace prayer—silence and prayer. Hallow the Name."

He encouraged us to buy and read Abraham Joshua Heschel's book *The Sabbath* when we got back to Maryland. "And then reread it. Let Heschel soak your imaginations in all the ramifications of Sabbath-keeping."

We did buy the book, read it, and reread it. We quit taking a "day off" and began keeping a "Sabbath," a day in which we deliberately separated ourselves from the workweek—in our case being pastor and pastor's wife—and gave ourselves to being present to what God has done and is doing, this creation in which we have been set down and this salvation in which we have been invited to be participants in a God-revealed life of resurrection.

We kept Monday as our Sabbath. For us Sunday was a workday. But we had already found that Monday could serve quite well as a day to get out of the way and be present to whatever. But now the "whatever" was recontextualized in an unforced yet intentional way of prayer. The content of the "whatever" didn't change much, if at all. It certainly didn't become a "religious" day in any conventional sense. It was a day of nonnecessities: we prayed and we played.

Our Sabbath-keeping became ritualized. After getting the children off to school, I prepared a simple lunch of sandwiches and fruit. We took our day-pack, walking sticks, binoculars, and appropriate clothing for whatever weather faced us—rain, snow, sunshine. We drove to a trailhead, usually not more than thirty or forty minutes away.

Jan read a psalm and prayed (I had initiated the prayers on the congregation's Sunday Sabbath; she initiated them on our Monday Sabbath). We entered a morning of silence, an Emmaus-walk silence in which we listened to Jesus. After three hours or so we found a rock alongside the river or a fallen tree in the woods, broke the silence with a spoken prayer, and ate our lunch. And then we talked: observations of the kingfisher and wood thrush, red fox and beaver, bloodroot and trailing arbutus; conversations of the past week; reflections on Sunday's worship. Old memories jogged out of the silence. We paid attention to the creation week that we had just lived through. We paid attention to the holy week we had just lived through. It always turned out that we had missed a lot. Each Sabbath became a day of remembering, becoming aware of where we were, who we were—the gifts of God for the people of God. We talked all the way home.

I knew that Jan and I couldn't do this by ourselves. We needed help. In particular we needed the help of our congregation. I wrote them a letter: "Why your pastor keeps the Sabbath." I told them about our decision, moving from "taking a day off" to "keeping the Sabbath holy." I wrote to them:

> *We need your help if we are going to keep a Monday Sabbath. This is a day to recenter our lives on God and God's work and God's presence. We spend our workweek telling you about God, serving you in the name of God, leading you in the ways of God. But we need a protected day to simply pay attention to God ourselves, to not be in charge, to let God be God for us, to develop habits of being present to God at all times and circumstances. It is not easy in our noisy, hyperactive American culture. Would you help us? We need your help to keep a Monday Sabbath. Jan and I are ready to respond to you any time of day or night, on any day of the week—death, accident, crisis. Don't ever hesitate to call us. But if it can keep until Tuesday, call us on Tuesday. We will do our best to protect Sunday as a day of rest and prayer and leisure for you. We will do our best to keep Sunday uncluttered—no committee meetings scheduled for Sunday—a day of not-doing so that you will have sanctuary time to notice what God is doing, listen to what God is saying. We'll help you keep a Sunday Sabbath. Help us keep a Monday Sabbath.*

And the congregation did help us. We rarely got a request to do anything on Monday—maybe a dozen times over the twenty-five years of doing this with them.

I never preached from the pulpit on Sabbath-keeping. What I did each year was write to the congregation a variation on my Why-your-pastor-needs-your-help Sabbath letter. I didn't think guilt would serve as an appropriate goad for Sabbath-keeping. I didn't think Sabbath-keeping could be imposed on a congregation. Jan and I wanted to change, as quietly and indirectly as we could, the unsabbathed culture in which we all lived. But first of all, starting with ourselves, we wanted to recover the practice of Sabbath-keeping. Every Monday we went to the rivers and woods with our "pick and shovel prayers," keeping Sabbath.

# 27

## SISTER GENEVIEVE

Two or three months after I had entered the womb "a second time" and come out as a pastor, I removed all of my academic diplomas from the wall of my study and replaced them with the framed portraits of three men whose company I wanted to keep as I lived into my newly realized vocational identity. I was not exactly putting the world of academia behind me—I would always be on familiar terms with that world and would participate on the fringes as an adjunct professor and visiting lecturer—but it was no longer my vocational home. The diplomas verified my vocation in terms of the world of intellect and learning, classrooms and libraries—professor. I anticipated that my life now as pastor would be worked out in quite different conditions—intimate relationships, a tradition of holiness, and the cultivation of souls. The world of learning was still there in all its glory, but my vocation now was not about the learning itself but about integrating learning into prayer and worship and the ordinariness of everyday living. Sanctuary, workplaces, and households would provide places to keep my vocation local and personal.

My picks for mentors were John Henry Newman, Alexander Whyte, and Baron Friedrich von Hügel—the company I would keep to stay in touch with the conditions in which I was now working. The three, though long dead, were no strangers—I had been in prayerful conversation with them for a long time—but now I embraced them as colleagues, not just as admired ancestors.

One phrase of Newman's had resonated for years in my memory: "The people of Birmingham also have souls." That phrase now became personal. The sentence was Newman's reply to a friend who vehemently protested his leaving Oxford University for Birmingham, England, to gather together a few priests and start a small school for boys in the working class world of steel mills and hard labor, a world without a shred of culture, a world indifferent to learning. At the time, Newman was widely considered to be the leading intellectual at Oxford, maybe in all of England. His influence was magisterial in the Church of England. He wrote magnificent sermonic prose and sacred poetry. He was the primary theological voice at the time (it was the middle of the nineteenth century), giving shape to the church's thinking. His name was on everyone's lips. Then Newman converted in midlife to become a Roman Catholic priest, abandoned Oxford and its elegant surroundings, his place of intellectual prestige and religious influence, and chose to spend the rest of his life in the Birmingham of belching steel furnaces, teaching boys in an ugly neighborhood where no one read books. Newman in Birmingham? It was like Einstein leaving Princeton to start a school for street kids in the Bronx.

I was no Newman, but I loved the world of Newman—the storied antiquity of Oxford, the finely honed intelligence crafting sentences of beauty. And though I was no longer aspiring to be a professor on a campus of shaded lawns and venerable buildings, I thought it not out of the range of possibility that in a few years I might become the pastor of a university church where I would be immersed in a culture rich in tradition and art. That fantasy was aggravated during these badland years by discovering that in the cultural flatland of suburbia the people to whom I was pastor had no interest in books or the life of the mind. *TV Guide* seemed to be the only reading material in evidence in the homes I visited.

Newman *chose* Birmingham for his work. I didn't choose suburbia. It was given to me. And now, as the energy of the early development years of Christ Our King Church was waning, I was becoming dissatisfied with the gift I had been given and was looking around for a new challenge, a challenge that included at least some intellect in it. It was while daydreaming this new fantasy that I tripped over this sentence that had caught my attention when I first read it years earlier but had been lying dormant in my memory: "The people of Birmingham also have souls." You don't have to be an Oxford don to have a soul; you don't have to be interesting to have a soul; you don't have to have leadership potential to have a soul. I was rebuked out of my fantasy. *Souls.* If Newman could do it, I could at least try. Birmingham souls. Suburbia souls. I needed to renew my conversations with Newman, cultivate a way of understanding these men and women in my congregation in terms of who they *were*, not in terms of how they either interested or bored me, not in terms of what I could make of them—but *souls*. Which I did.

Baron Friedrich von Hügel had long been a significant voice in my life. The world of religion teems with naive superstition, mean-spirited polemic, and unscrupulous deceit. Writing and teaching on the spiritual life brings out the worst in a lot of people, ranging from the superficially trivial to celebrity showmanship to idolatrous fads to the devil showing up as an angel of light. It isn't long before pastors learn that a lot of people lie in the name of God. In this confusing melting pot of the neurotic, infantile, and religion-as-commodity, von Hügel is conspicuous for his sheer sanity. Like Newman, he was English, but he didn't have a job or position. He was a scholar, studying and annotating old manuscripts and writing on the spiritual life as a layperson. He lived on a modest, private income with his wife, three daughters, and dog, Puck.

Word had gotten around, and men and women came to see him for counsel and direction as they sorted out their lives in matters of love and faith and obedience. But mostly he wrote letters. He wrote letters to me. They weren't addressed to me—he died seven years before I was born. But as I read the letters, I realized that they were, in fact, addressed to me, a pastor searching for a language and disposition for discerning a whole and healthy way of life as I lived with my congregation. He was wary of working up enthusiasm for Jesus ("nothing was ever accomplished in a stampede"), warned of simplistic, impatient "solutions" to living to the glory of God ("please, no cutting of knots"), and insisted over and over that every soul is unique and cannot be understood or encouraged or directed by general advice or through a superficial diagnosis using psychological categories ("there are no dittos in souls").

In my prepastor days I had learned much personally by reading von Hügel. Now I was letting his letters form in me a pastoral way of using language that was conversational—not condescending, not manipulative, but attentive and prayerful. Not instructional, preparing my parishioners to pass examinations on matters of sin and salvation. Not diagnostic, treating these unique souls as problems to be fixed. Now as I read and reread and reread, I was letting von Hügel soak me in holy mysteries, so that as I talked and listened informally, conversationally, without pastoral self-consciousness, I was inviting people into the ways of God that are "past understanding," not just instructing them in how to get across the street without stepping into moral mud puddles. I recognized this as holy wisdom, knowledge distilled into reflexes and synapses, knowledge *lived*. I needed to keep company with this man. I didn't want to be a pastor who talked too much, who knew too much. I didn't want to be a pastor who treated souls as dittos.

Alexander Whyte entered my imagination and became a companion as the pastor I was not yet but wanted to become. Not as a ditto. In the same way that souls are not dittos, neither are pastors. And Whyte was safe that way—there was no way that I could copy him. He was a pastor in Scotland a hundred years preceding me, in the late Victorian era in a culture that was stable, still defined by habits of churchgoing and a common morality. Those conditions had long ago been eroded in the secularized America in which I had become a pastor.

But I needed a pastor. I was new at this. The requirements of organizing and developing a new congregation provided a sufficient harness for keeping me connected with what had to be done to get started. But when those requirements had been completed, I realized there was not an adequate interiority to support the work I was doing. To adapt and reverse C. S. Lewis's famous line, my outside was bigger than my inside. I installed Alexander Whyte as my pastor.

At six o'clock every Sunday morning, I read one of his sermons that he had preached from the pulpit of St. George's Presbyterian Church in Edinburgh.

I had already prepared the sermon I would preach that day—now I let him preach to me. I did that for the next twenty years of Sundays. The quality that I wanted to absorb, and did, I think, was the fusion of scripture and prayer, prayer and scripture, or something more like scriptureprayer and prayerscripture. It was this fusion of God speaking to us (scripture) and our speaking to him (prayer) that the Holy Spirit uses to form the life of Christ in us. It was all the same thing, the listening and answering, that provided the core of worship in Whyte's practice. He had a truly biblical imagination. The entire biblical narrative came alive when he preached—not explicitly, but the tone and the allusions developed a storied coherence around every text. As I sat under my pastor's preaching, scripture ceased to be a sequence of texts and became a seamless story. And I was a participant in the story.

After his death, his son-in-law wrote a biography of him—one of the great pastor biographies. I mined it for access to his character, to his interior, to the kind of interior that I knew was required to maintain a pastoral vocation with integrity. It soon became clear that there was no pretense in the man. He took his pulpit seriously, he took his congregation seriously, but he didn't take himself seriously. When a newly ordained seminary graduate, commenting on his long and distinguished life as a pastor of St. George's Presbyterian, asked him for advice as a young pastor starting out, Whyte said, "Relieve yourself as often as possible, and take a long vacation." He was not given to pious clichés. I liked that.

I had grown up in a Christian culture that gave a great deal of attention to feelings. I had one pastor when I was an adolescent who always greeted me with "How are things with your soul today, Eugene?" The first few times the question left me stuttering and tongue-tied. I hardly knew I had a soul. Mostly I had hormones. But after seven or eight of those encounters that left me scrambling to salvage some shred of feeling that I could offer to validate my soul, I quit trying. I soon realized that before I had stumbled through the few clichés that I had picked up in his company, he had lost interest in my soul, if he ever had any in the first place, and was on to other matters—a divine-healing mission trip to Cuba that he had just returned from in triumph, an elk-hunting party that he was getting together for men of the church that (after some prayer) he was now generously inviting me to join, a deal on tires that he had just learned about that I might want to look into for my newly acquired used car.

And it wasn't just that pastor. In my church culture as a whole, examining your "soul" was a way to measure the God content in your life. Soul was a kind of internal thermometer you could consult to find out where you stood on the Laodicean spectrum of spirituality: cold, lukewarm, or hot. High on every pastor's agenda was keeping people "on fire" for Jesus. Worship in general and the sermon in particular were bellows for blowing smoldering embers into a blaze.

But now that I was a pastor myself and finding ways to survive in the badlands, I realized that emotions were not a very reliable witness to the presence of God in my life and that the pastoral manipulation of emotions in others had a very short shelf life.

A friend introduced me to Sister Genevieve, the prioress of a Carmelite monastery: fourteen nuns living a life of contemplative prayer together in their convent, hidden away in a forest of beech and oak trees, the first Carmelite foundation in America. I had never known a nun before. I don't think she had ever known a Presbyterian pastor. We were about the same age. We became friends. I would occasionally visit with her in her monastery. She had meals with Jan and me in our home and at times came to stay with us in Montana for a few days of retreat and rest.

Conversations and a developing friendship with Sister Genevieve extended my conversation with my three mentors from the cemetery into a larger circle of sympathetic friends, a living tradition that she and her nuns practiced, a way of understanding the soul and the nature of prayer that turned out to be essential to me for surviving in the badlands: prayer as a way of life, not a discrete discipline that one practiced, as I had been taught, to "make room for God."

In one of our conversations, Sister Genevieve must have detected something in my language that betrayed a romanticizing notion I had developed regarding her convent of nuns, vowed to a life of prayer, protected from the noise and interruptions of the outside world—a holy community in a holy place. She said to me, "Eugene, is it difficult to be married?"

I replied, "Certainly. It's the hardest thing I have ever done. I lived twenty-five years as the center of my universe, and then suddenly I was no longer the center. There was another, Jan, who had also been accustomed to being the center. It took us both by surprise—you can't have two centers. Yes, it is difficult. Why do you ask?"

"How would you like to be married to thirteen women? Some of these nuns can be real bitches."

So much for romanticizing the contemplative life.

In another conversation, we had been talking about the Lord's Prayer. I interrupted the flow of conversation by saying, "Do you know the petition that I have the hardest time praying, entering into, knowing what I am praying?"

"Of course—'Deliver us from evil.'"

"How did you know that?"

"Oh, you Protestants. You are so naive about evil. You know everything about sin, but nothing about evil—the prevalence of evil, the persistence of evil especially in holy places, like this monastery—and like your congregation. The mystery of evil. You make cartoon characters out of evil so that you don't have to deal with it in your own households and workplaces, crouching at the door every time you open it. Or else you deny it and label everything that is wrong with the world as a sin you can name and then take charge of getting rid of."

It was in these conversations that I was introduced to the sixteenth-century reformers of Carmelite foundations in Spain: Teresa of Ávila and John of the Cross. The insouciant earthy spirituality of Teresa and the richly sensual poetry of John.

My theological education had pivoted on Martin Luther and John Calvin, brilliant and comprehensive thinkers, writers, and exegetes of scripture. They taught me to think largely and passionately about God and the scriptures. For them, reforming the Christian life was primarily (but not entirely) a matter of recovering right thinking, understanding doctrine, interpreting scripture. Teresa and John worked from the other end. They took up matters of the soul, reforming Christian living by taking seriously the life of prayer and recovering the ways of prayer. They gave themselves to discerning the illusions and pitfalls that interfere with receiving what God is giving and reducing prayer to a self-help project with no concern for relationship and love, adoration and mystery.

I had received a theological education adequate for preparing me to be a professor in the classroom, dealing with truth and knowledge—"faith seeking understanding" (Anselm). But now I was a pastor, and a great deal of my life consisted in dealing with souls as they went about their lives in households and workplaces. Scripture and worship and gathering a congregation I was ready for. But the life of the soul and the attentiveness of souls to God that is prayer I had taken for granted. It was simply assumed, peripheral to my training, pretty much limited to being addressed by the offhand question, "Well Eugene, how are things with your soul today?" And now I was being introduced to a vast world that I had known only in books, by Sister Genevieve, who, with her nuns, was living that world, a world in which Teresa and John were major voices. Teresa and John treated the soul and praying rightly with the same disciplined care as Luther and Calvin took with the scriptures and believing rightly. This was something more like "faith seeking holiness." The more I got to know them I realized that my three "framed" mentors—Newman, von Hügel, Whyte—had drunk deeply from the same artesian springs that had nourished Teresa and John.

In the badlands I had been incrementally realizing that there is far more to this Christian life than getting it right. There is *living* it right. Learning the truth of God, the gospel, the scriptures involves understanding words, concepts, history. But living it means working through a world of deception, of doubt and suffering, a world of rejections and betrayal and idolatry.

We don't grow and mature in our Christian life by sitting in a classroom and library, listening to lectures and reading books, or going to church and singing hymns and listening to sermons. We do it by taking the stuff of our ordinary lives, our parents and children, our spouses and friends, our workplaces and fellow workers, our dreams and fantasies, our attachments, our easily accessible gratifications, our depersonalizing of intimate relations, our commodification of living truths into idolatries, taking all this and placing it on the altar of refining fire—our God is a consuming fire—and finding it all stuff redeemed for a life of holiness. A life that is not reserved for nuns and monks but accessible to every Dick and Jane in every ordinary congregation.

In my conversations with Sister Genevieve I realized that I knew a lot more about scripture and truth than I did about souls and prayer. I also realized that for me as pastor, souls and prayer required an equivalent demand on my attention as scripture and truth. This is what pastors are for—to keep these things alive and yoked in everyday life.

I couldn't have been given a better or more personal introduction to what I so much needed if I was going to be a pastor in the badlands than Sister Genevieve taking me into the living tradition rooted in Teresa and John.

Sister Genevieve and Teresa and John took seriously what I had been taking, rather superficially, for granted. I had assumed that my vocation was preaching and teaching the truth of the gospel and encouraging people to do what they had been told. I had no idea that matters of the soul and prayer had an equivalent demand on my attention as doctrine and scripture.

Teresa and John were theologians every bit as "theological" as Luther and Calvin. But they used a very different language. Teresa told stories; John wrote poems. They were saturated in the same scriptures as their contemporaries a thousand or so miles to the north, and as theologically astute. But they, instead of arguing and defining and interpreting, were expressing and witnessing and insisting on the presence of God no matter how you felt about it—or if you felt anything at all. Luther and Calvin were trying to make the truth clear, which they did wonderfully. Teresa and John were trying to deal honestly and discerningly with the experience of God when it wasn't plain, insisting that there were necessary obscurities and shadows to be embraced if we were to grow into mature holiness. That we cannot have God on our terms, domesticated to our requirements, reduced to our ideas of what God should be doing. Prayer was our immersion in the way that God is present with us whether we understand or like it or not.

More than anything, my widening circle of mentors was becoming personal—*this* is what it is like to pray, to live a life of faith and love, to be detached from a life of self and become souls free for God.

Teresa's earthy spirituality is free of pious pretense. As I was getting to know Teresa, I was told this story. She is sitting in a privy with a prayer book in one hand and a cinnamon roll in the other. The devil appears to her, scandalized at her irreverence. He sanctimoniously reprimands her. She responds, "The sweet roll is for me, the prayers are for God, and the rest is for you."

John's poetry is richly sensual. Today he is recognized by many as Spain's greatest poet. His lines spill out with metaphors and similes—he uses the material and physical world, including its considerable beauties and unavoidable pain and suffering, to make a piece of art out of the soul and prayer.

His reputation, too often reduced to "the dark night of the soul," with connotations of grim austerity, is misleading. Most of his writing is a commentary on his poems, drawing us into all that is involved in pursuing a life of love on God's terms, not ours. It is true that he often warned us not to get addicted to "a spiritual sweet tooth," but that is no more than you would expect from someone who is warning us not to reduce the life in Christ to an infantile preference for something on the level of popsicles and boxes of Valentine chocolates.

Together, under the tutelage of Sister Genevieve, I found these Spanish saints absolutely essential for pursuing a pastoral vocation through the badlands and beyond. I was coming to visualize Luther and Calvin as mountain people, scaling the heights, taking in the horizon, and Theresa and John as valley people, tilling the soil, going to the market, cooking meals. I needed all of them, my congregation needed all of them.

# 28

## ERIC LIDDELL

Well along in these badland years I began noticing around me men and women running alongside the roads and in the parks, people my age, my peers—lawyers, doctors, businesspeople, teachers. I hadn't run for seventeen years. I assumed that after graduation from my university, my running days were over. I had always loved running and running races—the middle distances and mile were my events. I loved the easy rhythms, the relaxed sense of being physically in touch with the earth under my feet, the texture of the weather, my body working almost effortlessly in long cross-country workouts.

A running world had opened up when I wasn't looking. Emboldened by what I saw around me, I began to run again. I subscribed to the magazine, *Runner's World*. Jan and I each bought a pair of running shoes (Adidas) and were immediately impressed by huge strides accomplished in the technology of running shoes. After a year or so, Jan decided that running was not her thing and dropped out. She was later replaced by our son, Leif, who was winning cross-country races for his school.

It wasn't long before running had established itself as a ritual. Every day in the late afternoon I would run five miles—it took about forty minutes. But there was far more to it than aerobic breathing and oxygenated muscles, more than the running as such. There is a meditative dimension to long-distance running: the uninterrupted quiet, the metronomic repetitiveness, the sensual immersion in the fragrance of trees and flowering bushes and rain, the springiness of the soil on park trails, the Zenlike emptying of the mind that felt like a freedom to be simply present, not having to do or say anything. Was I also running out of the badlands? It felt like it. Things were coming together. It felt like I was becoming reacquainted with my body. Another detail in the arrival?

From my schooldays, the Scottish runner Eric Liddell had been an idol of mine. He was a natural companion, a person who integrated running races with a Christian identity. I loved his statement "I believe God made me for a purpose, but he also made me fast. And when I run, I feel his pleasure." As running was again a part of my life, I was feeling that pleasure in a fresh way. I also admired his refusal, out of reverence for God, to ever race on Sunday.

After a couple years Leif and I every month or so would compete in a 10K race somewhere in Maryland, accompanied by our cheerleader wife and mother. The most memorable of those races took place about an hour away north, in Amish country near Lancaster, Pennsylvania. Leif and I were pretty evenly matched, but I always won. A couple months before the Lancaster race, Leif's friends told me that he was training extra hard and planned to beat me in Lancaster. And so I, without saying anything, began to put in extra miles, mixed with "speed play," to make sure that didn't happen. The day came, and the three of us drove to the site of the race. The course began in the university sports complex with a lap around the track. Then it was mapped through the Amish farms through the countryside. There were ten hills. We started out running side by side. Leif was a stronger runner than I, and so going up the hills he pulled out ahead. But I was a better downhill runner and passed him. We exchanged leads ten times on those ten hills. As we approached the end of the race at the stadium, I knew I would have to increase my lead if I was going to win. And so I did. I thought that the race ended when we entered the stadium. I had timed my final sprint for that anticipated finish. But the end of the race included a final lap around the track. I had a quarter of a mile left. I gave it my all, but there wasn't much "all" left. On the last stretch I heard Leif coming—I knew it had to be him. Down the last stretch he passed and beat me by twenty yards. All the time he was passing me, I could hear Jan in the stands, yelling, "Leif, you can't do that to your father!" But he did. And he did it fair and square.

It was probably the most satisfying loss of my life. And he was completely modest in victory. He didn't crow. But later I couldn't help but notice a classic Oedipal quality to the event.

After several years of this, I got more ambitious—I started to run marathons. A marathon for a distance runner is the ultimate race: 26.2 miles. Far more than simple endurance is required; it is an art form—pacing, diet, mental readiness—a dozen things can go wrong in the three hours or so of running. Every year I would train for and run a marathon. And then I decided I would run the Boston Marathon, in my mind, and many others', the granddaddy of all marathons. But there was one problem. Not just anybody can run the Boston. You first have to qualify by achieving your qualifying time in another recognized marathon. Qualifying times are adjusted to your age group. When I turned fifty, my qualifying time was raised to three hours and twenty minutes. I thought I had a chance at that and so started getting ready—it takes at least six months.

As I was looking for a marathon that was geographically accessible and fit into the time frame needed, the only one I could locate was the Philadelphia Marathon in November (the Boston is always in April). But there was a huge problem—I wouldn't be able to do it. It was held on Sunday. Eric Liddell would not have run it on Sunday. I couldn't run it on Sunday.

At the next meeting of my ruling elders I told them of my disappointment. "Sunday? Why can't you run on Sunday?"

"Because Eric Liddell, a world-class runner and a Christian, would never run on Sunday." I told them of my youthful and now lifelong admiration of

Liddell and of my respect for his reverence of the Lord's Day. There was no way that I could run a marathon on Sunday.

"Haven't you watched the movie *Chariots of Fire*—all about Eric Liddell?" They had, but they had missed the part about Sundays.

A half-hour discussion heated up. They wanted me to run the Philadelphia Marathon. "Eric Liddell was a Scots Presbyterian—they are strict about that kind of thing; we're American Presbyterians—we would be honored if you would represent us. You have our absolution, and our blessing."

And they reminded me that they had the authority to do this. They were, remember, my *ruling* elders. I accepted their ruling and went into training.

We booked a hotel in Philadelphia and drove up on Saturday for the Sunday race. Saturday evening all the runners assembled in the hotel for registration and a supper of pasta. Pasta, and lots of it, is the supper of choice before a marathon. Early Sunday morning, having long since deleted Eric Liddell from my pastoral imagination, I joined the runners to be bussed to a small village where the race would begin, twenty-six miles out in the country north of the city. Jan kept the Sabbath by going to worship at a nearby church.

The autumn day was bright with sunshine, but cool, ideal running weather. Several hundred of us gathered at the starting line. About five miles into the race we entered a small village. Loudspeakers were ranged along the curb. Suddenly the air was full of the theme song from *Chariots of Fire*. And Eric Liddell. I had forgotten all about him. And now here he was. The first thing I thought of was that I was betraying my friend—my faithful companion across the years in running races. But guilt, as it turned out, proved to be the perfect energy supplement. As I crossed the finish line, the electronic, digital clock on the steps of Independence Hall, confirmed by Jan and her greeting, gave me the verdict: I had qualified for Boston.

Five months later I ran the Boston Marathon. But the Boston is always on Monday. I ran that one guilt free.

# 29

## "WRITE IN A BOOK
## WHAT YOU SEE . . ."

Pastor John of Patmos provided the biblical DNA that gave me my identity as pastor. In the badlands that identity was given texture as I became a writer. The apocalyptic angel who was sent by God to deliver the vision, the Revelation of Jesus Christ that John saw on that memorable Lord's Day, said to him, "Write in a book what you see . . ." *Write what you see.* Writer and Pastor were two sides of a single identity for John. It was not as if he added writer onto his vocation as pastor or pastor onto his vocation as writer. Pastor was not his "day job" and writer, the work for which he is best known in the church today, his real job. Nor was pastor his real job, the work for which he was best known in his own seven churches, and writer a mere moonlighting diversion. Writer and pastor are the same thing for John. It was in the badlands that I realized this about John—pastor and writer. Right foot, left foot: pastor, writer.

I had identified with John, *Pastor* John, for years now. I had understood the Revelation as a work I would later learn to name as spiritual theology—entering into the *lived* quality of theology, writing my way into the primary substratum of life that involves taking the immediate conditions of everyday life—family, work, place, feelings—into the scriptures and gospel story and making a home there. Entering into reimagining and repraying scripture in the details of daily living personally and relationally and *in place,* right here, right now.

And it was in the badlands that I realized this about myself: pastor and writer. Not writer competing for time from pastor. Not pastor struggling to integrate writer into an already crowded schedule: pastor and writer, a single coherent identity.

I had always written. In high school and university I had thought I would one day be a novelist. My first published writing was a letter to the editor in our local newspaper, supporting an unpopular stance my high-school English teacher was taking in opposition to a school-board policy. It was the first time I saw my name signed under something I had written. I liked it. I wrote a column in my university newspaper, wrote poems that never quite came off, wrote an occasional article or essay for a periodical. I liked to write. When something I wrote was published, it was confirmation that I was a writer. But I was not a real writer. Up until then writing was a way of telling others what I knew, or what I felt—I was passing on information or feelings. Writing was a way to get published. In the badlands I became a writer.

The badlands, this desert time for probing the interior of my pastoral vocation, continued to do its work. I was getting into the guts of who I was as a person. I was leaving the performance mode in which I had done pretty well up until then. I found that there was a way of writing that I had only peripheral acquaintance with and never pursued—heuristic writing. I began to sense that my writing was at some deeper level a conversation with scripture. At the same time a conversation with my congregation. But conversation, not explaining, not directing. I was exploring the country, this land of the living. And I was taking my time. I hadn't set out to do this. I had neither model nor goal—at least I didn't think I did. It was a way of writing that involved a good deal of listening, looking around, getting acquainted with the neighborhood. Not writing what I knew but writing into what I didn't know, edging into a mystery. This, I was learning, was what real writers did. Novelist Kurt Vonnegut described this writing as walking through a dense forest in the dead of night with a pencil flashlight between your teeth, about two feet of the darkness illuminated before you as you worked your way from word to word.

Heuristic writing—writing to explore and discover what I didn't know. Writing as a way of entering into language and letting language enter me, words connecting with words and creating what had previously been inarticulate or unnoticed or hidden. Writing as a way of paying attention. Writing as an act of prayer. In the badlands the act of writing was assimilated into my pastoral vocation, revealing relationships, drawing me into mysteries, training me imaginatively to enter the language world of scripture in which God "spoke and it came to be," in which "the Word was made flesh and dwelt among us." And it became a way of writing in which I was entering into the language world of my congregation, their crises and small talk, their questions and doubts, listening for and discerning the lived quality of the gospel in their lives. Not just saying things. Not just writing words.

I came across something that Truman Capote wrote, with a sneer, on the work of a popular novelist: "That's not writing, it's typing." About the same time, I read Emily Dickinson's pronouncement, "Publication is no business of the poet." Capote exposed much of what I had been doing as "typing"—using words to manipulate or inform or amuse. Dickinson rescued me from a lust to be published.

I began to understand the sacred qualities of language. My work as a pastor was immersed in language. There was hardly anything I did that did not involve language: the Word of God provided not information but revelation. Jesus told stories and taught and prayed, not to entertain us or inspire us but to draw us into a participating, believing, listening, loving way of life that was, above all, local and personal: prayerful. I wanted to do that too. A way of using language in which God, whether implicitly or explicitly, had the first word. And I began to understand that the way I used language involved not just speaking it and writing it, but listening to it—listening to the words written in scripture, but also listening to the words spoken to me by the people in my congregation. In the badlands I realized that the largest part of language has to do with listening, not speaking—and certainly not "typing."

I started paying attention to poets and novelists and artists, the way they wrote about what they were doing as writers and musicians and painters, weavers and potters and sculptors. I made friends with the world of art, the work of the artist. I embraced artists as allies. They took a place alongside the theologians and biblical scholars in my formation: art as a school of pastoral formation, the pastor as artist. My artistic medium was words, written and prayed and preached.

A little girl with the old-fashioned name of Charity gave me the word that opened up the way in which "writer" came to be absorbed in my pastoral formation during those badlands years.

Charity, at the time I met her, was a plump, bold, cute, and highly verbal five-year-old. She lived in a city halfway across the country. I knew her through her grandparents. When I visited in their home, I sometimes would get to talk with Charity. It was her grandmother, Brenda, who told me this story. Brenda had taken the train to visit her daughter and son-in-law, Charity's parents. Charity's other grandmother had left the day before, after an extended visit, returning to her home in New England. I had never met this other grandmother but knew she took her grandmothering duties very seriously.

The morning after my friend Brenda's arrival, Charity came into her bedroom at five o'clock, crawled into bed with her, cuddled up, and said, "Grandmother, let's not have any godtalk while you are here, okay? I believe that God is everywhere. Let's just get on with life."

When Brenda told me that story, I knew that Charity was onto something. It coincided with the awareness that was developing in the refining fire that was tempering my pastoral vocation in the badlands. It was the word "godtalk." What Charity was onto was that *life* is the country that Christians live in, frequently named in the Psalms as "land of the living." And what she was also onto was that when the life leaks out of what we say and write, teach and pray—especially when we are using sterile, lifeless language that objectifies words like *God, Jesus, prayer, believe*—we are left with nothing but godtalk.

I am interpreting Charity's five A.M. greeting to her grandmother as an accurate and honest response to a way of life that somehow gets language used in relation to a holy God disconnected from our ordinary lives, language that gets flattened into ideas or advice or rules—unstoried godtalk. Charity missed something essential in her first grandmother's way of talking that she was hoping her second grandmother would supply. She missed the life: "Let's just get on with life."

Charity was asking for a relationship with her grandmother in which God is not depersonalized into godtalk but rather comes across as a personal presence alive in their dailiness, a dailiness in which God and life are organically one in both speech and action. Charity was still living in that unself-conscious, spontaneous childhood world in which everything is still immediate and personal and relational. Soon enough that relational connectedness and personal immediacy would be abstracted into ideas, into acts in the service of roles, into persons reduced to a function instead of a presence.

When Charity is thirty years old and the disconnect has happened, I wonder who will challenge and demand, "Let's get on with life, okay?" Another child? Quite possibly. Children are primary witnesses in these matters. Isaiah's "a little child shall lead them" seems right. Children are our first defense against the deadening and flattening effect of words that disconnect God and life. Friends and teachers and parents are sometimes helpful. But more times than not, these are the very ones who turn out to be major contributors to godtalk.

So who takes responsibility for keeping Christians alert and present to everything and everyone around us, keeping our language grounded, incarnate in this vast and always God-personal world of creation and salvation? And not in grand abstract generalities but in detail? Who are the men and women who take on the holy vocation of defending the community of the resurrection from the dreaded godtalk?

Maybe writers who take responsibility for keeping language in circulation, free from cliché and slogan and mere utility? Maybe pastors who take responsibility for keeping the language of faith fresh and personal and relational? And maybe me, pastor and writer, writer and pastor, taking responsibility for keeping language in circulation as the spoken and written Jesus-word, a biblical word of revelation and not godtalk *about* the revelation? How about me, pastor and writer, writer and pastor, writing in the fear of the Lord, using language with a holy reverence, keeping the spoken and the written word organic to the biblical language of revelation, a language of participation, inviting my hearers and readers into holy mysteries and not godtalk?

These were badlands questions that brought out the sacredness of language, all language, as the common ground worked by pastors and writers. These were the questions that gave me the vocational assignment as a writer of *lived* scripture, *lived* theology.

Just as John of Patmos earlier had given me my identity as pastor, he now gave me my identity as writer. In the badlands, as I was slowly finding myself put together, living into who I had been becoming all my life, I was now acquiring a language adequate for expressing it.

In the badlands I was searching out for myself the interior dimensions of pastor, acquiring coordination and agility in the language of revelation, a language that developed out of conversation with scripture and congregation. I had been writing all my life but I had never written quite like this before. I was writing still, but now I was not so much shaping words into sentences to use to tell people what I knew or what God said—Charity's godtalk—but a language that was shaping me. I was gradually acquiring fluency in the vocabulary and syntax used in the "land of the living."

The pastoral identity I began with was clear enough: I knew that this is not a religious job; it is who I am vocationally. And I had made an adequate launch—gathered a congregation and built a sanctuary for worship. But the badlands made it apparent there was far too much of it that had not been assimilated. Too much was still on the outside—a framework to work in, a harness to keep me and the work connected, but not the thing itself.

I knew what I didn't want to be and do. But the badlands made it clear that there was too much that still hadn't jelled within. I knew that I did not want to be a pastor who took on the responsibility of "running this damn church." I didn't want to be a religious professional whose identity was institutionalized. I didn't want to be a pastor whose sense of worth derived from whether people affirmed or ignored me. In short, I didn't want to be a pastor in the ways that were most in evidence and most rewarded in the American consumerist and celebrity culture.

Now things were coming together. And writing was one of the ways. I wrote. I wrote what I was seeing. I began to get a sense that my writing was at some deeper level a conversation with scripture. At the same time it was a conversation with my congregation. But conversation—not explaining, not directing. I was exploring the country. And I was taking my time. I hadn't set out to do this. I had neither model nor goal—at least I didn't think I did. It was a way of writing that involved a good deal of listening, looking around, getting acquainted with the territory, the land of the living. At some point I started getting a sense that I was following in the steps of Pastor John of Patmos as he picked up his pen in obedience to the angel's command, "Write in a book what you see . . ."

John on Patmos; me in the badlands: *Write what you see . . .* I kept probing my life, my "intently haphazard" years pondering "Shekinah" clarities that emerged as a congregation was formed and as worship shaped us as pastor and people. But I had gotten ahead of myself. The badlands gave me the time and motivation to learn and write a language that wasn't just saying something that was true or important or attention-getting but that was in *conversation* with scripture and congregation. All language, all true language, is not so much communication, getting something said accurately and persuasively, adding to the information and knowledge that can be put in a library. True language has to do with communion, establishing a relationship that makes for life: love and faith and hope, forgiveness and salvation and justice. True language requires both a tongue and an ear.

Pastor John of Patmos showed me the way. He wrote what he saw. His *Revelation* is the result. It is a thorough immersion in and the last word in what is often named Spiritual Theology, *lived* theology, comprising the entire scriptures and the witness of the communion of the saints. I will always be a mere apprentice to St. John, and he will always be my mentor. What I have come to see and continue to recognize is that if I had to put in a single sentence what I have learned from John regarding the way he wrote what he saw, it is this: godtalk—depersonalized, nonrelational, unlistening language—kills. In the land of the living it is blasphemous, whether spoken from pulpits or across the breakfast table. Pastors and their congregations can't be too careful in the way we use language, this sacred language, this word-of-God language.

What is conspicuous about John, pastor and writer, as he "wrote what he saw" was that he was totally, personally immersed in his congregations, their strengths and weaknesses, testings and difficulties. At the same time he was mindful of the political and economic world in which they lived, the killing and suffering and evil. And then taking all of this into account, with his incredible imagination he gathered his congregations into the great drama of salvation and provided them with a story that rocks with Amens and Hallelujahs. And not a cliché in the entire book. Nothing abstract or impersonal. Everything *lived* in the towns and villages in which they are living.

That was getting inside me now. I was entering into the *lived* quality of theology and scripture, writing my way into the primary substratum of pastoral life that involves taking the immediate conditions of everyday life—family, work, place, feelings, weather—into the scripture and gospel story and making a home there. Entering into, reimagining and repraying scripture into the details of daily living, personally and relationally, *in place,* right here, right now.

And here is something that never ceases to astonish me. Pastor John of Patmos knew his Bible inside and out. The Revelation has 404 verses. In those 404 verses, there are 518 references to earlier scripture. But there is not a single quote; all the references are allusions. Here was a pastor and writer who was absolutely immersed in scripture and submitted himself to it. He did not merely repeat, regurgitate, proof-text. As he wrote, the scriptures were re-created in him. He assimilated scripture. Lived scripture. And then he wrote what he has lived. His book is certainly not "typing."

A few years after I got out of the badlands, I wrote an article on Annie Dillard's book *Pilgrim at Tinker Creek,* a book that was awarded the Pulitzer Prize. I recognized it as a tour de force in spiritual theology. I made the comment in my article that there was hardly a page in the book that didn't have an allusion to the Bible, yet there was not a single quote. Her publisher sent her a copy of the journal that contained my article. She wrote to me, "I have been treated very generously by my reviewers. But nobody has ever noticed (at least no one has mentioned it) that the book is saturated in scripture. I wondered if anyone ever would. Thank you for noticing."

———

There was no sharp line of demarcation that marked my exit from the bad-lands, but at some point—it had been about six years—I realized that some-thing was different. It didn't happen all at once. The effects were cumulative. I found myself more at home with myself, more put together. Previously un-connected parts of my life were connected, integrated, fused. I emerged with a lighter step. I had survived. It had been a time in the refining fire, a time of chastening, a purging of ego, the Spirit moving over and through my life and vocation, making a cosmos of it. It was in the badlands that all the parts of my identity connected, fused, coordinated—like an adolescent making the transition to adulthood. What so much of the time had seemed like an endless overcast day of drizzle began to open up with breaks of sunshine and starlight: glimpses of badlands beauty.

The annual Montana holy-land pilgrimage offered a leisurely setting for melding the intensities of my early spiritual heritage with the responsibilities of my newfound vocation. Ian's austere, craggy, no-nonsense Scottish High-lands theology, fragrant with the scent of heather, gave me a large Trinitarian God framework in which to understand and take seriously the lives of my congregation and my work with them without being crowded out by their needs as well as my own. The Monday Sabbaths with Jan, in silence and prayer and conversation as we remembered the apparent chaos of the week's scripture and neighborhood gossip, unexpected betrayals alongside unantici-pated grace, in the maddening, unsorted mix of saint and sinner that is the congregation, the dull and the delightful, and so much more, allowed us to see (but not always) the making of yet another seven-day work of creation and salvation.

Almost imperceptibly an organic fusion was accomplished between Jan's early years of Presbyterianism in Alabama with an insurance executive for a father and my early years of Pentecostalism in Montana with a butcher for a father. That gave us a broad place in which to understand and practice our marriage. Sister Genevieve and her nuns opened a window on a community way of life in the Spirit that was joyful and content but that was also deeply experienced in handling death and the devil. Eric Liddell's showing up and recovering the importance of running entered the rhythms of my body as a way of prayer, staying in immediate touch with the creation. And all the time I was acquiring a feel for language as revelation and poetry under the aegis of John of Patmos, written and spoken and listened to, getting inside the world of scripture and congregation and pastor.

I had been in formation as a pastor for much of my life. Those years of growing up in what now seems to be the sacred space and stories of Montana catalyzed in Pastor John of Patmos at the conjunction of sanctuary and classroom in New York—the end that I had started from. Pastor. Pastor Pete.

Marriage to Jan opened up an entirely new dimension to the pastoral vocation—hospitality. Our home—a place of hospitality. Congregation as a place of hospitality. Welcome and meals and conversation. The appointment to be a new-church development pastor in Maryland sealed our vocational identity. Three years of exploring our workplace in a congregation of saints and sinners, constructing a sanctuary, finding a vocational community in the Company of Pastors, and being immersed in all the details of worship and prayer while cultivating a culture of hospitality confirmed that pastor was both who we were and the work we were given to do.

But without those years in the badlands, I would never have become a pastor, at least not the pastor I'd earlier had a vision of being, a John of Patmos pastor, the pastor I had hoped I might be.

Looking back now, I see myself in those prebadlands years as a Labrador puppy, full-grown but uncoordinated, romping and playful but not yet "under authority," oblivious to its master's command: "Sit." The only verbal signal that the puppy was capable of responding to was "Fetch," which sent him galloping across a field, catching a Frisbee in full flight, and returning it with wagging tail, ready for more.

In the badlands I learned to sit.

## A LONG OBEDIENCE IN THE SAME DIRECTION

I now knew that I was in this for the long haul. Beginnings get things started, but what comes next makes the story, in this case, a vocational formation. By now I had a pretty good sense of what the long haul consisted of for me. I knew where I was, living on the local American ground of suburban Maryland. And I knew in a deeper and more tested way who I was: a pastor married to a woman in "holy orders," prepared to stay and cultivate our vocation in the congregation where we had been placed and see if we could get something to grow.

The phrase that gave us focus was "a long obedience in the same direction." I had come on the phrase while reading Nietzsche. This was the decade of the sixties, and there was a lot of talk and writing about the death of God. Nietzsche was often cited as the philosopher who had proclaimed the death of God, and now a lot of people seemed to be taking up the assignment of preparing for and conducting the funeral. I hadn't read Nietzsche since college days and wanted to find out what the excitement was about.

Early on in my reading I came upon this sentence: "The essential thing 'in heaven and earth' is . . . that there should be a long obedience in the same direction; there thereby results, and has always resulted in the long run, something that has made life worth living." That struck me as a text I could live with. I saw myself assigned to give witness to the sheer *livability* of the Christian life, that everything in scripture and Jesus was here to be lived. In the mess of work and sin, of families and neighborhoods, my task was to pray and give direction and encourage that *lived* quality of the gospel—patiently, locally, and personally. *Patiently:* I would stay with these people; there are no quick or easy ways to do this. *Locally:* I would embrace the conditions of this place—economics, weather, culture, schools, whatever—so that there would be nothing abstract or piously idealized about what I was doing. *Personally:* I would know them, know their names, know their homes, know their families, know their work—but I would not pry, I would not treat them as a cause or a project, I would treat them with dignity. Preaching, of course, is part of it, teaching is part of it, administering a congregation as a community of faith is part of it. But the overall context of my particular assignment in the pastoral vocation, as much as I am able to do it, is to see to it that these men and women in my congregation become aware of the possibilities and the promise of living out in personal and local detail what is involved in following Jesus, and be a companion to them as we do it together.

Later I wrote a book using Nietzsche's phrase as the title, *A Long Obedience in the Same Direction.* It never received the headlines that Nietzsche's death-of-God pronouncements garnered, but quite a few people read it. I sometimes amuse myself by imagining Friedrich Nietzsche, who is now long dead himself, showing up in my study as I am writing my books. He looks over my bookshelves and sees part of a sentence he wrote as a title on one of the books. He learns that I wrote the book. He beams (although I do have trouble imagining Nietzsche *beaming*). How pleased he is to find that I have kept his wonderful sentence in circulation into the third Christian millennium.

Then he takes the book off the shelf and looks through it. His face furrows into an angry frown. The old atheist was convinced that Christians, by promoting the weak and ineffectual Jesus, kept the weakest, spiritually diseased, morally unfit and inferior parts of the population alive and reproducing. They were a malign influence on civilization and would be the ruin of us all. He thought he'd delivered a deathblow, and now he finds us still at it.

I love imagining him standing here angry and appalled, his walrus mustache smoking, astonished that these weak, inadequate, ineffectual, and unfit Christians are alive still, and still reproducing.

My editor didn't like the title. "Obedience," he argued, was a dull word— "dead in the water" was his phrase for it. It didn't fit the ambience of contemporary American religion. I held out: it was a protest word against the fad-chasing, self-centered individualism of American spirituality. I wrote him a letter: "I know we aren't used to this. We have grown up in a culture that urges us to take charge of our own lives. We are introduced to thousands of books that we are trained to *use*—look up information, acquire skills, master knowledge, divert ourselves . . . whatever. But *use*? Well-meaning people tell us that the Christian gospel will put us in charge of life, will bring us happiness and bounty. So we go out and buy a Bible. We adapt, edit, sift, summarize. We then use whatever seems useful and apply it in our circumstances however we see fit. We take charge of the Christian gospel, using it as a toolbox to repair our lives, or as a guidebook for getting what we want, or as an inspirational handbook to enliven a dull day. But we aren't smart enough to do that; nor can we be trusted to do that. The Holy Spirit is writing us into the revelation, the story of salvation. We find ourselves in the story as followers of Jesus. Jesus calls us to follow him and we obey—or we do not. This is an immense world of God's salvation that we are entering; we don't know enough to use or apply anything. Our task is to obey—believingly, trustingly obey. Simply obey in a 'long obedience.' "

My editor gave in. Thirty years later the book is still selling at a brisk rate. But the real point is that if even Nietzsche saw the necessity of lifetime obedience, we have a much greater investment in the long obedience in the marathon of following God.

# 30

## MY TEN SECRETARIES

Meanwhile, in the words of my friend Tom, I had to "run this damn church." I didn't take any great delight in administrative work, but I knew it had to be done. The church was not financially capable of hiring a secretary, but I was spending too much time being the church secretary. I didn't know what to do.

I have a pastor friend, Dave, who, when he doesn't know what to do, grabs his fly rod, gets into his pickup, and drives a couple miles to the Blackfoot River, where he spends a couple hours fly-fishing. He claims it works better than prayer. Sometimes, he says, it *is* prayer. When I don't know what to do, I read a murder mystery. Murder mysteries are the cleanest, least ambiguous moral writing that we have. All the while you are reading, no matter how confused you are about motives or the significance of clues, you know that eventually the murderer will be identified and justice done. Just stay at it long enough and everything will be sorted out.

Faced with the task of dealing with the congregation's administrative needs, I went to my study and reached at random for a murder mystery. I don't now remember the title or the author. Early in the book, the detective is engaged to solve a murder in a small village in the Lake District of England. He soon realizes that these people are highly suspicious of outsiders and he would never get to first base asking questions. So he posed as a scholar looking for a quiet place in the country to pursue a writing project that involved considerable research. He needed the help of a team of typists. He put a notice in the local paper inviting applicants for the work. Out of the several applicants he selected five elderly women, all widows, who had lived in the town all their lives and seemed to know everyone, both living and dead. He hired them and put them to work in a room together, typing excerpts from various books, while he sat in the next room with the door open, posing as a writer.

The work was humdrum and boring for the women, but the pay was good, and the "writer" didn't seem to be very demanding. It turned out that the women were also gossips, keeping track of the story lines of the village people. After a couple weeks at his listening post, he had gotten from the women all the information he needed to solve the murder. And reading the murder mystery had given me just what I needed to solve the church's administrative needs.

I visited several women in the congregation. Most were elderly widows; a few were homemakers whose children were in school. They would be my "typing pool." I decided I needed ten, two for each day, Monday through Friday, from ten till three. Mostly I wanted someone to answer the telephone, prepare and mail a newsletter each Wednesday, and type and reproduce a worship bulletin every Friday. I divided the administrative work of the congregation into five parts, and assigned them to the five days. The work was not that demanding—we were still a small congregation—so I wanted two "secretaries" each day so they could keep each other company. I asked Irene, who had some organizational skills in office management, to coordinate the work. Her three boys were all in school.

My secretaries not only took care of many of the administrative details of the congregation, but they also provided an informal social setting for sifting out the news of what was going on in people's lives, keeping me in touch with circumstances that were useful pastorally. The system of volunteer secretaries lasted for twenty-five years, happily and efficiently. One Monday a man called from California to talk with me. I wasn't in, and he didn't leave a callback number. He called each day following, still not leaving his number. On Friday I was there to receive his call, and he said, "I've called you every day this week and got a different secretary each day. How many secretaries do you have?" I told him "ten."

He exclaimed, "Wow! You must have a huge church."

After twenty-five years the congregation had grown to a size that required an administrator with the skill to keep all the details together. We could also afford the salary by then. But I missed my ten secretaries.

# 31

## WAYNE AND CLAUDIA

Wayne and Claudia had six children, ranging in age from eight to seventeen. This was a second marriage for both of them, each bringing three children into the marriage. A new job for Wayne at the Martin Marietta aircraft plant brought them to our town. They visited our congregation one Sunday and asked me to come over that week and get acquainted. We set Wednesday evening. They told me they wanted a place where their children could get a moral foundation built into their lives. They were both up front with me about their motivation—this wasn't about them, but about the children. Wayne let me know that he was an atheist. "I don't have anything against religion; I just don't need it. But we will be with them on Sundays." Claudia likewise made no pretence of being interested in God, but she was an organist and would be glad to help out with the music if we needed her.

That's how it started. They were in church every Sunday with their children. Once in a while Claudia would play the organ if our regular organist was ill or away. But they were not easy people to like. Wayne was a physicist who knew a lot and talked a lot about the lot that he knew. And he had answers to everything. Claudia was sharp-tongued and didn't endear herself to anyone. The children seemed nice enough but were awkward socially.

I welcomed them to our congregation. This was going to be a challenge.

When I became a pastor, I resolved on a double focus for keeping my vocation on track: worship and community. At this point in my "long obedience," that resolve had been thoroughly tested and had developed an extensive root system. It had to if it were to survive. The religious culture of America that I was surrounded with dismayed me on both counts. Worship had been degraded into entertainment. And community had been depersonalized into programs.

By the time I arrived on the scene as a pastor, the American church had reinterpreted the worship of God as an activity for religious consumers. Entertainment, cheerleading, and manipulation were conspicuous in high places. American worship was conceived as a public-relations campaign for Jesus and the angels. Worship had been cheapened into a commodity marketed by using tried-and-true advertising techniques. If so-called worshippers didn't "get anything out of it," there had been no worship worth coming back for. Instead of calling people to worship God, pastors all over the country were inviting people to "have a worship experience." Worship was evaluated on the "consumer satisfaction scale" of one to ten.

It struck me as a violation of the holy, a secularization of the sacred. Taking the Lord's name in vain. I determined to reintroduce the rubric "Let us worship God" for my congregation, and then really do it. I knew this wasn't going to be easy. The entertainment model for worship in America was pervasive.

And community. The church as a community of faith formed by the Holy Spirit. Church in America was mostly understood by Christians and their pastors in terms of its function—what it did: build buildings, become "successful," change the neighborhood, launch mission projects, and create programs that would organize and motivate people to do these things. Programs, mostly programs. Programs had developed into the dominant methodology of "doing church." Far more attention was given to organizing and giving leadership to programs than anything else. But there is a problem here: a program is an abstraction and inherently nonpersonal. A program defines people in terms of what they do, not who they are. The more program, the less person. Church was understood not in terms of personal relationships and a personal God but in terms of "getting things done."

This struck me as violation of the inherent personal dignity of souls. The abstraction of a programmatic approach to men and women, however well-meaning, atrophied the relational and replaced it with the pragmatic. Treating souls for whom Christ died as numbers or projects or resources seemed to me something like a sin against the Holy Spirit. I wanted to develop a congregation in which relationships were primary, a household of hospitality. A community in which men and women would be known primarily by name, not by function. I knew this wouldn't be easy, and it wasn't. The programmatic methodology as a way of developing community was epidemic in the American church.

When Wayne and Claudia arrived with their children, we were ready for them.

Early on, Jan and I decided to lay the groundwork for a life of congregational hospitality by beginning in our own home. Whenever we had six to ten people who were to become members of the congregation, we invited them to our home for an evening of conversation. Jan prepared light refreshments, and we would get acquainted. I had already been in their homes, getting acquainted with them on their home ground in conversation with them regarding their faith and the church of Christ. Now I wanted them to experience our home. We listened to one another's stories—the places we had come from, the work we were doing, our children and interests.

We talked about our experience of church, pastors we had known, Christians we had admired, difficulties we had encountered through the years. I wanted to provide a setting and atmosphere in which we could get to know one another in personal ways that were not stereotyped by the work we did or the roles in which we functioned. I wanted to set a precedent for our life together by getting acquainted with one another by name, not by function, to understand our life as a worshipping congregation by what we would be receiving from one another and from God, not in terms of the responsibilities we were expected to fulfill. I wanted to provide a safe and congenial place for gathering to talk about faith and doubt and Jesus. And I wanted them to get acquainted with Jan and me, what our life consisted of when they didn't see us in church, something of what the life of a pastor and family looked like.

Before the evening was over, I told them of the covenant groups that we had developed in the congregation, ten or so persons who met weekly or biweekly in homes for conversation and prayer. This was one of the major ways we had to develop personal relationships in the congregation—getting to know one another in the context of our homes. It was our way to continue the conversation that got started every Sunday in worship as we listened to God's Word and God listened to our prayers. It was our way to get people into one another's homes in settings where relationships could deepen naturally and spontaneously.

What I was hoping for was that the people would begin their life in our congregation in the hospitality of our home and the covenant groups and that gradually their homes would develop as local islands of hospitality in the suburban world of isolation and loneliness, the "lonely crowd" that was getting so much attention by sociologists.

The covenant groups worked pretty well in getting people together for conversation, but as such they never developed into anything that I could discern as a haven of hospitality that pervaded the congregation. The covenant groups provided seeds, but hospitality as a way of congregational life came in increments that, to begin with, took us by surprise. Like Wayne and Claudia.

In our worship the congregation gave witness each week to what we believed by reciting the Apostles' Creed. An elder led the congregation: "Let us say what we believe . . ." Wayne always said the first two words, "I believe"—and then shut his mouth. Out of the corner of my eye I always watched him, intrigued— I wondered what he might be saying under his breath while the rest of us were confessing that we believed in God the Father and Jesus Christ, his Son, and the Holy Spirit. Six months or so after they began attending our church, I observed one Sunday that Wayne didn't stop with "I believe" but continued: " . . . in God the Father Almighty . . ." I kept an eye on him. It continued on successive Sundays. What was going on here? And then in a couple months, I observed the addition of "Jesus Christ, his only Son our Lord . . ." About ten months into this I saw Wayne complete his confession with "I believe in the Holy Spirit . . ."

Throughout this time I never had a conversation with Wayne regarding his professed atheism and this slowly "developing-by-increments" confession of belief in Father, Son, and Holy Spirit.

Then a couple weeks after I had seen him complete his confession of faith, as he was leaving worship, he said, "Pastor, I want to be baptized. Can we talk about it?" We talked about it. He told me about his slow and cautious working his way into a believing life. I told him that I had been watching it happen. He was surprised that I had noticed. He didn't know that he was being observed. The next week he was baptized, to the surprise of a number of those he had offended over the past year by his know-it-all atheism.

A couple years later Claudia was diagnosed with cancer. It was far advanced by the time it was discovered. Within six weeks she was dead. Six months later Wayne's job was terminated. After several months of unemployment, the bank foreclosed on his mortgage. He and his six children were homeless.

Mark and Nancy, his neighbors, who were also members of our congregation, invited Wayne to move in with them until he could get his feet on the ground. Marcia, the oldest child, had just graduated from high school and joined the Air Force shortly after her mother died. Cheryl's Spanish teacher, Henry, and his wife opened their home to her. Jan and I took the remaining four, Gloria, Scott, Steve, and Jerry, into our home. Our daughter, Karen, shared her room with Gloria. I converted our basement, the same basement that a few years before had been the church sanctuary, into a dormitory for the boys.

Acts of hospitality proliferated. First of all in relation to Jan and me. Meals brought in, thoughtfulness expressed, encouragement given. As the months continued, signs of it spread throughout the congregation. The months turned into years. Claudia's death precipitated a hospitality sea change in the congregation that continues to this day, a robust hospitality.

I had been pastor of Christ Our King Church ten years when the Wayne and Claudia stories were lived out in our community. Ten years of nonmanipulated worship; ten years of nonprogrammed community. These ways of worship and community, so un-American, had been working themselves into the soul of the congregation and into my soul gradually, slowly, but also deeply.

Neither Wayne nor Claudia had been easy to affirm or care for or like. The conditions that provided for a confession of faith like his and hospitality like this had been in formation inconspicuously but pervasively for ten years: Wayne's confession, slowly formed without anyone's (except my) noticing, Sunday after Sunday; a community's hospitality gathering sinew and intent quietly, mostly unnoticed, and then catalyzed by Claudia's death into a way of life that would continue to shape the character of the congregation another forty years, flourishing still.

A way of worship that was nonmanipulative. A way of community that was nonprogrammatic. One of the things I relished about being a pastor was being immersed in these ambiguities, the *not* being in control that allowed for the slow emergence of insights and resolve that developed into confessions of faith, and the unplanned, spontaneous attentiveness "one to another" that over the years became a culture of hospitality.

# 32

## JACKSON

The telephone rang. I picked it up. A woman's voice: "Pastor, I have a prob-lem. Can I come and talk with you?" Variations on that introduction are numerous in a pastor's life. What would it be this time? She interrupted my hesitating silence, "Maybe not a problem—it's a good problem." And then she introduced herself, "This is Donna. Remember me? I was Leif's kindergarten teacher a few years ago."

I remembered her. Attractive and alive with enthusiasm. In Donna's first year of teaching, my wife had been a volunteer teacher's aide in her classroom one day a week. She had also become acquainted with our daughter, Karen, in a pottery workshop they both attended. Jan and Donna liked each other and developed a casual friendship. One day, having greeted each other at the gro-cery store, they were making small talk, and something Donna said prompted Jan to say, "Why don't you come to church some Sunday?" Donna laughed. "Sunday is a blue-jeans day for me—I don't think I'd fit." Jan said, "Karen always wears blue jeans to church. I think you would fit in just fine." Through the years when they would meet in a store or on the street, there would be some banter that usually included a reference to blue jeans. But she never came to church.

"Yes, Donna, I remember you. So what is this good problem?" She told me she had a friend, an old friend from high-school days, who thought he had become a Christian and asked her if she knew anyone he could talk to about it. She thought of me, although we had never met face-to-face (but I had seen her in action while visiting her classroom).

"Can I bring him to meet you?"

After school the next day she brought Jackson to meet me in my study at the church. The three of us got acquainted. I learned that Jackson had recently come back to his hometown after several years' absence, the last five of which he had lived in the federal prison at Leavenworth, serving a sentence for trafficking drugs in and out of Mexico. He had been released from prison and now was serving out another six months of probation in which he was able to work through the week but had to spend the weekends in the local jail.

Then Jackson told me what had happened three days earlier, Sunday night, in his jail cell. "In the middle of the night I woke up, and my cell was full of light—a kind of pulsating light. It lasted maybe five minutes, it seemed like a long time. And then it was dark again. I was still in my bunk wondering what had happened, and then it came to me: 'I think I'm a Christian.' But I have no idea what that means. I don't know any Christians. Donna thought you might be someone I could talk to." He assured me that drugs were not involved. "I haven't used cocaine for over five years."

We agreed to meet for lunch every week and talk about what it means to be a Christian.

I soon learned that everybody in town knew Jackson. He had been the most accomplished athlete the local high school had ever graduated. He had a personality that exuded "juice," an infectious friendliness that was irresistible. When he entered a room, everyone there knew it, a kind of charismatic presence apart from anything he did or said.

Jackson had flexible hours. He was a used-car salesman, so we went to out-of-the-way restaurants and diners after the major lunch traffic had subsided, and we talked about faith and Jesus and prayer and just what went into being a Christian.

After about six weeks of these meetings, Jackson said, "Don't Christians pray before they eat?" I said that, yes, most do.

"Well, why aren't we doing it?"

I said that since he wasn't used to this kind of thing, I didn't want to make him uncomfortable by imposing my practices on him.

"If this is what Christians do, we better do it."

So I prayed before we ate. Then one week I said, "Jackson, you pray this time." He looked at me hard, stared in disbelief. And then he bowed his head and prayed. He prayed a long time. When he finally said Amen, he looked up and said, "I've never done that before."

From then on we prayed by turns. One week it was Jackson's turn to pray. We had ordered soup. After the soup was served, he bowed his head low over the soup. The waitress brought bread she had forgotten earlier and said, "Is something the matter with the soup?"

Jackson, with his head still bowed and with his eyes tightly shut, turned his face toward her and said, louder than he needed to, "We're praying."

There was no way to be an anonymous Christian when you were in the company of Jackson.

One week Jackson came with a question about some tracts that had been left in his jail cell. "What's a tith-ee?" A tith-ee? I scrambled to understand what he was asking. And then I got it—"tithe." I told him it was a practice of giving 10 percent of your income as an offering to God in worship.

"And Christians do this?"

I told him that not everyone did, but that there was precedent for it in the Bible and many Christians used it as a guideline.

"Now that I'm a Christian, I think I better do it. Since I'm in jail on Sundays, how about if I give my offering to you every week? And tell me again, how do you pronounce that funny word?"

And on and on it went. Exploring all the nooks and crannies of Christian practice. Getting the inside story of being a Christian. Figuring out just what this life of believing and praying consisted in. Learning how to read the Bible, not just to learn something but to engage in a conversation with God. I learned a lot, too, getting the inside story on what the Christian life looked like when encountered for the first time.

When the six months stint of his weekends in jail ended, he became part of our congregation and worshipped with us. He brought Donna with him. They both wore blue jeans.

Jackson was a recovering alcoholic and drug addict when I met him. He had developed his cocaine habit when he was serving in the military in Vietnam. One of the conditions of his probation was weekly attendance at AA and NA meetings.

Word began to get around in the subculture of recovering addicts. Largely because of Jackson, our church was becoming the congregation of choice among recovering addicts in our county who were motivated to find out more about their Higher Power.

One Sunday after the benediction, a woman introduced herself and then said, "What's going on here? I looked around and counted the people I knew. I felt like I was in an AA meeting."

"So how did you know we were here?"

"Jackson told me."

An intriguing thing about this for me was that I had learned early on that I was incapable of dealing with alcoholics and had taken the counsel of a man who had spent much of his life working with them not to even try. He told me I was too sympathetic, too compassionate, totally naive about the addictive personality. When I protested that that's just the way I was put together, he said, "Eugene, that's what I mean. Addicts lie a lot, and you believe every lie they tell you. Addicts deny a lot, and you accept the denials without questioning. Don't try to help them. If you feel you have to do something, send them to me."

I thought back through my life, wondering what it was that incapacitated me from being any help to the alcoholic. And then I remembered my paternal grandfather—an alcoholic. He was a carpenter who lived in Seattle, in Ballard, a Swedish immigrant neighborhood. When his drinking got out of control, which it did periodically, my dad would get a call from his sister: "Come and get Papa. Dry him out."

And my dad always did. He'd drive to Seattle, get his father, and bring him to Montana to live with us for three or four months. There was always a carpentry project for him to work on. One summer it was building a garage. Another it was enclosing our front porch, in effect adding another room to our house. He never talked much, but I liked being around him as he worked. I asked him for stories from Sweden, but he either couldn't or wouldn't do it. But he didn't exactly ignore me. Instead, with his jackknife he produced miracles of whittled tops from empty spools of thread and animals from scrap lumber and gave them to me. He let me get tools for him and carry boards.

Sometimes he would disappear, and my father would get a call from a bartender, usually in the middle of the night, to come and get him, passed out. One summer he was gone for three days and when found was incoherent and raging, with snakes and spiders crawling all over him. I added a new term to my vocabulary that year: delirium tremens, the dread d.t.'s. His sick room was my basement bedroom. When I would enter to get an article of clothing, he would wail, "Grog, grog . . . Eugene, grog, please, some grog . . ."

The next summer he died in a bar in Seattle. We drove out for the funeral. I was eleven years old. When we filed by the open casket, I saw that one cheek was a massive bruise. And then this: his daughter, my Aunt Helen, fell on the casket, cradling his face in her hands and sobbing, "Papa, Papa, Papa, oh, Papa, oh Papa . . ."

I think now that every alcoholic I have ever met was my grandpa. My father's patient, uncomplaining, futile rescues; my grandpa's helpless inability to tell me stories of Sweden and my helpless inability to give him "grog"; my aunt's uncontrollable sobs bathing his face with her tears. No wonder all this emotion and loss and sorrow incapacitates me from dealing with the alcoholic.

It is a huge irony that I ended up as a pastor to so many recovering alcoholics. But "recovering" is the key word here. These men and women, I think without exception, know the difference between dealing with alcoholism as a problem, which they are doing in their recovery, and living a life of faith in Christ as a gift and accepting me as their pastor as they do it.

Eventually Jackson and Donna asked me to marry them. They wanted a simple wedding with no guests, just Jan and me. But they did want some music. They both loved country music. "How about a song by Emmylou Harris?" She was a favorite of theirs.

I suggested something more in keeping with the new life they were now living. "How about 'Farther Along'—what I think of as Christian country?" They agreed.

So after the prayers and scripture, the exchange of vows, and the blessing, Jan and I, accompanied by my five-string banjo, sang

> *Farther along, we'll know all about it,*
> *Farther along, we'll understand why;*
> *Cheer up, my brother, live in the sunshine,*
> *We'll understand it all by and by.*

Considering their new beginning and the long road ahead in their marriage and their life in Christ, it seemed an appropriate wedding song for Donna and Jackson.

When Jackson writes to me now he signs his name "Jackson 'Farther Along' Nelson."

# 33

## THE ATHEIST AND THE NUN

The dean pulled me aside as I was walking to my classroom. A Thursday evening, the first class in the spring semester. In his hand he held a roster of the students enrolled in my class. He pointed out one name, "I thought I ought to warn you. This guy has been coming here for years. He claims to be an atheist. Worse, it turns out that he is an obnoxious atheist. I have no idea why he hangs around this place. Be wary."

I had no trouble identifying him even before he gave his name. Burly, with a full black beard. His torso seemed too large for his legs. He walked with something of a swagger. I learned later that his friends called him Bear. It was easy to see why.

The setting was St. Mary's Seminary in Baltimore. Each spring semester for twenty-two years on Thursday evenings I taught a course there. I was an adjunct professor in their Ecumenical Institute. The Institute offered night classes for men and women who were doing supplementary or continuing education.

Having made my decision to be a pastor and not a professor twenty-six years earlier, I never second-guessed that decision, never looked back. But the invitation to give courses at the Ecumenical Institute, as it turned out, was neither diversion nor detraction from my pastoral work. It contributed a kind of reinforcement, an enrichment. It gave me a supplementary congregation very different from the suburbanites I gathered for worship each week and with whom I lived as a companion. My classes were multiethnic, a gathering of people off the streets of Baltimore from missions, New Age cults, workers with the homeless, men and women who hadn't found their place, looking for a place. Some were Christians looking for guidance and stimulus in sharpening their witness and understanding. Some were professionals bored with professionalism. They kept me in touch with an energy that seethed in the city but also with its poverty and crime. My sense was that all of them were looking for God but often didn't have a name for what they were looking for. Their language and their stories protected me from being lulled into complacency by suburbia.

The seminary also maintained a connection with the life of the mind, a devout community of intellectual seriousness that did not exactly flourish in my congregation, homes in which there was a TV in every room. St. Mary's Seminary trained priests for holy orders. It was the oldest Roman Catholic seminary in America. I had a couple friends who were professors on the faculty. The life of the mind, the *theological* mind, flourished here. The library was elegant. The conversations were lively. A few hours a week at the seminary were enough to keep my mind engaged with the life of the Spirit, the Word of Life, a living link with the life of the mind.

The pastoral vocation in America is always in danger of becoming flabby with consumer religion and lazy with clichés. Those years and hours at St. Mary's Seminary provided a defense against both the flabbiness and the clichés.

This semester my course was A Theology of Ministry in the Workplace. There were eleven students. I introduced myself. We got acquainted—their names, what they did for a living, and so forth. Then I gave an orientation to the course. The working assumption was that ministry is what we do for a living, all of us, any of us. It is not a specialty work for pastors or priests or missionaries. As we met together around this seminar table, we would describe what we did for a living and see if we could find ourselves as workers in a workplace in the biblical story, a vocation of salvation. We would use Jesus's words in John 5:17 as our text: "My Father is still working, and I also am working." The Gospel of John as a whole would provide background and resource.

"The major requirement of the course is to write a paper on your personal assessment of the theology of a ministry that you are in. Each will present a paper in class. That will be the text that we will discuss. I'll orient you through the first three weeks; the fourth week you will take over, read your papers, and discuss them. I'd like you to start thinking about it. After these three orienting lectures, one of you will have to be first. That's a disadvantage, I know, but somebody has to do it. Any volunteers?"

Bear volunteered. "I already know what I am going to write about, 'A theology of work in the social security administration.' That is my place of work."

Pretty clever. I wondered what he would make of that. But obviously he could get by without mentioning the name of God.

The class fell to, discussing possible topics. They were to have chosen a topic when we came to class the following week. Discussion was animated. Except for one woman, a nun. She taught fifth grade in a parochial school. About fifty years old, plain, sullen, lumpish. She said nothing. Attempting to get something started with her, I asked, "Why are you taking this course?"

"It's not my idea. Faculty requires it—continuing education."

The next week she didn't have a topic. She said, "I don't have a ministry."

"Josephine, didn't you tell me when we were talking before class that you ran a bingo game every Saturday for the elderly in a nursing home?"

She was curt. "That's not ministry, that's penance." I backed off.

The next week Bear said he wanted to change his topic. "My father is dying; I want to write about my father and me."

Well, at least it was going to be personal.

The next week, the week before Bear was to read his paper, he announced, "I've changed my mind; I want to write about myself. 'The theology of my ministry to me.'"

Interesting progression: from an institution, to a dying father, to . . . himself. What was this going to be? I was mindful of the warning the dean had given me. What was Bear up to? Was he going to be his own God?

We all found out the next week. Bear read his paper. He had written a confession of faith. He wrote about his years of coming to the Ecumenical Institute, attracted in a vague way to God and theology and church, but also defended with the heavy armor of atheism against anyone's attempt to convert or get close to him. The Institute seemed safer than going to church—more anonymous. He traced his change of topics from the impersonal social security system to his personal relationship with his father and now to his relationship to God. He wrote of his pose as an atheist—how at first he just took delight in getting attention as an atheist in a theological school, but how for the last year or so the zest had been draining out of the charade. Those years of being de-personalized by the depersonalizing social security system in which he worked slowly uncovered a desire for something more intimate as he found himself wanting to spend time with his dying father. He talked of how the text for the course, the parallel between the Father working and Jesus working, kept swirl-ing around in his imagination. And then thinking, "Why not go all the way? Why not God? Why not Jesus?"

Bear wasn't showing off. There wasn't a hint of swagger in his voice. He had acquired considerable agility in handling theological language in his years of night classes at the Institute, but he wasn't putting it on display, not trying to impress us. Except that we *were* impressed, all of us by now involved in his confession—an altar call, no less.

Bear set down the conditions that prevailed for the rest of the semester: honest, probing, vulnerable, prayerful, and personal. And Christian. We all got practice in using language theologically in ways that didn't reduce God to an idea or an abstraction or a foil. Each week we listened and discussed another paper that gave witness to God in the local, God on the job, God in the home-less, God in the people around us, God in and with *us*.

Those Thursday evening conversations continued through the spring se-mester, our lives, mine included, validated in our workplaces, energized by what we were learning to recognize as the Holy Spirit.

Except for Josephine. She never entered the conversation. She sat there, shy and withdrawn. The one person at the table who didn't "have a ministry." I never challenged her silence. Now I was the shy one—I didn't feel privileged to invade whatever was going on within her.

The final paper in the seminar was given by Josephine. I didn't know she was going to read. She told me just before class. She had picked up on my earlier noticing that she conducted a bingo game for the elderly every Saturday at the nursing home. She took that as her work. As she read her paper, we were brought into a semester of Saturdays in which she reverently and lovingly served Christ to those old men and women. We all felt like we were in that nursing home with her. We were astonished. Timid Josephine! She covered the nakedness of Jesus in an old man. She wiped the spittle from the face of Jesus in a woman. We couldn't believe our ears. She observed that the bingo cards were the same shape as the Mass cards used at worship on Sundays. And that the bingo chips were the same size as the communion wafers. She reimagined that bingo game as the Eucharistic Mass. She was the officiating priest. The calls of "bingo" that punctuated the room were liturgical responses. The last line of her paper was "Saturday is the holiest day of the week."

# 34

## JUDITH

Judith is an artist. Her primary medium is textiles. Most of the time she begins her work with raw cotton or wool. She cards, spins, dyes, and then weaves her fabrics. Her weavings are usually on a small scale—a nest of bird's eggs, a portrait of David's Abigail, three crows—which she frames and gives as gifts to her friends. She makes her living by repairing tapestries in museums in Philadelphia, Baltimore, and Washington D.C.

Judith had an alcoholic husband and a drug-addicted son. She had kept her life and her family together for years by attending twelve-step meetings. One Sunday, she was about forty years old at the time, she entered Christ Our King Church. She came at the invitation of some friends she knew from her meetings— "You need to come to church. I'll meet you there." She knew nothing about church. She was raised in a morally upright home but had no acquaintance with institutional or formal religion. In her family the word "God" was not a part of its working vocabulary. She was well read in poetry and politics and psychology and knew a great deal about art and artists. But she had never read the Bible. If she had heard the stories of the Bible, she had paid no attention. As far as she could recall, she had never been inside a church.

Something, though, caught her attention when she entered this church, and she continued to come. In a few months she became a Christian and I became her pastor. I loved observing and listening to her. Everything was new: scriptures, worship, prayer, baptism, Eucharist—*church!* It was a tonic to me to hear and see through her excited perceptions everything that I had lived with all my life. All her questions were exclamations: "Where have I been all my life? These are incredible stories—why didn't anyone tell me these! How come this has been going on all around me and I never knew it!" We had delightful conversations. We became good friends.

Meanwhile her primary community was made up of artists. Painters and poets and sculptors, mostly, with a few of her twelve-step friends sprinkled in among them.

After four years or so of this, I moved across the continent to take up a new assignment. Letters replaced conversations. The following is a portion of a letter that is a witness to the interiority, the "insides" of what church feels like to a newcomer:

*Dear Pastor: Among my artist friends I feel so defensive about my life—I mean about going to church. They have no idea what I am doing and act bewildered. So I try to be unobtrusive about it. But as my church life takes on more and more importance—it is essential now to my survival—it is hard to shield it from my friends. I feel protective of it, not wanting it to be dismissed or minimized or trivialized. It is like I am trying to protect it from profanation or sacrilege. But it is strong. It is increasingly difficult to keep it quiet. It is not as if I am ashamed or embarrassed—I just don't want it belittled.*

*A longtime secular friend, and a superb artist, just the other day was appalled: "What is this I hear about you going to church?" Another found out that I was going on a three-week mission trip to Haiti and was incredulous: "You, Judith, you going to Haiti with a church group! What has gotten into you?" I don't feel strong enough to defend my actions. My*

*friends would accept me far more readily if they found that I was in some*
*bizarre cult involving exotic and strange activities like black magic or*
*experiments with levitation. But going to church is branded with a terrible*
*ordinariness.*

*But that is what endears it to me, both the church and the twelve-*
*step programs, this façade of ordinariness. When you pull back the veil*
*of ordinariness, you find the most extraordinary life behind it. But I feel*
*isolated and inadequate to explain to my husband and close friends—even*
*myself!—what it is. It's as if I would have to undress myself before them.*
*Maybe if I was willing to do that, they would not dare disdain me. More*
*likely they would just pity me. As it is, they just adjust their neckties a little*
*tighter.*

*I am feeling raw and cold and vulnerable and something of a fool.*
*I guess I don't feel too badly about being a fool within the context of the*
*secular world. From the way they look at me, I don't have much to show*
*for my new life. I can't point to a life mended. Many of the sorrows and*
*difficulties seem mended for a time, only to bust open again. But to tell*
*you the truth I haven't been on medication since June and for that I feel*
*grateful.*

*When I try to explain myself to these friends I feel as if I am suspended*
*in a hang glider between the material and immaterial, casting a shadow*
*down far below, and they say, "See—it's nothing but shadow work."*
*Perhaps it takes a fool to savor the joy of shadow work, the shadow cast as*
*I'm attending to the unknown, the unpaid for, the freely given.*

Judith gets it right. Nobody has any idea what she is doing. She feels apologetic about that. But she embraces what she is given—that seemingly fragile
hang-glider church suspending her in the mystery: "the unpaid for, the freely
given." She is an artist of church: "Don't look at me—see the shadow down
there. Look at the shadow work. You might see what God is doing." She knows
so little about church, yet she knows what it is. She is an artist who knows about
the invisible that energizes and shapes visibility, the Spirit that keeps aloft the
ligaments and sinews and fabric of the hang glider that she is strapped into, this
seemingly fragile church that casts on the earth what she calls shadow work.

# 35

## "INVISIBLE SIX DAYS A WEEK, INCOMPREHENSIBLE THE SEVENTH"

Every Sunday after a morning of leading my congregation in worship, I walked the quarter of a mile home. My next-door neighbor was often working in his yard and always greeted me cheerily, "Well that's done, pastor. A one-day workweek. Must be nice." I was welcomed home to the neighborhood with that greeting followed by a chuckle for thirty years. He always said it as if he had just thought it up on the spot.

I never minded too much. Evan was a good neighbor and a practicing Catholic. Our wives were friends, and our children were playmates. Whenever he said it, I remembered a more elegant version of his quip that I heard from a Scottish Presbyterian elder who had grown up in the Highlands, where "pastors were invisible six days a week and incomprehensible the seventh."

I don't know about the incomprehensible part, but the fact is that pastors *are* invisible six days a week. The only time that most of the people in our congregations see us at work is when we are leading worship on Sundays. There are a few other occasions when we do our work in public—conducting a funeral, blessing a wedding, preaching at the high-school baccalaureate—but when we visit the sick, only the sick person and his or her family knows of it. When we write a letter, only the person who gets it knows. When we pray, only God knows.

Most if not all of the people to whom we are pastor are very visible in their work: teachers in the classroom, businessmen and women in their places of employment, physicians in their surgeries and consulting rooms, checkout clerks in grocery stores and stockbrokers working the phones, policemen on patrol, and politicians on the campaign trail. The people they serve know if they are on the job or not and have a pretty good idea of whether they are doing it satisfactorily.

But not pastors. Away from the sanctuary, the people to whom we are pastors see us only in bits and pieces in settings and among people where the word "God" is more likely to be used as an expletive than in prayer. A great deal of our most important work is done behind the scenes. What people observe on Sunday is only the tip of the iceberg. The harmonies and rhythms that give solidity and weight to what everyone sees taking place in the sanctuary are slowly and incrementally formed in the ocean depths of the lives of both pastor and people. I thought it would be useful to find ways to convey something of the invisibilities that held our lives together as pastor and congregation as a people of God when we were not visibly together, something of what undergirded what they saw on Sundays and the occasional glimpses we had of one another on weekdays.

I wanted to let them in on, as much as I was able, the "invisibilities" of my life as their pastor, invisibilities in which they also were involved, even though not listed on their job descriptions as engineers and homemakers and students. Being a pastor is not a solo job. It might look like it on Sundays, but that is far from the truth. I wanted to find ways to develop a corporate congregational identity that had some sense of the formational harmonies and rhythms that kept our lives together. I wanted to counter the rampant American individualism, ice floes bouncing around on the surface of the water, "tossed to and fro by every wind of doctrine." No—we are an iceberg, a church, and most of what makes us what is seen on Sunday as we move rhythmically and easily with one another, efficient and graceful in response to God, is invisible.

What do pastors do between Sundays? What do lay Christians do between Sundays? I wanted to develop a congregational awareness that was shaped under the influence of Sunday worship and that then infiltrated the hours and days of the week implicitly in every workplace and household. I wanted to develop a pastor/people relationship that included all the days of the week, weekdays on a par with Sundays. I wanted them to know what I did between Sundays as I prayed for them by name, studied the scriptures so that I could translate them into the language and circumstances of their lives "between Sundays" and lead them in acts of worship that give depth and ballast to their lives wherever they are and whatever they are doing. I also wanted to know what they did between Sundays, living out in their dailiness what they had received in word and sacrament in the Sunday worship.

I began with a negative. Sunday worship was not the place to tell them, at least not explicitly, what I did when they didn't see me. Sunday worship was not a platform to put on exhibit what I did when out of their sight and make sure they knew how important it was. Sunday worship was about God and about inviting them into what God was doing in the world and in their lives. I wanted to be as inconspicuous as possible. Invisibility, of course, was not an option. But I would not call attention to myself or to what I was doing when I was out of their sight.

I began to deliberately imagine ways that I could convey how intricately our lives are involved with one another's even when, maybe especially when, we did not see one another. Much of this would be done indirectly, by manner and tone. But I thought that writing a weekly congregational letter might help. I used it to develop a congregational awareness of who we were when we weren't in church together.

**A**men/Yes. In one of the first services of worship in our basement, the "catacombs" era, our two-year-old daughter, Karen, was embarrassed when she was the only person in the congregation who responded with an audible Amen to the Amen with which I concluded my prayers from the pulpit. She did it because she was used to it—we always concluded our table prayers this way. Later in the service I mentioned this family practice of ours, and since we were now meeting as a family of Christ in the basement of our home, would they join my family in concluding the prayers with an audible amen. This is not standard practice with Presbyterians. But they did. They are still doing it. A simple thing, but I was pleased at how much energy it released into the act of worship.

But there is more to the story. In the early days of learning language, daily adding new words to her vocabulary, Karen asked what Amen meant. I said that it was a word that meant Yes. When we say Amen, whether at the supper table or in church, we are affirming the prayer that another offered: "Yes, that's right. I'm in on this too."

She said, "So why don't we just say Yes?" I told her that she could if she wished. But the people who had started the Christian church in the first place said Amen because that was Yes in their language, and Christians have just kept doing it. And Jesus was very fond of the word and said it a lot.

From then on, sometimes she would say "Amen" and sometimes "Yes" and sometimes "Amen Yes."

I especially liked the Amen Yes. Every time she said it, I was reminded of Paul's words to the young first-generation church in Corinth: "Whatever God has promised gets stamped with the Yes of Jesus. In him this is what we preach and pray, the great Amen, God's Yes and our Yes together, gloriously evident. God affirms us, making us a sure thing in Christ, putting his Yes within us."

I named the weekly congregational letter *Amen/Yes*. It arrived midweek, keeping us tethered to the Sunday just past and the Sunday soon to arrive. I would use it to keep us in touch with one another, pastor and congregation, under the aegis of "the great Amen, God's Yes and our Yes together." It would be a single page, front and back, so it could be read easily. I would not use it as a newsletter, posting schedules, meetings, programs, activities—it would not be a bulletin board. I would use it to shape a congregational imagination in which we embraced one another as peers in the Christian life, to develop congregational and pastoral rapport. I reported brief conversations that provided texture in our life together. I put in a lot of names, knowing that names are the most personal words in the language and therefore verbal building blocks for relationships. I reflected on what I was doing when they didn't see me. I reflected on what they were doing when I didn't see them.

I wrote it every Tuesday. The church secretaries mailed it out every Wednesday. A deliberate use of language to connect Sunday language with weekday language, weekday language with Sunday language. Sometimes I would insert a deliberate mistake or inaccuracy to see if they were reading it. They were.

**The Unbusy Pastor.** The seed that germinated into the weekly *Amen/Yes* had been planted the year after we completed our three-year postulancy. As a congregation, we had achieved critical mass, we were self-supporting financially, we had built a sanctuary that gave visibility to our worshipping presence in the neighborhood. It was the beginning of what I earlier called the badlands era in which the euphoria of establishing a church had gone flat, the adrenaline of being involved in a challenging enterprise had drained out. I had worked hard for those three years. The congregation had worked hard. We couldn't sustain it.

Except that I tried. I formed committees. I made home visits. Longer hours. A longer workweek. Just a few years previous to this, Roger Bannister, the first four-minute miler, wrote his autobiography in which he described life following his high-profile athletic celebrity. He wasn't breaking records anymore. He compensated by working harder and harder. He described himself as a carpenter who "made up for his lack of skill by using a lot of nails." That was me. I had tried to slow down. I had tried to relax. But I was afraid of failing. I couldn't help myself.

One evening after supper, Karen—she was five years old at the time—asked me to read her a story. I said, "I'm sorry, Karen, but I have a meeting tonight."

"This is the twenty-seventh night in a row you have had a meeting." She had been keeping track, counting.

The meeting I had to go to was with the church's elders, the ruling body of the congregation. In the seven-minute walk to the church on the way to the meeting I made a decision. If succeeding as a pastor meant failing as a parent, I was already a failed pastor. I would resign that very night.

We met in my study. I convened the meeting and scrapped the agenda. I told them what Karen had said twenty minutes earlier in our living room. And I resigned. I told them I had tried not to work so hard, but that I didn't seem to be able to do it. "And it's not just Karen. It's you too. I haven't been a pastor to this congregation for six months. I pray in fits and starts. I feel like I'm in a hurry all the time. When I visit or have lunch with you, I'm not listening to you; I am thinking of ways I can get the momentum going again. My sermons are thrown together. I don't want to live like this, either with you or with my family."

"So what do you want to do?" This was Craig speaking. His father had been a pastor. He knew some of this from the inside.

"I want to be a pastor who prays. I want to be reflective and responsive and relaxed in the presence of God so that I can be reflective and responsive and relaxed in your presence. I can't do that on the run. It takes a lot of time. I started out doing that with you, but now I feel too crowded.

"I want to be a pastor who reads and studies. This culture in which we live squeezes all the God sense out of us. I want to be observant and informed enough to help this congregation understand what we are up against, the temptations of the devil to get us thinking we can all be our own gods. This is subtle stuff. It demands some detachment and perspective. I can't do this just by trying harder.

"I want to be a pastor who has the time to be with you in leisurely, unhurried conversations so that I can understand and be a companion with you as you grow in Christ—your doubts and your difficulties, your desires and your delights. I can't do that when I am running scared.

"I want to be a pastor who leads you in worship, a pastor who brings you before God in receptive obedience, a pastor who preaches sermons that make scripture accessible and present and alive, a pastor who is able to give you a language and imagination that restores in you a sense of dignity as a Christian in your homes and workplaces and gets rid of these debilitating images of being a 'mere' layperson.

"I want to have the time to read a story to Karen.

"I want to be an unbusy pastor."

This had turned into something of a harangue. I didn't know that so much sediment of discontent had accumulated in the previous six months. The six elders had listened patiently.

"Why don't you just do it? This is the way you started out with us. Nobody complained, did they? As far as I know, everyone was delighted. The people who didn't like you this way have left. So what's stopping you?" This was Jason, a retired colonel—a problem-solving mind, impatient of ambiguities.

"What's stopping me is that I have to run this church."

"Why don't you let us run the church?" This was Craig again.

"Because you don't know how."

Mildred was less than tactful. "It sounds to me like you aren't doing such a good job yourself. Maybe we could learn."

They did. And I did. Instead of a resignation that night, we had a reorganization. We spent the next hour discussing how to go about this. When the evening was over, they had taken over "running the church." They assured me they could handle this. All of them said they had learned the "running the church" aspects in their own jobs, professions, and careers—"on the job." Each in his or her own way said, "Trust us."

We agreed that from then on I would attend no committee meetings. I would continue to moderate the monthly session (the meeting of elders), but that would be it. If they needed me to meet with them or their committees as a consultant for twenty minutes or so, they would invite me. The hands-on work of running the church—how and when and who—was their responsibility. The energy flowing around the table was palpable.

Two weeks later there was a meeting of the stewardship committee. It was budget time. Important decisions would be made. I was at home and restless. I picked up a book, but I couldn't concentrate. Karen didn't ask me to read a story with her. After thirty minutes of pacing and fiddling, I walked to the church and into the meeting of the committee. They were seated around a table. I pulled up a chair off to the side. They looked at me inquiringly. I said, "I wasn't doing anything this evening. Just thought I'd stop in and encourage you."

Jim, the presiding elder, an insurance agent, said, "You don't trust us, do you?"

Taken aback, I said nothing. And then, "I guess I don't. But I'll try." I left. I didn't go back.

Trusting them wasn't easy for me. For these three and half years of new church development I had been the leader. Things had gone well. I liked being in charge. Jim's remark when I showed up at that budget meeting hit the mark.

I *didn't* trust them. But I had said I would learn. And I did, but it took me a while. Sometimes they made plans and decisions I didn't particularly like, but I knew I couldn't have it both ways. If they let me be the pastor I wanted to be, I would have to let them be the elders they wanted to be. Mildred was right: I hadn't done such a great job of running the church. I let them do it. It turned out that they were perfectly capable of learning on the job.

And that was it for "running" the church. I did my part when asked. Occasionally I would offer a suggestion or write a note. But no more committee meetings. Over the next twenty-six years and two more major building campaigns, growing to a congregation numbering five hundred, still no committee meetings.

With their blessing I was free to cultivate the "invisibles" that made up so much of my pastoral vocation in the long obedience. They made it possible for me to be an unbusy pastor.

An unintended consequence of this decision, now that that I was unbusy, free to be the pastor that I had spent much of my life becoming, was that I now had energy and time to pay attention to the work of the men and women in my congregation in *their* workplaces. They were helping me in my workplace. I developed an imagination now to help them in theirs. Together we were restoring dignity to the term *laity*: we were in this together. Running the church was not a full-time job for them. They spread the work throughout the congregation, trusting others to help them do the work in the same way that I was trusting them.

As we did this together, the conviction spread through the congregation that one of the most soul-damaging phrases that had crept into the Christian vocabulary is "full-time Christian work." Every time it is used, it drives a wedge of misunderstanding between the way we pray and the way we work, between the way we worship and the way we make a living.

One of the achievements of the Protestant Reformation was a leveling of the ground between clergy and laity. Pastors and butchers had equal status before the cross. Homemakers were on a par with evangelists. But insidiously that level ground eroded as religious professionals claimed the high ground, asserted exclusive rights to "full-time Christian work," and relegated the laity to part-time work on weekends under pastoral or priestly direction. A huge irony—the pastors were hogging the show, and the laity were demeaned with the adjectives "mere," "only," or "just": "He or she is *just* a layperson."

As we together were making the transition, I to unbusy pastor, they to full-time Christian teachers and bankers, homemakers and farmers, I wrote a reflection for *Amen/Yes*.

> Most of what Jesus said and did took place in a secular workplace in a farmer's field, in a fishing boat, at a wedding feast, in a cemetery, at a public well asking a woman he didn't know for a drink of water, on a country hillside that he turned into a huge picnic, in a court room, having supper in homes with acquaintances or friends. In our Gospels, Jesus occasionally shows up in synagogue or temple, but for the most part he spends his time in the workplace. Twenty-seven times in John's Gospel Jesus is identified as a worker: "My Father is still working, and I also am working" (Jn. 5:17). Work doesn't take us away from God; it continues the work of God. God comes into view on the first page of our scriptures as a worker. Once we identify God in his workplace working, it isn't long before we find ourselves in our workplaces working in the name of God.

For months afterward when visiting in a home, I would notice that that paragraph had been cut out and pinned on a bulletin board or attached to a refrigerator door. I took it as evidence that we were becoming a congregation of Christians who were confident of the dignity of our vocation, which was identical both within and outside the church sanctuary.

I was reading Herman Melville's *Moby-Dick* at the time. There is a turbulent scene in which a whaleboat scuds across a frothing ocean in pursuit of the great white whale, Moby Dick. The sailors are laboring fiercely, every muscle taut, all attention and energy concentrated on the task. The cosmic conflict between good and evil is joined; chaotic sea and demonic sea monster versus the morally outraged man, Captain Ahab. In this boat, however, there is one man who does nothing. He doesn't hold an oar; he doesn't perspire; he doesn't shout. He is languid in the crash and the cursing. This man is the harpooner, quiet and poised, waiting. And then this sentence: "To insure the greatest efficiency in the dart, the harpooners of this world must start to their feet out of idleness, and not out of toil."

Was this a confirmation to cultivate what I had named an "unbusy pastor"?

A harpooner? Pastors are in a position to be reminded daily that there is something radically wrong with the world. We are also engaged in doing something about it. The stimulus of conscience, the memory of ancient outrage, and the challenge of biblical command place us in the anarchic sea that is the world. The white whale, symbol of evil, and the crippled captain, personification of violated righteousness, are joined in battle. History is a novel of spiritual conflict. The church is a whaleboat. In such a world, noise is inevitable, and immense energy is expended. But if there is no harpooner in the boat, there will be no proper finish to the chase. Or if the harpooner is exhausted, having abandoned his assignment and become an oarsman, he will not be ready and accurate when it is time to throw his javelin.

The metaphor, harpooner, was starting to get inside me. Somehow it always seems more compelling to assume the work of the oarsman, laboring mightily in a moral cause, throwing our energy into a fray that we know has immortal consequence. And it always seems more dramatic to take on the outrage of a Captain Ahab, obsessed with a vision of vengeance and retaliation, brooding over the ancient injury done by the Enemy. There is, though, other important work to do. Someone must throw the dart. Some must be harpooners.

Melville's harpooner found company in my imagination with Jesus's metaphors that feature the single, the small, and the quiet—salt, leaven, seed—that have effects far in excess of their appearance. Our culture publicizes the opposite: the big, the multitudinous, the noisy. Is it not, then, a strategic necessity that some of us deliberately ally ourselves with the quiet, poised harpooners, and not leap, frenzied, to the oars?

The metaphor is not perfect. No metaphor is. But harpooner continued, and continues, to serve me well for cultivating quietness and attentiveness before God and my congregation on the voyage in which Moby Dick and Captain Ahab seem to be calling all the shots

**The Mess.** "What do you like best about being a pastor?" The question came from a young woman, Stephanie.

"The mess," I said.

A group of seminarians from a nearby school—there were ten of them—had asked me to lead them on a thirty-six-hour retreat. They were about to graduate and enter into the vocations they had just spent years preparing for. For three of them, being a pastor meant starting over in a second career. They wanted to spend a couple days in prayer and conversation as they anticipated what was ahead of them.

My answer, "the mess," was unpremeditated. It stopped the conversation. But sometimes a spontaneous response reveals something important that had never surfaced just that way before. But *mess* wasn't quite the right word. I backpedaled. "Well, not exactly a mess, but coming upon something unexpected that I don't know how to handle, where I feel inadequate. Another name for it is miracle that doesn't look like a miracle but the exact opposite of miracle. A slow recognition of life, God's life, taking form in a person and context, in words or action that takes me off-guard. Theologian Karl Rahner was once asked if he believed in miracles. His reply? 'I *live* on miracles—I couldn't make it through a day without them.' Still another name for it is mystery. Pastors have ringside seats to this kind of thing. Maybe everyone does, but I often feel that pastors get invited into intimacies that elude a more functional and performance way of life."

Morris, an engineer who had spent twenty years calculating structural stresses and reading blueprints, asked me to elaborate.

"Okay. If we take the visibilities of Sunday morning as normal, the grid against which the rest of the week is evaluated, we will not be prepared for what does not qualify as normal—for the mess, for the disorder, for failures and disappointments, for suffering and death, for bursts of beauty in a falling-apart life. We are in charge of Sunday morning. People expect us to keep their belief systems coherent. People expect us to represent moral law and order in the community. We have adequate time to prepare ourselves for what is to be said and sung. The choir may sing out of tune. A screaming infant may need to be removed from the sanctuary. But mostly there are no surprises.

"But once we leave the sanctuary and are no longer calling the shots, we are functionally invisible. Our Sunday visibility no longer defines us. We live in a messed-up world, and the people to whom we are pastor are involved in the mess. We become witnesses to what cannot be seen or heard by a people whose senses are blunted by secularity, by *oughtness*, by a job description."

I had a letter stuffed in my pocket that I had received just before coming on this retreat. I pulled it out and read a portion of it. It was from a pastor friend who was giving me a report on his son, Richard, who was completing his first two years as a pastor. His summary sentence was that his son was "experiencing the syndrome common to many new pastors, impatience with people's slowness or unwillingness to change."

I asked these seminarians who were about to become pastors what they thought of this new pastor's "impatience with people's slowness."

They were getting into this now. I sensed a change in the tone of our conversation. Instead of talking about what they *did* as pastors, they were now talking about who they *were* as pastors.

Stephanie, who had kicked off this part of our conversation, interjected: "I'm not very patient with Richard's impatience. I wonder how many miracles he has missed in his impatience."

Morris again. "This is good, helpful. Now that we are talking this way, I realize that for those twenty years that I was an engineer sitting in the pew each Sunday, I never had a patient pastor—they were all trying to get me 'with the program,' shape me up, get me, as they put it, 'involved.' I don't want to become a pastor like that. I don't think that is what pastors are for."

Several times in the course of our conversations Matthew had compared what he was understanding the pastoral vocation to be to the life of an artist— potters and musicians and writers. He himself was a poet who had just had his first slim book of poems published. He was noticing a lot of parallel between poets working with words and pastors working with souls—that just as every poem is unique, so every soul is unique. "If we just copy rhythms or rhymes, we end up with doggerel verse." I added to his poet analogy the words of my long-dead friend, von Hügel, that "there are no dittos in souls."

Irene hadn't said much in our conversations. But she had been doing a lot of note taking. A consensus seemed to be emerging, and we were nearing the time for departure. I asked her if she would tell us what we had been saying. She was shy, hesitant. Then she said, "I don't know if I can do that. Let me tell you what I have been saying, without saying anything aloud. When I get a congregation, I want to be a patient pastor. I want to have eyes to see and ears to hear what God is doing and saying in their lives. I don't want to judge them in terms of what I think they should be doing. I want to be a witness to what God is doing in their lives, not a schoolmistress handing out grades for how well they are doing something for God. I think I see something unique about being a pastor that I had never noticed: the pastor is the one person in the community who is free to take men and women seriously just as they are, appreciate them just as they are, give them the dignity that derives from being the 'image of God,' a God-created being who has eternal worth without having to prove usefulness or be good for anything. I know that I will be doing a lot of other things too, but I might be the only person who is free to do this. I don't want to be so impatient with the mess that I am not around to see the miracle being formed. I don't want to conceive of my life as pastor so functionally that the mystery gets squeezed out of both me and the congregation."

I asked Irene if when she got home she would write out what she had just said to us and mail it to me. The above is what I received in the mail a week later. If I were to be asked for a brief word of counsel to the pastors of America, this is what I would say. I would give it this heading: *Pastor Irene's Manifesto*.

**I** remembered an incident that had taken place in Athens the previous spring. Jan and I with another couple had been in Israel for a couple weeks and were returning home with a stopover of a few days in Greece. One day we were strolling through the Parthenon on the Acropolis. I was telling Jan and friends Greek stories. After a while I noticed a young woman and man following us, listening in. At one point the woman said to me, "Can we walk with you? We started out with a guide but got bored—he didn't tell us any stories. So we dropped out. Would you mind?" We welcomed them to join us. Her name was Roxanne; his, Mark.

We finished up on the Parthenon and walked down to the city streets. For the next couple of hours we explored the city. When we got to the Areopagus, I talked about Paul's preaching his sermon on the Unknown God.

Roxanne said with surprised excitement, "Paul was here? I didn't know Paul was here. What was he doing here?"

And then Roxanne asked me, "What do you do? Are you a history professor?"

I said, "No, I'm a pastor."

She said, "Oh, pastor. I knew that it must be something good!" She grabbed my arm and held on.

Pastor—it must be something good: an affirmation of who I was from someone who didn't know who I was. I wasn't used to this. Very few people know what a pastor is when he or she is not doing something socially recognized as pastor.

Then she told us her story. She was on a trip through Europe by herself as a gift on graduation from her university in Quebec. She was French speaking—all her English words were spoken with a French pronunciation. She had been reared as Catholic but had drifted away from it in university. While in France she had happened on the ecumenical Christian community at Taizé and recovered her long dormant faith. She decided that she no longer wanted to continue as a tourist but would turn her trip into a pilgrimage. She went to Spain, walked a few pilgrimage miles on the Camino de Santiago, prayed at St. Teresa's Ávila and St. Ignatius's Manresa.

Rome was next, with its churches and holy sites. Having run out of pilgrimage sites, she had come on to Greece. She met Mark, an American, on the train, and they were now traveling together. She didn't know that there were holy places in Greece, didn't know that there were early churches established here, didn't know Paul had been here. Suddenly she was back on pilgrimage again, visiting and praying at the places of her spiritual origins. And now she had met a pastor, of all things. She was full of questions, brimming with enthused curiosity, as she reinforced her newfound identity as a Christian.

And now, a year later, as we were finishing up our retreat, the Roxanne story came to mind as a way of reinforcing our identity as pastors when we are not self-conscious of being pastors. Much (most?) pastoral work takes place when we don't know we are being pastors.


## "LET US WORSHIP GOD"

Meanwhile, the most visible thing I did each week was stand before the congregation in the sanctuary on Sunday and say, "Let us worship God." Sunday worship anchored the week. The act of worship, letting the scriptures be authoritative as the text to live by for the rest of the week, the recasting of our collective lives in answering prayer, the meeting with one another as brothers and sisters—not competitors, not threats. It was not only the most visible, it was also the most important thing I did. But there was a great deal of invisibility beneath that Sunday visibility.

Claire was a new Christian. She was vice-president in a Baltimore bank and a recovering alcoholic. After she had been with us for five years, she was promoted and assigned to a bank in Philadelphia. When a person or family left our congregation, the last Sunday they worshipped with us we had a service of dismissal just before the benediction, prayed a blessing, and presented them with a framed photograph of the church sanctuary that had been taken by one of our artist photographers. The week after we had done this with Claire, she came to my study to reflect on her years with us as a new and developing Christian. It was a totally unanticipated way of life for her. She had never worshipped in a Christian congregation. I asked her what the most difficult thing was for her in the service of worship.

"The silence. You say 'Let us pray,' and then you don't say anything for maybe twenty or thirty seconds—but it seems forever. I couldn't handle the silence. I'd get all anxious and fidgety. I almost quit coming I was so uncomfortable. And then after a couple months I calmed down. Then I started liking it. And now, when you finally start praying, I say inwardly, *Oh, not yet, pastor. I'm not ready yet.* I guess I thought that worship was something I had to do, or it was something you were doing. It was in worship that I became quiet and listening and present before God for the first time in my life. And the silence was my way in. Those twenty-five seconds of silence were better than any of your twenty-five minute sermons."

Eunice always sat a couple pews behind and a little to the left of Claire. She was there every Sunday for twenty-six years. When she left the sanctuary after the benediction, she always handed me a folded piece of paper that she had torn from the worship bulletin and said, "This is what you preached today." After the first few times, I knew it was not a good idea to look right then at what she had given me. Later in my study, after all the worshippers had left, I would read what Eunice had written, her summary of my sermon in ten words or less. "Don't quit, tomorrow's another day" . . . "Keep smiling, it's going to be okay" . . . "Don't let the bastards get you down" . . . "There's light at the end of the tunnel" . . . "This is your lucky day" . . . There was never any mention of

God or the scripture text or her own soul. The sermon that I had spent seven or eight hours preparing reduced to something that could just as well have come out of a fortune cookie. Maybe it did. In the privacy of my study I crumpled the paper and threw it, with considerable irritation, into the wastebasket. But after a couple years I got over it and replaced my irritation with a grudging thanks for this tangible weekly evidence that for at least one person in the congregation I had not been incomprehensible, only misunderstood.

# PART IV

## GOOD DEATHS

**I think that the dying pray at the last
not "please" but "thank you."**

*—Annie Dillard*

Jan and I were visiting a Benedictine monastery, Christ in the Desert, in New Mexico. One of the brothers was leading us on a path from prayers in the chapel to the refectory where we would have lunch. The path led through the cemetery. We passed an open grave.

Jan said, "Oh, did one of the brothers just die?"

"No, that is for the next one."

Three times a day, on their way from praying together to eating together, the monks are reminded that one of them will be "the next one."

And I was reminded that there is a long tradition in the church's life that the pastoral vocation consists in preparing people for "a good death." That tradition does not flourish in the American church. The widespread "denial of death" (Ernest Becker) that suffuses American culture now permeates the Christian church. But death, whether as metaphor, "I die daily," or as physical fact, "Blessed are those who die in the Lord," is given a lot of attention in our scriptures.

Resurrection does not have to do exclusively with what happens after we are buried or cremated. It does have to do with that, but first of all it has to do with the way we live right now. But as Karl Barth, quoting Nietzsche, pithily reminds us: "Only where graves are is there resurrection." We practice our death by giving up our will to live on our own terms. Only in that relinquishment or renunciation are we able to practice resurrection.

*A beech tree in winter, white*
*Intricacies unconcealed*
*Against sky blue and billowed*
*Clouds, carries in its emptiness*
*Ripeness: sap ready to rise*
*On signal, buds alert to burst*
*To leaf. And then after a season*
*Of summer a lean ring to remember*
*The lush fulfilled promises.*
*Empty again in wise poverty*
*That lets the reaching branches stretch*
*A millimeter more toward heaven,*
*The bole expand ever so slightly*
*And push roots into the firm*
*Foundation, lucky to be leafless:*
*Deciduous reminder to let it go.*

# 36
## THE NEXT ONE

The first baptism I performed in the underground sanctuary of what would soon become Christ Our King Church was of our son, Eric. Later he became a pastor who baptized. The baptismal font, from which I baptized him into the death and resurrection of Jesus, had been given to our new congregation-in-formation by an older Baltimore church. It was over a hundred years old at the time of Eric's baptism. It was constructed of substantial oak, a solid piece of liturgical furniture that, along with the oak communion table given to us by that same church, rooted our congregation in generations of acts of worship on Maryland soil, proclaiming death and resurrection. Baptism is our first basic intimation of death—first a dying and then a resurrection in Christ.

We were new at this: worship and baptism and Eucharist. But we weren't starting from scratch. The baptismal font and communion table had been brought over from Scotland in the mid-nineteenth century by a Presbyterian pastor sent to form a congregation in Maryland.

Steve and Sarah were both seniors in college. They had grown up in our congregation. I was the only pastor they had ever known. For the last couple years when home on vacation they would come—sometimes singly, sometimes together—and talk with me about becoming a pastor. "How does it feel . . . what exactly do you do . . . when did you decide to do this?" This was spring vacation. Graduation was imminent. It was time to make decisions about what they would be doing the rest of their lives. Their opening question this time was "What do you like best about being a pastor?"

"Baptisms and funerals."

On another occasion, when I was on retreat with the seminarians, I had answered that question with, "the mess." This time it was "baptisms and funerals." Sarah and Steve said they expected something more on the order of "Leading worship and preaching." Maybe if I had taken time to think about the question, I would have said that.

We talked about it. Leading worship and preaching is certainly the most conspicuous thing I do. But my spontaneous response touched on something basic about pastoral work that is not conspicuous. That is what we ended up talking about that day—that most pastoral work consists in pointing away from yourself to something other than you.

I had never articulated it just this way before. "You are at your pastoral best when you are not noticed. To keep this vocation healthy requires constant self-negation, getting out of the way. A certain blessed anonymity is inherent in pastoral work. For pastors, being noticed easily develops into *wanting* to be noticed. Many years earlier a pastor friend told me that the pastoral ego 'has the reek of disease about it, the relentless smell of the self.' I've never forgotten that."

This was new territory for Sarah and Steve. The three of us discussed it for the next hour, how a clamoring ego needs to be purged from the pastor's soul. From every Christian's soul for that matter, but pastors are at special risk. Baptisms and funerals are especially useful in this purging, acts of worship in which the pastor is most inconspicuous, almost incidental to the real action. All the attention and all the emotions are focused on the one being baptized, the one being buried. Baptism—buried with Christ, a relinquishment, a death, and then raised into a life that practices the resurrection of Christ. The funeral—a death that is a witness to resurrection. At neither baptism nor funeral is the pastor front and center. Get used to it.

That same baptismal font from which Eric was baptized in Maryland has since been placed in the church study of his congregation in Washington State. Placed alongside desk, books, telephone, and computer—the usual parapher-nalia of the pastor's study—that baptismal font, where he got his start in this death-and-resurrection business, now grounds and centers his daily work in the death of Christ. Also resurrection, but first, and don't forget it, the death.

At funerals Eric always uses the phrase "[name] has completed his (her) baptism." The death that becomes resurrection. At the baptismal font, at the graveside. I like that—dying with Christ, raised with Christ.

The telephone call was from my brother. "If you want to see Dad before he dies, you better come quickly." I did want to see him. Jan and I took the next plane to Montana. I told my congregation that I didn't know when I would be back—my father was dying, and I wanted to be with him in his death. He had been ill with cancer for a couple years. As it turned out, we were with him for ten days.

My mother was in advanced stages of Alzheimer's. Jan took care of her. Our daughter, Karen, was working as a freelance artist in Helena. She drove a couple hundred miles to be with us and to take care of the meals and laundry. I took care of my father, who was in a lot of pain. A public-health nurse came to the house and taught me, practicing on an orange, how to give morphine injections. He had difficulty walking—mostly I had to carry him.

We had never been very close. He gave most of his attention to his meat-cutting business. I was covetous of his attention but never got what I wanted. But in these ten final days of his life, I received a full measure of the intimacy that I had missed growing up. It was more than enough. I was with him con-stantly, giving him his morphine injections and carrying him. The intimacy went deeper than the physical—a retroactive *soul* intimacy.

My brother and sister and I were with him through his last night. And God was very much with us. He died as the spring sun was rising. We read Psalm 90 with him. As he died, we were all able to be with him touching and holding him. As the undertakers removed his body from our home, an osprey circled above the ponderosa pines, giving its distinctive cry. We all heard it as a benediction. My brother and brother-in-law were both pastors. The three of us conducted the funeral. A good death.

Eight months later my mother died of a heart attack while sleeping. My sister and brother, with their spouses, had been taking turns caring for her. Our family of pastors again conducted the funeral of our mother. She had been ordained as a pastor years before any of us were. While I was reading the scriptures, tears erupted. I tried to hold them back, then gave in. I remember thinking, "All these people get to grieve, now it's my turn," and let it come, sobbing uncontrollably. After thirty seconds or so, I recovered my composure and finished what I was doing. After the benediction, I didn't want to see anyone and slipped into a room just off the chancel. My daughter, Karen, came in and sat beside me, without words, putting her hand on my thigh. And then a man I didn't know came in, put his arm across my shoulder, spoke for three or four minutes in preacher clichés, and prayed. After he left I said, "Oh Karen, I hope I have never done that to anyone."

"Oh Daddy, I know that you would never do that."

She was very gracious. But I *had* done that—thankfully though, not for a long time.

Back in Maryland, resuming my pastoral work bracketed by baptisms and funerals, the impact of these two funerals, these good deaths, began to seep into my consciousness more personally than ever. I reported the deaths to my congregation. The legacies of death. The phrase "good death" became a part of the congregation's vocabulary. My father, a priest in his butcher shop, giving me my first sense of congregation; my mother's songs and stories, instilling in me a pastoral imagination.

I was the oldest child. My parents had always been ahead of me, clearing the way, showing the way. And now they were gone. I suddenly felt vulnerable, naked, exposed. I had conducted many funerals, but none had brought these feelings to the surface quite like these two. I was the next one.

# 37

## WIND WORDS

I was walking down the seminary hallway to give my lecture. As I passed the president's office, he bounced into the hall (Sam is nothing if not ebullient), took my arm, led me to a mahogany leather chair across from his desk, and sat me down: "Eugene, why don't you come here next year and be our pastor-writer-in-residence? You would love this place."

No small talk, no preamble. Abrupt, energetic, to the point. His energy was infectious.

I had only met President Calian the day before when I arrived at Pittsburgh Presbyterian Seminary to deliver lectures over the next three days. In seven months I would be unemployed. But he didn't know that. I didn't know what I would do to make a living. I didn't know where we would live.

I asked him how he knew I was planning to leave my congregation. Jan and I hadn't yet told anyone.

"I didn't know. Didn't know you were free to do this. Intuition, I guess.

After last night's lecture and seeing you just now, it seemed to me a perfect fit. It seemed the right thing to do to ask you. We can't give you any money, but we have a furnished apartment and you can take all your meals in the refectory. You will have no duties except to team-teach a theology course with me for one semester. But if you don't have a job lined up and don't have a place to live, I think I'm the providence of God in your life right now."

That's how we ended up at Pittsburgh Seminary for the academic year 1991–92.

The previous summer while we were in Montana reflecting on and assessing our lives in the sacred space and time of our annual holy-land pilgrimage, we found ourselves wondering if we were sensing a change in the air. Since the time of my Pastor John of Patmos conversion to a pastoral vocation in New York City, Jan and I had never imagined not being a pastor and pastor's wife. And we had never considered being pastor in another church. But that summer we found ourselves wondering if our vocational life was beginning to take a turn.

Fatigue was part of it. The congregation was manageable, about five hundred. But we had now lived in the neighborhood for twenty-eight years, and a lot of people who didn't have a pastor considered us their pastor—a "working congregation" of at least a thousand. And that was not manageable. But writing was also part of it. I had never felt any conflict or tension between being a pastor and being a writer. The vocational yin and yang were pretty well integrated into the way of life that Jan and I had lived for thirty years. But for the last couple years I had written almost nothing—the immediate demands of the day-by-day life of the congregation that I was accustomed to being absorbed into the larger rhythms set down in Lord's Day worship and then improvised in the salvation melodies and creation riffs between Sundays were feeling more like interruptions—intrusions.

So we decided to make this pilgrimage month a time of listening, listening, really listening to the Spirit, the Wind Words. Our listening post was the edge of a cliff overlooking our amphitheater lake where the acoustics were ideal for listening to the Wind Words. Every day at noon before we prepared lunch, we spent an hour listening and talking, discerning and paying attention: *Come, Holy Spirit.* By the time we returned to our church in Maryland that summer, we had made our decision: in one year we would leave our congregation. We didn't know how we would make a living but assumed writing would be involved. We didn't know where we would live but hoped that the Pacific Northwest might provide a home—our three children had already moved there. But however the details worked out, we would leave our Maryland congregation.

We also decided not to say anything to anyone for nine months. We would use the nine months as a buffer to test the authenticity of our discernment. We consulted with two families who knew us well. Otherwise we carried on as usual—"until death do us part." If the decision held up, we would tell the congregation after the nine months. That would give us three months for leave-taking. In August, twelve months after listening for the Wind Words at our Montana listening post on the cliff, we would leave.

Four months into our assigned time of discernment, our younger son, Leif, came home for Christmas vacation. We told him that this might be our last Christmas together in this house. We hadn't told anyone yet but would probably be leaving midsummer. He was doing graduate study at the University of Colorado in Boulder, studying creative writing with the novelist Ed Dorn—his launch into a writer's life in poetry and fiction. One day as we were talking about the writer's life, he said, "Dad, novelists only write one book. They find their voice, their book, and write it over and over. William Faulkner wrote one book. Charles Dickens wrote one book. Anne Tyler wrote one book. Ernest Hemingway wrote one book. Willa Cather wrote one book."

I wasn't quite sure I agreed, but he obviously knew more about the subject than I did, so I didn't say much.

A few days later, he said, "Remember what I said about novelists only writing one book? You only preach one sermon."

I protested. "I don't repeat myself in the pulpit. I work hard on these sermons. Every week is new, the world changes, the lives of these people are changing constantly. And each sermon is new, these scriptures personalized into their language and circumstances. I live with these scriptures; I live with these people. My sermon is a way for them to hear their stories integrated into

God's story, or God's story integrated into their stories. Either way it's a story in the making—new details every week, new in the telling, new in the making."

That stopped him. He changed the subject.

On Christmas morning we had our traditional breakfast of Jan's freshly baked Swedish tea ring and shirred eggs with link sausages. Then we opened our gifts. When I opened Leif's gift for me, I exclaimed, "Leif, cowboy boots! How did you know that I've always wanted cowboy boots?" (Cowboy boots are expensive. How did he, a penurious student in graduate school, afford this?)

"I've been watching you for years, Dad. Every time I come home, take off my boots and throw them on the floor, you are right there, fondling them, trying them on. I thought it was time you had your own. But there are strings attached. You have to wear them in the pulpit on Sunday."

"I can't do that. Wear cowboy boots with a pulpit robe? I can't do that. It wouldn't be, well . . . *fitting*, appropriate. Pastors are supposed to be inconspicuous, not call attention to themselves. If I showed up in cowboy boots, that's all they would see. Worship of God would go out the window. And the sermon? Forget the sermon. Cowboy boots would trump the text. No, I can't wear cowboy boots into the pulpit."

Leif had quit listening. "Sorry, Dad. That makes me feel bad. It looks as if this will be the last time I will hear you preach at Christ Our King. I was thinking that the cowboy boots would give it a touch of celebration. Mark an era. Guess I'll have to take them back."

I did wear the cowboy boots on Sunday. Leif was right—it did mark an era. And if not a celebration, at least a hint of jauntiness. But I was also right—there was more whispering in the pews about the boots I was wearing than listening to what I was saying.

After Sunday worship as we were having lunch, Leif said, "Well, Dad, that was your sermon. I've been listening to that sermon all my life. Your one sermon, your signature sermon."

This time I changed the subject.

Later that week, Jan and I drove Leif to Baltimore–Washington International Airport for his flight back to Colorado. I was wearing my cowboy boots. In the course of our preflight small talk Leif said, "When I get back to Boulder,

I think I'll look for another church. First Church is too big—I don't know anybody; nobody knows me."

We didn't hear any more about changing churches. In a telephone conversation three months later, I remembered what he had said at the airport. "By the way, Leif, have you found another church?"

"No. I tried a bunch of them but I'm back at First Church. None of those other pastors had found their sermon."

Oh. So *that's* what he meant.

The decision to leave did hold up. We anticipated it would be extremely difficult—uprooting ourselves from all the emotional attachments and well-developed intimacies that gave such a rich texture to our lives. Leaving this place of worship and witness where God had faithfully revealed himself and God's Spirit had created so much resurrection life. But as it turned out, leaving our congregation was surprisingly easy. Effortless almost. They expressed a decent sadness at our leaving but nothing hysterical or melodramatic. It seemed a confirmation that this was the right thing to do, not only right for us but also right for the congregation. And the cowboy boots were the appropriate footwear for returning, as we then anticipated, to the West.

# 38

## FYODOR

I had no way of knowing it at the time we said our good-byes to our congregation that seeds sown several years before were going to produce a new congregation, but a congregation that would take us a while to recognize as such. The seeds were translations into an American vernacular of parts of the New Testament and Psalms that I had been doing for several years for my congregation. They were occasional, piecemeal, local, pastoral work. But some of them had been published through the years in the context of other things that I was writing. I thought of them as *pastoral* translations.

On April 30, 1990, I received a letter that would eventually give us this new congregation. The letter was from the senior editor at NavPress who had read some of these published fragments, inviting me to translate the Bible into contemporary, vernacular American English. He began by telling me that he had read a book I had written on St. Paul's letter to the Galatians. What he liked most in the book, and the part he couldn't get out of his mind, was my translation of Paul's Greek text. He told me that he had made copies of the sections of translation, taped them together, and had been carrying them around for a whole year now, reading Galatians to his family and friends. He was getting really tired of Galatians and wanted to see if he could get me to translate the entire New Testament.

I was intrigued, but didn't take the suggestion seriously. Translate the *Bible*?

"Sorry," I said. "I'm glad you like it. But I'm a pastor. It took me two years to do that—and Galatians is one of the shorter books in the New Testament. And besides, I did it as a pastoral act."

I had sensed that these people to whom I was pastor were slipping into a kind of Americanized religion in which they were becoming conformed to the security systems and consumer satisfactions of the culture around them. I wanted to recover the energetic vigor of Paul's insistence on living original lives in Christ, not lives sustained by hand-me-downs from the culture. Subtle signs had been accumulating for some time that these people to whom I had been a pastor for twenty years were losing their sharp sense of Christian identity. I wanted to tell them again who they were, free men and women in Christ: "for freedom Christ has set us free!"

Galatians is Paul's freedom letter. I spent two years teaching and preaching Galatians, hoping to free their Americanized imaginations for living freely in Christ. As I was doing that, I translated Paul's Greek into my congregation's American, the language they used in their workplaces and around the house— "Christ has set us free to live a free life. So take your stand! Never again let anyone put a harness of slavery on you."

For a number of years I had also translated from Hebrew several psalms for my congregation into what I thought of as "American." But I didn't think of it as translation. It was a pastoral act, a way of teaching them to pray. Sometimes I did it for a single individual as a way to provide guidance in prayer. A common difficulty in developing a life of prayer is trying to be "nice" before God, using polite language, telling God what we think he wants to hear. But the psalms, the prayer book of the Bible, are not at all nice or polite. The Hebrew in which they were first prayed and written is a rough language, down-to-earth, very little of which we would designate "spiritual," and certainly nothing pious. The Hebrews used the same language when they prayed that they used to scold their children, buy and sell in the market, praise the beauties of mountain and stream, eagles and doves, and complain bitterly of injustice and betrayal. They didn't have a special language for prayer and another for everything else. One language—business language, social language, street language, prayer language.

So I wasn't entirely a newcomer to the world of translation, but the translation I had done always had been in the immediate context of my congregation, a local pastoral act getting the lived, colloquial quality of these ancient Hebrew and Greek originals into the American words and metaphors and syntax these people had been using all their lives.

Translating the Bible apart from the congregation that I was leading in worship, teaching and preaching, was something that would never have occurred to me.

Three months after that April 30, 1990, letter Jan and I made our tentative decision to leave Christ Our King—the month of the "Wind Words." In the year that followed, the decision to leave was thoroughly tested with numerous confirmations along the way. Our last Sunday was July 21, 1991. It was turning out to be a good death.

We were nearing the end of our twenty-nine Christ Our King years. Meanwhile letters continued to be exchanged between me in Maryland and the editor in Colorado. Interest picked up on my part, knowing that I would soon be free to take on this serious assignment if the editor continued to be serious about it. The editor, soon to be *my* editor, made suggestions. I provided drafts.

We met for the first time on August 27, 1991, at a daylong meeting in Colorado with the NavPress staff and senior editor who had proposed the translation. The editor had an impressive Dostoevsky beard, gray and flourishing, that conferred considerable authority. After sixteen months of saying a tentative maybe, Jan and I said yes to the proposed translation. With that yes my work for the next year came into focus: I would translate the New Testament and Psalms into "American." In the process I would discover that I again had a congregation.

From then on, between ourselves, in awe mingled with affection, Jan and I referred to our editor as Fyodor. We would work together for the next ten years, an intense collaboration that became *The Message*. In the process a deep, enduring, and prayerful friendship was established.

And a bonus: we already had the gift of the appointment as pastor-writer-in-residence at Pittsburgh Presbyterian Seminary for the academic year 1991–92. It turned out to be a most congenial, hospitable, and God-fearing place to do the translation.

Just as I had earlier discovered that I had been a pastor all my life without knowing it, I now discovered that I had been a translator for a long time without knowing it. As I set out to translate the New Testament and eventually the Old Testament into contemporary American, I found that most of the work had already been done. The translation, *The Message,* grew from the soil of thirty years of pastoral work. Planted in the soil of my congregation and community, the seed words of the Bible germinated and grew and matured. When it came time to do the actual writing there in Pittsburgh, I felt that I was walking through an orchard at harvest time, plucking fully formed apples and peaches and plums from the laden branches. There is hardly a page in the Bible, this lively revelation of God in Christ, that I had not seen lived in some way or other by the men and women, saints and sinners, to whom I was pastor—and then verified in my neighborhood and culture.

I lived in two language worlds, the world of the Bible and the world of Today. I had always assumed they were the same world. But my congregation didn't see it that way. So out of necessity I became a "translator" (although I wouldn't have called it that then), daily standing on the border between two language worlds, getting the language of the Bible that God uses to create and save us, heal and bless us, judge and rule over us, translated into the language of Today that we use to gossip and tell stories, give directions and do business, sing songs, and talk to our children.

And all the time those old biblical languages that I had spent several years teaching in the seminary thirty years before, those powerful and vivid Hebrew and Greek originals, had been working their way underground in my speech, giving energy and sharpness to words and phrases, expanding the imagination of the people with whom I was working to hear the language of the Bible in the language of Today and the language of Today in the language of the Bible.

# 39

## THE PHOTOGRAPH

We arrived in Pittsburgh in a Penske rental truck with a few housekeeping goods and an old photograph. The first thing we did after unloading was place the photograph on the kitchen table—a faded photograph curled at the edges, mounted in a cheap dime-store frame. The face in the photograph was my maternal grandfather, Andre Hoiland.

My grandfather Hoiland died twenty years before I was born, so I have no memory of him. But by being given Hoiland as my middle name, I have kept the name in circulation. I knew only two things about my grandfather. He came to Pittsburgh in 1900 to work in the steel mills. When he had saved up enough money, he returned to the family farm in Stevanger, Norway, and brought his wife and nine children to America. This time he bypassed Pittsburgh and continued by train to Montana, where some Norwegian neighbors had immigrated to earlier. The second thing I knew about him was that he told troll stories, stories that then continued to be passed on and elaborated on by my storytelling aunts and uncles and mother.

His photograph was on our table because we, like him, were in Pittsburgh as a stopover in this transition interim in our lives. He was fifty-eight years old when he arrived in Pittsburgh; I was the same age when I arrived ninety years later. Most mornings, eating oatmeal cereal and rye toast, Jan and I imagined what his life must have been like in the steel mills, the huge shift from a farm overlooking a pristine Norwegian fjord to being buried in the noise and heat and ugliness of mill work where three polluted industrial rivers—Allegheny, Monongahela, Ohio—joined. Immersed in a new language, separated from his children and wife—what was that like?

We were experiencing, though not so radically, some disorientation of our own. The photograph on our kitchen table, flanked by salt and pepper shakers, marked Pittsburgh as a historical site in our family—my grandfather in Pittsburgh, a significant place of transition. We were not complete strangers in Pittsburgh; my grandfather had slept there. But we didn't know exactly where in Pittsburgh or for how long (maybe two years?).

But the troll stories spilled out details that kept us familiar with the names and participants in a geography, immigration, and work that now included us. Grandpa Hoiland left a heritage of storytelling in the family. My uncles and aunts and mother told troll stories, embellishing the story trove of their father. It was a treasure ample enough for us to get in on the inheritance.

The basic Hoiland troll story from which all the troll stories developed was of a troll named Skogen. It was adequately capacious to keep all the family members together in a welcoming bouillabaisse of narrative.

When the Hoiland family immigrated to Montana, they brought Skogen with them. Trolls are mischievous creatures, pranksters who delight in playing tricks on people, but endearingly playful, tumbling and romping like kittens and puppies. They are two to three feet tall and have a tail. It is well documented in ancient runes that trolls are a uniquely Scandinavian mutant of the basic human species. They are all over Norway and Sweden, living in caves and other shelters, and usually, despite their mischievousness, put up with by Norwegians. The Swedes, not nearly as tolerant, treat them as pests.

When the Hoiland family left Norway, they knew they would never see a troll again. The children clamored and begged their father to find a way to bring Skogen, their favorite troll, with them. Papa Hoiland finally, but reluctantly, gave in. But it would have to be clandestine. Nobody must know.

So they built a chest with breathing holes to keep him alive but hidden on the voyage. They carried an enclosed bucket of lutefisk, the national dish of Norway, to feed him. But there was a problem. Trolls, playful and adorable as they are, stink. Trolls are elusive and mostly stay out of sight. They are usually detected by their body odor. Four sons, Reuben, Sven, Ernie, and Egil were assigned the responsibility of moving the chest around the ship's deck so that the troll stench would not attract attention. Their strategy was to always keep it in position so that the wind would blow any smell out to sea, away from where people were gathered. They did a good job. They arrived in New York harbor with Skogen undiscovered.

From New York they took the train to Montana. From the train station, they hired a wagon to take them to the lake where some Norwegian friends had preceded them and secured some lakeshore land. They camped there until they could obtain housing. They opened the chest and released Skogen from his cramped quarters. After all those weeks of confinement he simply went wild, leaping and somersaulting, climbing trees and jumping into the lake. He was the first troll ever in Montana, probably in the entire country. But he was also an illegal immigrant, so they had to keep him out of the way, which wasn't all that difficult since he was naturally shy and reclusive. But when it was just the family there, he had the run of the place and made the most of it.

That was the basic Skogen story from which my grandfather's imagination developed an endless stream of troll stories, turning into a complex mythology of tales that included all the brothers and sisters as they became Americans. The distinction between the troll and my uncles and aunts wasn't always clear. Probably all the stories had some kernel of fact to them, but in the telling and retelling, it was anybody's guess what it was. By the time I heard the stories from my mother and uncles and aunts, my feeling was that every detail was true in some sense or other, but maybe not factual. This was oral family history in which everyone participated as they went along. By the time I became a father and grandfather, I had entered into the mythmaking myself and was making free with embellishments of my own.

"What's that funny looking branch on that tree, grandpa?" I was sitting with three of my grandchildren on the lakeshore about fifty feet from a twelve-foot cliff that my children and now my grandchildren jumped from, making cannonballs in the lake. A Rocky Mountain juniper grew at the edge of the cliff, and one of its branches was bare and drooped with the weight of some kind of diseased growth at the end of it—a thick round ball of needles about ten inches in diameter. Seven-year-old Lindsay had asked the question.

"That's Skogen's tail."

"But how did it get there?" This was five-year-old Sadie.

Time for a new troll story. "When my grandparents arrived here from Norway with their nine children and the troll Skogen, they found this place on the lake—it looked just like Norway—and built a cabin. You know a few Skogen stories. This is one of my favorites. You'll remember that trolls are mischievous and like to sneak up on people and play practical jokes. Skogen was like all trolls that way. His tail was longer than most, and he was very vain about it. He was forever grooming it and admiring its reflection in the lake.

"But he had also picked up a bad habit since arriving in Montana. When people were swimming in the lake, he would sneak up on them underwater and bite off a toe, or a finger, or part of an ear. It wasn't such a big thing, and because they all loved Skogen so much and had so much fun with him, they indulged him. All my aunts and uncles walked funny because of missing toes. Uncle Reuben leaned back on his heels, like he was trying to keep his balance with a strong wind at his back. Obese Aunt Ursala shuffled. Uncle Egil listed to one side. My mother had only half an ear on her left side, but most people didn't know it because she kept it covered with her hair.

"One Sunday after church my grandfather invited the preacher to come and have dinner. After the chicken and dumplings, they all went for a swim. Skogen was excited—all those toes in the water! But in his excitement at having the preacher there, he got carried away and bit off the preacher's leg right at the knee.

"Well, that was too much. Skogen had gone too far. All my uncles and aunts started chasing Skogen. He ran up onto the cliff and jumped into the water. As he jumped, his tail got caught in the juniper tree and was ripped off. Skogen got away, but his tail is still there, as you can see. Skogen was very vain about his tail. To be seen without that tail would be too humiliating—he just couldn't bear it. So he has never been seen since. But every once in a while you can smell him, just a whiff of troll stink, and so we know he is still around.

And every once in a while we would learn that a guest who had been visiting, on returning home, would realize that there was a toe missing."

Lindsay, who got this started, said, "Grandpa, is that true? Does Skogen really like body parts?"

"No, Lindsay, I just made it up."

"Are you sure?"

"I'm sure."

I did my best to reassure her. But it was a week before she would get into the water, and then only with great caution.

Pittsburgh, with my grandfather's photograph for company, marked the transition from being a pastor with a congregation alive with stories to being a professor of classrooms of students I didn't know and who didn't know me. Later it would be primarily as a writer of books for a congregation of readers whose faces I would never see, whose voices I would never hear, reading books by a man they would never see or hear. I thought my days as pastor were over. The loss was palpable. Like a death, like I had left the still waters and green pastures of pastoral life (*pastural* life?) for life in the desert. Jan and I were not at all reluctant to do this. Energies were accumulating as we anticipated our new assignment. We knew we couldn't continue the rigors, both physical and emotional, of being pastor to a congregation. All the same, we were aware that it would be a transition involving both gain and loss.

The year in Pittsburgh provided the time, place, and community to translate the New Testament and Psalms into *The Message*. As that work was coming to completion, we were invited to join the faculty at Regent College, Vancouver, Canada, and spent the next five and a half years there teaching spiritual theology. Sam, the Pittsburgh Seminary president, with his wife, Doris, had us for dinner in their home the evening before we set out for Vancouver. He asked, "What will you miss most about not being a pastor?"

"The intimacy, being a part of everyone's story and having them be part of ours. That daily blending of ordinary and salvation life, the conversations that so often develop into prayers. This incredible company of friends following Jesus. Creating forms of worship and hospitality that unobtrusively subvert the secularity and individualism of the culture."

I had never thought of it quite that way until I said it. But there it was. Not entirely, of course. But I had grown up in a family of storytellers. I had been a pastor in a community of storymaking. The text I lived by, the Bible, was a long, deep immersion in a way of life that was rendered in story.

Story is a way of language in which everything and everyone is organically related. Story is a way of language that insists that persons cannot be known by reducing them to what they do, how they perform, the way they look. Story uses a language in which listening has joint billing with speaking. Story is language put to the use of discovering patterns and meanings—beauty and truth and goodness: Father, Son, and Holy Spirit. In the seemingly random and disconnected pieces of experience and dreams, tasks and songs, promises and betrayals that make up daily life, words and sentences detect and reveal and fashion stories in places of hospitality.

# 40

## DEATH IN THE DESERT

Unlike my grandfather, who, after collecting his family from Norway, immigrated to Montana, when we left Pittsburgh the next day, Jan and I went to Canada, across the continent all the way to Vancouver and Regent College, where I was installed in the recently endowed James Houston Chair of Spiritual Theology. On our arrival at the bed-and-breakfast we had booked, our hostess greeted us with "Welcome to godless Canada, this godforsaken desert."

Undeterred by the gloomy welcome, we easily found West Point Grey Church within walking distance, where we worshipped with a hundred or so Christians each Sunday. And we soon discovered that we were only a twenty-minute walk the other direction to the Spanish Banks, an extensive sandy beach on English Bay. It didn't take us long to establish our Sabbath ritual: worship with the Christians in the morning; return to our apartment and prepare a picnic lunch; then walk to the Spanish Banks, spread a tablecloth on the sand, and eat our lunch in the company of the godless Canadians.

In our thirty years of keeping Sabbath together we had simplified our definition of Sabbath-keeping to three words: pray and play. On Sabbath we would do nothing that was necessary, obligatory, "useful." We would set the day apart for the unfettered, the free, the unearned. Pray and play.

On our first Sunday lunch on the Spanish Banks, we were struck by the vigor with which the Canadians participated in at least 50 percent of Sabbath practice, these Canadians that our bed-and-breakfast hostess had alerted us to as godless. They knew how to play. We had never been in the midst of such a riot of play—ever. Frisbees sailing, kites flying, volleyballs set up and spiked, kayaks and canoes and sailboats. Maybe we were being introduced to a form of symbiotic Sabbath-keeping: we were helping one another. Each Sunday Jan and I prayed in the morning to kick things off, and the Canadians picked up where we left off and played all the afternoon.

The observation was more than playful. It provided a point of vantage for noticing the trajectory of intentions that had been set in motion long ago, now ripening into maturity. Our bed-and-breakfast friend's use of "godless" and "desert" to describe our new country revived an old memory. When Jan and I were first married, we had talked seriously of dedicating the last ten years of our working life by offering ourselves as missionaries to a seminary in a third-world country. Now, after a month or so in Canada, we realized that the third world we had intended to go to thirty years before had come to us. The students with whom we were working were from Zimbabwe, Kenya, South Africa, Brazil, Argentina, Korea, Japan, Indonesia, India, Sri Lanka. Our student body was thoroughly international. If we were in a godless country and a spiritual desert, we *were* missionaries.

But a godless country? A spiritual desert? Well, maybe. But that was nothing new for us. We had started out as pastor and pastor's wife to form a Christian congregation in the 1960s, the decade of the funeral of God. The death of God was written up in the obituaries of newspapers and periodicals all over both Europe and North America. Pollsters were busy issuing monthly reports on the precipitous drop in church attendance. There was widespread panic, especially among pastors, at times verging on hysteria.

If God were dead, the church couldn't be far behind. Life-support systems were being proposed right and left to keep the church going. "Relevance" became the mantra of choice. New forms of church organization were proposed. Innovative strategies of public relations, misnamed evangelism, were launched with impressive fanfare. Worship was replaced by entertainment. Statistics trumped kerygma.

Didn't these people, especially the pastors who were driving ambulances with their sirens screaming from church to church, from conference to conference, know anything about death? A *good* death? Didn't they remember Jesus's words that "unless a grain of wheat falls into the earth and dies, it remains just a single grain; but if it dies, it bears much fruit"?

The Negev in Israel is a barren, featureless, and seemingly endless stretch of wilderness. There are no mountains, no rivers, no trees. Understandably, it is not a popular destination for people who go to Israel to get a feel for the biblical world. But that is why we were there, Jan and I, with a few friends, to get a feel for the biblical world. We walked in the Negev for five days. For the first day we didn't see anything—there was nothing to see. And then gradually, bit by bit, detail by detail, the emptiness of the desert began to show us a fullness that we had not anticipated.

It was our guide who insisted on the walking. "You don't get this by taking pictures. You have to make the trip." And the way you make the trip is on foot. "You acquire the biblical story mostly through your feet, only peripherally through your eyes and ears." My friend Arthur introduced me to the Spanish poet Machado's line, "The way is made by walking."

And so we walked—for five days. We walked through the landscape in which our faith was formed. Abraham walked here and built altars. Isaac walked here and dug wells. Moses walked here and herded sheep. We walked and assimilated through our feet the obvious but slowly comprehended realization that faith is formed on unimpressive ground, among invisibles, with few distractions.

We took a bus north to the Galilee and resumed our walking. Another five days of walking. We walked from village to village to village, Capernaum to Bethsaida to Chorazin and back to Capernaum, the "evangelical triangle" that served as the home base for Jesus's preaching and teaching. There is nothing left of these towns but ruins, but the ruins show that they were small towns and probably not of any political or historical significance since there are no ruins of forts or palaces.

It doesn't take many days of walking through the Negev, that seemingly godless and godforsaken desert, to realize that it might well be the least propitious piece of geography on earth on which to form a people of God that would "bless all the families of the earth." And it doesn't take long while walking in the "steps of Jesus" in out-of-the-way Galilee to realize that he chose to work with a few run-of-the-mill working-class people to launch and live out the story that is the gospel, the good news that is the kingdom of God.

Thirty years earlier, Pastor John of Patmos had supplied me with the imagination that served as the ultrasound that identified my nascent vocation as *pastor*. He continued to provide me with images that took the sting out of "godless" and "death." Godless Canada and America's dying church didn't seem all that different from Abraham's Negev and Jesus's Galilee. Robert Browning, one of our great poets, wrote a long and great valedictory poem on John that he named "Death in the Desert."

By this time we were used to godless and godforsaken, to death and deserts. Jan and I had been living among the godless in godforsaken deserts all our lives under the patronage of Pastor John of Patmos. Barth again: "only where graves are is there resurrection." We rather like the company.

Amen Yes.

# AFTERWORD
*Letter to a Young Pastor*

*Dear A—,*

*Your letter revives a wonderful memory—those years of vigorous correspondence between your father and me. The last mention he made of you in his letters was that you had "flunked churchgoing." I urged him to be patient. His death a year or so after that prevented me from knowing the outcome but his patience must have paid off since here you are, ten years later, not just back to "churchgoing" but for the last five years now pastor of a church, or as you put it, "finding my way as a pastor."*

*And yes, I would be honored to receive and respond to your letters, a welcome sequel to the letters your father and I exchanged. But I am not sure you can expect answers from me—think of it as something more like a conversation between two friends who share this pastoral vocation on the Way.*

*Your phrase "finding my way as a pastor" sets up resonance within me. As I look back on a lifetime in the pastoral vocation what I remember most is a kind of messiness: a lot of stumbling around, fumbling the ball, losing my way, and then finding it again. It is amazing now that anything came of it.*

*As we enter into conversation regarding just what goes into making up a pastoral vocation, one thing that comes to mind is the uniqueness—being a pastor is unique across the spectrum of vocations. Not better, not privileged, not anything special, but unique in society as a whole, also (but maybe not quite so much) unique in the company of the people of God. Not much transfers from other vocational roles to who we are, what we do.*

*One aspect of that uniqueness is that we make far more mistakes in our line of work than other so-called professionals. If physicians and engineers and lawyers and military officers made as many mistakes in their line of work as we do in ours, they would be out on the street in no time. It amazes me still how much of the time I simply don't know what I am doing, don't know what to say, don't know what the next move is. The temptation in that state of being is to determine to be competent at something or other. Unfortunately, there are many "ways of escape" in which we can exercise and develop areas of administrative or therapeutic or scholarly or programmatic competences in the church and in so doing avoid the ambiguity of being a pastor.*

*But I also had a sense much of the time (but not by any means continuously) that "not knowing what I am doing" is more or less what it feels like when I am "trusting in God" and "following Jesus." The position in which the church has placed us by ordaining us to this vocation means giving witness to what we don't know much about and can't explain—living into the mystery of salvation and holiness.*

*Here's a Psalm phrase that has given me some helpful clarity in the midst of the murkiness: "Blessed is the man who makes Yahweh his trust, who does not turn to the proud, to those who go astray after false gods" (Ps. 40:4). The "proud" for me in this context are those pastors who look like they "know what they're doing"—who are competent and recognized as such, who have an honored position in society and among their colleagues. And going "astray after false gods" amounts to living in response to something manageable, turning my vocation into a depersonalized job*

*that I can get good at. I'm probably reading more into this text than it*
*warrants, but it has given me a couple of images ("proud" and "astray")*
*that set off little alarm signals when I have sensed that I was betraying or*
*avoiding the uniqueness of pastor.*

*As I reflect with you on my fifty years in this pastoral vocation, it*
*strikes me right now as curious that I have almost no sense of achievement.*
*Doesn't that seem odd? What I remember is all the little detours into*
*"proud" and "astray" that I experienced, the near misses, the staggering*
*recoveries or semirecoveries of who I was and what I was about. People*
*who look at me now have no idea how precarious it felt at the time, how*
*many faithless stretches there were.*

*In retrospect, I think that the two things that preserved the uniqueness*
*of pastor for me were worship and family. I knew in my gut that the act*
*of worship with the congregation every week was what kept me centered*
*and that it needed to be guarded vigilantly—nothing could be permitted*
*to dilute or distract from it. And I knew that family provided the only*
*hope I had of staying grounded, faithful, personally relational, in the daily*
*practice of sacrificial love.*

*Maybe those things as such don't make pastor unique—everybody*
*has to deal with them. But our vocation is very public in what we do*
*in relation to God and a life of love. That public exposure opens up the*
*possibilities of either bluffing our way or constructing a way of life that is*
*competent but quite apart from trusting God or braving the intimacies of*
*love. People watch us. They see and are influenced either for good or bad*
*by the seriousness and reverence in which we order our response to God*
*(the showcase for this is Sunday worship); and they notice the way we live*
*with our families and friends—they see or don't see forgiveness and grace,*
*blessing and patience in our body language, gestures, and offhand remarks.*

*The daily, inescapable reality is that in neither of these areas, worship*
*or family, are we in complete control. If we try too hard we end up being*
*self-conscious, substituting our ego and performance and reputation for the*
*very thing we are committed to doing.*

*Is that enough for a start? Even though we have never met personally,*
*because of my long friendship with your father, I feel we are part of the*

*same family, which, of course, we are. But also companions in finding our way as pastors in this American culture that "knew not Joseph" and doesn't quite know what to make of us. That makes for lonely work. We need each other.*

*The peace of our Lord,*
*Eugene*

# ACKNOWLEDGMENTS

Three friends introduced me to the genre of memoir and guided me into imagining that I might be able to write one. Rick Christian, my agent and president of Alive Communications, was the first to suggest it and give me the confidence that I could do it. Ken Gire, a veteran writer and trusted friend, guided me through the initial stages. Jon Stine provided continuous insight and encouragement throughout the writing, from the first paragraph to the final period, testing each word and sentence for truth and accuracy. Memoir is new territory for me. I have always written from a text, mostly a biblical text. To have my vocation as the text felt awkward. I needed a lot of help to get past the awkwardness.

My editor, Michael Maudlin, and his staff at HarperOne gave assuring and expert counsel in revisions and made a better book out of what I handed to them. Don Ottenhoff, director of the Ecumenical Institute at St. John's Abbey, provided encouragement and direction when he didn't know he was doing it. David Wood probed my imagination for connections between pastor and writer.

No one achieves and continues the vocation of pastor by himself, herself. These are some of the pastors, writers, artists, and their spouses among whom I have found faithful and prayerful companionship: Tom and Debbie Abbot, Terry and Daphne Anderson, Dan and Anne Baumgartner, Arthur and Lorna Boers, Tim and Nancy Brown, Tracie and Marty Bullis, Matt and Julie Canlis, Kim and CC Crispeno, Michael and Nancy Crowe, Marva Dawn and Myron Sandberg, Peter and Tonya Erickson, Miles and Karen M. Finch, Kevin and Karen P. Finch, Constance FitzGerald, O.C.D., Lu and Peter Gerard, Diane Glancy, Dave and Debbie Hansen, Bill and Mollie Hopper, John and Skip Houdeshel, Trygve and Kristen Johnson, Faith and David Jongewaard, Paul and Rhoda Jones, Andy and Shawna Kennaly, Annemarie Kidder, Peter and Jenny Klenner, Endi and Kati Kovacs, Gisela Kreglinger, Jack and Linda Leax, Tom and Shirley Little, Steve and Laura Lympus, Bill and Valerie Mangrum, Hugh MacKenzie, Terry and Suzette McGonigal, Perry and Betty Monroe, Linda Nepsted, Cuba Dyer Odneal, Virginia and David Owens, Joyce and Ed Peasgood, Eric Peterson, Karen Peterson, Ken and Polly Peterson, Leif and Amy Peterson, Dean and Darlene Pinter, Wayne and Georgia Pris, Steven and Amy Purcell, Murray and Lynda Pura, Richard Shreffler (His Holiness), Alan and Brenda Reynolds, Luci Shaw and John Hoyte, Ray and Joan Sheck, Dan and Grace Ellen Schiel, Tom and Lollie Smith, Paul and Gail Stevens, David and Pheadra Taylor, Jeff and Kris Teeples, John and Lillian Toews, Steve and Bonnie Trotter, Cliff and Christine Warner, Louise Wheatley, Jeffrey Wilson, Ian and Madeleine Wilson, Bill and Mavis Wiseman, David and Jennifer Wood, Fred and Cheryl Wood, Jim and Cathie Wolfe, and Philip and Janet Yancey.

And congregation—the primary context in which the pastoral vocation is practiced. Because so much of my vocational life involves confidences that are privileged, lest I transgress inadvertently, with the exception of my family, I have changed most of the names and some of the circumstances. But I have done my best not to alter or embellish the truth that I am telling. I have told in other places and circumstances a few of the stories included here. At the time of the telling, I was not aware that they were part of a larger story. But in the course of writing this account of my pastoral formation, they surprised me by finding their place in a coherent narrative, a story with plot and texture.

# The Cop Was White As Snow

# The Cop Was White As Snow

by

## Joyce Spizer

INTERCONTINENTAL PUBLISHING

ISBN 1 881164 83 7

1st American edition: 1998

Typography: Monica S. Rozier
Cover by: Rosemary Boyd of Document Design, Laguna Beach, CA
Printing: BookCrafters, Fredericksburg, VA

---

**Library of Congress Cataloging-in-Publication Data**

Spizer, Joyce
    The cop was white as snow / by Joyce Spizer. — 1st Amercian ed.
        p.    cm.
    ISBN 1–881164–83–7 (alk. paper)
    I. Title.
PS3569.P59C66  1998
813'.54—dc21                                                        97–39430
                                                                            CIP

# The Cop Was White As Snow

## Acknowledgements
(in order of appearance in the life of this book):

*Lt. John Schaefer* with the Cypress Police Department, without whose guidance, honest answers and friendship, this book could not have been written.

The real *John Blackburn*, my loving cousin, whose resemblance to Johnnie Blake is more than coincidence.

*Susan Slinger* ... the sister I never had.

My closest friend, *Adele Alterman*, who knows my darkest secrets and loves me anyway.

*Ray and Jean Manning*, dear supportive long-time friends.

*Les and Elaine Page*, whose encouragement and constant nagging kept me going.

*Gary Gorman*, Long Beach Fire Department, whose editing in the rescue chapters helped create some of the scarier pages.

*Lt. Patrick Gildea*, Huntington Beach SWAT team, who held me hostage in an old school bus and taught me how to use an AK47.

*Sue Grafton*, a lady in every sense of the word, who acknowledged me for my efforts in "J is for Judgement" and who always has time for me.

"Whodunits," our mystery critique group, *Linda Leydekkers, Phyllis Krishan, Jo-Ann Coller*. And especially my dear friend, *Louann Murray, PhD*.

*Joan Oppenheimer*, author, teacher and mentor extraordinary.

A new friend, *Det. Gary Bale*, of the Orange County Sheriff's Department, who edited the seventh draft.

To author and fellow NWA/SCC member, *Doris Elaine Fell* (Till) who spent a long Saturday in January with me, completing the 10th version.

*Rosemary Boyd*, fellow NWA member and graphic artist, for her beautiful artwork which graces the cover.

*Maureen*, God bless you dear friend. You know who you are.

And last, but not least, many thanks to: All my friends in the cheering sections at SIC, NWA/SCC, RWA, Professional Writers League of Long Beach and Round Table West.

*Dedicated to*
*My Dearest Friend, Lover and Husband,*
*Harold,*
*without whom my life has no meaning.*

*—be thou as chaste as ice, as pure as snow,*
*thou shalt not escape calumny.*
Hamlet to Ophelia, Act III, Scene 1

# *Prologue*

Camellia Walker's high heels sank into the loose soil beside the freshly dug grave. She shivered as she pulled a torn newspaper clipping from the pocket of her wallet and shook it open.

## TWO OFFICERS FOUND DEAD

### William (T-Bone) Walker and David Frasier Services.

HARBOUR POINTE—Dual funeral services will be held at 10 A.M. Friday morning at Harbour View Memorial Park, for two Harbour Pointe police officers. William Walker was found dead Sunday at Scotchman's Cove. David Frasier was discovered sitting in a car in his garage on Saturday. The coroner's office reports each officer died from a single gunshot to the head. The suicides appear unrelated. Walker was reportedly despondent over the death of his wife, Carole, who died last year after a long bout with cancer. Detective Walker will be buried with honors. The Harbour Pointe Police Department, where he served for thirty years, will provide . . .

She did not have to read the rest of the article. Lies were not worth reading.

∞ **1**

A week after the funeral, Mel drove her vintage SL Mercedes back through the gates of the Harbour Pointe Cemetery and followed the twisting, narrow road to the family plot. Today shafts of sunlight filtered through the leafy, fragrant cypress and eucalyptus trees and the willowy oleander bushes. The cemetery took on the appearance of an open-air cathedral with the light beams bouncing off the ground in front of her father's grave marker. The slimy wilted wreaths and stale odors of flowers lingered there to spoil the effect.

Above, the wind whistled through the orchestra of greenery. A lone bird balanced on one thin limb and sang. How could he sing his happy song to her breaking heart?

Last week she had walked over the grave markers, not risking a sprained ankle in the sinkholes in the sodden earth. Today she stepped cautiously around the tombstones and ran her fingertips across the protruding granite memorial, catching the morning dew as she did so. Divorced. Her only child dead. Her parents gone. She had never felt so alone, so childlike, so angry. Camellia Walker, an orphan.

She whispered angrily, "I won't believe you committed suicide, Dad. I promised Mom I'd take care of you and we were much closer after she died. I can't understand it. Tell me, damn it. What the hell happened?"

Mel's voice had risen and she glanced around, hoping no one overheard. Her fingers twisted strands of short, curly auburn hair, a nervous trait from childhood.

Three family plots dotted this section. With her left hand she scooped a handful of soil from her father's grave and dribbled the loose dirt back and forth over the fresh mound. Mel then turned to her mother's grave and sprinkled more damp soil. An aged gray granite tombstone belonged to her freckle-face son, Willie, whose robin blue eyes were closed forever by a hit-and-run driver . . . only six years old and so full of life . . . playing ball in the front yard. *How harmless and how senseless. Where is the bastard who drove off and left him calling his mother's name?* This time she mixed a prayer with the rich black soil.

From somewhere behind her, Mel heard footsteps crunching over fallen twigs and she lowered her voice. "This gnawing in my stomach won't go away. I'm so damn mad at you. At me. At the world right now."

Mel felt a sharp blow to the side of her head. "What the hell?" she gasped.

She sprawled backward. One of the men pressed his legs over hers and grabbed at Mel's flailing hands.

*Something black on my head . . . I can't see. Oh, my God! I'm choking.* Her fingers probed between her neck and the darkness.

*A cord around my neck . . . hard to breathe . . . too weak . . . lots of pressure . . . no connection between hands and brain . . . Please . . . someone help me.*

A man's voice said, "Get the purse. Maybe it's in there. She has to have something with her."

Noises, scuffling. Car keys, coin purse and compact clicked as the purse's contents fell. Spanish gutturals exchanged between two men, as Mel managed to get one fingertip under the cord.

*God, I need air.*

Her feet worked free and she kicked wildly, hoping to connect with the assailant's knees.

"*Nada, amigo, nada*," one man said to the other.

A piercing series of three sharp sounds interrupted the assault.

*Oh, thank God. My beeper.* "Help me. Someone help me."

"Shit, man. *Vamanos*."

They threw her to the ground, shoulder first. She rolled onto her stomach. Mel grappled at her neck until she found one end of a cord and yanked it. A choking spasm followed as the rope loosened. When she pulled the greasy dark thing off, it appeared to be a black hand-made denim hood. Mel took one long deep breath and knelt on both knees while biting one broken fingernail.

She heard a car engine race and tires squeal just beyond a large bank of eucalyptus trees to the rear of the cemetery.

Mel coughed and inhaled the strong odor of ozone left by freshly mowed grass watered too often. *The bastards got away.*

Another three short static bursts from the beeper made her jump. She crawled to the purse, turned it upside down and shook. Nothing fell out. She rifled through a small pile, pushing aside used tissue, pens, paperclips, lipstick, keys and wallet. A black pager lay under it all. She pressed a button and cried as the familiar number appeared. Her father's office. She had called it thousands of times over the years.

Mel got to her feet, limped toward her car parked at the curb, leaned on the edge of the passenger seat and rubbed her bruised throat again. Then she opened the glove compartment, withdrew a 9mm Beretta and checked the magazine. With feet pressed against the curb and the gun in her lap, she grabbed the car phone and hit redial number two.

After the second ring, she heard a brawny male voice.

"Harbour Pointe Police. Homicide Division. Xavier Ramirez here. How can I help you?"

"Hi, X-Ray. Mel here. Boy, am I glad you called." A tear rolled down her cheek as she coughed.

"Where are you? I've been trying to reach you for an hour. You sound out of breath."

Mel glanced at the broad green velvet cemetery that stretched out before her. "I'm here with Dad." She paused, "And Mom and Willie."

"Are you all right?"

Another pause, another cough, "I just got mugged."

"Mugged? I'll get a unit on the way."

"No. I'm okay, X. Your call interrupted the attack."

"You're alone?"

"They're long gone."

"Maybe not. Get outta there. Right now."

"Can't. I haven't had time to check my purse to see what's missing, but I'm fine. Really." She drew in one long deep breath and slowly exhaled.

"I'm sorry. Geez, I should have come with you. You sure you're okay?"

"Just pissed off. What'd you need?"

"Well, I didn't mean to interrupt your grieving time. Call me when you're back on the road again."

"I'm leaving now. I don't know if this is something you ever get used to," she said.

Mel glanced back at the new mound of dirt, and then the older tombstones clearly etched in her memory with the names she loved.

CAROLE LOMBARD WALKER
BELOVED WIFE AND MOTHER

and

WILLIE ARCHER
BELOVED SON AND GRANDSON
FOREVER SIX

And now, soon, another name added to the gray granite.

WILLIAM WALKER
BELOVED HUSBAND
FATHER, GRANDFATHER AND
DEDICATED POLICE OFFICER

"What'd you need me for?" she asked.

"This probably isn't a good time to talk, Mel."

"It's about Dad, isn't it?"

"We should go over some of the evidence surrounding your dad's death." He cleared his throat, "The investigation, so far, makes it fairly clear that we have a uh . . ."

She interrupted him, her voice shrill. "He did not commit suicide, X-Ray! Don't you dare say that." Her hot, flushed cheeks tingled. Barely able to swallow, she inhaled and exhaled.

"Mel, get a grip, would you? I don't like it any more than you do. Hell, you know your dad was my best friend. Shit! I'd be in prison or dead myself if it hadn't been for T-Bone."

"Then you haven't forgotten."

She slapped the mouthpiece closed, tossed the phone and the black hood onto the front seat, slammed the passenger door and walked back to the family plot. Mel placed the gun within reach and using both hands, crammed the lipstick, keys, tissues and note pad into the purse, then she picked up the billfold. *Great, just great. No credit cards, no money. That's what I need. More bullshit in my life.*

Mel's gun remained poised in her left hand, purse strap over the right shoulder, until she returned to the car. She fumbled for the ignition switch, gritted her teeth and fought back the tears. Anger churned below the surface, like a pot of her mother's pinto beans ready to boil over.

She resisted the temptation to look back and drove down the narrow lanes of the cemetery until she reached the nearest boulevard. Mel steered the car toward Pacific Coast Highway like a mad woman trying to make the opening of a once-a-year sale.

She opened both windows, allowing her hair to tangle in the wind, to clear away some of the mental clouds. She pushed the radio buttons several times. "If I hear one more Christmas carol, I'm going to scream," she said to the radio. She twisted the dial with her bruised fingers until loud and wonderful music from a fifties station helped her regain control.

*I've gotta make a plan. I'm an insurance investigator, for God's sake. This 120 pounds of energy knows how to gather and analyze facts. I need to be as objective as possible and try to remove my emotions from all this shit. One thing I know for sure. After today, I have to be more careful. It's up to me. I know Dad didn't commit suicide. No way.*

She pounded the armrest and smiled wryly for the first time since his death.

*That's it. I can do this. I'll go home and set up a file on William Walker. A profile on everything I know about him*

16

*and what others have told me. A full investigation outline.*
*So many things to do. Why doesn't this damn holiday traffic*
*get out of my way?*

Instead, she had to follow all of the out-of-state "snowbirds," bumper-to-bumper as they snaked down Pacific Coast Highway toward Laguna Beach. Lucky snowbirds . . . living in Canada, or the Northern United States, enjoying the change of seasons of spring, summer and fall, but not winters. Their winters are spent in warm California.

To her right the stormy ocean crashed against the frothy churning surf. Inside, her turmoil was just as violent. She grabbed a small, hand-held recorder from the side pocket of the driver's door and began dictating notes. For the first time, she realized that with her investigative background and her contacts, she held the methods and means to resolve this issue once and for all. The only people she loved were permanent residents in a cemetery.

"I must remain the young me who'll never grow old until this is resolved," she said into the recorder. "This new file will be the biggest and most important case in my life."

∞**2**

Mel placed the recorder between her knees, balanced a can of soda with one hand and steered with the other. Her voice trembled as she spoke, "William, also known as T-Bone

Walker. Wife, Carole Lombard Walker, named after the famous movie star. Their only child, Camellia, also known as Mel. Family born and reared in Harbour Pointe, California, located thirty miles south of Los Angeles and situated on the Pacific Coast near Newport Beach. Carole died of breast cancer after a lengthy illness. The following year, William was found dead on a remote bluff at Scotchman's Cove . . . a single bullet wound in the mouth." She spoke into the microphone for a few moments longer, then clicked it off and laid it next to her on the console.

She entered Harbour Pointe that once was a clean, quiet, crimefree beach community with small one-story Mom and Pop boutiques lining each side of Pacific Coast Highway. The Spanish colonial motif with salmon colored tiled roofs reflected the city's rich cultural heritage. The burgeoning immigration from the south had newspapers throughout the country calling Orange County, "Northern Mexico."

She followed traffic past downtown toward the suburban area where taggers had painted creeping black and green vines of graffiti along the adjacent freeway sound-barrier walls, cement block fences and the beautiful old mission style buildings.

*I'm very proud of Dad*, Mel thought. *He walked a beat, rode a motorcycle and drove a patrol car, long before he became a detective. He knew all the gangs, guns, drugs, crime and general uneasiness which oozed from the city's pores, threatening the well-being of its citizens.*

Her mental game plan continued to develop for the next twenty minutes, until she reached the gate leading to her street on the coastal side of Pacific Coast Highway. A few moments later, she pulled into a circular driveway in front of a two-story California Mediterranean home with pale peach stucco walls and matching tile roof. Wild bougainvillaea rich with carmine and carnation pink blooms scaled the walls and smothered one corner of the house from the flower bed to the chimney. A FOR SALE sign faced the street. The double-wide white lacquered front door was unlocked.

"Rosa, it's me," she yelled as she shoved it open.

"*Si*, Mel. Rosa is upstairs. I'll be down in a few minutes. You need to eat."

"*Si. Mucho* hungry. Anything ready?"

"Sure. I ate already, but there is lots for you. Check the ice box, please."

"*Gracias.*"

Mel kicked her shoes off, leaving them in the marble entryway and dropped her purse next to the stairway. She walked to the downstairs study which doubled as a library and the only office of Walker Investigations where she and Johnnie Blake, a fellow investigator, shared space and work. There, she flipped through the Rolodex under "C," picked up the telephone and dialed the 800 number. As she waited for a customer service rep, she held a heart-shaped glass frame. Mel smiled through fresh tears at the picture of Willie, at age two, sitting in his rocker, wearing his blue spaceman pajamas and hugging his ragged little stuffed teddy bear. After a few "yes" and "no" answers, all department store and bank cards were cancelled and new ones ordered.

She moved through the home she loved so much into the living room. The heavily mortgaged house was part of a divorce settlement from her ex-husband, Attorney Taylor Lawrence Archer. A payoff for not shooting him when she caught him cheating with some blonde on the white moliere bedspread.

She dropped into an overstuffed orange and blue chair and propped her feet on the coffee table. The couch was covered with contrasting material adding pink and green to its tropical design. The realtor told Mel that the open airy rooms, majestic ocean sunsets and her personal touch had made the house more marketable. The broker hoped to sell it quickly so Mel could go on with her life, debt free.

In the kitchen she gathered a hodgepodge of snack foods; turkey sandwich, diet drink, and a small cluster of fresh cold grapes. Elbowing open the sliding door, Mel inhaled the fresh air swirling about the back patio, dropped into a cushioned deckchair and popped a grape into her mouth. When the house sold, she would miss the breathtaking orange and gold sunsets across the Pacific Ocean. Her home sat high on a rocky cliff, far enough from the sand to muffle the voices of passing lovers, but close enough to hear the pounding, boiling surf.

Rosa came to the patio door, smelling of vanilla and wiping her hands on an apron.

Rosa pushed her wavy black hair from her face with the back of one hand. "You need something more, then?"

"No, *gracias*. I'm fine." She rubbed her neck.

Rosa hesitated, "You sound hoarse."

"It's nothing."

"You want me to get the Christmas decorations out?" she asked, her coal black eyes full of concern.

"No. Not this year."

"Maybe you'd feel better, Mel, if we put bright lights outside. Tony could hang them."

"It definitely wouldn't make me feel better, Rosa. Maybe next year. Looks like Tony's been here today. He planted our favorite flowers. I love impatiens too. They are beautiful."

"*Si.*"

"He's sweet on you, Rosa. Is he your fella?"

Rosa blushed. "No way. He isn't my type. I want a professional man. I don't want my children to grow up on welfare or working like the *cholos* who live on my block. I'll do better."

"How can you do better when you're working here? I can't afford to pay you for even these few days."

"My mother told me to watch over you, like you take care of me."

Rosa's mother, Analynn, and her family immigrated to America from El Salvador. Analynn worked for the Walker family and, when she retired, Rosa assumed the household duties.

"I'm responsible for you," Rosa said, "and I owe you so much."

"What?" Mel asked.

"You got me that attorney to set up my cleaning company so all my family can work with pride."

"Rosa, you're like the sister I never had. I'd do anything for you."

"I feel the same way."

Mel smiled, thinking that Tony certainly had a crush on Rosa. He seemed to schedule his time when he knew Rosa would be here.

"Rosa, do you have a tattoo?"

Rosa laughed, "No," she said emphatically, "and I won't lose my virginity to someone like Tony. His arms are scarred with daggers and barbed wire. Not my type."

"Have I told you how lucky I feel to know you and your family?" Mel called through the screen door.

"Say it with *dinero*, Miss Mel," Rosa responded.

"Boy, are you a sassy today. Did I have any calls?"

"Yes. X-Ray called. I ask him to try you in the car." She added, "Now there's a very nice man. He still married?"

"You do have your sights set high, Rosa. No, he's divorced now. You interested?"

Rosa giggled and disappeared into the house, leaving Mel alone with her thoughts.

Mel toyed with the moisture dripping from the cold drink can and stretched her long legs across an adjoining chair as she pondered the investigation ahead. How could she juggle her already busy schedule? How long would it take? Could she support herself? Would the house sell?

She laid her head back on the chair, rubbed her throat and her tired burning eyes. How would Dad conduct this investigation, she wondered. She wanted to be objective. She demanded the truth. For the moment, she needed a nap.

Mel slept until dusk, brought back to consciousness by a phone ringing. She yawned, stretched and leaned over the patio table patting the glass top in a haze until she found the source of the noise.

"Walker Investigations. Mel Walker here."

A gravelly male voice said, "That was a warning."

A spot at the nape of her neck was sore where it had balanced on the metal headrest. She massaged it, "What?"

"At the cemetery."

"What are you talking about? Do you have the right number?" The sleepy fog in her head had not yet lifted.

"Miss Camellia Walker, daughter of a cop, we know where you live."

She froze now. *Jesus.* The guys from the cemetery. She tried a defensive move hoping to offset a chilling fright setting in. *They do know where I live.* "Oh, nice gift asshole. Want your black hood back?"

"Naw. We got something else for ya, if you don't give it up."

"What are you talking about?"

"Don't play little girl with us. What's your price?"

"I don't play games. I just don't know what you're talking about."

"Think about it."

"I am, and I think you mugged the wrong person."

"There was no mistake," he snarled. "We want it NOW."

"What? What is it?" She asked, more confused than ever. "You already have my maxed-out credit cards. I only have a few bucks in my checking account."

"You have something from your old man. It's the book and we want it back. We'll be in touch."

The man hung up, leaving Mel shaking her head and trembling in the night air. She had hoped they mugged her at random. She had nothing else to give. *What book would she have from her dad that two gang types would want?* Something in the tone of his voice troubled her. She crossed her arms about her chest and shivered.

Rosa had long since gone home and left a short note on the breakfast room table.

"A nap is good. So is food. Dinner in the icebox."

Mel locked the patio door behind her and drew the drapes. She checked all the windows on both floors. They were secure. Mel punched the house alarm on while retrieving the gun from her purse nearby. She paced back and forth as she munched on another grape but couldn't concentrate.

*Get a grip. I have more important things than food on my mind. I now have two problems . . . staying safe from those assholes and focusing on my new project.*

She rinsed a used glass, poured some iced tea and went to her office. The phone rang again. She paused before answering it. *Could be the assholes again.*

"Walker Investigations, Mel Walker."

"Is Johnnie Blake in?"

*The voice is female. Must be business.*

"He's on assignment in San Francisco. Should be back in the office by the end of the week. If you'll leave your name and number, I'll have him call you." Mel stirred papers on the desk and found a pencil.

"Is that you, Mel? This is Betty, in the DA's office. I'm returning Johnnie's call on the Derrick matter."

"Yeah. You working kinda late, aren't you?"

"Not when we're a month from trial and all witnesses haven't been served."

"Can I help?"

"No, just ask Johnnie to call me."

"I'll see that he gets the message."

As the call ended, Mel glanced around the crowded office. Working together had proved quite a feat . . . Johnnie's desk messy, hers . . . normally neat.

*Darn,* she thought. *My kingdom for a place of my own.*

* *
*

Johnnie Blake. She wished he were here. Johnnie had answered her ad, several years ago, when she needed a second investigator for her expanding business. She needed him now. His specialty, investigating death penalty cases, complemented her own insurance work. His even disposition, high standards and strong work ethics paralleled her own. The fact that he was homosexual enhanced his charms in her eyes and kept everything in the right perspective. All business.

She stepped over files stacked on the floor, shuffled through a mass of papers on his institutional style dark pine desk, opened and closed two file cabinets before finding the right instruction manual . . . a copy of the murder book, the one cops use when investigating homicides and other deaths. She remembered the blue file folder contained shake cards, things you record so the clues will not get lost. The cards keep the facts organized.

She sat at her small oak corner desk and for the next twenty minutes, searched through every police procedure she could find, but the answer to her question, "how to start?" eluded her.

She picked up the telephone receiver and hit the pound button and the #1.

"Harbour Pointe Police Department, Detective Xavier Ramirez. How can I help you?"

"Hi. It's me again. Glad I caught you."

"Just walking out the door. Are you okay? Did the mugger get anything?"

"Yeah. All the damn credit cards and my license. I've cancelled the cards, so all I have left is DMV."

"But, you're okay?" he repeated.

"My throat's a little sore, that's all."

"Catching a cold?"

"No, dummy. It was those two guys . . . at least. One of them put a hood over my head and tried to choke me."

"You didn't tell me that."

"It's nothing."

"Nothing? Sounds like assault and battery to me."

"They settled for my credit cards and my address."

"Do you need me?" X-Ray asked.

"No, really."

"Mel, do you feel better?"

"In a way. Say, I took a new assignment today."

"That's great. What's it about?"

*Oops!* She wasn't ready to share *that.*

"Uh, later, X-Ray, when I have more time, okay? All I can tell you is, it's one of those murder versus civil action type of cases. I'm going to coordinate the civil part."

"If it's a murder in our department, maybe I can help."

*Now for a really big lie.* "It's a suspected homicide, but not your jurisdiction. But, I sure could use some ideas. Like . . . how an investigation might begin from your side. How do you get ideas on what might have happened? Things like that."

X-Ray was quiet for a moment. "The first thing we do is 'secure' the scene of the crime and call in the forensic unit. They gather the evidence, tag it, photo and dust, you know."

"I know the basic stuff. I was thinking more along the lines of what isn't public information. What do you do that the public wouldn't know about?"

"Ever hear of 'chasing a shadow'?"

"Nope. What's that?"

"Sometimes when we get a really weird case . . . Say the crime didn't happen at the victim's home or office, we recreate the crime from the victims starting point prior to his death and follow his path to his death. We call it 'chasing a shadow'."

He added, "That's dangerous, though. I wouldn't want you doing something like that, because you wouldn't have access to the deceased's home or office. And I sure wouldn't want you arrested for a 459 at the scene of the crime."

"Don't worry about me breaking and entering. I wouldn't be that stupid," she replied.

"If it's something I can help with, I'll send a uniform with you. Where'd it happen?"

*I feel another whopper coming on.* "Ventura County. I don't have the file right here in front of me." She shuffled some desk papers for sound effects. He was getting too close for comfort. "I really appreciate your help, X-Ray. As I get into this, I may call again."

"When can we talk about T-Bone? I have the initial forensic material. We should sit down and go over it."

She cut him off, fearing he would put two and two together. "Listen. Can I get back to you in a day or so? I'm just getting into this new case."

"Sure. No problem. Let me hear from you. I'll be glad to drop by the house if you'd be more comfortable talking there. Let me know. Love you, lady. Call me if you need someone to talk to."

"Love you too, X . . . soon."

\* \*
\*

She hung up, smiling. *She did love that hunk.* X-Ray's muscled brown body barely made the department height

27

standard at five feet eight inches. Mel used to tease him about his long curls, now close cropped to meet the department's regulations. He was the younger brother she had always wanted. His life began in a barrio in South Central Los Angeles. All four of his brothers had been killed before they reached age twenty. He jumped into a gang, as a lookout, at age six, and progressed to petty theft before his ninth birthday.

His nickname, X-Ray, came from his ability to see truth through the cleverest fabrications and to understand what survival was all about. Despite his early childhood, he avoided a serious police record for a long time. Then one day, during a sting operation, he had been caught, along with other gang members, trying to sell some stolen stereos to the police. But he made one big mistake. He tried to sell the goods to T-Bone Walker, Mel's father. T-Bone had cuffed the thirteen year old at the scene and brought him home instead of to jail. Carole made him clean up and fed him and the family instantly fell in love with this tough little waif.

When X-Ray discovered how a family unit worked, he never left. He lived in the Walker's garage apartment and completed his education. T-Bone helped X-Ray get a job at the local service station and enrolled him at the police academy. X-Ray followed Walker to Harbour Pointe Police as a young cadet.

* *
*

Mel had not slept a full night since that murky night, a week ago. And she could not sleep now. Her father did not kill himself, and she would not be able to sleep until this was resolved once and for all. She had to face the truth, whatever it was. If not to set it free, then to satisfy her morbid curiosity. She would chase the shadow tonight.

∞*3*

The quarter moon created the perfect mood to "chase a shadow." Just after midnight, Mel turned down the dark noiseless lane, pulled along the curb and parked in front of a small frame house with a detached garage. Grabbing a black sport bag, she exited the car, glanced up and down the quiet street, and then made her way stealthily along the driveway to the front door. The night air swirled with odors of stale fish from a nearby pier.

Like the rest of this Harbour Pointe street, the house remained deadly dark. Even in the hazy street light, the neighborhood's age was easily discernible. She stumbled over roots from tall, thick peeling eucalyptus trees which had burst through the concrete walkways. Leaves piled in the yards, tossed there by Santa Ana winds.

Paint flecked off the exterior walls of her father's beach home, exhibiting a unique weathering pattern. Even the windows were pitted and scratched from blowing sand. The warped shake roof lifted and twisted as it nodded toward the west beach. Moss glistened on the eaves facing north.

At the porch, Mel withdrew rubber surgical gloves from her bag. They were the kind with talc powder inside. She slid both gloves on and pressed them down snugly between her fingers. She rechecked the hands and palms, concerned her long nails might have punctured the rubber. Satisfied, Mel reached into her bag and pulled out a small black metal pick. Being an investigator had certain perks. No law abiding citizen had access to such wonderful tools.

Yellow and black CAUTION POLICE ribbon criss-crossed the faded blue door. Drawn tight on all facia around the door, the tape sealed the entrance from intruders. Mel's fingers rubbed the tape's ends back and forth several times.

"Ah, perfect," she whispered sarcastically, as one side slipped off the door's fascia without tearing. Tricky.

Inserting the pick between the door jamb and the door, Mel placed her right hand on the knob. She checked the street once more. No dogs barking. No one stirring. She slid the tool down toward the lock and with one swift mechanical move, turned the knob and pushed. The door popped open. Mel cocked her ear again. She heard a sound . . . it came from her chest . . . heavy breathing and a bell beating heart. An instant later, she was inside.

With her back to the door she closed the blackout curtains and pulled a small flashlight from the black bag.

*What I need is a drink.*

Mel stepped gingerly across the living room to a small portable bar, switched on a lamp, cut off the flashlight and returned it to the bag.

*Oh! The great makings for a vodka and tonic.* She poured a stiff drink in a plastic tumbler and walked into the kitchen for ice. One long swallow emptied the entire glass.

The alcoholic blend startled her with a jolt. She coughed, added more ice, and returned to the living room.

The alcohol played tricks on her mind. Shadows criss-crossed the knick-knacks and furniture, creating fuzzy wall images. Well-beloved photos covered the walls and the piano. A wave of sadness taunted her. Camellia remembered playing chop-sticks on this piano as a small child. How she had hated music lessons, especially the exercise scales for limbering tiny fingers.

*Stop it Mel. Get a grip on yourself. You've got to be objective. You must be Mel the investigator now, not Camellia the daughter.*

A man's home now. No bouquets of flowers. No lace dollies. But she could still detect T-Bone's masculinity . . . the pungent odor of his nasty cigars . . . gun cleaning oil. *Where was the gun?*

She bent over a nearby desk and flipped the switch on a lamp. After checking through the drawers and cubby holes, Mel found no gun. She sank into the deep crumpled folds of the maroon leather, desk chair with her legs drawn up to her chest.

The ball bearings of the claw feet squeaked across the scarred wooden floor as she adjusted the seat to the height of the desk. The chair fit as if it had been made for her.

"Ah, memories," she murmured and exhaled one long breath. She raised the glass and drank to the bottom, until the remaining ice portions fell and she devoured those too. She set the glass down hard on the desk top, thrust her hair back and stood. Her hands trembled as she walked around the chair and pushed it closer to the desk.

Mel walked into the master bedroom, the room this man had shared with a woman for many years.

*A wonderful woman.*

Carole Walker's flowery pink curtains and matching dust ruffles with a solid pale green comforter warmed the master bedroom. The vanity with assorted perfume bottles and blow dryer remained undisturbed. *This man had loved Carole so much.* Mel walked to the dresser and touched it. She found no dust. The room had been kept as though Carole might return any minute. T-Bone had been waiting for his beloved wife.

*You're the investigator Mel Walker. Keep focused, damn it. You're chasing a shadow.*

Mel removed her outer clothing, folded pants and blouse and placed them in the bag along with her panty hose and shoes. She wanted no evidence left behind.

She stepped to the closet and fingered through the shirts, until she found her father's favorite white one. Mel removed it from the hanger and put it on.

Buttoning the plain cotton shirt, she chose a gray serge suit one with a thin gray stripe. A typical cop suit: cheap, plain and lightweight. His tummy had been bigger than she remembered.

She rolled up the pants to fit her trim, five feet, six inch frame and selected the tie he had worn to Carole's funeral, a horizontally striped gray and red tie. Her eyes stung as she recalled standing on a chair behind her father . . . an eleven year old . . . who helped Dad tie that Windsor knot. The knot he could never quite get the hang of.

*Keep focused, Mel Walker. You're a PI now.*

Inside the closet, from a hook holding two belts, one the Sam Browne issue, Mel chose the plain black, imitation leather belt and cinched it way past the loops and holes.

She opened the top drawer of the dresser. The socks lay neatly folded in half, side-by-side, according to color. *Dad . . . so methodical . . . just like his work and his life.* Mel selected a gray pair, wiped more tears away with the toe ends and sat on the end of the bed to put them on. While slipping on a scuffed pair of Buster Browns, she recalled . . . T-Bone had told her all street cops swore by the rubber soled, quiet comfort these shoes afforded flat feet. They were smelly from steamy summer days in the California heat; Mel's nose winced as the odor, like that of dirty gym socks, wafted over her.

She located his back-up .38 inside a gun safe hidden behind a mirror in the closet. Cold steel and powerful. In the mid 80s, most large police departments like LAPD changed to the 9mm Beretta automatics, but Walker had been comfortable with the six shot revolver. The grips were worn to the right and she was left handed. But, when Mel gripped it, a salacious sensation sizzled through her. It wasn't the gun that killed him, but it would do for her.

Slipping the holster over her right shoulder, she adjusted the belt loop to fit her smaller frame. Mel slipped the gun halfway out to make sure it fit and checked to see if it was loaded.

She pulled on the coat, curled up the sleeves and folded the white silk square neatly inside the jacket pocket. She tilted her head and studied the reflection in the mirror.

*Boy, these clothes are heavy. Why did I ever bitch about heels and hose?*

Mel flipped the bedroom lights off and headed for the kitchen, where she stuffed paper towels into the shoes to fit her size eights. She turned out all the lights to the living room and touched the front door knob before remembering the glass.

"Where'd I put it, for God's sake?" she muttered, taking out the flashlight, returning to the bar and then to the desk area. *There.*

Mel grabbed the glass, stuffed it into the valise and wiped the small water ring left on the desk using the cuff of T-Bone's coat.

Angry at her careless mistake, she slammed the front door. A neighborhood dog began to bark. His intruder bark.

"Hush, Brutus. It's just me," she whispered.

Mel took each end of the ribbon and resealed the door, giving silent thanks for sticky tape. She dashed to the car, stubbing her toe on the cracked concrete.

The Mercedes coughed and sputtered and finally caught. Without turning on the headlights, she sped out of the subdivision before any of the neighborhood watch could get her license plate number.

Now the trick was not to get stopped by the local police . . . no speeding or weaving . . . no infractions. That would be hard to explain. She could just imagine the cop's face when he stopped a thirty-something-divorcee-orphan-woman, dressed in man's clothing and toting a gun. Not to mention failing to pass any test for blood alcohol.

*What was she worried about? This is California, for God's sake. Any dress code goes and no explanation needed.*

She calmed down, put on a Vivaldi tape and roared south on Pacific Coast Highway, the negative reflections bombarding her again . . . the nightmares, the still shots the coroner flashed before the Grand Jury, photos of what was left of his head. The bloody dark mass near his salt and peppery brown-haired scalp, his eyes closed and a faint smile . . .

After Carole's funeral, T-Bone said, "I'll always be here for you Camellia. We still have each other."

*Dad didn't kill himself. He wouldn't let me down.*

And a promise Mel made to her mother as she lay dying in the hospital bed, all the tubes pumping life-sustaining liquids through her veins The body, incredibly wasted, frail . . .

Mel had held her mother's head in her arms and made a last promise, "I'll watch out for Dad. I'll take care of him."

*But, Mom, I did let you down! I'll make it up to you. Tonight.*

The gnawing ache in the pit of her stomach spasmed. Pulsating pains under her left breast . . . the thudding beat of her heart.

Near the Date Stand south of Corona del Mar, Mel braked the SL and swerved into the right lane around slower traffic as she anticipated the turnout for an unmarked dirt road ahead. Even in daylight it was not that easy to find. Only the glider guys who scaled sheer cliffs would venture across this area. It was much too high for the beach bunnies and sun worshipers.

She turned into the lane and checked for rocks and pot holes. Two wild brown rabbits darted across her path. Mel swerved, just missing them both. Sweat sealed her father's shirt between her body and the seat back. Mel flashed the headlights to high. The palms and fern tentacles reached out for the car, lashing at the fenders and doors as she passed.

Recent rains left a mud-pie lane as the SL slipped through the shiny black goo creating new ruts along the way. The lane curved left and right in a series of blind turns for less than a mile passing thick pampas plants, tall palms and monkey grass until she reached a broad clearing that opened onto a parking mesa. No one would find a body here for days.

The crashing waves on the rocks below masked the sound of the engine. She turned off the motor. The alcohol buzz left her with a sense of warmth and comfort as she reached under a sweaty armpit and patted the holster. She pushed both sleeves of the heavy jacket to her elbows.

Mel turned off the headlights and stepped into the cool breezy night air. *Damn, the ignition key,* she thought when she heard the insistent beeping. She slammed the door.

Perspiration rose across her thick brown brows matting the bangs to her forehead. Beads of sweat trickled down her back. The .38 felt cooler in her hands this time. She tightened her fingers on the grip.

*Yes, this is right. This is it.*

Crouched on the cool sand, Mel tried to find the spot. Here are the fire pits and boulders X-Ray told her about. She recoiled. Mel believed this to be a crime scene. She positioned herself between two large boulders and sat cross-legged.

Then saying aloud, "Please forgive me!" she placed the barrel in her mouth. With both hands on the trigger, she closed her eyes, grimaced . . . and squeezed.

Harbour Pointe Police Department protects seven square miles, serving the southern California community of forty thousand plus, full and part-time residents. Those seven miles run parallel with the Pacific waves, north and south if you believe the atlas . . . east and west if one is a native.

One would not think fifty police officers could effectively patrol this area because of its proximity to Laguna and Newport Beach and their arty and aquatic activities. On Easter weekends and during the Laguna Art Festivals, they do not have to cope by themselves. Other police departments are eager to send in auxiliary forces to escape the sweltering heat of the inland precincts during call up periods.

Police headquarters consists of a one story, white-washed, earthquake-and-bomb-proof vault. Even with its nearness to the ocean, air conditioning is a must with all the hot bodies coming and going.

The Chief is a hard-boiled career oriented tough cop named Murdoch. Under him, three captains supervise six divisions and twelve bureaus. A large contingent of civil service workers and a state-of-the-art communications system add to his frustrations.

Chief Murdoch likes the new technology . . . he just has no clue how it all works. In quality, Harbour Pointe's 911 system ranks second in Orange County and its officers are second to none. At least that is what Mel's father had espoused.

She had heard it so often, she had begun to believe it, that is, until his death. Now her faith was shaken . . . not destroyed, but damaged. Chief Murdoch, Mel's godfather, held her to his chest when she was an infant . . . the fresh woody scent of his aftershave.

Mel burst through the squad room door. Stale cigarette smoke and smells of rancid coffee and sweat filled the testosterone-laced atmosphere. This is the meeting she dreaded. The first since the funeral.

"Princess. God, it's good to see you." The burly chief lumbered toward her and crushed her in a gigantic bearhug. "I'm glad you came."

Mel smiled. No change in aftershave . . . still woodsy. As soon as he hugged her, the chief released his hold and stepped back. He brushed thinning gray hair away from his forehead, then hung his index fingers into belt loops and hitched up both sides of his pants until he had given his ample stomach shelter under the belt line.

In the middle of changing shifts, the midnight crews still worked on reports while the eight o'clock briefing group milled about the room. Cops were everywhere.

They stopped answering phones, quit talking and poised motionless to view their chief, tears forming in his eyes.

He tried to compose himself, then said, "We've pretty much cleaned out his desk for you. Are you here to get T-Bone's things?" He removed his glasses and wiped his eyes. She knew he was buying time to regain control.

"That and more," she replied. "Where's X-Ray?"

"On the computer, I think," he said. "We had a 914-S first crack out of the barrel this morning. X-Ray's running some ID."

"Thanks, Chief." She stepped closer to him, "You know, the other cop, David Frasier, may have been a suicide, but not Dad. Don't you dare close the file on him yet."

Murdoch took a step back, his bushy eyebrows raised by her response. In a warm voice he replied, "Mel, I understand how you feel. I've experienced a loss too. Not like you, of course, but two very fine officers . . . on the same day. T-Bone was my hero. Now he's gone. How do you think that makes me feel? I missed all the trouble signs . . . twice. They ate their guns, for God's sake." He covered his mouth with the back of his hand. Mel wished they both could take back the suicide conversation. "Damn it, honey, I always put my foot in it, don't I? Geez, I'm sorry." His balding head drooped.

Mel doubled her fist and jabbed his chin with a love tap. "And I didn't mean to tell you how to do your job, Chief. Right now, I need X-Ray."

She waved and shot people with her index finger as she walked past the cluttered desks and toward the computer room. Cops throughout the room muttered their condolences and a "Hi, Mel," as she passed. A few stepped forward to shake her hand and give a love pat on her shoulder.

Her father had trained most of them, knew all their kids, and their grand-kids, too.

Mel opened the door into the computer room and found X-Ray concentrating on a black-and-white screen. The computer beeped like a road runner with an urgent message.

"Hi, guy, we gotta talk. Dad . . . did not . . . I repeat, DID NOT commit suicide."

This outburst startled the young Hispanic. He spun the chair around to face her and replied, "Walker, let it go.

We're working on it as hard as we can. Two suicides in one week generate a lot of paperwork."

"I don't give a shit about your paperwork, X!"

"Don't you think it's still hard for me too? Give us a break, hon." His voice softened, he stood and touched her cheek. "What's that on your neck?"

"The impression from the cord."

"What'd you mean, the mugging was nothing? The bastards left a mark on your neck."

"I'm fine. Forget it."

"I worry about you."

His eyes were the color of milk chocolate candy kisses. He ran his hands through short black hair, then reached out to hug her. She responded. They stood almost head to head. She was comforted by his strong, firm hug. Mel closed the door behind her, leaving the two of them alone in the room, like at home when they were young and had secrets to share.

"X-Ray, I 'chased his shadow' last night. I did it!"

"Dammit, Walker. That's not only dumb, it's plain stupid! Leave the police work to the experts, will you? I told you, we've covered every possible aspect of this case. Why don't you concentrate on your insurance and fraud work and leave the police work to us? Give it up, hon. I know the toxicology and the forensics ain't back, but that takes eight to sixteen weeks. We know what the report'll say. T-Bone ate his gun! Then it's a matter of paperwork, and 'Case Closed'!"

Her gut tightened, she sniffed and gulped, "Don't patronize me, X-Ray. I re-created the crime, like you said. Forget all the evidence you found involving him in cocaine trafficking. The evidence must have been planted. Dad would never do anything illegal and he would not have killed himself that way. Work on this angle . . . what other reason could there have been for someone to kill him?"

"I don't know and I didn't want to believe it either. T-Bone involved in cocaine! But, it's true. Shit . . . I'm as mad as hell, maybe even more so than anyone here, including you. But the evidence is what it is and you have to let this go."

"No, X-Ray, no way! Remember Dad used to say 'the cop's gone C-A-D-S on us?' Break the word down. The elements just aren't all there and they'd have to be. Dad said so."

"Walker! The indications are all there." He continued, counting on his fingers as he spoke. "We found evidence of Corruption, Alcohol, Drugs and, of course, the Suicide: C-A-D-S. The house and car were filled with clues. You're not being objective. We've done all we can do for now. You have to let it go and, like my AA sponsor says, 'Let go and let God.' I love you, lady, but you have to get on with your life."

Mel squared her shoulders, narrowed her eyes. "I'll prove every one of you wrong if it's the last thing I do," she gritted. Then she turned and stormed out. The soundproof glass surrounding the room shuddered in reverberation as the door slammed behind her. "I won't let it go," she told herself.

She paused at the oldest desk in the room, the one unlike the others that were modern and gun-metal gray. T-Bone's noninstitutional, wooden desk bore marks from cigarette burns, initials gouged deep into the pecan and phone numbers in various shades of black and blue ink.

During its lifetime, it held enough secrets for thousands of police procedural novels.

She grabbed a large and over-filled moving storage box from the top of the desk and paused to catch a name plate that toppled out. A black silk ribbon draped diagonally across the face of the metal piece read, *Det. William Walker*.

Mel turned to go, but a chubby, middle-aged civil service employee, a distasteful little "wannabe" named Agee, stood in her path. He was in charge of property but she always felt he sniffed more of the property than he secured. He ran one hand through his greasy black hair and, with the other, gave Mel a large manila folder with several seals and stamps on it.

"This is, uh," he snivelled, "T-Bone's evidence envelope."

She drew herself up to full stature and responded, "Where's the register? Don't I have to sign for his things?"

"Oh, yeah, I forget."

He dropped the envelope on the desk and used that hand to pick his nose as he returned to the property room. Her last vision of Agee as he disappeared behind locked doors was of him wiping his crumpled uniformed shirt with the same hand.

Mel reminded herself not to shake hands with the nasty creep. She declined several offers for coffee, sat the box back on the desk and ran her fingers along the desk edges, alone with her memories.

Two Hispanic homeboy types with plaid, long sleeved shirts tied around their waists, straddled chairs at nearby desks and talked to several weary cops anxious for their shifts to end. Mel realized the handcuffed duo were glaring at her. She shifted from one foot to another, placed a hand on one hip and glared back.

One was tall, thin and lanky. He was most likely a product of too many drugs and too few meals. His long brown hair was rubber banded at the base of his neck and a thin hairnet covered his head from forehead down to nape. Colorful red and green tattoos with scripted letters carved statements into both shoulders, wording Mel couldn't decipher at this distance.

The other one, also slightly built, appeared somewhat younger only more agitated. He sported a similar tattoo on each arm.

They continued to "act out," shuffling their feet, making cat noises, trying to catch her eye. She ignored them.

X-Ray entered the room holding a printout and glanced up from the paper in time to catch the two boys moving their chairs in unison which made a loud squeak that brought everyone's eyes to them.

X-Ray approached Mel. "This is the home of punks, skunks and drunks. Those are the punks. They love making scary shit." He patted her on the arm. "That's Lozano and Alfie Ramirez . . . brothers . . . no relation to me, thank God. They're really nice perps and they're here snitching somebody for some 'good time'."

"Confidential informants?"

"Yeah, they're CIs. What's not to love about a system where guys with records rat on people that we want higher along the food chain . . . which in turn gives them credit for the next time we bust 'em."

"That's for shit. Necessary, but shitty. Why are they in cuffs, if they're so harmless?"

"Oh, they're not harmless, but they're friendly. We cuff 'em on the street and here in public so they won't be spotted as snitches. We'll cut 'em loose when we get the info they have, and they'll tell everybody they were questioned and released. No harm, no foul."

"Right."

"In fact, they were CIs for T-Bone. Gave up some bad people to T-Bone and me. Want an intro?"

"No thanks. I'll pass for now." Mel made a mental note, *CIs for Dad. Mm.*

She turned her back on the Ramirez brothers and nodded toward the property room door. "Where is that turkey?"

"Probably scratching his ass somewhere. I'll get him," X-Ray replied.

Seconds later, Agee returned, holding a pen in one hand with a clipboard in the other.

She pulled a ballpoint from her father's box.

"Ya oughta check the contents, you know," he said. She scribbled her name and address on the empty line beside the notation, *"Personal property of Det. William Walker."*

She swallowed hard and took the envelope. "I trust you."

He shrugged and turned to go, giving her one last insult. An evil smell followed him as he blew wind from her to the property room door.

A slight chuckle and harrumphs could be heard throughout the room. The guys were used to this kind of filth. They lived with it and worked in it.

Mel placed the envelope on top of the pile and grabbed the box. The officers stood aside. She rebuffed all attempts

44

to help and instead, walked proudly through the squad room hugging the box saying, "No, thanks."

Even the police department had snowflakes hanging from the ceiling and Christmas music playing.

*Shit, I hate holidays. I hope Dad's appointment book is here. It might, at least, tell me who saw him last.*

## ∞5

The evening seemed unusually crisp as Mel drove her car along the eucalyptus-lined lane toward the Dotson's annual boat party. Patty Dotson had been her best friend since junior high school when they were considered the odd couple of their social scene.

Patty's parents were wealthy socialites, philanthropic by nature and great money managers. Patty was well grounded emotionally. After graduating from Stanford, she had fallen in love and married into another wealthy family. Mel, a klutzy peasant, whose father was a cop and mother a housewife, attended local junior college and married a two-timing lawyer.

The prospect of attending another annual Christmas party that was traditionally a dull event, caused her mind to wander as the night played out before her a satisfying way to end the evening.

*What if, tonight, my asshole ex-husband drank to his usual excess and fell backwards, unnoticed somehow, into the murky waters of the Newport Bay and disappeared forever?*

She giggled as this fantasy developed in her mind. Mel spent a fortune getting her hair done. A rare treat for her. She did not normally waste money on current hair styles, so the SL top remained up. She was unlike so many plastic-faced ladies in southern California. A wash and a blow-dry usually served her naturally curly, short hair well.

She rounded the bend and neared the English Tudor home that sprawled across the end of a cul-de-sac. A lavish display of Christmas lights and decorations, Patty's tribute to wealth, indulgence and the holiday season, caught her vision.

Parking was at a premium on the narrow, harbor-front streets and a white-coated valet stood by.

As she neared the front entrance, soft jazz spilled into the night, followed by smells of basil and pasta . . . an Italian caterer. *Maybe it would be a good evening, after all.*

Mel slipped from under the steering wheel, and took a claim check from the valet. She smoothed the lines of the black silk dress. The black matching high heels slipped on the Palos Verdes stone steps. "Might have known, slick as oil when wet. Remember to be graceful," she told herself. "Take small steps and hold your stomach in."

The sound of her heels made a counterpoint with the live music as she approached the double, wide, panelled doors and stepped across the threshold into a marble vaulted foyer.

Dozens of attractive well-dressed people, many of whom she did not recognize, stood in clusters . . . everybody talking, nobody listening. The air, thick with cigarette smoke, perfumes, and jazz sounds assailed her senses. Much to her amusement, a shrill laugh trilled periodically above the crowd noise.

"Gawd, I have to get out more often," she murmured to a perfect stranger; then took a deep breath and pressed forward into the crowd.

Jason, the butler, met her at the door, smiled, and without comment offered a vodka and tonic with a lime twist.

Jason and his wife, Bessie, had worked for the Dotson family since Mel and Patty were in junior high school. Though Jason and Bessie were English and, a bit stuffy outwardly, they had always spoiled the girls who enjoyed their warm and special relationship. They would sit in the Dotson kitchen for hours, doing homework, eating Bessie's scones and jams and listening to stories of merry old England. Tall, lean Jason always wore gray. Bessie, a bit more fleshy, favored gingham dresses and ruffled white bibbed aprons.

Bessie carried a large silver tray filled with stuffed celery, caviar, artichoke hearts with chopped mushrooms and some little shrimp on toast. She offered Mel a napkin and encouraged her, with a wink, to take more.

"Since you made them, I will have another," Mel said, reaching for seconds. She could hardly hurt Bessie's feelings. Bessie had been trying to put weight on Mel's size eight frame since the tenth grade.

Hearty laughter caught Mel's attention. Turning toward the living room, she spotted a man, dressed like a cowboy, standing with Patty. Patty excused herself and joined Mel. They exchanged the usual "Los Angeles kissing-the-air" gesture.

"Who's the guy you're talking to?" Mel asked.

"The one with the wonderful smile?" Patty said, waving toward the source of their gossip.

"Yeah."

Patty grabbed Mel's hand and led her through the crowd. As they approached him, his grin widened and a deep chin cleft disappeared. With his aquiline nose and neatly trimmed black hair, he was the kind of man who could double for a matinee idol. His eyes were the color of crystalline blue that was usually seen only in the movies. The eyes drew Mel closer.

Under a black dinner jacket, a starched white tuxedo shirt covered his broad shoulders. A perfectly creased pair of Levi's best encased his lankiness with pointed-toed boots completing the picture.

"Mel, I want you to meet Lucas, my Texas cousin I've told you about. I finally convinced him to move his business to southern California. Houston's wells are dead, fenced, locked and closed. The future of the oil brokerage business is here, my dear. And even better, he too, is single."

With that, Patty released her grasp on Mel's hand and disappeared into the party.

Mel felt herself blush as she shook Lucas's hand. Lucas held her hand a moment longer than she thought necessary, but must not have realized it, because he looked down at their grasp and turned loose so fast that the effect was comical. They both smiled.

Mel spoke first. "What did Patty actually do, to convince you to come to Tinsel Town?"

"I'm relocating my oil business to the west coast to coordinate new acquisitions with some offshore business," he drawled. "The move to California will be good if I'm to expand. The oil is here and so are the deals. But I must admit to you, I dislike California already."

"I'm a native and I assure you, there are one or two nice things about this place."

"Would you personally be responsible for changing my opinion about California?"

"Sure, anytime." She possessed an uncanny knack for speaking her mind before engaging her brain. After only a second of remorse, she smiled again, glad she'd gone to the extra effort this evening, after all.

Their elbows touched as people continued to fill the room, invading their space. She felt a tingly shock somewhere inside.

The guests jostled toward the best possible view walking between the bar and the giant windows through the French doors leading to the deck. Someone bumped her elbow sloshing a bit of her drink. She turned, expecting an apology. "Oh, it's only you, Taylor." Mel looked away, knowing she would not get any apology from her ex-husband.

But, Lucas persisted. "Can you watch it fella? You made her spill her drink." He put his arm around the area of her shoulder, not touching, but protecting her space.

Taylor responded with a snide retort, "She can hold her liquor. You don't have to worry about her."

With that, Lucas stepped forward. She stood between them, her drink jiggled and a few drops flew onto the exposed bosom of the "drop-dead" blond who quickly clung to Taylor's arm.

"Lucas, this is Taylor Archer," said Mel.

"I'm her ex-husband," Taylor replied.

Lucas stepped back, and both men nodded to each other in acknowledgement. Neither extended his hand.

Taylor used his drink napkin to wipe the spots from the plunging neckline of his escort. "And this is Natalie Williams."

Mel knew the name, quite well. Taylor had worked his way through law school serving summonses for the William's firm when Mel worked for Natalie's father as a paralegal. Taylor's great sense of humor and stories about the clients was what first attracted her to him. They married and she supported the family until he passed the bar. Then, Taylor became a lawyer in the same firm and Mel quit working to become a full-time mother for Willie.

Taylor never forgave her for Willie's death. But, how could she watch him every moment? A hit and run driver's car jumped the curb, rutted through the front yard and ran over Willie who was playing ball, not ten feet from her parents' front door. The marriage splintered after that, and Taylor began to drink and stay out late.

*It wasn't enough that he slept with his secretary in our home, now he's dipping his pen in the company ink, sleeping his way to the top of the company letterhead. The boss's daughter. Would he ever learn?*

Now, Mel and Lucas found themselves ferried along with the crush. They soon faced the twinkling Christmas lights which draped rooftops of homes across the bay. Boats brightly decorated with this years "angel" theme paraded just beyond the deck.

"I'm sorry that one of your first impressions of California was meeting my ex. He's one of our hundreds of thousands of lawyers. She's the boss's daughter. Actually, as California divorces go, ours wasn't as messy as others you hear about, and he's usually there for me when I have problems."

"As Texas divorces go, mine wasn't so clean. Children?"

"We had a son, Willie. He died several years ago. And you?"

"I'm sorry. That must have been terrible for you both. No, my ex-wife wanted to be a career lady. She would not give up the pursuit of her PhD long enough to get pregnant." Lucas frowned at his empty glass.

The crowd forced them ever closer until she recognized his cologne. "I love Aramas," she said.

"I like your Joy."

Mel felt Texas-sized goose bumps on her arm.

They laughed together.

Another nudge to Mel's elbow interrupted the mood. This time, her arm flew forward and she spilled her drink onto the black and white Brioni jacket of a tall, distinguished, gray-haired gentleman.

The man turned, as if to protest, and then exclaimed in his best "I went to Harvard" voice, "Why hello, my sweet Mel."

He wrapped his long arms around her and gave her a bearhug.

"Patty said she'd invited Taylor, but never mentioned you were even in town." He blurted without waiting for a response, "He's here. Have you seen him?" He held a drink in one hand and vigorously rubbed his nose with the other as if trying to stop an itch. He talked as fast as a runaway train.

Ignoring his question, Mel tried to brush her drink off his back with her cocktail napkin. "Lucas, I want you to meet an old family friend and my former employer, Jeffrey Williams. He's one of the few really nice attorneys I know. JW, this is Lucas, from Texas."

The two men shook hands. JW held his elbows tight against his body so his drink would not spill again. He commented, "Patty has fabulous parties and this is the finale. This is the 'A' party in Orange County for the Christmas season. How do you fit into this picture, Texas?"

"Patty's my 'kissin' cousin and I never knew she was such a socialite."

Mel interceded, "I saw Taylor with Natalie, JW."

"Yeah, they're an item, now. I know I spoiled her rotten, but I believe Taylor might be good for her . . . tame her somewhat."

*It wouldn't hurt his career either.* "Yes, they may be good for each other, JW, and they both deserve some happiness." She then leaned over and hugged his arm snugly. JW scratched himself furiously, and she released her hold on his free hand.

"We need to go over some papers on T-Bone's estate. Want to drop by the office Monday or Tuesday and go over them with me?"

She stared into the bottom of her glass and guzzled her drink with one long slurp. "Yeah, probably Tuesday, if that's okay with you?"

"Fine. I should be in all day, but if something comes up, I'll have Lil call you and save you the drive in."

"Great. See you then." Mel peered into the far depths of her now empty glass.

JW said, "Well, nice to have met you, Lucas . . . see you Tuesday, Mel." He rubbed his nose again and excused himself to get another drink. Mel found herself alone with Lucas.

"Do you really want to see a boat parade? I'm hungry. Wanna stay and eat here, with all these chattering strangers, or is there a nice little Italian place near here? Someplace we can talk?" Lucas roared over the deafening noise.

"Patty makes me come to these affairs every year. Look, I have some great lasagna at home. We won't be missed."

Mel and Lucas shouldered their way through the revelers who looked at them like they were crazy for relinquishing their front row spots. Mel spotted Patty and waved goodbye. Lucas blew Patty a kiss. But Patty motioned them to join her in the kitchen.

The smell of fresh garlic bread filled the air in Bessie's kitchen as Mel and Lucas entered the kitchen. Patty said, "Too much noise out there for you, huh?"

"Yeah. If you don't mind, cuz'n, Mel's sold me on some pasta at her place."

"Are you kidding?" Patty said, smiling.

Bessie and Patty both grinned, approvingly, and Bessie threw a bag of loose salad greens along with a loaf of french bread, dripping with garlic and butter, into a large shopping bag. Lucas rounded the corner of the kitchen's center counter holding two bottles of the Dotson's best Chianti.

In a few seconds they reached the front door, gasping the first fresh, cool air they had breathed all evening. They both fumbled for their parking stubs and giggled like kids playing hookey.

"I have a GM rental car," he added, "but it's a convertible."

Mel responded, "Mine's what they call a California Ford, but what the hell, I'll put the top down. Let's take my car. It'll be parked out front. I can bring you back later."

True to California custom, all the expensive cars were parked at angles facing the street. Each Mercedes, Rolls, BMW and some specialty kit cars were on view. Mel's car was first in line.

She tipped the valet handsomely and winked at him knowingly as her thanks for the fine parking space, then folded the cloth top into the trunk storage area and snapped the cover in place. She carefully placed the food and wine on the back seat and jumped into the car. The SL roared to life and Mel pointed out landmarks of interest as they cleared the gated community and sped along Newport Boulevard toward Pacific Coast Highway.

"Patty tells me you're an investigator. A private eye type?"

"Naw. I do insurance fraud, lots of wrongful deaths, a few intellectual property rights, things like that. I do have a PI working with me though. He specializes in death penalty cases. Name is Johnnie Blake. JB's on a case in San Francisco and should be back tomorrow. I've got a new assignment for him."

"Were you born in California?"

"Yeah. My home's in a small city south of Newport called Harbour Pointe."

*My dad was murdered there.*

Mel's salon hair style swirled like a tornado as she steered through the traffic caused by the boat parade. Extra officers directed the annual Christmas madness. Barbra Streisand sang some old Broadway hits on tape. Mel leaned forward and turned down the volume.

During a break in both the music and traffic, she surveyed the clear, dark sky. Her mouth turned down slightly.

Lucas leaned over, smiling. "You're going to change my mind about California, remember?"

That got her attention. She smiled. A small one, but a smile nonetheless.

"I was actually thinking about how refreshing it is to breathe air I don't see nor taste. For a change, the night air is clean and crisp. But, you must be used to fresh air, coming from a coastal city like Houston."

"You haven't been to Texas in a long time, Mel. The oil industry has caused a lot of pollution. Houston can hold its own against LA any day on any issue: air, crime, corruption. We're not virgins anymore ... if we ever were."

"Really? Maybe it's that we get all the publicity ... nationwide, anyway. I have that California state of mind that we're the worst."

"How far are we from Harbour Pointe? You have me totally lost," Lucas said, changing the subject.

"It's past Corona del Mar, probably another ten minutes; of course, depending on the traffic." Red taillights, strung like Christmas lights, filled both lanes as far as the eyes could see. She stopped.

Lucas chuckled. Mel jumped in, "Yeah, yeah, I know you have traffic too; this is nothing."

"Well," Lucas admitted, "this is not nothing. Our traffic is a bitch. But I must say, LA is the biggest parking lot I've been exposed to west of New York and north of Mexico City."

Mel nodded and, after waiting her turn, merged into the flow of traffic going south on Pacific Coast Highway. "So you've been to California before?"

"Many times. I usually stay in a hotel at LAX, conduct my business and get back on the plane the next morning."

"And I need to fill in the blanks between LAX and the rest of the city, huh?"

"Right."

"Been to Catalina?"

"Only in the song." He began to sing, "Twenty six miles across the sea . . . "

"Oh, God and you can sing too." She laughed.

"I can line dance, bait a line, sing a line."

"What a line." She threw back her head and they both laughed.

Corona del Mar had rolled up the streets for the evening. Some couples strolled along, holding hands and glanced into the darkened windows. "Corona del Mar has great little boutiques and art galleries, but window shopping's nice too."

"Unlike most men, I like shopping. Can you fish?" Lucas asked.

"Like Ahab."

"I knew that."

After clearing the picturesque part of the community the highway opened to rolling hills and more traffic. With Mel's foot on the accelerator all the way, the car sped on past Crystal Cove and the Date Shop. They drove another two minutes before she entered a guarded gate, removed her plastic key from above her visor, inserted it into a silver box and punched in a code.

She nodded to Jeff in the guard house as the brass gate rolled to the right. Jeff raised his hand and waved her through.

"These are lovely homes. Do you have an ocean view?" Lucas asked.

"Yes," she replied, "I got the house in the divorce. Well, I didn't GET it exactly, but you know what I mean."

"I sure do," he said to the breeze outside his window.

They rounded the corner and entered the last street before the cliffs . . . six homes in a cul-de-sac.

"If you came home drunk, it'd be easy to miss your house," Lucas said.

Pale pink stucco homes sprawled over every lot, each with identical darker pink tile roofs. The houses were two stories high with circular driveways. Looming before them stood majestic manila; red and purple queen bougainvillaea climbing the walls toward the tile roof.

With a start, Mel leaned forward in her seat and slammed on the brakes, bringing the SL to a screeching halt in the middle of the street. Lucas, caught unaware, rocked forward with his arm on the dash. They were all alone on the road.

"What's the matter? Are you all right?" He yelled and gulped for air.

"The lights . . . the lights are on in the house!" She glanced around, "I turned out all the lights before I left for the party, and Rosa's gone for the evening."

"Who's Rosa?"

She turned the car lights off, drove to the curb two houses away, grabbed her purse and removed a handgun. Lucas, eyebrows raised, gripped the dashboard and gulped, again.

"Wait here, okay?" She took off running, without waiting for his acknowledgment.

Lucas jumped out of the car and ran to catch up with her. "You're not going in there without me."

She kicked off her shoes, leaving them scattered in the street. Lucas and Mel matched step for step as they crossed the circular driveway toward the towering front doors. The massive carved oak doors stood wide open.

"Damn," she said between her teeth.

Mel, now in her stocking feet, crouched and looked around the front yard, then ran to the side of the right-hand door. Knees bent, she raised the gun and grasped it with both hands, aiming chin high. She motioned for Lucas to be quiet and remain outside. Mel glanced into the front hall, then ducked back.

Taking a long breath, she stepped across the open threshold and out of Lucas's sight.

The stairs were to the left inside the door. Mel crouched there to regroup, her gun still in position.

*God, all the lights in the house are on. The door was open! So why didn't the damn alarm go off?* She crept forward to the edge of the step.

*SHIT.* Inside, the scene looked as if an earthquake had hit the living room: furniture overturned, lamps broken and pictures lopsided.

Mel swung back toward the stairs and ducked into the half bathroom under the stairwell. "All clear," she whispered, marking the room off her checklist.

With her back to the door casing, Mel entered the dining room and hunched down. She heard sounds from the kitchen. A kitten . . . meowing. *I don't have a cat.*

She tilted the gun forward, cocked the hammer and moved cautiously toward the kitchen doorway.

The fluorescent lights in the kitchen blinded her as she neared the threshold. It took a few seconds to adjust to the brightness before she entered. The meowing continued.

*A cat . . . in pain.*

Mel hunched even lower and then, as her father had taught her, jumped into the room, yelling, "Put your hands in the air. I have a gun and I'll blow you away."

But, the only movement came from the gun in the air. She turned to the right. There on the floor beneath the end of the counter, lay Rosa's shoes. Mel would not have thought that unusual, except that there were feet in those shoes . . . Rosa's feet.

"My God, Rosa! What happened?" Mel knelt and touched the back of Rosa's head to lift it, but withdrew her hand when she spotted blood on the floor. She held Rosa's wrist. A strong pulse . . . but unconscious.

Mel quickly stood and reached for the telephone. A shadow in the doorway caught her eye. She swung the muzzle of the gun around and pointed it directly against a man's cheek . . . Lucas. With a deep sigh, she lowered the gun.

"You could be a dead man." She scowled, loud and firmly. "I asked you to stay outside. I have a real problem here."

"I see that. How can I help?"

She pointed to the telephone. "Thanks. Dial the pound sign, then the number one. When someone answers, ask for X-Ray and tell him Mel has a code two and a 907N at home. I need to finish checking the house." Her jaw and teeth ached from the grinding she had given them.

"She's alive and should be fine if we can get help."

Lucas grabbed the telephone and dialed as instructed. On the second ring, a man answered. "Harbour Pointe Police Department. X-Ray here."

Lucas whispered, "Mel has a code two and a 907N at her house." He placed the receiver back on the hook.

Rosa lay motionless, but moaned softly, as a small pool of blood from the side of her head formed near Lucas' feet. He held her hand and checked her pulse. "Hang in there, little lady, help's on the way."

Mel moved three steps into the breakfast room and glanced outside the windows to check for intruders. Unfortunately, the bright lights inside made visible only shadows . . . cast by the trees in the planters . . . the queen palms. The pool and spa broadcast bright wavy shadows on the king palms against the back planter wall.

Her mind must be playing tricks on her. *Did something move? Were palm fronds blowing in the ocean breezes?*

She turned, and placed her back against the archway, glanced around and with one bold step, found herself square in the middle of the brightly-lit living room.

Pillows from the couch lay strewn on the carpet. The end stands, coffee table, lamps, and sofa had been upended and tossed about the floor. The contents of drawers lay spread over the off-white carpet. Thousands of bits of paper-like confetti covered the room. Several pieces of crystal vases lay broken. Pictures on the wall hung askew; others were knocked onto the floor. Her precious *Etude II*, the one real piece of artwork she owned, lay face down.

Mel stepped gingerly over the debris. Her dry mouth made it hard to swallow. "Who in the hell would do this?"

Outside she heard noises. The troops had arrived.

She hesitated, one foot on the bottom stair, both sweaty palms clasping the gun tighter.

From outside, she heard, "Halt! Police! Stop! Stop where you are and put your hands in the air." Mel lowered her gun and rushed to the front door.

∞ 7

In the middle of the cul-de-sac, cops' guns were trained on Lucas as he dropped Mel's shoes and raised his hands above his head, palms forward.

A short and well built Hispanic guy stepped out from behind an unmarked car with his Magnum drawn and pointed at Lucas' face. He sprinted toward Lucas forcing him face down on the ground while two other uniformed officers patted Lucas' pockets, front and back.

Once handcuffed, the officers pulled Lucas by the shirt and belt loops bringing him to his feet.

The first thing Lucas said was, "You've got the wrong guy, I'm a friend."

The leader of this group demanded, "Then why were you holding Mel's shoes? Why is her car here in the street? And what have you done with her?"

"She's in the house playing Dirty Harriet. I heard you guys coming and I came out to help you find the house. There's a woman unconscious and bleeding in the kitchen."

"She's got her gun out! Oh shit! Move in, guys," the officer ordered. They turned to approach the house when Mel stepped onto the porch and waved the officers inside.

The ground appeared to shake. The deep bass motor of an approaching red fire unit, complete with hook and ladder, caused it. The truck entered the street and parked at the curb. A red paramedics van arrived and parked ahead of the patrol cars.

Two motorcycle officers directed traffic, dispatching units, like party guests in a receiving line, to the front of Mel's house. The red-and-white siren lights strung across their bars, clicked as they spun. All personnel, with weapons drawn, positioned themselves in an area of safety behind their units, or in the bushes, and aimed their weapons at Mel's front door.

Over the crackling sound of the police dispatch radios, the sound of a Sikorsky Black Hawk helicopter hovered inside the housing tract, its blades chattering.

The paramedics grabbed their equipment boxes, telephone and backboard and ran into the house.

One officer, notepad in hand, asked, "Now tell me again, what you're doing here?"

"I tried to tell the other officer, sir. I'm a friend of Mel's. I was here with her, not trying to steal from her."

"Right!" The officer pulled Lucas's driver's license out of the billfold asking, "And your name is?"

"My name is Lucas Donovan. She and my cousin are good friends. I'm not the bad guy here. Can't you believe me?" he pleaded.

* *
*

The moment was interrupted by the paramedics pushing a gurney with a partially covered body on it. Mel followed, speaking to the attendant who held the IV, as she affectionately patted Rosa. The medics loaded the patient into the rear of the van and pulled away from the scene.

Lucas called out, "Mel? Over here!"

Mel scanned the scene, trying to spot him. When she did, she quickened her pace, "Oh my God, Lucas. I'm so sorry."

"Murdoch, there's been a mistake here. This is my friend."

"Yeah, that's what he's been telling me," Murdoch said. He unhooked the keys from his belt and removed the handcuffs from Lucas's wrists.

Lucas grabbed his wallet and stuffed it into his hip pocket, grumbling. He rubbed both wrists trying to restore circulation.

Mel explained to the officers, "I went to a boat parade party at a friend's house on Balboa. Rosa left hours before I did."

"When did you leave?" X-Ray asked.

"I haven't been gone more than one and half . . . two hours at most."

"Was anybody else here?"

63

"No. When I left, I turned out all the lights and set the security alarm."

"Is this how you found the house when you got back?"

"Yeah, the doors wide open, and every light in the house turned on. What a damn mess! And Rosa bleeding on the kitchen floor. I don't know what the hell happened."

She crossed her arms to control her shaking.

The rest of the officers came out of the house and joined the throng. Mel introduced Lucas.

"Everybody, this is Lucas. He's Patty Dotson's cousin from Texas. He was a new friend. But after tonight, I'm not too sure." The entire ensemble, motorcyclists, uniformed and plain clothed officers, reached into the circle, recited their last names and shook Lucas's hand. The one who had handcuffed Lucas and patted him down, smiled and nodded with an apologetic handshake.

Good naturedly, Lucas said, "I'd be a fool to give you up as a friend. What with your entourage." He smiled as he put one arm around her waist.

She returned his smile and the policemen dispersed into their units. In a few minutes the area cleared. Only X-Ray and the crime scene unit remained. X-Ray stepped toward Lucas and stuck out his right hand.

"Hi, I'm X-Ray. I'm Mel's best friend."

Lucas smiled. "Wow, you got those guys here in a hurry."

"You bet. We're family."

Mel vacillated, taking a step or two toward her car and then one or two toward the house.

Seeing her dilemma, X said, "Why don't you let the CSU finish here and I'll drive you over to Harbour View to see Rosa. Everything else can wait. The mess isn't going anywhere."

Lucas added, "And don't forget to reset the alarm."

"Yeah, okay. Good idea. Give me a minute will you?" Mel said.

As she disappeared into the house, X-Ray turned to Lucas, "Well, nice to meet you. Have a good stay while you're in California."

"I'd like to say 'Goodnight' before I go," and he quickly added, "if you don't mind? Only thing, I don't have my car here. I drove here with Mel."

"We'll drop you off, of course. Where? On Balboa?"

"Yeah."

"No problem."

They turned toward the house. Mel stood in the driveway and spoke to a crime scene officer who was wearing surgical gloves and lugging a large black suitcase. She gave him something, and walked toward the two men.

X-Ray spoke first, stepping in front of Lucas as Mel neared. "We're going to drop Lucas off first, to get his car."

Mel said, "Why don't I just give you the keys to my car and you can bring it back tomorrow?"

"Are you sure you won't need it?" Lucas asked.

"Positive. I have days of cleaning ahead of me."

"Do you want me to wait with the officer you left in the house?" Lucas asked.

"Thank you, but that won't be necessary. He's the fingerprint guy and I just gave him an extra set of house keys I can pick up later."

"Well, I'll see you in the morning then, Mel," Lucas drawled as he accepted the keys. Lucas bent over as if to give her a peck on the cheek, then pulled back and stuck out his hand, instead.

* *
*

During the drive to the hospital, a haze settled over the coastal area, like a low gray cloud. Mel told X-Ray, "What a great welcome to California for Lucas. Helicopters, police cars, paramedics, fire truck and guns. Some first date."

X-Ray chuckled, "That poor cowboy. Bet that was his first time to be handcuffed and searched."

"Honestly, X, you guys came in like an army assault unit."

* *
*

Within ten minutes the lights of the hospital parking lot appeared through the light coastal haze. X-Ray parked his unmarked unit in the designated police area.

He and Mel entered Harbour View Hospital through the double wide emergency room doors that parted electronically to greet them. Mel hesitated before entering. Two family members had entered these same doors, and exited in black body-bags.

She shivered and folded her arms against the chill. X-Ray responded by putting one arm around her shoulders and nudged her through to the warmth and light inside.

But Mel didn't feel the warmth nor see the lights. She smelled the antiseptic odor that, to her, signalled death.

A television blared in one of the waiting rooms. People huddled in small family groups consoling each other and waiting for medical updates on their loved ones.

*... old memories and lots of tears.* The emergency room triage nurse walked on noiseless rubber soles as he

approached them in the large corridor, interrupting her thoughts. The nurse, in surgical greens, carried a clipboard that had a pencil swinging from a short cord.

"May I help you?"

"Yes," Mel said, "we're looking for a friend, Rosa Castillo. Can you tell us where she is?"

"Yes, as a matter of fact, she was in Mm-m-m," the soft-spoken black man scanned his list as he spoke. "Yes, she was in emergency C, but I believe her tests are complete and she's been transferred to the trauma floor. I'll get you her room number."

He entered a small alcove with wire reinforced glass view port and tapped something in a computer. Within seconds he returned.

"Yes, she is in room 333."

"Thank you." The two walked down the corridor into a waiting elevator.

At the third floor, as the elevator doors opened, Mel darted ahead of X-Ray into the corridor to the left. They did not pause at the nurse's station which buzzed with medical activity and urgency. She needed no directions. Her mother had died here. So had her son, Willie. *This is the Walker floor,* she thought.

At room 333, Mel pushed through the closed door and found herself facing what looked like the drill sergeant of all nurses. The vision in white stood at least six feet tall with thick rounded shoulders. From a strong square jaw, the nurse barked, "The patient is heavily medicated. You can't come in here! Doctor's orders." Both massive hands with chubby fingers extended outward, halting their progress into the room.

"I'm family. It's not a problem," Mel said and she walked past her to Rosa's bed.

"You don't look like a Castillo." Sergeant Nurse said with emphasis on the "eo."

*And you don't look like a nurse,* Mel thought.

By this time X-Ray had caught up, and entered the room. He looked up, into the nurse's steel blue eyes. Any other person of his size might have been intimidated by the tall white barrier, but his training and instincts pressed him onward. He, also, brushed past her and approached the bed where Mel stood wiping Rosa's brow.

The nurse shrugged and pulled the door closed behind her, mumbling.

Rosa dozed. A large bandage covered her head. Her face was covered with bruises. In response to Mel's touch, Rosa opened her eyes. Mel patted her brow and whispered, "We're here, X-Ray and I. You're in the hospital."

Mel moved the IV aside to check Rosa's hospital bracelet, "Ah, Dr. Townsend. You're in good hands, Rosa. Is there anything you need? Anyone I can call for you?"

"No, Mel. I'm fine. When I first got to this bed from the emergency room I called my family. I'm fine. Really."

*"Si, como no! Ya basta con tanta plactica. Cuenteme con todo el detalle que puede todo lo que paso? Observo vd. quien le pego a vd? C como eran estas personas? Que nunca les habia visto antes?"* X-Ray queried rapidly.

Mel, overwhelmed by this outburst, yelled, "Wait a minute! Hold it! Let's have that again. In English! That is, if Rosa feels like answering some questions."

"Don't fuss over me, Mel. Really, I'm okay. Sure, I can answer questions."

X-Ray turned to Rosa and said, "Repeating for the native, Rosa, I said 'Enough of these niceties, tell me in as much detail as you can, what happened? Did you see who struck you? What'd they look like? You ever see 'em before?' "

Softly, Mel inserted, "First, why did you come back to the house? When I left to go to Patty's party, you'd been gone for over an hour."

"I forgot the grocery list. It was in the kitchen. I came back to get it."

"Was the house still dark and locked?"

"Yes, and the alarm was on, too."

"So before you went in, did you see anything unusual outside, like a strange car or people . . . anything?"

"Street quiet like normal. I see nothing. I parked on the street, so the oil wouldn't leak on the driveway."

"We don't need this much detail, Rosa. Just tell us what happened." X-Ray said.

"Okay. Then I use key and open the door and push the keys to turn alarm to 'off'. I go into the kitchen with no light on 'cause I know my way very good in the dark."

Rosa exhibited her Mexican Sarah Bernhardt impression, very low, soft and dramatic. X-Ray shifted from one foot to the other and leaned closer to Rosa's side.

Mel sensed his agitation. She reached over and patted his hand.

Rosa continued, "I get to the kitchen. Still no light on. I put my hand on the kitchen counter to get grocery list. I think I turned around. I'm not sure. Then I hear a voice say like, 'Where is it? Where'd she hide the damn thing?' Then BOOM! I get hit on head one maybe two times. And, wake up in the ambulance when I hear a loud siren over my hurting head."

When she paused to breathe, Mel took the lead. "Did you see anyone? Recognize anyone?"

"Not see anyone, just go BOOM, BOOM."

"How many?" X-Ray implored.

"*Dos,* I think . . . maybe more; I'm not sure."

"Hispanics, Anglos, Blacks, what?"

"I'm not sure about that, either, X-Ray. Maybe they Mexican. But not El Salvador. I know El Salvador." Rosa raised her head off the pillow. "Don't be mad, that I went in the house and left the door open. I thought I'd be there only a second." Her head dropped back. "Oh . . . " she moaned, her hand holding one side of her head.

"It's no problem, Rosa. You couldn't know . . . X-Ray, I think she's had enough excitement for tonight," Mel patted Rosa's arm. "Don't worry about medical bills. I'll take care of everything. Please rest. We'll be back tomorrow."

"Don't worry about that. My company pays for medical insurance for me and for all my family. It'll be okay."

Mel leaned over and kissed Rosa's forehead, then backed away smoothing the bed sheets. X-Ray touched Rosa's arm briefly, then joined Mel by the door.

Rosa added, "And don't worry about cleaning any messes. My whole family will be there early in the morning. My sisters and nieces . . . you'll be fine. I gave them good instructions for work to be done."

"Rosa you don't know what a mess those guys made. The house is in shambles. It'll take days, maybe weeks, to get me back in working order." She would worry later, how she was going to pay for all this extra work.

"Not to worry, now go eat and go home. First, you need to eat."

X-Ray followed Mel out of the room and closed the door.

"How'd she know I was starving?" Mel asked.

"Maybe that growling stomach was a clue," X-Ray replied.

"No shit. I wasn't even aware. That's embarrassing."

"No big deal. How 'bout Bernie's?"

They reached the elevator and the door opened. Out stepped Dr. Townsend, their family doctor since Mel was a toddler. He hugged Mel with his left arm and shook X-Ray's hand with his right. "Rosa's going to be fine. The x-rays are back and all the tests are okay. She has a mild concussion, needed a few stitches, but there's no inner cranial bleeding or clots. Nothing life threatening, but I want to keep her overnight as a precaution. She got hit pretty damn hard."

Mel loved Dr. Townsend. He had seen her through her measles, chicken pox and mumps . . . and Willie's too. Although an imposing six foot tall, he looked somewhat stooped tonight. His white, thinning hair had once been black as coal. He smelled warm, and comforting, like English Leather.

"We've got to stop meeting like this, Doc." Mel tried some humor.

"That's the damn truth," Doc replied, nodding his head in agreement.

X-Ray interrupted, "How many blows did she have to the head? Can you tell what weapon was used? Any other marks on her body?"

"Two. Over the right ear and above the back of the neck like a karate chop," he replied, demonstrating with his hands over his own head and neck. "Blunt . . . no other marks."

This time, Mel heard her long low growl.

"I gotta get this gal some food," X-Ray said. "We'll see Rosa again tomorrow."

"Good idea. Let her get some sleep tonight."

The doctor pressed a small white packet deep into Mel's palm. "You may need this later, for sleep. It's benzodiazepines. I'm assuming you're not pregnant. Don't drink or drive, but eat something first," he added and smiled.

Mel smiled, too. She had nodded during the instructions. The elevator door opened and they entered, leaving Dr. Townsend in the corridor. Mel turned to wave, but Dr. Townsend had already walked away from them toward the next emergency.

"We've got a long history, me and Doc," Mel said.

"Yep. Let's get outta here. I hate the smell of sickness around here. I wonder if they ever get it outta their clothes."

The emergency room doors opened as they stepped on the rubber mat. X-Ray spoke first. "Ever have a break-in like this before?"

"No. Never. That's one reason I wish I could afford to stay in that house. It's a gated community on the land side, bound by the ocean on the other."

"Does your ocean side have a gate?"

"Yeah. But it's got a combination type lock, which is changed every month."

"Any rentals in your neighborhood?"

"I don't know."

"We'll check it out."

They spent the trip to Bernie's trying to sort out the evening's events. X-Ray concluded, "I feel sure this is an isolated incident. But we'll know more about it when the forensic's report comes in. Hopefully, we collected some fingerprints too. Have you had any strange calls or letters? Anything that could be related to this attack?" He stopped for a light and turned to Mel who stared straight ahead, not speaking. "What are you thinking about? Did you hear me?"

Without turning, Mel answered, "I heard you. Strange calls or letters huh? That's your question?"

"Uh huh."

"Nothing I can't handle."

Bernie's was the favorite eatery for the Harbour Pointe Police Department. It won hands-down in taste tests, while losing handily in those measuring cholesterol. Bernie's had low lighting and dark paneling, the food was cheap and filling.

Bernie's single claim to culinary fame came from their 32-ounce steak. If one could eat the entire steak, with all the trimmings and associated condiments, the meal was free. Only her father held this revered position within the police department and on that spring day, Walker's nickname was born. Proudly scrawled on his picture hanging behind the bar, "T-Bone, June 1962."

X-Ray parked among other unmarked police cars behind Bernie's, and entered through the rear door, waving to three scroungy guys who sat in a large red plastic U-shaped booth in the far corner. The guys moved closer together, allowing room for the two to join them.

Cookie, Bernie's significant other, a sweet ... sometimes sassy lady, wiped her hands on a starched white apron as she approached the booth. Her carrot-colored bouffant, triple-long false eyelashes and Cleopatra black eye-liner belied her youth.

Mel smiled as Cookie neared.

"Hi, Mel. X. What'll it be?" she asked, snapping her gum. She attempted to blow a bubble. Her tongue stuck through the center preventing a full air vacuum. She used the eraser on the pencil to stuff the wad back into her mouth and popped smaller ones inside.

Mel and X-Ray glanced around the table. Everyone had black coffee. Chicken-fried steak smothered in brown gravy with fries and gobs of catsup completed the fare. The guys used Cookie's fresh baked biscuits to sop the gravy.

"Ditto for me," X-Ray responded twirling his index finger around the table.

"If I ate that at this hour," Mel interrupted, "my stomach would revolt. Not for me, Cookie. You have any soup left?"

"Sure, honey. I made fresh vegetable soup today with lots of beans. And I have some fresh cornbread," she added.

"Great. That'll be great. And a diet-something to drink. Maybe a small salad too, with your house dressing."

The three other guys mumbled amidst mouthfuls of food. One vocalized, "You gotta be kidding! That's pig food!"

"Thank you for sharing that with us. At least I won't have clogged arteries and heart attacks like you turkeys," Mel said.

"Anything else for you guys while I'm here?" Cookie shifted from one foot to the other, tapping her pencil on the note pad.

"Nope. We're okay," came the chorus in unison. They groused under their breaths and continued to scarf the food, without interrupting their conversation. Cops, like soldiers, learned to eat fast. Time was so precious and interruptions so frequent for them, that a meal became more fuel for the battle than food for the soul.

"Hey, we heard about World War III at your house earlier. What went down?" growled the burly undercover guy known on the street as "Daryl." Catsup dripped onto his graying unkempt beard and his already dingy, sweaty tee shirt.

X-Ray glanced around, making sure the room was full of friendlies. He hunched over the scarred formica table top and quickly and methodically gave them the details . . . mistaking Mel's date for a perpetrator and handcuffing him was the grand finale. Cops love that kind of thing.

All of them, including X-Ray, laughed so hard one of the older guys choked on his food. Mel slapped him on the back to help him catch his breath.

Mel remained stone faced. Feeling confused, weary, hungry and irritable, she crossed and unfolded her hands, which rested on the table top. Then, as their laughter subsided, they returned to the trough. "Oh, I get it," Mel said and started to giggle.

This action infected the guys and contagious laughter erupted. It took a few moments of small talk and stories of similar embarrassing moments, and then the five of them regained their composure.

The moment calmed as Cookie approached bearing a mountain of plates, which began at her fingers and terraced perfectly by overlapping each other all the way up her right arm to her shoulder. In her left hand Mel's plate spilled over with greens. Cookie didn't miss a chew of her gum, nor a beat in her step. She slapped the salad down in front of Mel and kept right on walking. She knew not to intrude on the inner sanctum of the police world. She was a "friendly" but she knew her place and maintained her distance. No questions plus no answers equals no loose lips, later. Mel knew Cookie followed the rules.

Mel devoured her salad ... hungrier than she'd realized. Cookie served more coffee. The guys burped into their napkins and pushed their empty plates back. The toothpicks came out all around and the jackets were unbuttoned. With heavy sighs abounding, Mel glanced around at this motley crew.

What a fearless trio; Daryl, Mikey and Whitey. Undercover cops, smelling like weeks in a rancid alley. They dressed in dark pants and jackets that didn't match. The frayed clothes were heavily stained.

Mikey, the youngest and cockiest of the trio, had transferred from the Los Angeles Police Department a few years ago. He was of medium build, but strong as a bull. His jet black hair screamed in all directions, as greasy as the remains on his plate. With eyes so piercing they could carve a tombstone. What he lacked in age he made up for in guts and grit.

Daryl and Mikey had gone through the Academy with X-Ray and, under her father's tutelage, had grown in experience and moxie. Buffed to the finest of muscle tone, nothing got past these two.

Daryl, the enormous bear on the force both in height and weight, had dark thinning hair and hazel eyes. He measured in at six feet, six inches, with two hundred forty-five pounds of muscle and twenty pounds of fat, most of which spilled over the belt line. As if he needed an equalizer, a magnum bulged under his right armpit.

Whitey's nickname matched his shock of pure white hair, now long, grimy and tied at the nape of his neck with an equal dingy leather strap. Even his eyelids and four-day-old beard were white. His eyes were the greenest Mel ever saw. His cheeks and nose reminded her of Santa. It resembled a blush red, fractured road map. A result of years of heavy drinking. It was the "A" in the CADS her father had cautioned her about.

*Dad's cheeks were not like Whitey's,* she reminded herself.

Whitey, with over thirty years with Harbour Pointe Police, was considered the "old timer," now that T-Bone had died. His concern for Mel exceeded everyone's, except for X-Ray. After all, Whitey had photographed her first steps during one of T-Bone and Carole's famous Sunday home barbecue dinners.

T-Bone and Carole's major contributions to the Sunday picnics at home, had been a sense of warmth and a loving family, an exception in most police departments. Carole, an outstanding cook, worked miracles on a cop's family budget and T-Bone was the master fire starter.

The picnics ended a few years ago, when Mel's son, Willie, had been killed while playing basketball in the driveway. They never found the driver. Despite the resources at hand, the trail became colder and colder as the years passed.

* *
*

The interrogation about Mel's break-in continued.

"Okay," Daryl asked, "what's missing? Do you have a safe . . . cash? What were they looking for? Any idea?"

"Listen, guys, I wear ALL my valuables. What you see is all there is." She pointed to her watch on the left wrist and to a gold ring with a small red stone. She turned her hands over palm side up, like a magician, showing she had nothing up her sleeves. She continued. "I carry what little cash I have. Insurance companies and attorneys pay me by check which I deposit weekly."

"Anything missing?" Mikey asked again.

"It's too soon to know," Mel said. "Rosa's family will be there first thing in the morning to start cleaning. Until that's done . . . and it may take a couple of days . . . I have NO idea. I didn't notice anything missing, no."

Whitey had a question. "Any room more messed up than others?"

"Yeah," X-Ray interrupted, "the office. Paper and files everywhere."

"What did Rosa get hit with? Anything we could fingerprint?"

"Nothing found at the scene," X-Ray responded. "The doc said it was a blunt instrument."

"Ah," added the cocky young Daryl. "Like Clue. I see it all now. Colonel Mustard did it in the kitchen with the candlestick. See how easy crimes are to solve? Next case."

"Could be a simple B and E, someone looking for something to pawn for drugs," said a weary Mel.

Cookie took the empty salad dish and placed a steaming bowl of belly-filling soup and cornbread in front of Mel.

"Aw, you know the cop business Mel. There are no coincidences. Did you check the area, X?"

"Yeah, my guys did. Mel lives in a gated community of some forty plus homes. You gotta have a key or a code to pass the front gate. The guard's there all evening. We haven't checked with him yet. There's easy access from the beach, hers was the only home hit in the past ten years, according to our records. You're right. This is no coincidence. But I haven't figured out the connection yet. We're working on it," he replied, patting Mel on the hand.

A beeper interrupted the discussion. Each of the guys checked their belt line. "It's mine," Whitey said.

He pushed a button, glanced at it and then at Daryl and Mikey, "Looks like the bait has bitten," he whispered. "Let's hit it. I may get to dump my humnet yet."

Crumpled money was thrown onto the table along with stained paper napkins. They scooted around the circular booth and stood, hitching their belts over very full bellies.

"Keep in touch, guys," Whitey told X-Ray and Mel. "We wanna follow with you on this one."

"We'll get those guys, and they'll be sorry," Daryl added.

X-Ray and Mel found themselves alone. X-Ray's dinner arrived.

"I'll bite," Mel said after eating in silence for a few minutes. "What's a humnet?"

X-Ray laughed. "It's narc speak for a 'hummer' day. You ever heard of that?"

"Nope."

"It's like a bummer day, when everything goes wrong. Only in the case of a narc, it's when he can't make a decent bust. The department made a truly ugly trophy called a 'humnet'. Whitey has had it on his desk for, oh six months, I guess. He can't pass it on until he gets a good bust."

"Well, I wish him luck. He's a neat guy."

"Yeah."

Mel slouched back in the booth, her head against the leather trim.

"You must be exhausted from your busy day, pretty lady," X-Ray said.

Cookie dropped the bill between the salt and pepper shakers.

"Let me get this," Mel said.

"No way. Your money's no good with me, woman." X-Ray calculated the tip, dropped more bills on the table and turned with Mel toward the back door.

Cookie brushed Mel's arm and whispered, "If there's anything Bernie and I can do, you gotta but ask, you know?"

"That's sweet of you both. I'll remember that. Thank you." Mel smiled and gave her a big hug.

At the car, X-Ray commented, "She knows better than to listen in, much less repeat what she hears in there. Boy, that really pisses me off."

"Let it go, X. She was just trying to help. No big deal."

"Yeah, right," he grumbled as the car growled to life and they exited the lot onto Pacific Coast Highway.

# ∞9

In minutes, they arrived at the guard gate. Mel gave X-Ray her code and the gates rolled apart.

"Jeff works from eight to eight," Mel said. "And he's very dependable and reliable. If the assholes didn't enter here, it was probably from the beach, like you said."

"There's no telling, Mel. We'll find 'em, don't worry."

Her eyes watered. One tear trickled down her cheek. She brushed her face with the back of her hand as they entered her driveway.

She opened the car door and leaned over to give X-Ray a goodnight peck on the cheek.

"You can forget that 'goodnight' shit. I'm here for the long haul."

"You don't have to do that. I'm a big girl." She straightened, half in and half out of the car.

"Two guns are better than one."

With that, he turned the ignition off, got out of the car and joined her at the front door.

"I'll sleep on the couch."

"You can sleep in Willie's bedroom. It's just as he left it. The twin beds are fairly comfortable. I even sleep there, sometimes." Her voice drifted off.

"Okay, whatever you say."

They entered the dark, quiet home. X-Ray flipped on lights. Mel turned the alarm from "interior and exterior" to "exteriors only" which sealed them safely in for the night.

"First, let's get some milk or I'll make some tea so you can get those pills down . . . that Doc gave you. You got any cookies?"

"Rosa always keeps cookies here," she called from the kitchen. She checked the water kettle on the stove top and pointed at the cookie jar on top of the fridge.

"Funny, isn't it, how musty a house smells when it's been turned upside down?" she asked.

"Yeah. I noticed it too. Guess I never thought of it before. But you're right. It's kinda like a mildew smell."

They grabbed cookies and milk for Mel, tea for X-Ray and cleared off a place at the dining room table.

"Don't you dare tell anyone I drink hot tea. It's a sissy drink for wussies."

"Ah, more blackmail material for me later. I'll save that," she teased. Mel lowered her eyes and voice and said, "Gawd, I miss Dad. Do you miss him X?"

"Shit yeah. I loved that guy. I loved him like the father I never had. T-Bone was the kind of dad most kids could only dream about. You and I . . . damn lucky."

"I miss picnics and barbecues with friends and family, going to the zoo, vacations . . . all that stuff."

"I can remember how we used to have long talks at the dinner table about our days at school. Even though he might be working on some gruesome crime, he always had time for us."

"Yeah. You don't really believe he ate his gun, do you X?"

"I certainly don't want to believe it. I admit . . . I saw no signs of corruption . . . I mean he wasn't living beyond his means, no long vacations, or tossing around a lot of money. Like he never let on to any problems. But afterward, at the house, we found a bank account book with monthly deposits well beyond his salary. Lots of alcohol around the house, some residue of cocaine on the coffee table and travel brochures to some very expensive locations. Remember what T-Bone said about C-A-D-S: Corruption, Alcohol, Drugs and Suicide? I just don't know." He shook his head and picked up his cup of tea.

"Well, I don't understand it, either. But I do know my dad. In spite of all that evidence, he never did use or sell drugs. I'd swear to that. Why, he would have killed me if I ever lifted a cigarette to my mouth, much less a drug stronger than aspirin, unless it was prescribed. Speaking of which, wonder what kind of pills Doc gave me, tonight."

She reached into her purse and found the small envelope. Inside were three white pills with Xanax stamped on them. "Xanax, huh? Good for short term relief of anxiety. Yeah, Doc gave me stuff like this before, you know . . . for all the funerals."

She shuddered and swallowed one oblong tablet with a sip of cold milk. "Gawd, what rotten years these have been. And now, I feel so lonely." She pushed the chair back and stood; picked up her plate and reached for his.

X-Ray said, "I'll get the dishes. I know how to load the dishwasher."

"You'll do dishes? Ah, more blackmail material. Do you need an apron, big guy?" She teased and tickled him in the ribs.

"Get laid, Mel." He dodged her next tickle attack.

"I wish."

"Anybody I know? Lucas, maybe?"

"Too soon to tell. Tonight was a hell of a first meeting." She walked down the hallway to make sure the guest room was picked up. She turned down the covers on Willie's bed. X-Ray made noise in her office. "Everything okay, X?"

"Yeah. The office is a bigger mess than I first thought," X-Ray replied. He entered the bedroom. "You didn't have to go to a lot of trouble for me. I can sleep standing up."

"I know that. I've seen it. But tonight you deserve a warm clean bed. After all, I have to take care of a guy who drinks tea and does the dishes."

"That's just too cute." X-Ray grabbed the two loose pillows and banged Mel about the head and body. She deflected blows and they giggled.

He threw the pillows back on the bed and Mel straightened them against the headboard. "Get serious, Mel. Tomorrow, first thing, you gotta work that office and see what's missing. Anything on the computer they might want like? Disks or files? Are you working on any big cases? You think this might have anything to do with your mugging in the cemetery?"

"Your c-o-p is working overtime. Take a break. See you in the morning." She leaned over the end of the bed and gave him a peck on the cheek.

"Fresh towels in the guest bath. Wake me early." Mel said.

She liked the idea of X-Ray sleeping in Willie's room.

Upstairs, she prepared for bed and paused at the intercom pressing it, "I love you, X. You're more than a friend. You're family."

A response bounced back, "I feel the same way, Mel. You're the sister I never had. Love you."

She pulled the covers to her chin and rooted for some warmth from the cold sheets. A blinking light drew her attention toward the night stand. It came from the telephone recorder. It was her personal and unlisted telephone number.

"Well, it'll just have to wait 'till morning," she murmured. The medication kicked in.

# ∞ 10

Earthquakes are California's alarm clocks and that morning was no exception. A small seismic shock, somewhere under the ocean floor, brought Mel back to the real world.

She scooted down into the warm bed trying not to wake up. Soon wonderful smells came wafting up from the kitchen. "He's a cook too?" She smiled, and reluctantly jumped into the cool air of her bedroom.

After a quick shower, she stepped into casual slacks, tennis shoes and a long loose shirt. She brushed her hair and applied a little makeup. The sobering remembrance of her trashed house quickened her steps.

At the head of the stairs, she blinked and wiped her eyes. The living room looked perfect. Everything in its place and anything broken, cleared away.

She bounced down the steps to the source of the bacon and coffee smells.

A charming little four-foot-something Mayan influenced-body barred Mel's entrance to the kitchen, "*Senora, I am Yolanda, Rosa's sister and vice-president of our company. We not wake you, huh?*" The slight Spanish accent made her voice sound delightfully exotic.

"No, Yolanda. The earthquake shook me. I needed to get up anyway."

The young girl peeked through thick, brown, straight hair which crowned her strong cheek bones and she pleaded, with both hands together, "Rosa kill me if I not here to serve you. She worry it was her fault those guys get in house because she leave alarm off." The enchanting accent and the melodic voice made it seem normal to drop the occasional word.

"How did you get so much work done, so quickly? I thought it would take days to get squared away."

"We work very fast, Rosa's family. We mostly through with the lower floor. You have lots of mess here. We work very quietly to finish. We not vacuum yet, though. That *Cholo* guy with the gun also speed up our work. He always grumpy this early in the morning?"

"I don't know, Yolanda. This is the first night he ever slept here." Then, looking around, she added, "I don't how I'm ever going to pay you all for this work?"

"Rosa said you are not to worry."

Mel hugged her. "*Gracias.* Where is the guy with the gun?"

"In your office, *Senora.* He not let us in there. We clean there last, okay?" she asked.

"That's fine, Yolanda. You can start on the second floor when you're ready. There isn't as much damage upstairs, but the police dusted for fingerprints. That's why it's such a mess."

"We know. Rosa told us about that dust. It needs a special cleaner. We ready for it. We went to the grocery first thing this morning."

"She doesn't miss a trick, does she? What happened to the broken stuff?"

"My cousin, Enrique, he found a carton in the garage. He put everything in box, for now. We lined box with a pillowcase to keep clean what you want to fix later, maybe. Enrique is working in the yard. He's not pleased with yardman. Is okay, *Senora?*"

"Sure, that's fine. Anything Enrique can do will be greatly appreciated. Wait a minute." Suddenly alert, "How did you know where things went? You have everything back in place."

"We go by hospital early. Rosa told us where she have pictures of each room, where everything should go. She have for vacation time when she break in someone, like new cousin, to clean."

"That woman. She's special. Well, I'd love some breakfast. Something smells good. Got any left for me?"

"All for you, *Senora*. Rosa gave me word on what you need to eat. Rosa is oldest sister. Oldest of ten. We not question Rosa. She the president."

"She bosses you too, huh?"

Mel walked toward the office and called out. "X, how about some breakfast . . . you hungry?"

At the door, the reality of the previous evening hit her squarely in the face. She raised one hand to her head and placed the other on a hip.

"AW, is this how Taylor saw you every morning? No wonder you're divorced. You look like ten miles of bad road."

"Thank you, X . . . hungry?"

"Sure, give me a minute. I'm trying to pick things up from the floor so you can start sorting and organizing."

"Well, I'm ready to eat." Mel walked toward the breakfast room. Along the way, two more young Hispanic girls giggled behind their hands as they guided her toward the back patio. There before her, lay a banquet fit for a cruise ship.

"Everything but an ice sculpture," she marveled, checking out the fresh fruit, breads and pastries, eggs sunny side up, waffles, bacon and sausage. Four kinds of juices plus milk and coffee and, of course, the pre-requisite refried beans, tortillas and homemade salsa completed the menu.

She turned to see a cluster of Rosa's relatives huddled inside the patio door, awaiting approval. X-Ray passed them and joined Mel.

"Wow." He said. "This is great . . . let's eat."

The family smiled with pleasure.

Yolanda turned. In Spanish she called out to Enrique, *"Enrique, limpia la cochina por favor."* She finished it in English to Mel that Enrique would clean up and join them for breakfast too. Dishes were handed out and the buffet line formed.

The door bell rang. Yolanda hurried to the front door.

No one seemed the least bit curious until Yolanda returned. Behind her, carrying a large box of assorted donuts, stood a very sheepish looking Texan. Lucas had returned, bearing gifts.

Everyone turned and caught the surprise on Lucas's face as he spotted the feast before him. Mel was reminded of the Littlest Angel with his humble gift as she rose to greet him.

"Thank you so much," she said, giving him the briefest hug.

She took the box and gave it to Yolanda who prepared a plate for the donuts in the center of the table. She also thrust a plate in his hands.

Lucas filled his plate and he and Mel reviewed the previous night's events.

Yolanda, the first to finish eating, cleared the table and emptied plates. When she got to the kitchen, X-Ray called out, *"Por favor,* change the sheets on MY bed too, Yolanda. When you have time."

*"Si, Senor,"* came a distant response.

Mel picked up the deliberate taunt. Lucas raised his eyebrows and looked down at his plate.

Yolanda chattered in Spanish to the younger girls. One grabbed a pail filled with rags and assorted cleaners and ran upstairs. The other stood in the middle of the living room holding a vacuum cleaner.

Yolanda returned to the patio door, *"Senora,* I can vacuum now? Is okay?"

"Sure. That's fine. Not the office though. I'll do it another day. It's a mess."

Yolanda nodded and disappeared.

Mel's attention returned to the conversation between the two men, now biographical in nature. It appeared to be the life story of Xavier (X-Ray) Ramirez, former life member of the TIO Gang, who jumped out of the gang and lived long enough to become a police officer, thanks to T-Bone Walker, detective, mentor, and friend . . . the long version.

Not wishing to hear all this today, Mel gathered her dishes and carried them into the kitchen where Yolanda scoured the stove top with a frenzy.

Mel set the dishes in the sink on top of others, soaking. Suddenly, a loud call for help permeated the air. It echoed throughout the house, octaves above the noise of the vacuum.

*"Policia, venga aqui ahora!"*

The entire house silenced. Everyone ran from every corner of the house and yard, converging on the stairway. X-Ray led the pack.

The medication had left some residue in Mel's brain. She stood for a moment, wondering if she had imagined that call for help. She turned, "Yolanda, did you . . . Yolanda?" She found herself alone in the kitchen.

"Mel, come here!" ordered X-Ray, sternly. "Quick!"

She ran to the source of his voice in her bedroom.

Everyone huddled in one corner. X-Ray bent over examining something on the night stand. Yolanda and the others consoled a shaking, agitated cousin. She spoke as

Mel crossed the threshold, *"Senora,* please don't be mad with Lily. I clean very good and hit button on recorder. It was accident."

Lily, crying, pointed at the table.

X-Ray firmly ordered Lily to be silent. "Mel come here. Do you recognize this voice?" He hit the rewind button on her telephone recorder and then played the message.

"Where is it, Bitch? You've been warned. We want it NOW. Don't make us kill you, too."

The phone disconnected. A dial tone followed.

No one spoke nor moved for a moment. Lily quit crying. They stared at Mel.

"If I knew what the fuck 'it' is, I'd give it to you. I'd even give the damn thing to that bastard!" Mel stated, shaking uncontrollably. The weight of several years of tragedy and loneliness set her head spinning.

*I wish I knew what it is that someone wants so bad. That sounds like the same voice from yesterday's call. I just can't be sure. I wonder if the "what" is worth dying for?*

She fainted.

∞ **11**

Mel floated on puffy white clouds above the earth, spinning and diving. She loved this free floating feeling.

*Am I awake or is this a dream? Why are Mother and Dad here? Not a mark of disease or death on either of them. Holding hands and dressed in white flowing robes. My God. Where is Willie? Willie? WILLIE?* A shock of something acrid and bitter, below her nose, something cold and wet on her forehead forced her over the high board of clouds into an Olympic swan dive straight into the abyss of reality. The heavenly judges awarded her straight tens. A perfect score.

When she opened her eyes, she found herself under the bedcovers and surrounded by three angels, X-Ray, Lucas, and Yolanda, who was reciting the Rosary.

"I'm not dying for God's sakes!" she shouted, pulling herself up on one elbow and snatching the wet towel from her forehead. "I'm fed up. I've had all the stress I can handle for this lifetime."

Lucas said, "Take it easy now."

"You're going to be just fine," X-Ray added.

"Lie there and you'll feel better in a few moments."

"Can we get you something to eat? Some tea?"

She hated mothering.

"What I'd like is some peace and quiet and some time to think."

"Sure. No problem." X-Ray motioned all occupants of the bedroom to leave. He added, "I didn't recognize the voice. It must have been muffled. Handkerchief or something. According to the clock, it came in at 10:30 p.m. About an hour after we left for the hospital. I have the tape with me." He patted his jacket pocket.

"Why don't you rest for a while?" Lucas suggested.

"We won't make any noise till you say, *Senora*," Yolanda rushed her brood through the hallway and down the stairs.

The house became unusually quiet, the pin drop kind of quiet. Mel laid her head back on the pillow. The thought banners, like headlines on the Goodyear blimp, flashed across her mind.

*Mel and Taylor divorced two years ago.*
*Mother died of cancer last year.*
*Willie killed in a hit and run accident three years ago.*
*Dad committed suicide last month.*
*Mel mugged in the cemetery.*
*House ransacked last night.*
*Rosa injured and hospitalized.*
*Threatening message on machine.*

"No coincidences. There are no coincidences," she murmured. She was having trouble staying awake long enough to analyze and capture those thoughts.

In an instant, she was transported back to the puffy white clouds. Safe. She could rest now.

# ∞12

Silence filled the house. Shadows stretched across the walls creating dark mystical creatures. At dusk, Mel floated back to earth. For a reality check, she washed her face, brushed her hair and went downstairs.

"Is it too early for a drink?" she called out, not expecting any reply.

"Here for you." Yolanda magically appeared with a serving tray. "I have tea for you."

Rosa had used good judgment, leaving her in Yolanda's hands. "I'd like to pass on the tea till after dinner. I could use a stiff drink though."

"Here. This best for you right now." Yolanda handed Mel a cup of steaming tea and returned to the kitchen, adding over her shoulder, "That Lucas guy on patio. He waiting for your wake up. He nice man. Very nice man."

When Mel reached the patio door, Lucas sat at the table, scanning through a book and drinking ice tea. "Are you my designated babysitter?" she asked.

"No. Well, actually, yes, I guess I am. No, I don't want to. You don't need a baby sitter. But X-Ray had work to do and he asked me to stay. Think of me as your bodyguard. It's Sunday. I had nothing better to do, anyway."

She shook her head. "Thanks. You really know how to make a gal feel good."

"That didn't come out right, exactly. But in any event, I'm glad to be here."

Mel smiled.

"Ah, guess you're going to live after all."

"No question in my mind." She took another sip of her tea, then stirred it with her lemon twist. Yolanda seemed to have missed nothing. The chamomile drink smelled like sweet apple. Chamomile, the comfort tea. *Perfect, almost a Rosa.*

"So, what's on the agenda for the evening? Want me to help you get organized? X-Ray did leave orders for the office to be cleaned and if anything's missing, he wants to know ASAP."

"I'll worry about that tomorrow," she replied in her best Scarlet O'Hara imitation.

"Not bad for a southern Californian, but don't give up your day job, lady."

Yolanda appeared with a fresh drink for Lucas and more hot water, "One more drink for you and you. Then you two have nice walk on the beach. When you get back, *muy bonito* dinner will be ready. Okay? Is okay with you, Miss Mel?"

"Great idea. But I hate to put you to that much trouble. I don't know how I'll ever pay you for the work you've already done. Do you ever go home, Yolanda? This has already been a long day for you."

"Rosa say, me stay until you eat tonight."

Mel nodded to Lucas. "Are you game? A walk on the beach with a new friend?"

"I'm not sure the walk is such a good idea."

"Why not?"

"X-Ray said for us to stay here and inside."

"Are you negotiating with me?"

"I'm not very good at it, huh?"

"Not very."

"Well, put it this way, X-Ray must have been concerned. He did leave me a gun." He said, patting the coat jacket.

"He did, huh? Well, cowboy, put it in your holster, and let's go, partner." She stood. But before she crossed from the table to the door, Yolanda appeared and handed her a Windbreaker. "You've got to stop being so perfect, Yolanda, or you'll give Rosa a run for her money."

"Oh no, Miss Mel. I make plenty mistakes. I break things. I lose things. I forget. Only Rosa is perfect. I only try to be perfect like her." Yolanda blushed slightly.

Mel put on the jacket and zipped it to the neckline.

Yolanda disappeared into the house and seconds later, Mel heard the vacuum. "Boy, she doesn't give it a break, does she? Bless her heart."

She grabbed his hand. "Come on, there's a shortcut to the beach."

They walked along the cliff to a small greenbelt area, then down well-maintained steps to the sand. Revived by two cups of tea and the halogen lights which blazed on standards every eight feet, Mel's mood brightened.

They walked for a few moments in silence, then Lucas spoke first. "I don't know what to make of you. You're a bit of a paradox."

"How do you mean that?"

"I mean it as a compliment."

"I'm no more complex than most people I know."

"For starters, you're very mature, but delightfully childlike. One minute you've very serious, and the next . . . funny."

"And you know others who aren't?"

"Oh sure. You aren't at all like the stuffy snobs I dated at Rice University. And I married one after graduation. You've been through a lot of shit recently. Despite all that, you're still here."

"I didn't know I had a choice."

They strolled along the water's edge, kicking small shells as they walked. He reached for her hand and looped their fingers together. Mel kicked at the sand. Her heart pounded at his touch. I like this, she thought.

They walked south for some distance, to the large boulders at the water's edge, and paused. Cool ocean breezes stirred the air. Low tidal waves crashed below the rocks.

Lucas found a flat surface, removed his jacket and smoothed it, motioning for her to sit.

"You're spoiling me, you know."

He grinned. "So, Miss Camellia, tell me more about yourself."

She found herself wanting to tell him about her inner fears. She didn't usually express her feelings. *When you're married to a lawyer it's never your turn.*

She began by recounting a short version of the past year, setting the major events in chronological order. She deliberately left out the gory details. She needed a friend and telling too much information might scare him away.

They sat and talked for a while, until, over the sound of the waves, a stomach growled. They both heard it. Mel was certain the rumble was hers. Lucas patted his belly. Together, they laughed.

"I'm starving. Even after that wonderful brunch." He glanced at his watch. The watch hands glowed in the dark. "No wonder we're hungry. It's 7:30. Let's start back."

"Sounds good." Mel took off her tennis shoes and he followed her cue. As he placed his jacket over her shoulders, she decided she could get used to this kind of attention.

They walked, their bodies gently touching, sometimes a hand, sometimes a swinging arm. She smiled, took a deep breath of fresh air and matched him, stride for stride.

"You know," he said," it seems to me the break-in and the phone call could, somehow, be related to your work. I think the rest of your problems stem from life's nasty little coincidences."

Before she could reply, shots rang out.

# ∞ *13*

A bullet whizzed past Mel's cheek. The report was so loud, she thought it was a Magnum 45. Both she and Lucas hit the sand.

He pulled the gun from his pocket and waved the gun slowly, back and forth toward the face of the cliffs above. "Do you see the shooter? I can't tell what's what."

Mel scanned the area and spotted purple flowering ice plants growing from tall pampas grass which lined the cliff's edge. *They could be shielding the attackers.* Her heart quickened. "There!" She pointed. "Over there." Two shadowy figures crouched in the ground cover. "I think they're the ones." She said. "They both appear to be armed."

Lucas lay beside her in the sand, flat on his stomach. He used his free hand to brace the other holding the gun. He returned fire. The figures scrambled back from the edge of the bluff, one of the dark shadows yelled out.

"Nice shot. I think you hit one of them."

Mel searched for their shoes in the sand, and Lucas grabbed her by the arm. "Forget the shoes. We'll find them tomorrow. Let's get back to the house, Mel."

"Can't argue with that," she replied and they both ran to the stairway near the greenbelt.

"Uh-oh, The stairs are as black as a well digger's lunch kit, Mel," he whispered. "Is there a another way back to the house? Or a phone?"

Mel looked around. Someone had cut off, switched off, or shot out the stairway lights. "Let's go this way toward the boardwalk. We should find lots of light, telephones and people. If we're lucky . . . maybe even a cop."

It took several breathless minutes for them to hurry across the deep cool sand until they reached civilization. The boardwalk lights were faded yellow halos. Mist spilled over the causeway covering scattered groups of lovers, walkers, skaters, strangers . . . and a cop.

Mel said, "Put the gun away. I don't want you to get arrested again this week."

"Right." He pocketed the weapon.

Mel began waving, wildly. As the bicycle cop neared, she recognized him. "JIM! Here! Over here!" she called. The policeman nodded, waved and ambled toward her, now pushing his bike.

In a few short gasps, Mel made it clear, "A 966 on the bluffs, above the boulders."

"Anyone hurt?" Jim asked. His hand reached for the button on his walkie-talkie.

"One of them, maybe. We returned fire and might have hit one of them," Mel said.

"Where's your gun?" Jim asked.

Lucas handed it to Jim.

"This is police issue, where'd you get it?"

"X-Ray gave it to me."

Jim called in. "We have a 966, with a Code 3. Yeah. Near Camellia Walker's home. On the bluffs." He shut off the radio. "You two wait here with me. Units are rolling."

Lucas and Mel plopped down on a park bench and wiped the sand from their feet.

Mel sat back and stared at the ocean. "Investigation #101, Rule Number One, Lucas. There are no coincidences."

## ∞ *14*

Officers unrolled their CAUTION POLICE yellow plastic tape both above and below the bluffs. Mel knew it would be morning before a complete search could be made of the area for clues and the spent cartridges.

A door-to-door search of the housing tract had yielded no leads.

*Second police visit in a week. The neighbors will love me.*

At midnight, the helicopter and the patrol units finally left, leaving only X-Ray's unmarked unit in her driveway.

X-Ray stood in the doorway shaking his head, "I can't tell you how this pisses me off."

"I'm sorry for the trouble, X."

"That's why I left a gun here, because, clearly, you might be in danger. I thought you'd use your head and stay here, *inside*."

Lucas interceded. "I'm not making any excuses mind you, but she's pretty hardheaded."

"You don't have to tell me," X-Ray added.

Mel stomped her foot, "You two don't have to talk about me like I'm not here. Okay, I made a mistake. You're both absolutely right. Going down to the beach was really stupid."

"Mel, I'm leaving one of our new officers here, tonight. He was tops in the academy. A fine shot."

"I don't need a cop here. I'll be fine," she said.

X-Ray ignored her, turned to Yolanda and, in Spanish, made it clear that an officer would guard them throughout the night.

Yolanda nodded her understanding.

X-Ray turned to Mel. "I know you're tired, honey. We're going to leave now, but Scott stays with you. No further discussion on this issue." X-Ray leaned back toward the driveway and called, "Officer Scott."

A clean-shaven, flat-topped young cop approached the door. He carried a long black canvas bag. Bold white letters identified this bag as POLICE property.

*A rookie, by golly. He probably still believes there's a truth and justice system.*

"Scott," X-Ray motioned, "this is Mel, her friend Lucas, and Yolanda's in the kitchen. I've made arrangements for Yolanda to stay over too. You are NOT to answer the telephone, nor the door tonight. You are NOT to exit this house unless it is engulfed in flames. Do I make myself clear?"

Goose bumps rose on her arms. *WOW, a side of X-Ray I've never seen.*

She acquiesced, "All right, tonight only. You're right, I am tired." She pointed her finger at X-Ray adding, "But just tonight!"

"One day at a time, Mel."

Lucas interjected, "Well, it's late. I have an early flight to San Francisco tomorrow. So I guess I'll be going."

He shook X-Ray's hand and waved at Scott, who was busily setting up the battlement in the dining room near the patio doors, then turned and thanked Yolanda for her kindness.

He added, "Mel, this has been the most exciting weekend of MY life."

"Ditto for me, Tex. How are you getting home?"

X-Ray said, "I'll run him home. It's no trouble."

"Thanks X-Ray. I'll take you up on that. Maybe we can stop for a bite on the way." His attention was drawn to Mel who rubbed her eyes and yawned. "Hey, you're fading fast. Can I call on you again?"

"The question is 'will you want to call me again' after tonight? After what I've put you through, are you a glutton for punishment, or what?"

"The Texas Rangers never give up, and neither do I," Lucas said, as he walked out to the porch. Then he turned. "Here . . . I almost forgot your keys." He tossed them to Mel and gave her a little salute.

Mel closed the door, and Yolanda directed her to the breakfast room. She pulled out a chair, seated herself and placed the napkin in her lap. With a sigh, she called out to Scott, "Hi stranger. Want to join me for a bedtime snack? You're welcome to join me."

The phone rang, causing her to jump.

Scott turned to the direction of the telephone. Mel pushed the chair back to get up and answer it.

Yolanda waved her back to the table, "No, I get, Miss Mel. *"Buenos Noches,* this is Walker residence. I can help you?"

Pause.

"Hello?"

Pause.

"Hello? Someone there?"

The young cadet jumped to his feet, ran to the telephone and grabbed the receiver from Yolanda. He demanded, "Hello. Who is this?"

There was just the sound of heavy breathing, then the dial tone followed.

Scott turned to Mel. "May not be related, but I'd better report this. Yolanda is there another phone I can use so Mel can eat in peace?"

Yolanda took him to the office, where they both remained for several minutes.

*Do they think I'm a dummy. They've been in there far too long. Yolanda's getting her instructions.*

"Who are you guys kidding! Not related! Get serious!" She yelled. "Do you guys think I was born yesterday?"

*Boy, somebody sure is pissing me off. What's next?*

Mel slept like a rotten log sunk deep in its own soil residue. If the telephone rang, she had not heard it. And, if there were problems, she did not want to know.

Mel sat on the edge of her bed trying to re-organize her brain. "Okay, so this is Monday. What else is it? I know I have something else to do. Oh, yeah. Today, I have to drive to L.A. to JW's office and sign the estate papers."

She stood and stretched saying, "UGH!"

A stroll in her walk-in closet addressed the second major decision of the day. "What to wear?" She yawned and stretched again.

As an investigator she had her "street" clothes and her "court" clothes. After careful examination of her minimal wardrobe consisting of some rather outdated suits, she selected a "court" outfit.

She laid a navy blue two-piece suit and pale blue blouse on the bed. She showered and washed her hair.

After dressing, she joined her overnight guests downstairs. Yolanda and Scott were huddled over buffet food left from Sunday. "I'm really ravenous, Yolanda. Any left for me?"

"Oh yes, *Buenos Dias,* Miss Mel. I have a plate for you and coffee. You need black coffee to get going, Rosa says."

"*Gracias.* How's Rosa feeling? Have you talked to her?"

"*Si.* I call this morning. She feel much better and should be home soon."

"That's wonderful. Next time you talk to her, please tell her I send my love. I'll try to get by the hospital, later today."

"*Si, Senora.*"

"And a good morning to you too, Scott. Is all quiet in the Walker house?" Mel asked.

"All secure. I hope you had a good night's sleep."

"I did, thank you. Anything you want to tell me?"

"No. The house was quiet as a mouse."

"Liar," she said.

"Sounded good to me." He replied not making eye contact.

"I'm not that dumb. BUT, I really don't want to know right now. I'm in good hands, and so long as you and X-Ray work it out, for now, leave me out of the loop. Okay?"

"That's what X-Ray said." Then, as if seeing her for the first time today said, "You're all dressed up. Going anywhere special? I'm not sure you're supposed to leave the house, yet."

"Now wait a minute! I have work to do and personal things, too."

"Let me check with X-Ray." Scott stood and walked out of the room. Mel ate breakfast alone.

Scott called out, "X-Ray wants to talk to you. Can you catch the kitchen phone?"

"Sure." She picked up the receiver. "Hi, X. How're you doing?"

"Fine. Understand you slept soundly. Where're you going?"

"JW's office in L.A. I have some probate and life insurance stuff to go over with him. I'll be gone at least half the day, 'cause it's a two-hour plus, round-trip drive. I may stop by and see Rosa, too."

"Is this a good time to be getting on the freeway?"

"X! 1955 was a good time to be on the freeway. Today I have things to do. Not just this morning, but for the rest of my life. Nothing is going on hold just because of some creep."

Silence.

"Gawd. You're as stubborn as Dad."

"Yeah, I had a great teacher, and I bet he's pleased I'm here to aggravate his beloved daughter in his name. Time, please?" X-Ray asked.

"I'm leaving right after breakfast. I should be home by two this afternoon, barring any mysterious slowing on the freeway. Look," she added. "How long is this going on and do I have to give you an itinerary EVERY day? I DO have a life, for God's sake."

"You're on a 'need to know' Mel. Sorry I can't be more specific."

"Does all this have anything to do with Dad's death?"

X-Ray replied, "Have a safe drive and call me when you get home."

"He hung up on me." She stuck her tongue out at the telephone receiver and slammed it down hard, almost missing its base.

Mel went to her office. Her purse and briefcase sat untouched among the havoc which surrounded the room. She looked around and said, "I'll deal with you when I get back."

She grabbed her keys and yelled, "Bye, Yolanda. Bye, Scott. Go home . . . both of you."

Their responses had been a resounding confidence building answer, "Sure."

Lucas had parked the car in the garage. No chance of booby traps or tampering with brakes, she dramatized.

Turning on the ignition she realized Lucas had filled her tank with gas and put Bette Midler's tape *Beaches* in the tape deck. *He shows great promise AND a nice tush. What a combo!* She smiled, backing out of the driveway.

The long hot drive to Los Angeles became a frustrating one, with one person in each car and each paying more attention to some personal hygiene or professional activity, than to their driving. One guy with a personalized plate that read ININIINC, spoke on the cellular phone, drove with one hand, while writing on some papers he had balanced on the steering column with the other.

With such a balancing act he should be in the circus, she mused, as her car inched past his. He smiled, and his lips broadened under a thick salt and pepper mustache. Remembering how much she liked the way mustaches tickled when kissing, she returned his smile.

All the activity in Mel's life had made her unaware of the offshore wind that had blown the smog away. The air smelled clean and clear. Now, she could see the rising snow-capped peaks along the San Bernardino mountain range, but it had not yet taken a choke hold on her lungs as she drove. The air conditioning only cooled the smog to make its digestion more palatable to one's lungs.

Traffic crawled along the Harbor Freeway, but Mel guessed the drivers were attempting to interpret the new graffiti left by weekend taggers, as opposed to there being any real accident ahead. This was a freeway which had not earned the respect of local artists. The cryptic letters *TWY* were repeated several times along one sound wall.

*Boy, they aren't kidding. They are Totally Wasted Youth. These kids ... not grown. This highway ... not completed, and both already dead.*

JW's office was located in a tall mid-Wilshire concrete monolith, dedicated to some hotshot Los Angeles developer. She drove down, down, down ... into the gray bowels of the parking structure, and pulled a parking ticket from the dispenser.

*I don't care for this underground thing. If an earthquake hit right now—POW—me and my little car.* Thirty-five floors in an express elevator popped her ears. She felt like a country girl come to the city for the first time, nervous and apprehensive.

The elevator doors slid apart and a large traditional reception room loomed before her. It housed four maroon leather couches and eight matching chairs. The room smelled of the floor's richly oiled dark wood, mingled with the Monday morning's fresh flower delivery.

She approached the massive carved oak reception front. On it sat the largest most beautiful vase she had ever seen. The scents from the torch ginger and tiger lily were pungent. Mel rubbed her nose.

"Morning, Cary," she spoke first.

"Good morning, Mel. I'm so glad to see you again. But not under these circumstances. I'm so sorry your Dad is . . . uh . . . gone."

*Having trouble saying he blew his brains out, Cary?*

"Thank you Cary. Is JW in yet?"

"Yeah. He's waiting for you. Let me call Lil to get him for you. Would you like some coffee?"

"No, thank you. It's been a long drive though and I'd like to get rid of some coffee. Let me catch the little girl's room first, before you call him."

Cary gave her the key. Mel had to laugh. How ludicrous to believe that here on the thirty-fifth floor of a mid-Wilshire building, a bum off the street would go to all this trouble to use the rest rooms.

*Secure potties. Only in L.A.*

Moments later, she returned, tossed the key to Cary and walked over and picked up the *Daily Journal*. She had browsed only the headlines when JW appeared. They approached each other and exchanged a warm hug.

"Good morning, Mel. Good to see you. Want some coffee?"

"No, thank you, Cary already asked. I'm fine."

He led the way along a long hall, past small work stations on the left, each containing a worker, a desk and computer. Associate's offices faced the window side of the building. At the end of the aisle, Mel and JW turned into a large corner office.

A typical attorney, JW wore a three piece suit with pinstriped vest, of course, in gray serge. A starched white shirt and diagonally striped tie completed his outfit. His wing-tipped black shoes had little holes in the toes. Ever since she was a little girl, she'd always wanted to stick little toothpicks in those holes, like her personal version of the hot foot.

She wondered why some lawyer, any lawyer, did not become a risk taker. Break out as an individual dresser instead of blindly following the herd. Mel walked to the window in his massive office. "Great view of the smog," she teased.

"Don't be a smart alec, Mel. Some days it's so clear you can read the downtown billboards."

"Sure, you can."

As they bantered, this gave her an opportunity to see all of his office ... traditional dark woods and maroon leather chairs with brass tacks. Behind the obscenely enormous desk, bookcases filled with brown and red California Civil Procedures lined one entire wall. Personal photos or plaques interrupted the line of books every so often. One pictured JW and her father in fishing gear. They each held a large freshly caught Alaskan king salmon.

At one side of the room, a cozy conference table completed the furnishings. The smallness of it seemed friendly.

She smiled. Someone, probably, had advised him on "how to market your office."

JW motioned her to the table. He pulled out a chair for her, then sat on the opposite side amid two fountain pens, some long yellow Benchmark legal pads, yellow Post-its and a neat stack of bluebacked stapled documents.

"Ah, technology. Ain't it grand?" she said out loud as she fingered one of the little pads.

"Yeah, these stickers come in handy for quick changes. I don't know what we did before all this," JW responded. "Now here are your papers to review and sign. I'll explain each one of them as we go through them. If you have any questions, please ask. They are not unlike those of Carole's that you and T-Bone signed last year."

"But Dad seems to have left a few more than Mom," she said, stirring through the sheaf of papers that faced JW.

"Well, it's the finality of a household isn't it? That's why there's a few more. But ... " He cleared the emotion which was creeping into his voice, "let's take these one at a time shall we?"

*I hate that "we" shit. He isn't going through it. I am. I have no mom, no son and now, no dad. God.*

She cleared her throat, "Shoot!" and immediately regretted her word choice.

An awkward moment of silence followed. He sneezed, then spoke. "Let's begin with this," he said, "the contents of the coroner's evidence envelope."

*Why weren't they released to me . . . the sole survivor and heir apparent, instead of an attorney?*

She was suddenly rankled and struggled to control her tongue.

"Here's his key chain and a safe deposit key." He handed them to her. "I checked the safe deposit box already and made a list of its contents. Nothing too important there."

Mel felt a slight prickling of her cheeks. "Can I have a drink of water?"

*I'll decide what's important here, you asshole.*

"Sure," he stood, went to the door and signalled for an aide to bring water.

He returned to the table and, either did not realize or just ignored her discomfort. "Here's his wallet, some photos, and his wedding band." He stroked her arm and continued.

After what seemed like an eternity, she had reviewed the will, the quitclaim to the house, and numerous life insurance applications for death benefits, including one from the government.

Her father had been a marine, a fine marine.

"You'll have some financial comfort too, Mel." He pressed more blue-backs in front of her. "Carole had a nice little trust that went to Bill, and now it's yours. The house is free and clear and we obtained the police release for you to take possession now."

*That "we" shit again. What business did he have presuming to "get" all these things for me? This is personal.*

"There are two sets of papers left to review, Mel."

Her mind wandered. She hoped that if the top of her brain blew off from the anger boiling within, his ceiling would not crumble.

"This is a Power of Attorney for you to sign. I'd like to continue as your personal counsel and, of course, should we need to make any decisions, major or minor, I'd like to have the POA on file."

"I'll take that paper with me and get back with you on that." She grabbed the sheets of paper and stuffed them into her open briefcase. "Next. Is there any money? Any cash?"

"Well, yes. Here's the passbook. He did have a moderate sized savings account."

*What? How could he? I spent a fortune of my own money funding Mom's medical bills towards the end. Dad was flat broke. He told me so.*

She threw the book in the briefcase.

"Next," she said.

"We've saved what is probably the most difficult for the last. These are Bill's police pension papers."

"Where do I sign?" She asked, leaning forward with one of the pens raised.

"Nowhere yet," he paused. "There's a complication."

"What kind of complication?" She felt the blood pulsating in the crown of her head.

"It's very simple, actually. One hundred thousand dollars, in federal funds, is available for death benefits unless . . . "

"Unless what?"

"If death is a suicide, there are *no* monies from the program."

The air hung thick, hot and still.

Perspiration now dribbled down Mel's back. She had reached the boiling point. She dragged the briefcase off the table.

"Okay." She replied, as lightly as her crackling voice could muster, "So, you'll get back to me on that?" She stood abruptly.

"Exactly." He sat there staring at a torn cuticle, then suddenly he stood and hugged her.

She did not hug back. What had started as a tight band across her brow was now a full-blown, screaming black headache. She needed to be free of this room, this man, this memory and this building.

She grabbed her purse and briefcase and headed for the door. "No need to walk me out. I know the way." She crossed the threshold, turned slightly, and added, "I know this has been difficult for you, too. Thank you. I'll have to talk to you later about all this."

"I understand," he responded. "Take care."

She walked the long narrow aisle toward the lighted EXIT sign, and focused on reaching it, to keep her from fainting.

"Oops!" A male voice echoed, as he bumped into her. "Excuse me, I should have signalled."

Mel dropped her purse.

He stooped to assist her and starred at her long legs. Then, as his eyes raised to the level of the hips and waist, he realized they belonged to his ex-wife.

"Hi, Mel." Taylor leaned over to kiss her gently on the cheek. His face flushed with embarrassment.

"You know, that I know, you were looking. Don't 'Hi, Mel' me. You were watching my legs. You never change, do you Taylor?"

"I can look. I'm not married you know."

"Thank you for reminding me of yet another wonderful event in my life," she replied.

"I'm sorry. This must be the paper-signing day, huh?"

"Yep. We're done now."

"Time for lunch? Maybe you can use a friend."

"Thanks. I'll take a rain check. Better yet . . . send cash."

He ignored her caustic response, choosing instead to change the topic. "X-Ray called JW this morning. Filled us in on your busy weekend." He motioned for her to join him within the confines of his office and out of gossip's way. She did.

"Do you have any clue who it is? Or what they want?" he asked.

She shook her head. "Not one frigging idea. You or JW have any thoughts?"

*After all it's apparent to me that JW went through all the contents of my life before giving anything to me.*

He shook his head, "No, sorry. We can't think of anything. Could it have to do with something in one of your files? You're getting into a lot of criminal stuff, I hear."

"No, I don't think it's my work. But, I really haven't had time to get the office cleaned yet. That'll be my next move."

"Lots of damage to the house?"

"No, actually. Looked like a tossed salad, but Rosa's cousins are there and they worked like beavers to get it back in shape."

He slapped the side of his head with his open palm. "How selfish of me. How is Rosa?"

"She should be home from the hospital soon. Doc Townsend took great care of her."

With that, there was nothing left to say.

She glanced at her watch, breaking the awkward silence. "Well. I've got to get outta L.A. before the Great Escape which starts about now."

He checked his watch. "I have a 'depo' after lunch I should get ready for."

He leaned over and kissed her on the cheek, again. She lifelessly returned the gesture.

Cary stamped Mel's parking ticket and before she reached the elevator, Mel gulped three aspirins and some water.

The underground parking area reeked with diesel fumes, oil and stifling heat. She had hoped to catch some fresh air, but coughed instead.

She drove up and around the circular multi-tiered parking ramp until she reached the street and the light of day. The car's air conditioner kicked in about the time the front wheels touched Wilshire Blvd. She inhaled, suppressing an urge to wail. Mel felt the tingle in her toes, moments before the scream came shuddering through her body, and burst forth from her mouth. She jiggled the steering wheel, ignored all traffic and the street panhandlers, and continued to yell all the way to the Rosecrans exit sign.

A freeway billboard sign that depicted a black hand and a white hand clasped together in friendship, along with a Rodney King quote, "Can't we all just get along," brought her back to reality.

The car phone rang. She pushed the button on her hands-free unit. "Hello." Her voice sounded weak.

"This is Johnnie. Where in the hell are you?"

"I'm on the Harbor Freeway, southbound, coming home. Where are you, turkey?"

"Trying NOT to get arrested by some young stud in uniform, at the front door. Please tell studly I'm a friend, not a foe."

"Oh, shit. Sorry, Johnnie. I forgot you'd be in today. You cannot fucking believe what a wonderful weekend I've had. Put him on the phone. Oh, and don't faint when you see the office. We'll work on it together. I should be there in about an hour and a half. Put Scott on the phone."

"Officer Holcomb here."

"Go home, big guy. The troops have landed. The finger's in the dam. All's right with the world. And Johnnie's gay, so don't bend over."

Silence.

Officers are sometimes slow, but rarely stupid. Mel smiled, realizing he was digesting this new information, especially the "bend over" part.

Then he responded, "X threatened me within an inch of my life if I even think of leaving this house until he gets here at the end of my shift."

"This must be more serious than I thought. Chief Murdoch wasting two entire shifts on little ole' me."

A beep interrupted them.

"Listen. I have another call on the line. Let Johnnie in. He's my partner, and a private eye and his gun's bigger than yours. Don't give me a ration of shit on this. Okay?" Without waiting for his approval, she pressed the disconnect button, repeating once more, "Hello."

A gruff and indistinguishable voice growled, "Lady, you gotta give it up or we're gonna off you."

"Wait! Don't hang up," she replied, afraid to lose the connection. "Listen. There's no way I can trace this call, so please hang with me a minute. Are you there?"

## ∞ 16

Nothing.

"Answer me damn it. Are you still there?"

"Yo. So talk."

"First of all, I'd like to thank you for fucking up a perfectly good weekend, and my life. Oh, and I got all your precious little gifts. You really didn't have to, you know."

"This ain't no fucking tea party, bitch! Get to the point."

"Fine. So let me make it perfectly clear that I don't have a fucking clue what the fuck IT IS you want. But, paint me a picture, give me your address, I'll put the damn thing in the mail today . . . whatever it is. I always pay my bills on time."

"Don't be coy bitch. It doesn't become you."

"Coy ain't got nothing to do with it you sonofabitch. I really don't have a fucking clue."

Mel realized the caller had muzzled the receiver and now whispered to someone in the background. She could not make out the words. Cellular phones don't receive the best connection on the Harbor Freeway. She strained, but only the static sputtered loud and clear. She waited.

"Your turn," she decided to say.

He singsonged, "Mel had a daddy cop. He was white as snow. And everywhere that Mel went, the cop was sure to go."

"You bastard! Now who's being fucking coy. If you think my father was somehow mixed up with coke, you gotta another think coming."

"You ain't that stupid, Bitch. He was holding and we want it. We want it all. The cash, the coke AND the book. And we want it now."

* *
*

Mel, the Mad Woman of Harbour Pointe, performed all parts of a three-act play the entire way home. She pounded on the steering wheel and the dash while screaming and crying in full fits of anger and desperation. She changed lanes several times, cutting others off and, at times, blazed new trails alone in the carpool lane in excess of eighty miles per hour. No one gave her so much as a second glance.

Mel looked down where several strands of hair had fallen, like snowflakes, into her lap.

*With stress levels this high . . . I'll be bald by midnight. Must tear this scab of stress away. Pull the top off the pressure cooker.*

Tired and relieved, Mel turned into her community entrance. As the car approached the wrought iron standard, Jeff gave his usual salutation and smiled.

"Hi, Mel. Lots of excitement this weekend huh?" He waved.

She shrugged.

Jeff said, "If there's anything I can do for you, call me. I know things have been rough at your place."

Mel, with eyes turned a wildly deranged hazel color, drove through the gates and down the street to the safety of her home, her garage and . . . sanctuary.

Entering the house through the garage she darted down the hallway calling out "Johnnie! Johnnie! Are you here?"

Johnnie stood at the office door, then stepped out into the hall with open arms. "Gawd, Mel, you look like shit. Did you go to town like that?"

"No. Silly. This is what happens when you go to town and see a fucking lawyer." They embraced and exchanged kisses.

She pitched her purse and briefcase in one corner of the office, jerked off her coat jacket, tossed it at the foot of the stairway and stepped onto the first riser, "I don't think it's too early for a drink. Get me a drink, would you Johnnie? You can't believe my fucking day. My fucking weekend . . . "

Johnnie walked to the bar area as Mel's last comment echoed, "My fucking life," then, sounds of shower water running.

Through the pulsations of the water, Mel could barely hear her own voice as it flooded down the stairs like ghostly images of white pain. She screamed and pounded, testing

119

the shower walls. As the water stopped, so did her tears and rage. "Now, I really need that drink."

* *
*

They sat on the patio with Mel's beaker of vodka and tonic and Johnnie's personal favorite, Chivas Regal.

The winter sun looked like open mini blinds, playing peekaboo in strips of light through the coastal haze. Twenty-six miles away, surrounded by slits of puffy orange clouds, the sun dropped over the Catalina mountains. By the time Mel elaborated every last detail of her "fucking" weekend, the sun had disappeared from the horizon. For the first two hours, Johnnie had not interrupted her. Now, he went back over several issues and asked one or two questions to clarify and organize the details in his mind.

Handsome, slightly built and wonderfully virile Johnnie. Although a few years younger than Mel, his experience in investigation superseded hers by centuries. His keen brilliant sense of deduction and reasoning exceeded her well educated background by miles. She loved Johnnie.

*Every woman needs a friend like Johnnie.*

After several drinks Johnnie became more verbose, expounding how he felt about "the fuckers" who had disrupted her life and their office.

Mel's head drooped. This gave Johnnie a chance to clarify a few more loose ends. "So this asshole on the phone says he wants the cash, the coke and the book." His voice trailed off as he seemed to digest this information, then looked up adding, "T-Bone was holding? Bullshit. Why, the guy even quit smoking cigarettes, remember? When your Mom got ill."

"Other than abusing food, which we all do," she patted her own stomach, "Dad never abused anything or anybody. And he sure as shit wouldn't use or sell drugs."

Silence.

"We need more ice," Johnnie said. He grabbed the bucket and entered the house.

"Make iced-coffee, would you?" Mel called to him. "I need some energy."

When he returned, he stretched his arms to the heavens and yawned. He rubbed his chest with both hands and said, lightheartedly, "I think we should interrupt this drunken evening for a word from our stomachs. How about some grub?"

"Haven't you eaten today?" Mel asked, pouring herself a glass of black coffee.

"Well, I grabbed some coffee in San Francisco and Yolanda brought me some lunch. But gawd, Mel, it's ten o'clock."

"Shit. I didn't realize it was that late." She stood. "Let's raid the ice box."

Johnnie pointed out, "Yolanda left two appetizing looking salads, covered with plastic wrap,"

"Ah, chicken salad and veggies." Mel smiled. "Perfect."

"Shoot. I thought there might be some fried chicken, mashed potatoes and gravy with peach cobbler for dessert," Johnnie joked as he looked for forks and some paper towels.

"Not this late at night," Mel responded. "That would go straight to the bottom of your gut. Here." She grabbed two bananas. "Great for potassium. That'll be dessert. Now shut up and eat your dinner, or you don't get dessert."

"Yes, Mommy," he mockingly whined.

"Icky," he added, as he munched the carrot and celery sticks. "I'm really dreaming of a Heath Bar Blizzard. The large size, of course."

"Right. Now, eat your carrots, Johnnie."

\* \*
\*

After dinner they did not re-open the wounds of the weekend. Instead, they spent another hour cleaning the office. "How shall we organize our day, tomorrow?" Mel asked.

"I'll tell you what let's do," Johnnie said, "I'll finish cleaning up the office and determine what, if anything, has been stolen."

"I doubt if anything is stolen, especially if the burglars are still trying to find *it*," she said. Mel sensed a renewed vigor in her and added, "Okay. First, you clean the office. Then, I'll set up new files, match mail to existing files, and later, review telephone messages."

"Sounds fair. But in the meantime what are your plans? The cleanup will take me a couple of hours."

"Well, now that I have a key, I thought I'd go by Dad's house early tomorrow morning and check things out."

"Want me to come along?"

"No. Maybe I should go alone this time." Careful not to hurt his feelings, she added, "Maybe you could take a break around noon and bring us some lunch. I thought I'd also box some things for charity. You know, start recycling some things."

"That sounds fine. What are you going to do with the house? Get it cleaned and ready to sell?"

"I'm not sure yet. It's paid for. And it's been repainted and in pretty good shape. I'm just not sure yet . . . "

She closed the conversation with a quick goodnight kiss and tousled through his brown, baby-fine hair with her fingers. She stared deep into his penetrating ice blue eyes and added, "Too bad you like guys."

He swatted her on the rear as she took one step toward the stairway. "How can you think of sex at a time like this?"

"Easy."

"I've heard that about you."

She laughed. "Good night, love."

"Night, Mel."

He switched the house alarm to "on" and retired to the guest bedroom. The telephone did not ring all night.

# ∞ 17

Mel opened her eyes, rolled over, and squinted to make out the fluorescent numbers on the clock on the nightstand.

"Aw. It's 6:30."

She threw off the covers, opting to forget any exercise today. Then, showered and dressed in faded, torn jeans, tennis shoes and a chambray shirt.

"Today I'll be bending over, loading and unloading things. That'll be enough exercise," she said aloud, justifying her actions as she tip-toed downstairs, grabbed her purse and keys and crossed the hallway to the garage.

Once on Pacific Coast Highway, only minutes to her parent's home, her stomach growled. "Well," she bargained, "I do need some energy."

Mel entered the drive-through and spoke into a faded clown's mouth ordering, "Coffee. Black . . . and a maple bar."

"That'll be, one . . . seventy-five at the second window."

"Gee. You're a ventriloquist too," she spoke to the gaping red hole.

"What?" Came a voice from the speaker.

"Nothing."

"Nothing? You don't want your order?" said the confused clerk.

"Yes, I want the drink and the sweet I just ordered."

"Well, make up your mind."

She grinned and shook her head, "What a clown." She was no match for the clown at this hour. Mel pulled forward to the second window, fumbled with her wallet and handed the pregnant clerk the exact change.

Mel grasped the sack containing her order, laid it on the adjacent seat and pulled back onto the highway. She reached for the drink, expecting it to be hot.

Cold. Ice cold.

She opened the bag and peered at its contents.

*A diet drink and a donut.*

"Ah Shit! The clown got me, after all." Mel chomped on the stale donut and grumbled the whole way.

* *
*

The sea gulls soared in a feeding frenzy overhead as Mel turned into her father's beach community. The pungency of today's catch-and-kill from the harbor docks several blocks away, filled the air.

She was born in this house that contained the mysteries of her youth, her mischief and the living, loving and dying of her son and parents.

With some trepidation, Mel turned into the asphalt driveway and stopped in front of the detached garage at the rear of the house. It was difficult to distinguish the grass from the dandelions and clover. Her Mother's roses and bougainvillea had taken on a wild, out of control, growing splurge. While not a priority, Mel pulled out her note pad and jotted *trim flowers* on her "to do" list.

This morning's quiet street reflected the inhabitants were either at-work yuppies, still-asleep retirees, or snowbird tenants.

Mel reflected on memories.

Wonderful memories.

She tried to keep focused by adding things to the "to do" list. The tall thick eucalyptus in the front yard spawned massive root tentacles undulating across the grassy lawn on its way to buckling the concrete walkways and asphalt driveway.

*FIX,* she wrote in capital letters.

The eucalyptus had shed profusely, not just onto this lawn, but to neighboring ones as well. She lined out *FIX* and beside it wrote: *REMOVE DAMN TREE.* She would replace it with some other shade tree. *WHAT KIND,* she also wrote, deciding she did not have a clue, nor enough energy to deal with it right now.

Despite her father's long days at work and long nights with his ailing wife, he had made sure that most of the deferred maintenance was attended to promptly. Then he ran out of money, and even borrowed from his pension plan.

*Now the house and yard need work. Lots of clean up. Paint Okay. Roof Okay.* "Well," she muttered to herself, "I've procrastinated long enough." She sighed, reached into the coroner's property envelope and removed a sticky set of keys. A pink and clay-like residue clung to the key's sharp edges. She rubbed her fingers over them to clean it off. *Keys to enter the house this time? How quaint!*

A beautiful, faded funeral wreath of white carnations and greenery lay against the front door. A gift from concerned neighbors.

She placed it to one side while juggling her purse, the key ring, notepad and pencil, trying not to drop any of them.

Mel ripped the caution tape entirely off the door facing and wadded it into a ball. She found a jumbled mess of mail and flyers on the floor inside the door, below the mail drop.

*The mailman resumed delivery,* Mel thought, as she knelt, gathered an armful and threw what she could on the desk. Some pieces fell to the floor.

"You're a later project," she told the bundle.

The house had a different aura in the light of day. Things did not feel as mysterious and dark as the last time. Mel opened the windows in the living room, kitchen and bedrooms, letting the ocean breeze blow the smell of death away.

*Was the house this messy? Funny, I don't remember.*

The fingerprint kit residue had blanketed the house with a dusty fine mist. Taking a quick memory walk through this wonderful home, Mel remembered the place as being bigger, larger than life. Now, she saw a wood frame, three bedrooms, one and one-half bath with living room, dining room, kitchen and detached two car garage with a small two bedroom apartment above.

"You're a mess!" she exclaimed. Standing in the center of the living room, Mel placed her hands on her hips and shook her head. "And I am thirsty."

Mel found a non-diet drink in the ice box. She needed caffeine.

"What am I going to do with this house?" She yelled, assuming some spirit from on high might answer this question.

She plopped down on the couch and inhaled a long hard swig, that fizzed up her nose, causing a gasp that triggered a violent coughing spasm. A cough . . . like T-Bone's . . . when he drank his cola. She saw him, sitting at the desk, working on daily mail.

In that moment Mel knew exactly what she would do with the house.

"This'll be my new office!"

She smiled, confident to have found the best use for something she was not ready to abandon. *Not now, anyway.*

Mel went to the telephone and called home, wanting to tell someone before she chickened out. *This is going to be a big project.*

Johnnie answered. "Walker Investigations. May I help you?"

"Hi," Mel said flippantly and somewhat giddy. "Guess what I'm going to do?"

"Nothing would surprise me, Mel," he came back equally glib. "Animal, vegetable or mineral? I need a clue."

"With Dad's house, silly. Remember where I am?"

"Oh, yeah. I recall. I'm the one who blindly volunteered to stay here with this mess and make some sense of it. Okay, I'll bite. What are you going to do? Turn the Walker house into a museum?"

"Close," she responded, breathing more heavily now. "Get in the car and come over, to the future home office of Walker Investigations."

"WOW!" was all he said.

"No shit. It's a good idea huh?"

"HUH?"

"Shit, Johnnie, get excited. It's really a good idea isn't it?"

"Well, you must remember . . . I'm the levelheaded member of our weird little twosome. I have to let this sink in a moment." He took a deep breath. "Okay, I'm on my way."

Mel hung up the receiver. *Okay, Miss Spontaneous, you're sometimes a bit rash.* She put her palms facing out and spun around the living room adding, "But, I know this idea is great."

She fussed around the desk for the next ten minutes, tossing all third class mail into a nearby black trash bag. While humming to herself, Mel made separate stacks for bills and sympathy cards she would answer later.

A car door slammed.

"Is that you, Johnnie? I didn't hear you drive up."

"Yeah, it's me." He stood on the porch and peered through the screen door.

"Come on in." Mel called out, "It's open."

Johnnie entered and glanced around. "It's my first visit since T-Bone's death." His body shook and he scrunched deep into a nearby chair, and held his head low over his knees.

"Are you okay?" She patted his shoulder.

"Yeah. This is very hard."

"I know. But, I think this idea is perfect. It'll be much better for me. Having an office away from home."

"Okay. If you say so. What can I do to help?"

"First," she asked, "How's the mess at home? Anything missing or tampered with?"

"Probably too soon to tell. All our files appear to be intact, and the disks, both main and backups, are there."

"How about my personal data?"

"Since your private accounting program has your secret code, and I don't know it, you'll have to check that, yourself."

"What about the correspondence file?"

"Shit, Mel. I don't have a clue as to your REAL life. I left all that crap for you to go through."

"OKAY, later on that. What I'd like to know is, does anything appear to be missing to you?" She spun the captain's chair around to face Johnnie.

"No," he shook his head adding, "nothing that I could see. I'm not finished. Remember, you called me away, so now that I'm here, let's focus on this new brilliant concept of yours. This is going to be our office?"

"Yes, the home office of Walker Investigations, Incorporated, Johnnie. Try to picture it will you?" She jumped up grabbed his arm and darted into the center of the living room still holding on. His upper body caught up with his feet as he tripped forward. He stood and regained his balance.

"OKAY, so the living room will be our reception area. Maybe we'll hire a secretary. We can use the sofa and some chairs for our clients and," she waved over to one corner, "maybe one or two file cabinets there. Then . . . " Mel dragged Johnnie once again. This time, to the dining room. "Right here, Johnnie, we'll leave the table and chairs here. You can bring your old California Civil Procedures, West Law, Black's, everything, out of storage boxes. This'll make a wonderful library."

Johnnie smiled, nodded his head and hugged Mel, acknowledging her efforts.

"Now the kitchen and breakfast room will be fine as they are, don't you think? 'Cause we'll still have need for coffee and cold drinks. Perfect!" She beamed with pride. "And now for the *piece de resistance*. The house has three bedrooms, right?"

"Right. Okay."

"One will be your office. One will be mine, and the other will be a combination conference room and storage area."

Johnnie clasped his hands on either side of Mel's face and smiled. "Mel, it's a great idea. Just think, I'll have my own office. And our clients won't have to meet in your home. We'll look much more professional. This is going to be great."

That deserved another hug as they walked back into the living room area.

Mel picked up the receiver and called home.

"Walker residence. Can I help you?"

"Rosa! What a surprise. What are you doing there? How're you feeling?"

"I'm feeling fine. Dr. Townsend, say I'm almost one hundred percent."

"So go home. I need you to get completely well. Do you need anything?"

"I'm fine, but not sure about fixing you some dinner before I go. You coming home now?"

"I'm calling, hoping to talk with Yolanda."

"She gone home. I'm back in charge now."

"Well, we don't need any dinner. Just take care of yourself. After all, you just got out of the hospital. Listen, I do have a project I can share with you." She drew herself upright and proudly announced, "We're going to make Mom and Dad's house the Home Office of Walker Investigations. You like that?"

Rosa replied without hesitation, "You will need help. What about the furniture and mess X-Ray's people left behind? You want to start today?"

"No. That's not necessary. Tomorrow will be fine. We'll make some decisions tonight about what goes where. I don't know how I'm going to pay you for everything your family has already done for me. Say, maybe you and your family could take some of Dad's furnishings, like the bed and dressers and stuff. And what you don't want, you can take to the swap meet. We'll work out the details later. Right now I just want you to rest. Is that okay with you?"

Rosa replied, "Also maybe paint the house and clean up the yard and get new carpets and . . . "

"Whoa! You're way ahead of me, Rosa. Make a list of your ideas. So will Johnnie and I. And we'll compare notes tomorrow morning and develop a plan. We may not even be able to start doing things this week. This is going to be a very big project, and will take some planning."

Her folks had lived here since their marriage. There was a lot of dust and memories to stir.

"No problem, *Senora* Mel. We fix everything just the way you like. Now you bring Johnnie and come home and I get some snack ready. Okay?"

Mel fingered some papers on the coffee table, as the conversation ended. At the bottom of the stack she found a travel brochure with no creases nor writing on it.

*Funny!* She had not noticed it there before. It looked new, brand new.

She turned it over.

*No mailing label.*

But it did have a rubber stamped return address from a Laguna Niguel travel agent. The tri-fold glossy advertisement showed colorful scenes of sunshine over sandy beaches, a lady resting in a hammock, and a happy couple drinking something blue out of a glass decorated with an umbrella.

Then Mel startled Johnnie as he focused on decorating the library area, "Shit! Can you believe this? Dad drank a lot of things, but he'd never drink something blue from a glass with a paper umbrella."

"What do you mean? What made you think of your dad drinking?" Johnnie asked, now by her side.

"I found this travel brochure on the table of a Caribbean cruise." Mel handed him the paper. He opened and closed it several times.

"As I recall, T-Bone wasn't a sun freak and hated to travel unless on family vacations."

"He loved camping and fishing and shady areas with lots of tall redwoods and woods to walk in . . . maybe a lake or two. But, the closest thing he'd get to water, was his morning shower and shave, and he only used the lake with a worm at the end of a rod."

"Yeah, I've heard him say that, lotsa times. T-Bone hated sunbathing. He certainly wouldn't have slowed down long enough to take any island vacation at this time in his life. Look here, the place boasts tennis and golf facilities, too. He hated that stuff. Hummp." He handed the brochure back to Mel. "Well, this isn't getting anything done. You want me to help you go through the mail or something? Anything?"

"No. I think I'll stay here for another hour or so and try to get some of this organized," she replied, motioning to the roll-top desk overflowing with mail.

"Why don't I go home and develop my list? I'll be there when you get home. We'll have an early night and get started tomorrow."

"Fine." Mel leaned over, kissed him gently and exchanged a warm hug. "You're such a dear friend."

When Johnnie left, she did not even hear the door close. Her mind swirled as she argued with herself. "Dad didn't have any extra money, unless . . . no, he wasn't doing drugs. But, where else would he get the money to travel? No. If he had planned to take a vacation, it wouldn't have been to the Caribbean. Something's very weird about this."

Darkness set in, by the time Mel finished going through the mail, writing checks, and cleaning the kitchen. She closed all the windows making sure her new office was secure. She loaded her car with some items to be reviewed later, then left for the short drive home. A wet, tumbling fog boiled and churned the air. It blanketed the windshield, interfering with her visibility. Mel turned onto Pacific Coast Highway south toward Harbour Pointe. The night chill caused a shiver from the top of her head to her tailbone. She locked the doors, adjusted the seat belt, turned on the heater and found an Oleta Adams ballad on the stereo. Secure as a foot in a sock, she hummed and sang softly, in the only way she knew—off key.

The mist played around her car's headlights, millions of shiny needles cascaded around her. The traffic slowed again. Mel's temples ached with stress, her jaws clenched tight. Without warning, the cars ahead, pierced into the white fog, disappeared from her vision completely, which left her alone on the roadway. Now alert to this aloneness, Mel checked both sides of the highway. The shoulders on each side . . . perfectly clear. No stalled cars . . . police . . . nothing.

She slowed, took her eyes off the road for an instant, to change radio stations, when the headlights of an oncoming vehicle startled her. She seized the steering wheel with both hands and cut the car to the right, screaming all the way over and down the embankment, "SHIT!"

A crowd developed from deep folds in the fog. A half-dozen cars and trucks stopped and people ran to the road's edge, trying to see through the haze, which combined with the dust from the recently airborne vehicle.

"Hey! Are you all right down there?" the first lady cried out.

"Fella! Please answer me. Are you all right?" A trucker clutching a rope, a flashlight, and a fire extinguisher, called out to her, as he clambered down the steep, muddy embankment.

"Help's on the way."

"Hang in there."

"We're on the way."

"Answer us!"

"How many people you think are in that car?"

"Two, maybe, huh?" others clamored in unison, joining the trucker's pursuit.

"Did someone call 911?"

"Yeah, I called. Anybody got a blanket?"

"Will some of you help me? I can't get the car open. I smell gas. We need to get him out of the car. Gimme a hand with this door, will you?"

A voice yelled from above, "I called the cops."

\* \*
\*

Mel's mushy mind thought it heard voices and prayed she'd be rescued in time. All the other senses . . . intact. The strong smell of gasoline rushed to her nostrils. Other odors, stirred the air like a mocha mudpie salad tossed lightly with some green grassy things, a hint of California poppies, maybe, with lobelia and the roadside forsythia. Along with that smell, something damp and sticky rolled down her left arm onto her forehead. I'm not sure which end is up, she thought.

* * *

"Hey!" a trucker called out as he reached her door. "It's a gal . . . and she's alive. Let's hurry here."

The trucker yanked on the driver's door which caused the car to shake sharply. The door did not budge. Other men joined him, using iron bars and other tools from their vehicles. A makeshift rescue going nowhere. The mist continued to thicken and the night drew closer, enveloping the rescuers.

* * *

Mel closed her eyes and tried to sleep, but the outside noises and movement kept her on edge and awake. She trembled. One stage of shock, she reminded herself. Glass shards from the windshield, and one or more side windows, covered Mel and the front seat.

She spent several seconds counting backward from one hundred by threes . . . an old trick Doc Townsend taught her.

"One hundred . . . ninety-seven . . . ninety-four . . . ninety-one . . . ninety . . . uh-ho."

Sirens blasted the night with a cacophony of different sound frequencies. The noise was thunderous.

"Which are which?" she asked herself. "One should be a police car . . . another, a fire truck. Maybe, the 'tool truck' with all those wonderful toys, like the Hurst equipment . . .

the jaws of life. Aw shit," she muttered. "Maybe, I'm going to die tonight."

Her body trembled. The coolness of the damp evening oozed through the broken windows, and sucked away additional body heat.

The sirens reached their peak. Suddenly, as if on cue, they ceased. Then voices, noises and flashlights broadcast across and down the embankment, where Mel remained trapped.

The smell of gasoline filtered through the mist. *It's getting stronger. Gas is leaking.*

"Fire, oh, my God, I'm going to burn to death. Okay, Mel, get a grip. Try to think of something wonderful you can do in the spring, like romp through a green meadow covered with fragrant flowers. Yeah, flowers like red, bottlebrush. Red ... fire ... shit."

\* \*
\*

The trucker backed away from her doors and passed the rescue baton to several firemen, who had rappelled down the slope, transporting more sophisticated life-saving gear. The firemen wore yellow turn-outs, hardhats and high-topped, black rubber boots.

"We're here to help you. What's your name?" one of them asked.

"Mel."

"Mel, my name is Greg. Where do you hurt?"

"My head is buzzing. I see blood and I think it's coming from one of my arms. It could be my head though ... I'm not sure. Can you get me out of here?"

One yellow-jacketed man yanked at the passenger door. It did not open. Greg put his hand inside the open window and unlocked the driver's door. It still did not budge. "Just try to remain calm, and we should have you out in a second or two."

Mel counted, "One thousand-one, two thousand-two." *I'm still trapped ... they lied ... so much for that second-or-two theory.* She remained quiet.

"Can we turn the car over?"

"The ground's too soft here. Let's put blocks behind the top so the car doesn't slide ... while we free her."

"Get me a booster line. There's way too much fuel flowing around here."

"Let's get the spectators back up the hill. We don't need another problem here."

"Are the cops here? We could use some crowd control."

"Yeah. They're putting out tape and cones now."

"Who's the smallest here?"

"Guess I am."

"Can you crawl in the back window?"

"I can sure try."

Greg came back to her door, carrying a box which resembled her father's fishing kit. He pulled out a stethoscope, wrapped the blood pressure cuff around her arm and inflated it. He put the earpiece in each ear and placed the end at the crook of her arm and listened as the air deflated on the cuff. Then, he placed the end just under her blouse in several spots near her breasts. He then took her left hand and held it, looking at his watch with the other. "Her BP is 90 over 60. The pulse is 110."

Mel heard a garbled message from the walkie-talkie.

"We need to stabilize your neck, so I'm going to put this collar around your neck. It's not very comfortable, but it'll keep your head from moving, and allow us to move you. Once we get the dashboard pulled back, you'll be able to breathe just fine."

She reached for one end of the collar.

"Let us do the work. Just remain still. We don't want your head to flop around."

The two men wrapped the hard plastic collar around her neck. She heard the velcro closure. Then one of the firemen put his hands on each of her knees, tracking her legs down to her feet.

"What are you doing?"

"I'm making sure you have no bleeding or compound fractures, and that the accelerator and brake are not binding your feet."

"Ouch."

"Are you okay, Mel?"

"I just want to get out of here."

"We're working on it." Then, to others Mel could not see, he said "Get ready to start your engine, guys. She's clear."

"Do you have anything to cover your head with, Mel? If not, we have a blanket."

"I have a jacket, but I'm not sure if I can reach it."

"Here. Let me check you again." He pumped the cuff once more and listened. "She's 80 over 50. Pulse still 110."

He released her arm. She felt around behind the passenger seat until her fingers found some leather, wedged there. She pulled and the leather piece got bigger and closer to her.

She raised it triumphantly for the fireman to see, half expecting applause, for she was now bathed with portable lighting.

"Great, Mel. Let me help you cover the upper part of your body. We're going to pull the dash back away from your legs and we don't want you to get cut by any more flying glass or metal."

She put the jacket over her head, but it fell off, hitting the car's headliner.

Nauseous and dizzy, her last intellectual thought before blissfully passing out was, "Shouldn't the mist be falling down, not up?"

\* \*
\*

After what seemed like an eternity, Mel opened her eyes. Her head experienced shooting pains, like strobe lights at a rock concert. Her left arm hurt, as she tried to undo her seat belt.

"We're going to have to cut the seat belt, Mel. Then we'll put this backboard under you. This will help us get you up the hill, without hurting you more. We'll be gentle ... we promise."

Screeching metal and a hideous pounding throb shook the car as the jaws of life gnawed at her dash.

The acrid smell of leaking gas filled the air within the confinement of the car.

"Hey, guys, let's get her out of here. Get that booster-line going. We need to disperse this fuel."

"Roger."

One man, with EMT embroidered on his pocket, reassured her, "You're going to be fine. But, please try to relax and not move your neck."

One of the men held a large, white-plastic backboard, with several black straps flapping freely at the sides, which he shoved through the opening onto the passenger seat.

Still another, used a knife and cut the seat belt. Then several hands gently lowered her onto the hard, cold backboard and the black straps were pulled taunt across her body.

"On the count of three. One, two, three."

The men grunted as they heaved the Stokes board, pulling her through the opening created by the jaws. They tethered the board to a rope, and moved Mel along the muddy embankment to the highway above.

Two EMTs worked on her, one on each side. Mel felt a jab of pain in a vein and some tape being applied around her arm, near her right wrist. *The IV . . . probably D5W . . . a standard on those emergency shows I see on TV.*

But, later, her scrambled brain had a vivid memory of them saying, "Start the WD40."

*I don't need greasing. Did I tell you that?*

One tech raised her blouse slightly, and placed a sticky EKG pad near her breast, and another one below that, on her lower rib cage area. The last pad stuck to her inner thigh. They cut her jeans.

*My best jeans . . . now they're shorts.*

Her left arm, the one without the IV drip, throbbed. She felt the cold circle of an instrument playing around in her blouse. She tried to resist with the sore arm.

"It's okay Mel. It's Greg. I need to keep listening to your heart."

"Okay. Ow."

"Do you hurt somewhere new?"

"I have a shorter list . . . for what doesn't."

"We'll take it."

"My legs. My legs don't hurt at all."

"Can you feel your legs?" He pinched her lower legs.

"Sure. They don't hurt."

"She has a couple of lacerations here and here."

Her eyes grimaced shut with pain.

"Any tingling?"

"All over. And all fingers . . . both hands."

"Her BP is 80 over 50. Pulse 98."

"Okay. Got it Greg?" he called out again.

"Got it," came a reply.

Her mind spun . . . noises crashing in on all sides . . . lots of lights flashing. Mel had no control over her life right now, so she did the best thing she could do under the circumstances.

She fainted.

# ∞*20*

The concept of time was not Mel's priority. *I want to sleep.* A siren . . . blinding light in her eyes . . . a stranger calling her, "Mel! Stay with us!" . . . and some ammonia wafting under her nose, all acted in unison to disturb her sleep.

"What!" She cried out. "Please get quiet! I have a horrible headache!"

"That ain't all, Mel."

A soft, rubber-gloved hand held a wet, damp compress on her forehead. "Do you know what day it is?"

"No, Saturday maybe."

"Are you allergic to any medications?"

"Cocaine," she hazily responded, then giggled with the emergency medical technicians and corrected herself, "I mean, codeine."

"We know what you mean," the one nearest her answered. "Is there anyone we can notify to meet us at the hospital?"

"My doctor is Dr. Townsend. My friend is . . . uh . . . call . . . uh . . . I guess, Xavier Ramirez at the Harbour Pointe PD. He's going to love this!"

"You know X-Ray?" came a voice from the foot of her gurney.

"Yeah, my dad is Detective T-Bone Walker . . . X is his partner. They've worked together for years." She responded in present tense, as though nothing had changed.

In the ambulance, the two-man team glanced at each other, shook their heads, and kept focused on Mel's most pressing medical needs at the moment. They continued to read her blood pressure monitor, swabbed and bandaged the blood and checked her IV. She shivered harder. They added another warm blanket.

*This is supposed to make me feel better. Now both arms hurt.*

The EMT closest to Mel said, "Mel. We knew . . . eh . . . know your dad. We need your help. For now, let's focus on you staying awake."

Mel was not aware of the warmth within the ambulance. She vaguely caught bits and pieces of the instructions going on around her. All worked in unison to make it noisy and bright. *I want it quiet and dark so I can sleep.*

The EMT repeated, "Mel! Stay with us. Don't you go to sleep. We have some tests to run. Can you feel this?"

The piercing noise inside the ambulance abated, as the ambulance slowed, and turned up a slight embankment. Attendants at the hospital opened the ambulance's back doors. The EMTs and two firemen jumped out and pulled out Mel's gurney with one swift motion, all the while chattering to the hospital attendants.

"Hi again, Paul. Busy night," one of the attendants said.

"Looks like. What have we got here?"

The gurney hit one jarring bump. They had crossed the hospital threshold.

"Female . . . thirty something . . . ITA . . . Single car rollover. Minor cuts and abrasions. BP's 75 over 50. Pulse 95. Some tingling in the upper extremities. Check the head."

"Trauma Room One. Get x-ray here. We need pictures," someone called out.

She wove in and out of consciousness, snatching up more bits and pieces of her diagnosis. The gurney was first pulled, then pushed to a brighter, noisier, colder room, where the EMTS passed Mel's IV onto the next relay team.

*This isn't the morgue. But, I need a nice warm bed, dark and quiet so I can hurt in silence.*

For the next few hours, Mel was bandied about, from room to room, and from one attendant to a noisy hall and then to another attendant, with interruptions consisting of terse remarks such as, "hold your breath please," and "can you give us a urine sample," then "just in case, let's type and cross match her blood."

\* \*
\*

144

Doc Townsend and X-Ray bent over her, one on each side, partially blocking the blinding light above her bed. Doc patted her left shoulder. X-Ray patted her right.

"Did anybody get the number on that truck?" Mel asked.

They both laughed leaned over to kiss her forehead at the same time and butted their heads together. This caused another burst of laughter.

"Guess you may not be the only one here with a concussion, Mel," Doc responded, as he rubbed his head and adjusted his eye glasses which were knocked half-off his ears.

"You're gonna be fine," X-Ray whispered.

"Could some of you guys clear out and let me have some sleep?" Mel begged the multitude of floating shadows that filled the small private room.

X-Ray and Doc Townsend turned their heads in each direction, then back to each other. They shrugged, and X shook his head.

Doc Townsend spoke first. "Mel, there's no one else here. Just me . . . X . . . and you."

"You've had a pretty solid hit to the head. But you're better off than the car," X-Ray chimed in.

"My car, oh my classic little car. How is it?"

"Oh shit!" X-Ray snapped his fingers, and ground his teeth. "Sorry, I shouldn't have mentioned that right now. Let's concentrate on you getting well. The car will be fine. It'll be good as new, like you, in no time. Right, Doc?"

"Right. But for now, you need some rest. We'll go over your injuries later, when you're more comfortable. Tomorrow we'll run a few more tests to make sure your head is okay." He leaned over and snapped on a little light at the end of his pen. He lifted her eyelids, one at a time, and repeated the reassurances.

"Will I bleed?" Mel asked.

"No. It's a non-invasive test we do at a facility near here. It's called an MRI."

"What's an MRI?" She asked.

X-Ray chimed in. "It's an air-conditioned coffin with stereo drums."

Doc Townsend slapped at X-Ray, chiding him, "It's no such thing." He smiled, drawing his hand to his chin, and added. "Upon further contemplation, I guess that's exactly what it is."

"Oh, thanks guys. I needed that."

Doc said, "What? Mel, you're not claustrophobic are you?"

"I hope not."

"We'll find out soon enough."

Then, X-Ray leaned over and kissed her lightly on the bandaged forehead and patted her shoulder once more. He and Doc tip-toed from the room. Mel snored before they closed the door behind them.

\* \*
\*

"So," X said, as they walked the hallway toward the lobby elevators, "how long you think she'll be here? A day or so?"

"Probably two, at the most. The concussion is slight, I hope. The MRI will rule out any internal bleeding. The arm is okay. A few stitches took care of that. And the cracked ribs are going to be uncomfortable for a time. What concerns me most are internal injuries, bleeding and the like. And, of course, the double vision like we just experienced with her. We should know better when she's had a good night's sleep."

"Want to get some coffee, Doc?"

"Too late for me, X. The Walker clan has given me too many sleepless nights already. I'll pass on this one and see you tomorrow. I suggest you get some rest, too. Believe me, with the medication she had tonight, she'll sleep better than either of us."

Doc chuckled, and shook X-Ray's hand, while masking an oncoming yawn.

"Don't do that, Doc, that's infectious." X yawned, too. "But I'd feel better if I got a cot and stayed with her . . . tonight anyway."

"Suit yourself X." He pushed the elevator-down button. "See you tomorrow."

The elevator door closed, leaving X-Ray alone in the lobby. He had something in his hand. "When we shook hands, he slipped me a packet of pills. What a neat guy." He stopped by the water fountain on his way back to the nurse's station. "Could I rent a cot, some sheets and a pillow for the night?" he whispered to the night-charge nurse. "I'd like to stay with Ms. Walker, if I can?"

The nurse, who had been writing in someone's chart, glanced over her reading glasses. "Doc Townsend already ordered that. They're making up your suite, as we speak."

"Thanks." He walked past two nurses exiting Mel's room.

One spoke. "All we have is a cot. But we left you clean sheets, a fluffy pillow and a thermal blanket. No charge for the fresh towels, wash cloths and toothpaste."

X-Ray removed his coat and tie, then, after brushing his teeth and washing his face and hands, he melted into the soft clean sheets. Both he and Mel slept and neither was disturbed by the eleven o'clock shift change, the two a.m. bed and blood pressure check, nor the IV change, until dawn.

* *
*

Mel stirred. *I can't remember when I hurt so bad. God . . . I pray that no one else got injured.* She tried to roll over on one side and get out of bed, but the sheets were wrapped tightly around her. *Help, I'm a mummy.*

She reached for the nurse's button loosely wrapped around the top rung on the railing and touched a heavily bandaged left arm. She laid the arm on the bed, and tried to reach over with her right arm, only to find it taped securely to a flat board, with an IV protruding from it.

"I can give that urine sample now. But, I'm a mummy. HELP!" Two nurse's aides came rushing through the door. Mutt and Jeff, a young, tiny blond and an older, larger, fuzzy white-haired one.

As the younger of the two neared the head of the bed, she asked, "Can we help you, Ms. Walker?"

"I need to use the bathroom and I can't move in this cocoon. Help me, please."

"Dr. Townsend left strict instructions that you were to stay in bed until after your tests this morning and he gets a chance to read them." The other nurse explained, as she tucked the pure, white sheets even more tightly around Mel's body.

The "Jeff" nurse filled her water pitcher from the faucet in the bathroom and walked toward Mel, giving her a small emesis tray and a toothbrush with paste spread thinly, on top.

148

"I don't think so," Mel protested. "With the IV going all night . . . I really need to use the bathroom."

"We'll bring you a bedpan," said "Mutt," who began a search for the silver bedpan.

"Where is it, Ethel?" She opened both palms to the heavens awaiting deliverance.

"It's usually kept in the vanity stand. Is it in the bathroom?"

"No, I didn't see it there," Ethel continued to foist both the emesis tray and the brush. Mel's death grip on the side rails made her knuckles white.

Mel muttered. "Now, how do you suppose I can brush my teeth AND hold that tray?"

Before either answered, "Mutt" left the room, and "Jeff" set the brush and tray on the bedstand, quietly following "Mutt."

"Now, I'm back where I started, and I still need to pee. DOES ANYBODY OUT THERE CARE!"

This time, no one came.

She pushed one side of the railing down and dragged the IV stand slightly away from the bed's edge. Mel rolled over and threw the bedcovers back, totally destroying the contour of the finely honed, military tri-folded corners on the sheets. She felt a sharp pain in her chest, but a quick peek revealed no stitches or bandages there.

She pushed herself off the bed with one big, "Oh-h God, that hurts."

The pale blue mini-gown was not tied at the neck, nor the back. She used the sore arm to pull the gown over her shoulders and cover her rear. Mel pushed the IV stand with the other, and shuffled with her cold, bare feet, all the way to the bathroom.

"This was not a good idea." She returned a few moments later, holding on to doorknobs, sinks, chairs and railing, all the way back to the bed. Dizziness and nausea washed over her. "Why does Doc have to be right all the time?"

She crawled gently back under the covers and a chill crossed her chest. Something drew her attention to the television screen. It was a large input/output chart, scotch-taped to the screen, with the words, *"Don't go anywhere, I'll be right back."* The note was signed with an *"X."*

*Joker.*

# ∞*21*

Mel dozed most of the morning, after two more unauthorized bathroom and shower trips, which resulted in a "final word of warning" from someone gray, gravelly and grouchy. The woman had the kind of face whose normal expression caused the edge of her lips to turn down in a permanent frown. The nurse removed the IV needle and bag, and lowered the bed railings.

"I take this to be a sign of recovery," Mel told her.

The nurse commented along the way, "It's too bad your friend can't write his name." She removed the in-put/out-put chart from the television screen.

Mel felt no compunction to explain THAT WAS HIS NAME.

Mid morning, two male attendants came into the room pushing a gurney. The tall, thin, dark-haired one with the protruding adam's apple wore a blue uniform. He took her chart and shoved it under the thin mattress at the end of the gurney. The other, identically dressed, had a blond ponytail tied with a leather strip covered in purple stones which matched the stone in his pierced earring.

*Does the stone match other pierced equipment somewhere else on your body?* She smiled.

"Miss Walker, can you get on the gurney by yourself?"

The perennial frowner appeared, pushing herself past the gurney and into the room.

"Yeah, she can move herself, with a little help."

"I think I'll be all right. Where're we going?"

"Dr. Townsend scheduled an MRI this morning," the nurse replied.

"But these don't look like hospital people."

"The MRI, because of its magnetic properties, isn't located in the hospital. It's down the street at an independent lab."

Adam's Apple added, "If it was here, it'd throw off all the radiation equipment. It has a magnetic pull of thirty thousand times the force of gravity on earth."

"Yeah. Big time pull, Dude," the other chimed in.

During this informal education, Mel pulled herself onto the gurney and they covered her with a sheet.

"We'll have her back in a flash . . . Jack," Ponytail said.

They pushed the gurney across the hall, into the elevator and down another hall to the emergency room exit and a waiting ambulance. She remained quiet, while the two young men exchanged silly weekend stories.

In less than five minutes, the ambulance arrived at the medical building. The men jerked on the gurney, and pulled her from the back of the ambulance. They entered through the back of the building into a long hall. Both attendants removed everything metal, including their watches, and placed them in small boxes which resembled safes, built into the wall just outside the testing room. They rolled her into the room and assisted her onto a cold, hard, white-plastic, curved bed and handed her chart to the technician.

"Good luck. We'll be back for you later."

"Bye, guys, and thanks for the ride."

Mel turned her attention to the technician who was a mousey little man with stooped shoulders. His small, fragile-looking head was topped with thinning, gray hair. He wore owl-like glasses with dark-rimmed frames.

"It's very important not to move during the test part so we don't have to do it over."

"Okay."

"I need to strap you in first." Despite his fussy gestures, he seemed to know his business as he carefully, but gently, strapped Mel onto the sliding board. He wrapped something around her legs, then her waist.

"Okay."

"Now be sure to keep your head very still." He placed her head in a white-plastic, halo crown. The top touched the center of her forehead.

"I will."

He pulled something from his crisp white, lab jacket. "Here. You'll need some earplugs."

He inserted them in her ears, patted her reassuringly on the arm and left her side for a moment. When he returned, he covered her with a thermal blanket which had been heated.

"That feels good. Thanks."

"You're welcome. Ever had an MRI before?"

"No."

"Well, the test is done in small increments of two to four minutes each. The entire test should take about thirty minutes total. It's very important and I can't emphasize that enough, to remain perfectly still."

"It looks pretty tight in there."

"It is. But if you want to talk with me, there's a microphone near your head. Although I'll be in the other room, I can hear you, if you have any trouble." He pushed his glasses onto the top of his head and rubbed his nose.

"What kind of trouble you expecting?"

"Are you claustrophobic?"

"I'm not sure."

"Well, we'll know in a few minutes."

"Will anything help me if I am? Claustrophobic, you know."

"You can close your eyes to make you feel better. A lot of people do. Ready?"

"As much as I'll ever be . . . I guess."

The technician patted her leg. The first sound she heard was the motor transporting her horizontally into the narrow tunnel.

*Oh, shit! It IS a small air-conditioned coffin. Mm, no noise though.*

In the faint distance, over the microphone, the tech said, "Remember, get still and comfortable and don't move till I tell you."

"Okay," she replied from her position deep within the bowels of the machine.

"I can hear you fine, Miss, uh Walker. Now the first part will take two and one-half minutes. Ready?"

"Ready." Her eyes squeezed tight. She felt cool air flowing over the small opening above her body, and wondered if the circus needed a new ejection act. *I'll call it, Private Eye Shot from a Cannon.*

*K knock. K knock. K knock.*

*Tom a toma. Tom a toma. Tom a toma.*

*Burr rap. Burr rap. Burr rap.*

*Doitathome. Doitathome. Doitathome.*

Even with the ear plugs, the drumming noise pierced the enclosure and shook the air around her.

She counted, "One thousand-one . . . two thousand-two. Three thousand-three."

In exactly four minutes, the noise abated and the tech's voice said, "Very good, Miss Walker. How're we doing?"

"You lied to me, you sack of shit."

"Excuse me?" he replied.

"I counted to two hundred and forty. That's way more than two and one-half minutes."

"Well." He thought for a moment. "But, did we start together?"

"That's the story of my love life. We both start together. We just don't finish together."

She heard laughter.

*That's good. Ole four-eyes has a sense of humor.*

"Okay, that's fair. So let's start again, shall we?"

One and one-half hour later, the coffin test ended.

The tech entered the room as the bed emerged from the tunnel. He smiled. Mel returned it.

"God, I hated that. Talk about claustrophobia."

"Some do better than others. You did fine, Miss Walker."

"Right."

"The guys are here." He turned and motioned. "She's ready."

"Hi, Miss Walker." A trim-waisted, broad-shouldered Hispanic smiled down at her. The gleaming white teeth against his dark skin took her breath away.

"Oh . . . hi."

"Need some help?"

"No. I'm fine. Where're the other guys? The ones who brought me here."

"They got an emergency run. Will we do?"

He stepped aside and a six-footer with wavy brown hair and light green eyes entered the room.

"Fine. Just fine."

The trip was much too short and the attendants were all business.

*Probably too young for me. I don't care. They have great buns, big smiles and, by damn, I'm through that damn test. What else can I ask for?*

* *
*

Lunch arrived, as did Doc Townsend, and seconds later, X-Ray. Doc conducted a brief exam including his famous little pen light trick in each eye. He poked and lightly mashed her abdomen with his stethoscope, then stood and pushed his eye glasses back on his nose.

"Well, what's the verdict, Doc?" X-Ray asked.

155

"Yeah, can I go home? I really need to go home!"

"Follow my finger," he responded, moving his index finger to each side in front her face while holding her head still with the other.

"I'll follow you anywhere, Doc, so long as it's outta here."

"Okay, well, the MRI results were normal. No fractures or clots. I'll let you go home today if ... you promise to stay quiet and rest for a few days. You've had a concussion and may experience some double vision and dizziness for a day or so. Some ribs are cracked. No laughing, coughing or sneezing, if you don't want to hurt more. And I'd like to see you in a few days to take those stitches out of the arm. Also, if you have any abdominal pain, call me immediately. The x-rays were fine, but there's always a chance of internal bleeding. Any questions?"

Mel shook her head. So did X-Ray.

"So, can I go home? Like now?"

"X-Ray, can you take her, if I release her?"

"That's why I'm here. Courtesy of the Harbour Pointe Police Department. Your chariot awaits, fair princess," he said with a sweeping bow with one arm extended toward the door.

"Well, if you both will give me some privacy, I'll meet you outside," she said. Her clothes smelled oily and were covered with smudges of dirt and small droplets of blood. *I don't care. I'm walking out of this hospital.*

A young, male attendant pushing a wheel chair, met her at the door and motioned to her. "I'm not sitting in that," she said.

"You must ... it's the hospital rules," the aide responded. X-Ray encouraged her, "Give the guy a break.

156

Sit down and don't give us any static. Doc gave me a prescription for some pain medication for you."

Moments later, seat-belted in and heading home, X-Ray broke the news to Mel.

"Well, we have good news and bad news."

"Let's get the bad news over with first. My car?"

"Yeah. I don't know if it can be repaired or not. A roll over is not the best way to treat a delicate old Mercedes. At least you had the hard top on and the roll bar kept you from being killed, but . . . " his voice trailed off.

"So where is it? Can I see it?"

"We had it towed to that restoration place in Newport Beach, off 17th Street. We saw his sticker in your door frame. I guess he knows the car's history better than anyone, huh?"

"Jelly? Yeah. If anyone can save it, Jelly can. What's the good news?"

"The good news is that the roll over caused your trunk to pop open. We found papers and boxes and shit everywhere. Lucky for you, we had the area cordoned off as an accident scene all night and the next morning we got a Conservation Crew detail from Juvie Hall there. So the county cleaned up your shit."

"What's so great about that? Will I get a bill from the County?"

"Naw, silly. One box, it seems had T-Bone's office stuff in it. I hope we got it all. It dawns on me that maybe what these assholes are trying to find was at the office. You know? Things from his desk."

"His notebook and files and shit?" She turned sideways in the seat asking, "Where is it, the box and stuff?"

"In my trunk. We'll go over it when I get you home . . . and quiet. Rosa's ready for you."

"I'll bet she is." Mel settled back in her seat and smiled, secure that the box held some key to this puzzle.

"How could I forget the box?"

"I wondered that, too. Maybe some of your anxiety about 'chasing a shadow' after I warned you about it, caused you to forget it."

"Yeah, that was about the same time, wasn't it? Did you see anything particularly noteworthy in it?"

"Hell no. I wanted to get it all picked up before the Santa Ana winds started today. Please be patient. We'll be there in a few minutes."

Mel let her head fall back on the head rest and closed her eyes. The music from the radio and the air conditioner hum, along with the sun beating through the windshield, made her feel warm, toasty and safe. She dozed.

* *
*

Mel suddenly realized that the motor was off and that the lovely music and cool air had vanished.

"I hate to disturb you, but we're home." X-Ray lightly shook her bandaged arm.

"What a nice ride. Thank you, X. You're a real friend. What would I do without you?" She got out of the car and held her good hand to her head, shielding her eyes from the sun coming over the rooftop.

He held her around the shoulders and they approached the doors which popped open, as if on cue. Rosa wiped her hands on her apron, then motioned for them to enter. Johnnie joined her at the door. They both reached out to accept Mel.

"Please, *Senor,* she is my responsibility now. Her bed's all ready for her." She motioned for X-Ray with her fingers, eagerly awaiting her charge.

X-Ray protested, "Please yourself, *Senorita* Rosa. I'm the one who brought her home. Let me at least help her upstairs."

Johnnie reached out for Mel, too. Her feet faltered over the threshold.

"Please, all of you," Mel interceded. "My head hurts, let's don't fight over me. There's plenty of me and I see six of you."

X-Ray and Johnnie left the room. Mel undressed and Rosa got her into bed, under the fresh, soft sheets. Mel nodded off before Rosa closed the bedroom door.

* *
*

Mel stirred, and turned over on her side.

*A shooting pain in my chest.* She gasped and woke up.

"Ouch!" The shadows of the afternoon cast protective ghosts on the walls around her bed. "Yeah, I have to be careful with those ribs. God that really hurts. All over . . . "

She pulled the sheet back, and cautiously pushed herself to a sitting position. Mel stood and boldly stepped forward.

"What a killer. I hurt so bad all over . . . I can't decide what to hold first . . . my head, my arm, my chest or my rib cage."

*So much body. So little time.*

Mel dressed and ran a comb through her hair. *Now, I need to manage those steps. Remember, it was you who insisted on a two-story home.*

As she approached the landing, Mel held her chest and squinted her eyes, taking in the scene unfolding in the

159

living room below. A wave of dizziness and nausea passed over her and she grabbed for the stairwell railing to keep from stumbling.

"Uh-oh."

*The living room is covered with papers and people. Why doesn't Rosa get that clean? I have house guests.*

Her guttural "uh-oh" startled X-Ray, Johnnie and Rosa below who were on hands and knees, doing something with papers. The noise caused all three to jump from the floor, and come running to the edge of the stairway.

"Settle down will you. I'm fine. I'm a little dizzy and hungry and . . ."

"And a lot sore," X-Ray intoned. "I could have told you that. You know, I've been through a few skirmishes myself, in my day."

"I feel like Norma Desmond on these steps."

"You look like her, too," Johnnie intoned.

"Thanks. Help me will you? Were there any witnesses? Anybody?"

"I wish . . . Mel, you were all alone. The people who stopped did not see the accident. And no witnesses stopped. We'll talk about it later, when you're feeling better. Rosa, let's get this gal some nourishment."

As he spoke, X-Ray came up the steps and extended his arm to steady her descent. She sat on the sofa and Rosa placed a television tray near the end of the sofa with some soup, a sandwich and a cold drink on it. Rosa, X-Ray and Johnnie once more busied themselves with the papers on the floor.

"How you doing?" X-Ray said, after she had finished her broth and part of the sandwich.

"Not bad for a basket case, huh?"

"Want something more to eat?"

"No thanks, Rosa. I could use a glass of water, though."

"Are you in pain? Need a pill?" Johnnie asked.

"God. You're worse than Doc Townsend. Always pushing those pills. I'm really sore, but all pertinent parts appear to be intact."

Rosa returned with a glass of water, which she sat on the tray. Rosa then gathered some of the dirty dishes and disappeared into the kitchen.

"Oh, Rosa, I'm not complaining . . . I know you've had quite a medical time of it too, but why is the living room so messy? I never saw the house like this. Can't Yolanda help?"

"It's not a mess, Mel. It's the property from T-Bone's desk. His personal things I told you about that were in the trunk of your car." X-Ray answered for Rosa.

"No shit. What can you make of it? Anything?"

"If I knew what it was they were looking for it would be a lot easier. What I did was make some stacks for you to examine."

He walked over, knelt on his knees and shuffled through several items with both hands. "These are really old and personal things you'd find in every cop's desk: old badges from visiting city cops, merit awards and some old pictures. Memorabilia, like ticket stubs, pins, coffee mugs . . . shit like that."

Johnnie added, "I started another box for those things you can go over some other time."

"Did you find any notebook? The blue one he always had with him? That might tell me what his schedule was like the months before he . . . uh . . . died?"

The doorbell rang.

Mel pushed herself up from the sofa when she heard Rosa from the kitchen, "I'll get door. You sit still, please."

Rosa opened the door. A tall someone stood behind an enormous bouquet of red and white carnations. All Mel could see were freshly pressed jeans and spit-polished, cowboy boots. "Oh," she exclaimed, "Lucas Donovan, come in please, how beautiful."

"I hope my timing is good. Patty told me you were hurt in an . . . uh-ho." He caught sight of X-Ray and Johnnie sitting in the middle of the living room surrounded by papers. "I hope this is a good time."

"No, we're busy," X-Ray grumbled, giving Lucas no eye contact, nor any other acknowledgement of his presence.

"Oh, don't mind him, come on in. How lovely and thoughtful."

Under his breath X-Ray added, "I brought her home from the hospital." Mel patted X on the shoulder as she passed him, approached Lucas, and gave him a light hug.

Rosa held the flowers away from her body, as water drops fell to the carpet. She carried them to the kitchen.

"Can we get you anything to drink?"

"No. I'm fine. I wasn't sure how you were feeling and I promised Patty I wouldn't stay too long. She and David send their best to you. How are you . . . really?"

"Well, Doc Townsend says I have a concussion, some broken ribs and this cut on the arm." She lifted her left arm and motioned toward the bandage. "Other than some dizziness, I'm fine."

"Doc said she shouldn't have any company. That she should remain quiet and rest." X snarled.

"Then, why are you here?" Lucas asked. "Are you her bodyguard?"

"Yeah, if you must know, I am. And right now we're in the middle of a homicide investigation."

It was the first Mel had heard X admit it was homicide, not suicide. She was not sure if the dramatics were real, or for Lucas' benefit.

"Well, maybe this isn't a good time. Listen, I've decided to stay in California for a while. So I got myself an apartment. A condo actually. I certainly couldn't keep imposing on Patty and David. So here is my new business card. I've written down my phone number." He gestured to a small white card, which he handed Mel. "When you get to feeling better, please call me. One of us still owes the other an Italian dinner."

Mel chuckled. "I'm not sure who owes what. But I'll take the initiative. I will call you in a day or so." She ran her fingers through her hair and hoped it was not as oily and grimy as it felt.

"Promise?" he asked.

"She promises." Both X-Ray and Johnnie mocked in unison, like children making fun of a young girl-boy conversation.

She swatted her hand behind her back, imploring the two guys to stop taunting Lucas. "I promise. A day or so at most. And thank you so much for the flowers."

Another hug and after a brief, friendly wave toward the two men on the floor, Lucas left the house. Mel shut the door behind him. "Honestly, you two are like little kids. That was embarrassing."

"Not for me. Was it good for you?" Johnnie asked, turning to X- Ray.

"I loved it."

"I'm sure you did." Mel responded. "Now, back in the pool. Where are we, and what is all this?"

"To answer your earlier question, I did find the blue notebook." X-Ray leaned over and picked up a frayed, soiled, narrow book from the coffee table. He handed it to Mel and continued, "Much of it is coded in initials, fairly crude and simple, like all cops. But . . . " he bent over another stack and sorted haphazardly through it. "I don't think that will help much without his calendar."

"And we're still looking for that," Johnnie added.

"Maybe the calendar was in his desk at home. I picked up a bunch of papers and mail there. It's in a large trash bag in the office." Mel braced her arms against the carpet and pushed herself off the floor.

"No, just sit there. I'll get it for you," Johnnie said, as he moved quickly toward the hall and the office beyond.

"It'd be clearer if we could organize his schedule and contacts on butcher paper, say across the office wall . . . like you do at the police department."

"Okay, sounds fine with me. Facts we know . . . and questions we have? Like that?"

"Exactly." A smile crept across her face, "And I don't want to do it here." She balanced both palms on her thighs sitting with her legs tucked under her, and leaned forward toward X-Ray. "Did you hear my great idea about Dad and Mom's home?"

"Yeah. Johnnie was telling me about it while you were sleeping. I think it'll make a great office. And I'm sure T-Bone and Carole would be proud of your decision."

"So many wonderful memories there, huh? Great barbecues and parties. Say, we could have a celebration barbecue there, and invite all the old gang, once we get the place painted and cleaned up."

Rosa quietly entered the room and asked, "When do you want us to get started? My family's very hard working and fast too. We can get it done very, very soon. Not a minute to lose."

"Let's give you and me at least a day more to heal. I think I want some things brought here. Some will stay there. Others can be carted away and I'll make a list of what needs to be purchased."

"We can start tomorrow, Mel. You can sit and give directions. We'll do everything," Rosa said.

X-Ray joined in, "I have to work tomorrow, but I'll come by for lunch and, of course, afterwards for the clean up."

"Come by where?" Johnnie asked returning to the room, dragging a large, black trash bag behind him. The bag was filled to the brim.

"Tomorrow's the day," Mel responded, rising to her feet. "We're going to start on the new home office. Can you help? What's your appointment schedule like?"

"One of us has to work, Mel! We've received several new assignments and naturally, mail and calls keep coming in on the pending stuff."

"Of course, we do, and I really appreciate you a lot, Johnnie." She added a hug, which he returned, causing her to wince with pain.

They dumped the contents of the trash bag on the dining room table and each of them stood alone on a side, searching for the calendar.

"Voila!" Johnnie said. "Here 'tis."

They gathered around him and scanned the pages, looking for the date of T-Bone's death. "Ah! Here's the last entry."

"What does it say?" X-Ray asked. He could not get close, what with Rosa on one side, and Mel on the other.

They all turned to X-Ray as Johnnie dropped the calendar to the table. Mel spoke first. "It says his last appointment before he was killed was ... with YOU, X-Ray!"

∞*22*

Mel tossed and turned in pain, anger and sadness. She pounded the pillow, now wet with tears. The sheets, blanket and duvee were twisted and lay in a single heap at the foot of the bed. The sun had long since risen when she heard whispered voices approaching the stairs toward her end suite.

"Rosa! Is that you?" She straightened her kitty-printed night shirt which had wound around her waist, leaving her white cotton bikini panties exposed.

"Yes, Mel. Did we wake you?"

"No. I'm thinking about getting up. What time is it?"

"About nine o'clock. I have some breakfast for you. Can I come in the room, please?"

Mel pulled the sheet up to her waist, and propped her head on two pillows against the brass-headboard. "Sure, come in."

Rosa opened the door, propped it with one foot, then half-turned into the hallway to retrieve the tray from the hall stand. Mel smiled. "You're dressed pretty casual today, even for you."

Rosa wore long walking shorts, a white tee-shirt and tennis shoes. A red bandanna bound her dark hair close to her head. The bandanna's small knot ended at the nape of her neck. The tray boasted a plate with wheat toast, scrambled eggs with salsa piled high, grits and a glass of orange juice. Some vitamins rolled around loose on the tray. A tall, thin vase with a single, reddish-orange hyacinth, freshly cut from her own back yard, completed the picture.

"We got lots of work to do today."

"But you and I need our rest. We're still recovering, you know? And . . . I can't afford you."

"Don't worry about the money. We'll work something out."

"Wow! That's some breakfast. I don't usually eat eggs." Mel protested.

"I know you don't like eggs. But, today's a very big day and you will need some energy for your body."

"Thank you, Rosa. Mm. It sure smells good." She unrolled the napkin and tucked it under her chin. Rosa set the white, wicker bed tray across her body.

Mel ate a bite of the eggs and salsa and let out an "Mm," once more. "I didn't realize how hungry I'd be this morning. You're a great cook Rosa. Better than your mom, I think."

"No one's better than *mi madre*. But I like to cook. Anyway, Yolanda cooked this morning." As Rosa spoke, she pulled the edges of the coverlet back and neatly folded it at the foot of the bed. "I think you had a bad night. Do you need some pain pills?"

Mel spoke with her mouth full, "No, I'm fine. Much better today."

"Now, at least, take your vitamins."

GULP.

"What a little fuss-budget you are! I'm ready to get started for the day. Who was that you were talking to in the hall?"

"My cousin here. She is young, but a very hard worker, too. She is finishing now with the upstairs windows. Then you get dressed and we'll all go together to the house. I sent my brothers ahead with the lawn mower and clippers. They should be done by the time we get there."

Mel placed the tray at the end of the bed and rolled off the side of the bed, stretching her arms and yawning as she approached the bathroom door. "Ow . . . that hurts. What am I going to do for a car?" She disappeared into the bathroom, turned on the shower, stripped and entered the shower stall, leaving the question unanswered.

When she re-entered the bedroom a few moments later, the bed had been changed. Fresh, colorful sheets and pillowcases covered the bed. The tray and Rosa were gone. The blinds and window were open, admitting morning, ocean breezes and clearing the stuffy, overnight air. The smell of ammonia affirmed that even her windows had been cleaned in her absence.

She wore long bluejean shorts which were ratty at the leg endings, and a tee-shirt proudly proclaiming victory of her new favorite NFL team, the Dallas Cowboys. She put on her tennis shoes and laced them. She stood. *I'm surprised how much better I really do feel today. What's it been, two days now since my little episode?*

Downstairs, a hubbub of activity which involved cleaning materials, buckets and paper towels, along with some baskets of what appeared to be food for the workers, were transported by various members of Rosa's family to several trucks and cars parked around the cul-de-sac.

"Ready, Miss Mel?" One of the young girls asked. "We ready for you."

"It sure looks like it. Yeah. I'm ready. Where's Rosa?"

"She left in first trip to house. I stayed behind to get you."

She ducked her head slightly, "I hope you don't mind going in my car. I put a blanket on the seat. It torn a bit."

Mel placed her arm around the girl's shoulder and walked with her toward the door adding, "No problemo, seorita. Vamanos!"

They both chuckled. With the alarm set, they closed the front door securely behind them.

* *
*

When they arrived at the Walker home, that same group of trucks and cars now surrounded her father's house, leaving one parking space in the driveway open for Mel's arrival.

The yard caught her eye first when she exited the ancient faded-blue Chevy. "Wow. How nice." She directed her voice toward several men who were in the final phase of bagging the grass, tree and bush trimmings into bundles with burlap bags. Several bags were already placed on the sidewalk in front of the house.

In return, they nodded "*gracias*" and kept sweeping.

The front door was wide open. Inside, each room in the house had one or two people in it, along with boxes and papers awaiting packing instructions. Some people had been delegated to the kitchen and breakfast room which was getting a thorough scrubbing. Others, unloaded boxes from trucks parked in front of the detached garage, near the back door.

"We're ready for instructions, Mel." Rosa greeted her, wiping her hair off her damp forehead. "Where do we start?"

"Well, first, we need to discuss finances. How do you feel about my idea the other day? I'm thinking we should remove all the furniture and things which don't belong in an office. What your family doesn't want, maybe they could take to the swap meet?"

"Barter for work is a good idea. You tell us . . . we move it." She hollered for all to hear, "And if you find personal things please place in a box in that room for Miss Mel to go through later."

"Let's start in the big bedroom . . . Dad and Mom's room."

* *
*

By noon, the bedrooms had been cleared of all furniture. Clothing, packed in boxes, were loaded in trucks. The personal items had been placed in bigger cartons and labeled for review by Mel at a later time. The living room had also been cleared except for the sofa, end tables and lamps which would serve as waiting room furniture. Her father's roll-top desk and captain chair had been moved to the center of the master bedroom and covered with a tarp, while the rooms received a new coat of soft, ivory paint.

"After painting, the carpet needs cleaning."

"And drapes, Mel?"

"I think I want tiny, ivory blinds for the house. But, for now these drapes will have to do." Rosa ordered the drapes and their linings removed from their rods.

"They will be washed today, ironed and rehung after the painting." Rosa said.

"Great," Mel said.

Rosa said, "We can do carpet probably by tomorrow or maybe later today." She raised her voice several notches, "Time to eat now. Lunch is ready." She waved her arms and gathered her flock toward the massive dining room table, which sported a bountiful lunch.

"Get your plates and drinks in the kitchen. After you get your food, we'll eat in the back yard." Everyone obeyed. No one questioned Rosa.

*Rosa, too, is now the head of her family. So young, yet so wise beyond her years.*

Sounds of Mexican music from a small radio played in the background. Several children danced and played with a small cloth ball containing dried beans. Lawn chairs had been unfolded and placed near the redwood table and benches. Everyone ate and jabbered in Spanish. Ravenous, Mel filled her own plate and sat at the redwood bench.

The children shyly played around her, but kept mostly to themselves and giggled a lot. Because of Rosa's insistence on conservation, several trash cans had been lined with bags and set out near the garage door, one for the paper goods, one for cans, and the other for general trash.

When Rosa's relatives finished eating, they dropped their trash in the proper bins and quickly moved to their next assignment. The men folded some jackets and other clothing under their heads and laid under the grapefruit trees for a quick siesta.

Back inside, boxes were being hauled to waiting trucks and the painters started on the kitchen. Mel carefully stepped over the tarp, which was splattered with wet paint. Rosa called to her from the dining room.

"Mel, this rug under the dining room table? We can take it to the cleaners? Okay?"

"Yes." Mel responded. "I want everything to be spick and span when we're through. It's an old carpet. Belonged to my grandparents . . . I think."

She heard the scooting noise as the chairs and table were being moved to release the rug.

"Mel . . . you know the combination numbers?"

"What combination?" Mel asked.

"The kind to open this!" Rosa held one end of the oriental carpet, and pointed at something under it.

Mel entered the room. Several girls made a path as she approached the corner near the break front. Mel gasped, "Where'd that floor safe come from?"

The front door had been left wide open as people walked in and out all day. But a sharp knock on the door startled all those in the dining room, causing Mel to jump.

"Hi. Anybody home?"

"Yeah. In here, X-Ray," she called.

He entered the living room, glanced about the crowd for a familiar face when he spotted Mel. X-Ray greeted those around him and walked toward the dining area. As he neared her side, his eyes were drawn to the area where the oriental rug was pulled back, exposing the safe.

"What the hell is that safe doing here?" he asked.

"Don't ask me! I was only born and raised in this house. I don't have a damn clue when or how the safe was installed. I was hoping you might know."

"Like T-Bone would confide something as personal as this to me." He and Mel knelt to touch the safe. It was recessed into the floor and a rich, dark, piece of matching hardwood floor fit neatly over it. Inset in the cover, a brass ring lay flat, making it even, so it could not be detected when covered with a carpet.

"It says, 'Harbour Safe Company.' Looks fairly new. I suspect it was probably installed after Carole's death. Did T-Bone leave you anything with any numbers on it? We'll need some numbers to . . ." X-Ray said.

"Silly. If I didn't know there was a safe, how in the hell would I know the numbers?"

"Okay. So we need a plan to try to open it. Let's try some combinations on birthdays and anniversaries and substituting numbers for letters for everyone's name. And let's keep a list so we don't waste our effort."

"I have a better idea! Let's call the safe company. Wouldn't they have the numbers? Something for a fail-safe type incident."

"That's not necessarily true. But it's not a bad idea. Where's the phone?"

Rosa brought the portable phone in from the kitchen and handed it to X-Ray. Without a word, she and her staff dispersed to other rooms, allowing X-Ray and Mel privacy.

X-Ray dialed the phone. "In Harbour Pointe."

*Pause.*

"I need a number . . . for the Harbour Safe Company."

He pulled his black notebook and pen from inside his coat jacket, and without speaking, copied the number.

He dialed again. "Hi. This is Detective Xavier Ramirez with the Harbour Pointe Police Department. I need to speak with a manager, the owner, anybody in charge."

*Pause.*

"Hello. Yes. This is Detective Xavier Ramirez with . . . oh, he told you. Okay. So anyway, I'm at the scene of a decedent's home searching for some evidence. We've discovered one of your floor safes. I'm with the decedent's daughter and she has no knowledge of this safe or its combination."

He strolled across the dining room holding the telephone, paused, then copied something on the notepad. X-Ray walked out of earshot and lowered his voice.

Mel could not make out his conversation. She shrugged, opting to let him handle this for the moment and entered the kitchen and got them both a cold drink. When she returned to the dining room, the telephone conversation had concluded. X-Ray scribbled something on his notepad, again.

"Well? Any luck?"

"Not much." X shook his head. "They installed it last year, and T-Bone paid cash for it. Each homeowner is responsible for the combination."

Mel's look of exhilaration changed to one of disappointment. "Did he or she recollect installing this one . . . at all? Maybe they remembered something. Anything?"

"He, Max, the owner, did remember this particular safe and put a note in the invoice that the owner would use four numbers rather than the usual six. So I guess it was coded to accept the four, because he charged T-Bone an additional $10.00 for that alteration."

"Well," she brightened, "that's something. We need to find four numbers, not six, huh? Right!"

She walked the length between what was now the reception area and the dining room and stared at the floor as if the numbers might magically appear on the hardwood knot holes.

"Maybe the numbers are in some of the papers I found here. Jesus . . . I must be losing my mind in all this excitement. We haven't cleaned out the locked cubby holes in his desk either. I haven't been to the safe-deposit box yet. Lord! I even forgot the box in my trunk until the accident. I must be coming apart."

She rubbed her hands vigorously and paced the length of the dining room, to the living area, and back again.

"Come over and sit down." X-Ray encouraged her, as he walked toward the sofa. "Remember, this has not been a good two years. Shit, honey, it's been at least five years since you've had some peace."

Rosa came through the living area and snuggled beside Mel. "We're ready to go home now. My family will come back tomorrow after church and finish painting the house and shampoo carpet." Rosa asked X-Ray, "Can you take her home?"

"Sure, I can." He added, "It's probably a good thing that tomorrow is Sunday. You can get a fresh start on Monday. but Sunday, you relax and play."

Rosa hugged her boss, then brushed Mel's hair back from her eyes with one hand, and patted her hands with the other. She stood and placed her hand on Mel's shoulder. "X-Ray's right. You play tomorrow. And I'll be home bright and early Monday morning with breakfast. For now, don't think about anything. Anything! Got it?"

Mel nodded at the ever so mature Rosa, and replied, "Got it." She sighed. "Thank your family so very much for such a great day. You got so much done. I have no idea how long it's been since this place had been cleaned this much or even painted."

Rosa shut the door behind her. "My favorite saying *Senora*, say it with *dinero*. Say it with *dinero*."

X-Ray changed the subject. "Say, I'm starved. How about dinner? Out."

"Only if you agree to tell me everything you know, eh, everything you can, about Dad's death. I think I'm ready for a double barrel of it now, so I can pull myself together and go back to the beginning, on Monday."

"Agreed. Now what are you hungry for? Italian? Mexican? Thai? Chinese? What?"

"Anywhere but Bernie's tonight. Mexican is fine. How about that little cafe on the Back Bay?" She brightened. "They have the coldest beer."

"TJ's? Sold." He went over to the safe cover and shut it and placed the carpet and table back over the opening. He double checked and locked all the windows and doors.

While X-Ray finished, Mel went to the bathroom, threw water on her face, blew her nose, and freshened her makeup over the sink. She stood by the front door with purse in hand when he returned to the living room.

* *
*

TJ's was located in a white, frame building at the end of the pier on Back Bay. Tonight's line of hungry customers waited their turn for one of the dozen tables in the dining area. Another line formed for take-out. If asked, most patrons might believe TJ's was an abbreviation of the famous border town, Tijuana. Few knew the initials were those of the owner, Tom Jones, a Welshman, like the famous singer who was his namesake. But this Tom Jones' motion was more in the shaking of the belly, than the swiveling of the hips. The aroma of fried onions and chili powder enriched the air inside the small restaurant.

"No *fumar*, Dorothea," they told the middle-aged Hispanic hostess. She wore a white, off-the-shoulder, peasant blouse and a full skirt with petticoats, that resembled a square dancer's costume. An added touch to her authentic costume were red, plastic flip-flops, which clearly exposed her partially painted, chipped, red toenails.

X-Ray ordered, *"Dos Dos Equis, por favor."*

"How've you been, Dorothea?" Mel asked.

177

"Fine. Just fine, Mel. We had a nice vacation. Got to see some of my family in Guadalajara. It was too damn short. Nice, but short," Dorothea replied.

"You guys deserved it. You work too hard. Is Tom here tonight? I haven't seen him in a long time, either," Mel asked.

"Sure. He's in the kitchen. I'll have him bring you some chips and salsa. Let me get you those beers." She disappeared into a room behind two swinging cafe-doors which were splattered with dried food.

Tom burst through the cafe doors balancing an overfilled tray. "Hi, you two. Glad to see you both." Tom transferred the taco chips and salsa and the two beers to their table, then placed the empty tray on the extra chair at the table. He leaned over and hugged Mel. He smelled like week-old cooking oil.

Tom wore an oversized, white and brocade-embroidered shirt with full sleeves, with a V neckline. A colorful sash under his large, overhanging belly held up his faded blue-jeans. Tom, too, wore the traditional flip-flops.

"Heard you two had a nice vacation in Mexico?" X-Ray asked.

"Yeah. Weather was great. But I didn't have time to get over to the coast and do any deep-sea fishing this time."

"That's too bad. Hey, maybe we can get a charter together with some of the guys at the station and go outta Dana Point some weekend."

"I'd like that. Sounds great. Call me," Tom said, moving away from Mel and X-Ray as new customers were seated nearby and called for service.

A quarter-round slice of lime stuck out the top of each beerbottle. Mel got a frosted glass. X-Ray did not.

"So. Let's order and get down to business." She grabbed a menu and scanned both sides for several seconds.

Dorothea, who doubled as the waitress, approached with pencil and pad in hand and tapped it for attention. "Are you guys ready to order? Honestly, honey." She leaned forward, fresh with the smell of plumeria and placed the palm of one hand on the table, "I don't know why you always read the menu. You always order the same thing." She smiled.

"I'm not sure," Mel responded, still holding the large menu.

"Of course, you are. Dorothea's right. You always look at every single thing and we always order the very same thing." X-Ray grabbed both menus. "We'll both have the number-two, combination platters and a side order of guacamole."

"Are we sure?" Mel asked.

"Yep."

Dorothea took both menus and left, shaking her head.

"Let's toast." Mel said. "What can we drink to? More bad luck?"

"No. No more bad news. Let's get to the end of this year, solving lots of crime, and making lots of money."

"Also, can we toast to getting laid?"

He laughed. "Yes. But NOT with each other."

"Done." They clinked glasses.

They drank and watched the incoming tide rising below the pier. Several sailboats maneuvered quietly toward their berths. Glimmering just behind their sails, the fading sun caught the boats' shadows just above the horizon. The once golden sun, now in shades of hot pink at the highest level of its arc, became smoggy and brown as its base touched the vista.

They sat for a few minutes without exchanging any words, drinking in the sunset.

Mel broke the silence, "Well. Where do we start?"

∞*24*

"Well," X-Ray said, "I have an envelope in the car for you . . . for after-dinner. I didn't think a review of crime scene photos and autopsy reports would be proper dinner-fare."

Mel leaned over the table with salsa dripping from the edge of her taco chip and replied, "Fair enough."

"As I told you before . . . eh . . . earlier, cops never believe in coincidence. But this case couldn't be clearer. All the evidence indicates . . . suicide."

*Cough.* Mel swallowed a piece of salsa that stuck in her windpipe and caught her breath, "Mm, lay it out for me, like I'm a idiot. One, two, three. A, B, C. That sort of thing."

"C-A-D-S, first, I guess."

"Okay."

"Corruption! T-Bone had several bank accounts with some unexplained large deposits. Not millions each time . . . mind you, but on his salary, much-too-much to be legitimate. JW tells me he found notes and passbooks in the

180

safe-deposit box that indicate regular deposits over a period of several months. Know anything about that?"

Mel expressed surprise. "I felt he never really needed any money, except what I loaned him during Mom's last months. I don't think he tried to borrow any money from the bank." She shook her head staring out into the night, "I didn't know anything about any money."

"Okay."

"Wait!" Mel said, as she grabbed X-Ray's arm. "Why didn't JW tell me about this money when I met with him and we went over Dad's financial matters?"

"We asked him to hold back until we got our initial work done and I could talk with you myself. We wanted to make sure you weren't . . . eh . . . involved in this too."

"You gotta be fuckin' kidding me, X-Ray! I don't know where I'll find the money to get my car outta hock, even if it CAN be repaired. Or pay Rosa and her family for all the work they've done for me. For God's sake, X, I have my house up for sale."

Her voice rose and patrons at nearby tables stared at them.

X-Ray patted her shoulder. "Don't worry about money. That's the least of your worries." He paused . . . then added, "Your Dad left you over two hundred K in cash."

Dorothea delivered their food.

Mel sat, white-faced and stunned. She whispered, "Two hundred thousand?"

"Since this is the biggest hit I have for you tonight, maybe it's best to finish dinner first and let that information sink in."

They ate in silence.

Two tears drizzled down her cheeks. Mel kept swallowing, hoping to keep her food down. X-Ray finished eating and ordered another beer.

Mel stirred her meal around the plate until the beans and rice were mush. The taco shell got so soft, it fell apart when she bit into it.

"You cops." She pushed her plate back, and laid her fork and knife across the middle. "You damn sure keep secrets."

"I take it you knew nothing of the money?"

"I swear." Mel shook her head. "He never said a word to me, at least, none that I can think of at this time. This is pretty complex. Shit. This is heavy shit. You never knew, but I loaned Dad a lot of money towards the end of Mom's life. He did everything he could to keep her out of the hospital and at home, with him. Nurses and medicine were very expensive. He didn't want to refinance the house. But, he was flat broke. Or so I thought."

"I guess learning YOU got big bucks now can be tough."

"I can't believe you said that, X! I swear, honestly, I swear." She grasped his wrist now and squeezed it for emphasis.

"I have to press, Mel. It's my job. It's a damn dirty job as they say, but I'm the one to break this to you. I had to see your reaction. I have to make sure our conclusions are accurate."

"Under the Asset Forfeiture Act, are you attaching the house and the money? Is that why you haven't told me about it before?"

"No. We don't have enough evidence . . . eh . . . any evidence for that matter, at this time. Nothing actually ties

T-Bone into any crime. The money is yours. That is, until or unless something concrete is developed."

"So the investigation is still ongoing?"

"Not officially."

"What exactly does that mean?" she said.

"The file is closed with SUICIDE-CLOSED stamped across it. But if we ever develop information which ties in corruption or drugs, you can bet we'll have to come back for the assets."

"In other words, don't spend it all in one place!"

She pushed the chair back and ran out of the restaurant, stopped at the pier railing, gulped for fresh air and tried not to heave her dinner into the ocean.

X-Ray glanced at the check, tossed some money on the table and caught up with Mel.

"You're white as a ghost. Are you okay?"

"No. But don't let that stop you. Let's get this out tonight. All of it . . . right here."

X-Ray counted on his fingers. "A, is for alcohol, right? You must admit he was a heavy drinker, Mel."

"All cops drink! Sure, Dad liked his beer, but gave up the scotch after Mom died," She paused, thinking, "and he never was so bad that he had to attend any AA classes."

"Interesting you mentioned that. Why did we find some AA schedules at his house?"

"What? Where?"

"On his desk, along with a lot of other mail."

"Did it appear to be something he just picked up or sent off for or got from someone?" Baffled, she struggled for clarification now.

"Agee told me that T-Bone knew he attended AA, and he asked Agee for the dates, places and times. Agee gave it to him."

"Well. Dad never told me. It was never a problem with us. Why didn't he share that with me?" She slammed her fist against the wooden railing.

Other patrons exited the restaurant. The line for dinner crowded them. X-Ray took her arm. They walked down the end of the ramp and he leaned against his car.

"Okay. So let's get to the drug part, the D thing."

With both hands on her hips, she stood, facing the accuser, demanding an answer.

"Drugs. Cocaine. While we never saw any real evidence of T-Bone's use ... in our day-to-day contact with him, several things are undeniable. First, we found some cocaine residue in the house. A couple of lines on the glass coffee-table top."

Mel opened her mouth and he raised his palm to her, "Wait until I finish. This isn't easy you know and I gotta get this out."

She nodded, and he continued.

"Next, we found some things in his notes that really bothered us. We found some dates marked in red ink. And beside those dates were numbers in kilos. A posting kind of record keeping."

Mel squeezed her eyebrows together.

"It seems to us that those were dates cocaine was taken in, and placed into envelopes in the evidence room."

"How does that tie-in? That's what he did for a living for God's sake. He caught drug dealers!"

"I know. I understand what you're saying. What makes it unusual is that the notes were not in the usual blue book he kept. Again, it was found in the safe-deposit box. As if he were trying to hide it from us."

"Maybe you got some bad guys in the police department and he was trying to catch 'em?"

"Not a chance. This is the cleanest department I've ever seen."

"Except for Dad, huh?"

"No! Mel, I don't mean to imply any wrong doing here. I'm trying to explain, like you asked, how we came to our conclusion."

"Well, just FUCK your conclusion, FUCK your whole conclusion."

She swung at him, fanning the air with her fists and luckily missing her mark.

He grabbed her arms and held them at her side, so she could not lash out at him again. He held her shaking body for several moments. The line of people outside the restaurant diminished. They stood alone in the filtered moonlight.

He cupped her chin in his hand, lifted her head even with his, and gently placed his lips on hers.

She did not resist. He did not press, nor was it urgent.

He then whispered, "I know it's lonely and I miss him too."

She responded with her arms around his waist returning the embrace. The slight wind from the ocean added a chill to the atmosphere. They stood together, listening to the waves lap against the dock.

Mel leaned against X-Ray's chest. He braced himself against the hood of his car with Mel still in his arms. She pulled back, startled to feel contact with a building pressure below his waist against her lower abdomen.

She stood quickly, as did X-Ray. He pulled his jacket across his belly to cover the rise in his crotch. They both chuckled and that blew into full laughter.

"I thought we said NOT with each other," Mel said, smiling.

"I lied," X-Ray replied.

"Forget it, big guy." She walked around to the passenger door. He unlocked it for her. A large, brown envelope was in the back seat. X-Ray reached over, retrieved it, and placed it in her lap.

She did not touch it all the way home. Her thoughts now bound into years of her own training. Investigation years, different from police work. Years of gathering and verifying facts, catching frauds and thieves. She decided that the first thing on her agenda, for the following day, was the purchase of some butcher paper.

The golden moon guided their way home. A slight off-shore breeze cleared the night. They rode in silence. The surf pounded to their right and on their left, a developer's orange and green earth-moving machines sat poised to poison the once-beautiful hillside. They pulled into her circular driveway minutes later.

"What are your plans for tomorrow?" he asked.

"First, I need to check with Jelly on the car. I hope it can be fixed. I'll get a rental unit in the meantime. And, I guess I'll go by my new office."

*I definitely don't want X-Ray to come inside. Not tonight. I have lots of things to sort out.* She leaned back into the open door with, "Thanks, X. For dinner, for your honesty and for this," she pointed at the envelope she clutched to her chest. "And for my kiss. And not necessarily in that order."

"My pleasure."

"Such a good friend. Thank you for understanding."

His last words as he pulled away from the driveway were, "I'll have some butcher paper delivered to the office for you tomorrow morning."

She cocked her head sideways as he disappeared out of the cul-desac, "Now, how'd he know what I was thinking?"

## ∞25

"Mel, telephone for you, please," were the first words she heard, as she approached the back patio after her morning walk.

"Hi, Mel here," she said, taking the portable phone from Rosa's eager hands.

"Do you know how to roll 'em or what?"

"Hi, Jelly. Gosh, you were the first one on my list this morning."

"You sound outta breath. Did I . . . eh . . . interrupt something, eh . . . personal?"

"Right. Turkey. Did my two mile stroll on the beach. And boy am I sore. But, I'll live. So what's the survival rate? Do I need to float a loan, or what?"

"Like I said honey, you sure know how to roll 'em. You want the long version or the bottom line?"

"Is it going to live?"

"Yep. For a price, all cars live."

"So, cut to the chase. How much and how long will it take . . . and can I get a loaner . . . real cheap?"

"Lots. Two weeks if I can get the parts. And tell me what color and I'll have a driver and car there in thirty minutes."

"Get the parts ordered. Give me an hour and bring me any color but black. I don't need black today."

"Deal. Ciao!"

"I love a man who knows his business," she said as she flipped the tennis shoes to the top of the stairway and pulled off her sweaty socks. She rubbed her sore arm and ribs.

"These stitches are ready to come out. They're starting to itch."

She walked toward the stairwell when the phone rang again. "Give me a break will you? Hello, this is Mel."

"Hi. Gosh! Taylor told me you were in a car accident, Mel. Are you okay? Is there anything I can do to help?"

"JW, hi. Aw, that's old news. I'm fine and the car will be, too. And what you can do to help, is quit lying to me."

"I guess the police department talked with you, huh?" he said, after a long pause.

"No shit. Gosh, with friends like you, who needs enemies?"

"I had no choice Mel. They made me promise, you know, in case you were also . . . eh . . . um, involved."

"As long and as close as you were to Dad, you KNOW he wasn't involved in any of those things."

"Mel. Does any of us know anything about anybody? Really?"

"I do." She replied while shedding her clothes. "Listen you caught me getting into the shower. I appreciate your concern. Don't think I'm being rude, but I have a busy schedule today."

"I understand. I only wanted to see how you were doing. One more quick thing. Let the lawyer in me add that that car accident, the other night, is the typical kind of situation you can get into. One more reason why you need to sign those papers for me . . . to protect you, you know."

"Right. I'll get back to you on that."

"You said that before."

She turned the shower on full blast, "I'm saying it, again. Bye."

* *<br>*

By noon she finished some errands and pulled into the driveway of her new "office" ready to work. Jelly delivered an oil-burning, gas-guzzling, faded blue bomb. It was so bent and battered it reminded her of a demolition derby she once attended. *At least the price is right—free. It should be, for what he is charging to repair my little car.*

She pushed with both hands and leaned hard against the driver's door with her shoulder, trying to open the crimped, bent wing. It squeaked like the jaws of life when it did budge.

She noticed something wrapped in a brown wrapper, like the Oswald rifle, lying on the front porch. She approached the house along the side walkway. As she neared, Mel noticed someone had scotch taped a business card to the package.

It was X-Ray's, with a short hand written note on back. *Here it is, as promised. Good luck!*

She had several legal-size boxes with her papers and some investigation files in the car. Rosa also packed her a lunch. It took several trips to unload the car. Lovingly, Mel carried in the bundle last. Inside the wrapper was a huge, heavy roll of butcher-paper.

She closed the front door and plopped onto the couch.

"Ouch. I really overdid it this time."

* *
*

The smell of fresh paint and ammonia combined to make Mel's eyes water. She opened all the blinds and windows.

*Neighbors might as well enjoy this smell, too.*

Two hours later, she had completed her work and put all papers and files away. Mel made a list for the safe combination numbers to be used later by anyone who came by the office and had any ideas. This she placed on the dining room table, with a pencil. She scrounged through the catch-all kitchen drawer and located several thumbtacks that she used to pin several large pieces of the white butcher paper against the walls in her office.

Using simple index cards in place of the regular murder cards, Mel developed a list of all the C-A-D-S clues X-Ray had given her, along with others she had questions about, and taped them to the right side of the paper.

She wrote random notes of things to be checked out later. These were taped to the left side.

One call to the telephone company changed the billing information, listing this number as the new one for the offices of Walker Investigations. It cost extra for the new system, so she could program the unit to dial at home.

Mel also hooked-up a new answering machine at the "secretary's" desk, and dictated a new, and more professional telephone message. She'd have to grow up now, and toss those celebrity impression tapes she'd gotten from Radio Shack.

"Aging is the pits," Mel grumbled, as more decisions were made throughout the morning. She made coffee, in case someone dropped by.

* *
*

The telephone did not ring until noon.

"Walker Investigations. How may we help you?"

"That is so cheery, I'm gonna puke."

"Oh, hi, Johnnie. Wait until you hear the telephone message on the recorder. Watcha doing?"

"Took a statement on that embezzlement case in Fullerton. They've got three more employees lined up who'll be taking lie detector tests later this week. How about you? Anything cooking?"

"Why don't you head over this way and we'll do lunch?"

"Want me to grab something? I haven't had much time to go grocery shopping for the office yet and I'm sure that hasn't been a priority with you."

"Well, actually, Rosa packed food today and there's lots of cold drinks in the ice box and fresh coffee is ready. Maybe I'll take a break and work on the safe combinations till you get here."

"Give me a half-an-hour, or so. You know that mysterious slowing we have on the 57 Freeway is a bitch this time of day."

"Any time of day," she answered. "See you when you get here."

* *
*

During the next thirty minutes Mel ran the most likely numbers that might open the safe. Her birth date. The address. Her father's social security number.

She heard a knock at the door.

"Come on in, Johnnie. This is home now, no need to knock," she called out. "I'm on the floor . . . in here."

"How's it coming?"

"Well. Here's the list so far, of what doesn't work. It certainly isn't any family member's birthday. Past or present. It isn't any anniversary, social security partial, or driver's license that I know. I also used numerical exchanges for letters in everyone's names, including first, middle and last, and I even reversed all the numbers."

"What about his badge number? One-O-One isn't it?" Johnnie sat cross-legged on the floor and pinched a bite of her tuna sandwich.

"I tried it, using the number . . . repeated it like, 1010 and then backwards . . . 0101. Also, the year he graduated from the academy, and his ranking in the graduating class. No luck. Nothing."

"Here, let me have a try. I have a few ideas."

He pulled a piece of blue scrap-paper from his shirt pocket and punched a few numbers.

"Watcha want to drink?" She asked, as she brushed crumbs from her lap onto her napkin.

"I'll take some coffee and maybe another of those tunas."

Mel stuffed the last bite of sandwich in her mouth and carried her plate and empty cola bottle into the kitchen.

She prepared a tray with two cups of coffee and grabbed another tuna sandwich and a fresh napkin. All she heard from the dining area was "shit" and "damn."

"What ISN'T working?" She called out.

"This address, your address, partial zip codes, variations of the telephone number."

"Good ideas. Trying them backwards, too?"

"Yep." He added. "Can you give me some of his banking account numbers and I'll try them?"

"Funny you'd mention money." She joined Johnnie on the floor and sat the tray between them.

"How funny?"

"He left bucks. Big bucks. Over two hundred thousand." She said flatly.

"Right!" He replied, chomping into the sandwich with vigor.

"No shit. That's one of the many things I need to check out. X tells me that Dad had several accounts I wasn't aware of."

Johnnie quit chewing. "Are you shittin' me?"

"I wouldn't kid you about a thing like that! You can't believe the investigation the police have done on Dad."

She waved her hand at the safe. "Let that be for now and we'll get back to it later. Come here. Let me show you."

He placed his list next to hers and stood to join Mel, holding his coffee and the remains of his sandwich. She walked to her office and settled into the chair in front of the roll-top desk.

"Don't let's forget . . . we need to add those numbers to the list of those that don't work."

Johnnie nodded, "Done. Say. What's this? New wallpaper? Nice touch. I especially like all the original photography." He grimaced and dropped the last bit of his meal into her trash can.

"Lost your appetite?"

"No shit."

"X-Ray gave me a copy of the police investigation last night."

Two walls had white paper tacked on them, one width across and two deep.

"This wall," she pointed behind her, "the one with all the writing and arrows, are all my notes. That's all I know right now. The other one is the police investigation file."

She fumbled with several key rings. She tried several of the keys on the desk's cubby holes. None worked.

Johnnie paused briefly beside the "picture" wall. "Mm, not too gory for crime scene photos."

"You have to remind yourself that it is a file, not a human being. And work it like anything else we do."

He scanned the initial autopsy and coroner reports which were also posted.

"Is this the whole file? Are some documents and reports missing here?"

"No, this isn't all." She laid the keys on her desk and turned toward Johnnie. "All I have is the death certificate, a copy of the evidence envelope, and the police report."

"How was the body discovered?"

"A surfer."

"Mm."

"Listen, Johnnie. It'd help me a great deal if you could keep working and reporting on my files, so I can resolve all this." She motioned to both walls.

"Things are a bit slow right now, so that's not a problem. I've been thinking about all this. I think I'm ready to leave your nest and find a place of my own. Maybe I could live here . . . in the garage apartment? I'll pay you rent and help with the utilities in exchange for some of my billings?"

She jumped up and hugged Johnnie. "What a great idea. That'd be perfect. I'll miss you at home, of course, but I realize you need your space too. You're such a love."

"It'd also give me more time to work on the safe numbers. Keep the house secure for you. Be here for assignments. I'll keep the lawn up. I'm really great with plants and flowers, when I have time."

She shook his shoulders, smiling. "Silly. Quit selling. I already said yes."

"I guess I had a few more assets I wanted you to know about."

"No shit. But I already knew that about you."

She kissed him tenderly on the cheek.

"How soon can you get here? My gosh, we completely forget to paint and tidy the garage apartment. That place has more old furniture and storage stuff in it, I believe. I haven't been in there in aeons. X-Ray and his Mom stayed there for several years. Maybe Rosa's family can help with that. I know she has the carpet cleaner scheduled for later this week. Now that the painting is complete, she wants everything to be fresh and clean for me."

"Well, I can do the painting myself and any repairs. I'm pretty handy to have around. I'll borrow a truck from a friend of mine and he'll help me move. So I could be here . . . maybe . . . by the end of the month."

"Fine. Perfect. If you need any supplies or groceries, give Rosa a call. She loves that mothering part. And she'll adopt you here, too."

"I'll be fine. It's something I want to do, and it gives me a project, too."

She turned to reach for the telephone. "Say! We can afford a secretary. Want a secretary?"

195

"Naw. Between me and the telephone recorder we'll be fine. I'll put an extension in the apartment first thing. Say, we didn't lose our typist, did we?"

"No, thank goodness. But maybe Barb can coordinate coming by here to get and drop off dictation, instead of the house now. You work out the details. I'll leave that to you."

"Deal."

"I'll be moving more of my files here from home later. But first, I have to solve this mess."

She glanced at her watch. "Say, there is one thing on the list I can check on today if you don't mind."

"Want me to go with you? Help with the list?"

"Thanks, Johnnie. But as they say in the old westerns, this is something I have to do alone."

"Well. Okay. Sure. I have some dictation to do anyway. And I'll call Barb and work on MY list. Hell. I've got a lot to do here."

* *<br>*

Mel drove to the Laguna Niguel offices of the travel agency whose brochure she had found at her father's house.

This was the first of her checklist items and she cautioned herself to be careful about exposing too much information or leaving a trail.

Through the plateglass store-front, Mel could see the small office. There were four black-lacquered desks. One appeared to be vacant. Advertising posters were plastered at angles across the walls. Several enticing cruise-line ads with miniature models of their ships enhanced a window display. An elderly woman straightened the travel brochures that lined a bright red bookcase along one entire wall.

"How much trouble can I get into? I'm not exactly impersonating a police officer."

She smiled and removed her father's police badge that was encased in a black-leather, fold-over wallet. It did not have his name on it. His card was on the opposite side, inside a narrow plastic slit. She slipped her own investigator's license over her dad's picture.

Mel opened the door and a blast of air-conditioning greeted her. A receptionist, whose hair was as blue as the ink on the back of the brochure, sat at the lead desk.

"May we help you, dear?" She took her granny glasses off, placed them on the desk and gave Mel her best, bleached-denture smile.

Mel reached into her pants pockets and pulled out her father's police wallet. She flipped it open, let the lady see the shiny part, then closed it.

"I'm investigating a homicide."

Her voice of authority must have filled the air, as another elderly lady, shuffling through some papers, came out of the back room. This gray-haired lady's smile and eyebrows were raised in a state of inquisitiveness.

"Yes?" the new one replied. "I'm Miss Helen, the manager. How can we help?" Miss Helen wore a lime-green, polyester pantsuit that pre-dated Carter's administration.

Mel loved the "can we help you" part.

"Thank you, Miss Helen. I'm inquiring about this brochure." Mel extended the paper to the polyester queen who approached her.

"I see our advertising stamp with our address on it. But it doesn't look like we mailed it out," Miss Helen said. "This is a typical ad we have, for the Caribbean area. This is a current year. You know, as opposed to older ones, because as you can see we have others here in the rack."

"In other words you throw older ones out?" Mel asked.

"Yes."

"So this one is about . . . "

"I believe it's about six months old." She turned to the other lady and they both nodded in affirmation.

"This one," Mel said authoritatively, "was found at a crime scene. Is there any way to find out how it got there?"

The woman turned it over once more and then shook her head. "No, I'm sorry. They are usually mailed out in an envelope or simply given out here." She added, trying to help, "Did you find an envelope?"

"No. Just the brochure. Do you keep a list of those you give out or mail out?" Mel asked.

"No, sorry. Possibly we handed it out. Do you have anyone's name?"

Ever the spontaneous investigator, she quickly opened her purse, pulled out her official-looking address book and scanned it intensely. "Mm, how about a William Walker? Do you have a client named William Walker?"

"I don't think so. Eleanor, check the computer for her, please."

The telephone rang. Miss Helen answered it, leaving Eleanor free to run the name through her computer.

A few seconds later, Miss Eleanor shook her head, "Nothing, dear."

"It's a fairly common name. Guess it doesn't sound familiar to either of you?"

They both turned to the other woman who shrugged as she continued her phone conversation.

"Mr. Walker was in law enforcement, too." She hoped this might help.

Eleanor paused biting the lower part of her lip. "Wait a minute." She placed her fingers under her chin. "Maybe I would recognize him, if you had a picture of him and if we handed it out to him?"

"Why is that?"

"Why, this is such a small community . . . mostly retired folks. We don't get much walk-in traffic that isn't familiar to us, you know, on a first name basis. And we *did* have a police officer a few months ago, as I recall now, come by for something from the rack. Although I can't be sure what island or country it was for."

Reaching once again into her bag, she pulled out a picture of her father from her wallet. He wore a suit and tie. She showed it to Eleanor.

"No, I'm sorry that isn't him. At least it doesn't look like him."

"How did you know he was a police officer?" Mel pursued.

"Why, dear, he was wearing his uniform."

## ∞26

Mel smiled. "Eleanor? Is that your name . . . Eleanor?"

The lady returned the smile. "Yes, dear."

"What days did you work, say . . . in November of this year?"

"I work part-time on Tuesdays and Thursdays only."

"Eight to five on those days?"

"Oh no, dear. I'm on social security and have limited hours I can work. Otherwise, I lose my benefits. I'm here from 10 a.m. to noon. Then I have lunch, come back at one-thirty and work until we close at four. And only on Tuesdays and Thursdays."

"Did you deviate from those hours or dates in November or December this year?"

"No, ma'am."

The supervisor raised herself to her full, five-foot-two height, interjecting proudly, "Eleanor is very reliable. She has a perfect attendance record."

"Wonderful," Mel replied. "It isn't often we find such fine and devoted employees like yourselves. Your boss is very lucky, you know."

There was a tingle in her stomach as she felt a plan was developing.

"You know I'd like to thank you for all your help. Can I return the favor?"

She moved more cautiously now, so as not to scare them off.

"Oh, no need to, dear," Miss Eleanor said, bobbing her fifties hair-do.

"Well actually," Mel formulated and continued, ". . . how about a personal tour of our local police department. Say, on a Thursday? I could pick Eleanor up at noon and we'll 'do lunch,' as they say in L.A., and I'll have you back here by one thirty."

"Oh," Eleanor squealed. "All those lovely men in uniform. I simply love those leather knee-boots."

Miss Helen's already wrinkled face continued to furrow deeper into her skull.

Mel did not miss the sign and added, "Oh. I meant that to include you too, Miss Helen. If you can, of course. I don't want to inconvenience you. You must be VERY busy."

"Oh." She clapped her hands in front of her bright, sparkling eyes and replied, "No trouble at all. We'd love it."

She glanced at Eleanor, who seemed a bit discouraged that Miss Blue was coming too. But she responded, none the less, and they both agreed that Mel would come for them about noon.

The ladies walked Mel to her car as they worked on the finer details of their impending trip. Mel reached the car parked in front of their office.

"I apologize for this old car. I had a slight accident in my car, and this is a loaner. It may not be much, but it was free."

"So . . . uh . . . why don't we meet you at the police department? I believe we have other stops to make on Thursday, anyway, and it'd be no inconvenience. Really. None at all." Eleanor said.

Both ladies grasped their hands together and rubbed them vigorously.

Mel smiled. "Sure. It's agreed then. If that's okay with you, I'll meet you there on Thursday. Ask for me if I'm not at the front door. The receptionist will find me."

She said her goodbyes to the excited twosome. They were discussing what dresses they would wear to the event.

Mel felt sure each would recommend the most unflattering to the other. She did not have the heart to tell them all the leather boots and uniforms would be on the streets and they had little chance of seeing any of those, no matter how much their hearts palpitated at the thought.

* *
*

She had one more appointment today. For his convenience, she scheduled it at low tide.

The drive to the Huntington Beach Pier Cafe was a comfortable thirty minutes along Pacific Coast Highway. Mel found a parking space at the curb. The city council priced parking there out-of-reach for a lot of working-class folks.

She dropped her last six quarters into the parking meter.

"How will I know you?" she had asked this witness on the telephone.

"I'll be the only surfer outta the water," he had replied.

That sounded simple enough at the time they talked. But now, as she shaded her eyes with one hand and scanned the blue-brown water and brown-gray frothy waves rolling toward the shore, she was not sure. Black shiny things dotted the dirty water like bobbing heads of seals gasping for air. She saw no shiny black things out of the water.

Passing on that piece of identification, she scanned the nearby parking lot for what had been described as a faded, old Volkswagen van.

That really did not narrow it down much. There were at least twenty vans with that description.

She kicked off her tennis shoes, grabbed them by the laces and tossed them in the back seat. Mel stepped quickly over the hot sand and asphalt until she neared the "surfer" area. This is a closed city where the surf boards stuck end-on-end in the sand, in a circle like fence columns, keeping the uncool out. Wet towels and plastic water bottles lay in the center of this circle that contained one sentinel, a young, bikini-clad blonde, lying on her nonexistent belly with her top unclasped.

"Don't you just hate that?" Mel said, in an effort to startle this potential groupie into action.

The girl did not even so much as move her head, "Naw. I'm not here for the water."

"Can you swim?" Mel had to know.

"Who wants to know?" This time she turned her head and put on her sunglasses.

"No big deal. I'm trying to make conversation. Say, I'm looking for a guy here."

"Ain't we all, lady. Ain't we all." And with that the glasses fell to the blanket and all Mel saw were indifferent, bleached tresses, much in need of a good hair dresser or a can of tomato juice.

"You looking for me?"

Startled, Mel turned. "Are you the surfer dude I talked to?"

"Yo, dudette." He gave her a high sign. "That's me."

Mel motioned for them to walk toward some afternoon shade afforded them by the vans. He matched his police report description. Five-eleven, about one fifty, stringy brown ponytail, and a faded tattoo, depicting a gecko on a surf board, on the right shoulder.

"As I told you on the phone, I'm doing some follow-up on the body you discovered, and I have a few questions."

"Got any ID?"

"Sure." She produced the wallet and flipped her way into impersonation again, counting quickly to three, so the badge would shine on one side, with the smile from her picture on the other. At the count of three, she shut it.

"Now." She said.

"Before you begin, officer. Like, I have a few questions of my own?"

She winced at the word 'officer.' "Okay. Shoot."

"This isn't going to take too long is it? 'Cause the swells are comin' in now and I'm missin' 'em."

"Not too long, if you let me get going."

"You know, I already answered a whole lotta questions to that other cop. That guy."

"Right. Well," she extended her best authoritarian stance and continued. "I need to cover a lot of the same territory as the last guy. We also retrace our steps and re-verify stories. Maybe you can think of something you didn't remember the first time, you know." She lapsed into his speech pattern to put him at ease.

"Gotcha. Also, I'm not gonna have to testify or anything 'cause if that's in your plan, lady, I'm outta here now and we'll both save each other some time."

"You won't have to testify for me. I swear."

*I'd swear to anything.*

She was not a cop. Or a lawyer either. But she tried her best to recall the hearsay rule, something about "against interest" rule, as she remembered.

"Okay. Let's do it."

She opened her black, vinyl file-folder and withdrew some photos. "Let's go over these together."

He shaded his eyes and stepped around, so they were side-by-side. He smelled like a wet, stale puppy dog. He pulled his damp, greasy, stringy pony-tail to the opposite shoulder and in doing so, splattered salt water on her and the photos.

She wiped them dry with the hem of her blouse, ignoring the droplets on her clothes and face.

"Now. How'd you happen to be at Scotchman's Cove that morning?"

"Is that a crime?" he said, abruptly.

"Don't be so defensive. It's only a question."

"Well, I already answered that question." He moved slightly away, his body language ebbed toward the water with each incoming wave.

*How about a bluff. It works sometimes.*

"Maybe you have something to hide, Dude? Why don't we go down to the police department so you won't be so distracted by the sun and the waves? Maybe you can see the pictures better inside a brightly lit interrogation room."

She hoped to appeal to his sense of freedom, yet not scare him off.

He did not respond right away. He kicked the sand, wedging his toes deeper until they disappeared beneath the surface.

"You don't have any wants or warrants do you?" Using her thumb and looking very stern, she pushed the button on her ball point pen, forcing the tip out.

"Oh man," he said, breaking a bit. "Geez. I'm sorry . . . oh . . . geez. Let's get this over with. Like, okay. Like, I was by myself that morning. I drove to the bluffs above the cove and got out my gear. I was going to dive for some lobster, but like . . . " anticipating her next question, "I got no lobster license, okay. So give me a friggin' ticket."

She replied calmly now, trying to work the story out of him. "Let's continue for now."

"I walked down the dirt road from the highway leaving my van on the shoulder. So, if any of my buddies came along they'd find me. Like, they could come along later . . . you know."

"Mm."

"I see this car parked near the mesa ridge."

He went into great detail describing her father's car, but she did not interrupt him for fear of losing him and his train of thought.

"Then I came around the rocks, dragging my wet-suit, and tanks and like . . . shit-stuff and I see this dude . . . and boy, was he dead."

"How'd you know he wasn't asleep? Like a drunk sleeping there?"

"He had on a jacket and slacks and shit. Like this photo here." He indicated the one on top. "So, I leaned over the rock and felt for a pulse. Zip . . . Zero . . . Nada, you know."

She shivered in the heat.

"So . . . like . . . I look around and saw nothing, nobody else. Like . . . I high-tail-it back to the van. I gotta CB and I called you guys right away, like a good citizen, you know."

"And?"

"I waited till you guys got there. The other cop asked me some questions, checked my ID, and let me go."

"Okay. So, here's the next picture." She gestured for him to take it. "See anything different in the picture, you didn't see there at the time you discovered the body?"

"Like, is this a trick question?" he asked, shading his eyes once more to make sure he did not miss anything.

"Nope. Is anything changed?"

"Nope."

"Now, I don't mean to help you here, you know, like coaching or anything . . . but look at the footprint area for me."

"Yeah. Okay."

"There were that many prints in the sand around the body?"

"Yeah. At least that many."

*That's strange. I thought those were made by the first point men on scene, or the forensic, crime-unit investigators.* "How can you be sure?"

"Well, like I also play a lot of beach volleyball, you know, and I couldn't help but see the sand around the body was all agitated, and I thought shit, he musta have put up one hell of a fight with those other dudes."

"Interesting observation, Dude." She wrote in her note pad. "Have any other thoughts?"

"Yeah. One wore tennies, I mean, you know . . . the other, who was barefoot, like me."

He raised one foot, maintaining perfect balance, and wiggled his sandy toes at her.

*Take a chance. We've come this far.* "You don't eh, like, know the brand-name of the tennies you saw, by any chance?"

"Lady, I can't do it all for you. You gotta do some figuring out yourself."

His hands gripped his waist, while he pinched non-existent lovehandles.

She patted his muscular biceps. "You're right. I do. Well. That about wraps it up for me. If anything else comes up, I know where I can find you."

He smiled. "Ciao." With that remark, he grabbed his highly waxed board and jaunted toward the water. No handshake and no goodbye.

*What a free, scared soul he is.*

She shook off the sentiment creeping into her mind, reminding herself that Willie could have become a teenager someday, and as much as he loved the water, could have become a surfer. She and Taylor and Willie used to take long walks on the sand, holding hands, hugging and having fun.

That thought caused another shiver.

\* \*
\*

On the way home, she stopped at the one-hour, photo shop and ordered two eight-by-tens, and asked the clerk to have them ready by nine the next morning. She also requested a larger photo of one of the bare footprints and one of the shoe imprints in the sand.

With emphasis, she told the employee, "Please isolate these footprints with the unusual markings for me."

Back in the car she placed a call.

"Orange County Coroner's Office. Can I help you?"

"Hi Sally. This is Mel. Is Barry there?"

"Oh . . . hi . . . Mel. Yeah. I'll get him for you . . . just a moment."

Music floated through the phone lines and she harmonized along with a Kay Starr favorite. She had a good friend in Barry Zabel . . . the shining star in the field of forensics for Southern California. *It doesn't hurt that he's also a hunk.* Tall, dark, and handsome and married, with six children. But he and Mel still shared great hugs in public places and that was enough.

Mel's thought processes reeled like motion-picture film. Barry knew all about her father. His name appeared on the autopsy report as the attendant witness.

*I have to move carefully here.*

"Hi Doll. How you doing?"

"Fine, Barry. Lonely ... but better. Thanks for asking."

"Got something cooking?"

"Yeah, I do, as a matter of fact. Busy tomorrow? About ten thirty or so?"

Paper noises combined with the cellular line static. The result was crackling and ear splitting.

"Huh. Right now, it's open. No bodies in cold storage. Unless we have a full moon tonight, I should be clear."

"Okay. So pencil me in, and I'll call you first, before I head out."

"Perfect. Is this personal or business?"

"Mm." *A nice round lie now.* "Business what else?"

"Bernie's as usual?"

"I'll be there. See you then."

* *<br>*

The phone rang.

She parked in her garage and even though she turned the key off, the engine continued to chug.

Mel picked the phone up from the front seat, answered it while her left shoulder and arm pushed against the creaking door.

"Hi. Mel here ... huh." She growled.

"Huh, to you too, Mel. Lucas here. Are you okay?"

"Fine. Just fine. This old clunker Jelly gave me may be free, but I'm not sure it's worth it. I can't get the driver's door open. I'm black and blue trying to get outta the damn thing. How're you settling in?"

"Great. Who's Jelly?"

"Jelly's the surgeon operating on my car."

*Humph. Her shoulder really pinched with that hit.* "Help! I'm being held captive by a car." She laughed.

"That's what I called about. I finally got unpacked and found my coffee pot."

"You got a condo . . . home . . . what?"

"A condo . . . on Balboa Island. Near you, I think. Nice view of the bay, anyway. I found other things, too, like dishes and cooking things. How about dinner tonight. At my place?"

"I must admit . . . since Rosa's been helping me. I'm not much of a cook, Lucas."

"I make a mean meat sauce. Can you boil spaghetti and butter some bread?"

"That, I can do. I can even stir salad-makings."

"And I'll treat you to a ride in a real car. I'll pick you up about seven-thirty. How's that sound?"

"Great. See you then. Bye." The engine finally died. "Thank God."

She grabbed her file folder and purse. With two more hard pushes, the car-door opened, creaking like a coffin lid in a scary movie.

Opening the garage door to the hallway, she called out, "Rosa . . . Johnnie . . . I'm home. It's me."

She and Johnnie had a code. It's their "Don't be scared it's just me" and "if I'm interrupting something important, put your clothes back on and hurry" code.

No response.

She dropped everything on the desk in the office and walked into the kitchen. Under the toe-tag magnet on the ice box was a short, cryptic note in Rosa's hand.

*I didn't fix dinner.*

*He's a nice man.*

*He likes you, I think.*

*See you tomorrow morning. Maybe not.*

*Now how did she know that?*

Wearily she climbed each stair step, removing shoes, socks and shirt, as she went.

A warm soak in the hot-tub on the deck could help her mood and her sore arm and ribs. She mulled over the day's discoveries.

Mel pulled the tub-cover back and checked the water with her fingers. *Fairly comfortable . . . but I need more heat.*

Mel flipped the heating switch on, while she finished undressing and found a fresh towel. She passed the night stand when she first noticed the telephone call-button blinking.

She lay across the bed with a pad and pencil ready to copy numbers and names, and pushed the replay button.

"Hi, Mel. It's me Lucas. I'm trying to catch you early. It's two o'clock . . . Let's have dinner tonight . . . My treat. I'll try to find you . . . Call me."

*So that's how Rosa knew.*

Mel spent twenty minutes fussing with her hair and makeup. On a normal day, Mel could brush, apply makeup and dress in less time than that.

Another twenty minutes passed before she settled on a pair of soft gray, silk slacks with matching blouse and a pink sweater. Mel also put on hose and short-heeled gray pumps. A splash of Joy, a glance and a turn in the full-length mirror inside the closet confirmed her inner thoughts.

*I'm ready for anything.*

She heard a car outside. She no longer heard the engine, but no one came to the door.

Seven fifteen.

She smiled. *He's early.*

At seven twenty-five, the door bell rang. Mel checked her handbag for tissues and walked to the door. Through the peep hole she saw Lucas' face.

He nervously brushed off some imaginary dandruff from his shoulder.

Lucas' first response as she opened the door was, "Wow! You look beautiful tonight, Mel."

Her eyes caught the dark blue of the alligator boots . . . then travelled past the snug-fitting, dark blue-jeans to the neatly pressed plaid shirt, finally landing on soft blue eyes. "Hi yourself, Tex. You look pretty yummy yourself."

They hugged briefly and cordially, then released their grasp.

"Mm you smell good, too," he added.

"Thanks. Let me set the alarm and I'll be ready."

She walked the few steps to the keyboard and pressed a few buttons.

"We have forty-five seconds to close the door." She reassured Lucas, shutting the front door behind them. He held her hand and walked her around to the passenger side of a pale silver, two-door Mercedes.

"Is this new?" she inquired. "This isn't the car you were driving at Patty's party."

"Say, you *are* a trained observer aren't you?" he smiled. "I just bought it a few days ago. I realized if I'm to stay here for a while, I might as well have a car here. A real car, I mean."

She commented, "Very pretty, Lucas. I love the smell of a new car."

"Me too."

"What kind of truck do you have back home in Texas?"

"How'd you know I have a truck?"

"I'm an investigator, remember?"

"Yeah," he chuckled. "It's a Chevy, with an oversize cab."

"Gun rack and all."

"Yep."

She smiled.

"Do we need to go by the grocery store and get anything?"

"No ma'am. I did all the shopping today and it's all unpacked and ready to go."

"Are you a woman's dream?"

"That's not what my ex said about me."

She was not sure she wanted to pursue unhappy memories for either of them . . . this evening, especially.

213

She leaned over and retrieved a small, cassette-tape box which she scanned through.

"See," he said, "I don't like only country music. You'll find a pretty good selection in those tapes."

"Barbra, Oleta Adams, Etta James. The Koz." She said, thumbing through them.

*A lot of my favorites.*

"Who helped you buy them?" she said, smiling knowingly at him.

"Does it show? It was Patty. She said these tapes were the stars you liked."

"It's very thoughtful of you to go to that effort."

He put his right hand on the passenger-seat headrest and smiled. "For you, Mel, anything."

She put a tape in and Etta James sang soft Billie Holliday jazz.

Only sounds floating through the surrounding speakers and out the partially opened sun-roof dispelled the silence. His hand dropped from the headrest and paused over her hand, which draped over the arm-rest between them. She made an effort to lace her fingers through his and once accomplished, he gave her an unobtrusive squeeze. They both smiled at the highway.

\* \*
\*

"What a great view you have," she said, scanning the inner bay and the setting sun over the horizon. Several sailboats motored into their slips. Crews scampered on board, working to release and fold the sails to the booms. Others grabbed the shore lines and prepared to moor.

"Thanks," he replied, joining her side. "I think if I watch this long enough, I could even get the hang of sailing myself, huh?"

"Maybe." She turned. "So. What can I help with?" Lucas removed his boots and left them by the door. She tossed her purse onto a nearby chair and kicked off her pumps.

"How about a drink? Vodka and tonic, I believe."

"Mm. You are good. And yourself? I probably know less about you, than you know about me."

He went around the bar and took a couple of cold glasses from a refrigerator bar, filling one with ice. She joined him at the bar and sat down on a nearby stool.

"White wine tonight. It's a Reisling . . . a California wine, I think," he said grasping the wine bottle.

"And Lone Star Beer on other occasions?"

"Nope . . . close though. It's an old Texas beer called Pearl. Stinks like hell. But, tastes great . . . at least after the second or third one."

He mixed her a drink and placed it over a napkin in front of her, adding a slice of lime. He uncorked his wine and poured the drink.

"I know what you mean. I like beer. Usually with Mexican food, though."

"That's that ol' sissy-beer like Dos . . . something . . . huh?"

"Or Tecate. Anything like that."

"It's still sissy stuff."

"I concede."

"Is that like 'give up'?"

"Sorta." She swivelled the bar stool around and faced the living room and large picture window.

"Ready for the guided tour?"

"Is this the two-dollar one?"

"Yep."

He led her into a short hallway where they walked through two bedrooms and one and one half baths, then back to the kitchen and a small dining room opposite the kitchen. The home appeared to be a model, decorated with muted peaches, blues and greens. The upholstery, drapes and throw pillows all blended with small modern designs of zigs and zags and little wiggly lines. The large plants were a dusky green and all either plastic or silk.

As they passed the large plastic fichus near the front door he explained, "I like green things, but dang if I don't kill this one, it'll be a miracle."

"I'm not good with greenery, either. If it wasn't for Rosa, my whole house would be brown."

"Here's the stereo. Pick out what you like to hear and join me in the kitchen."

After reviewing his selection and her options, Mel decided on a smooth listening FM radio station rather than changing tapes or CDs.

"Mm, great smells in there. Am I in the right home?"

"Yes ma'am, you are. My favorite uncle taught me this meat sauce recipe. He's from Louisiana and anything with Tabasco in it gotta be good."

"So . . . where do I start?" She said with her hands on her trim hips.

"First, an apron. Don't want to mess up that pretty outfit." He produced a full-bibbed apron from a nearby drawer and she turned so he could tie it around her waist. He lifted her hair, making sure it was above the apron neck lines.

*Mm. That was thoughtful.* She smiled.

She found butter and an interesting smelling jar filled with garlic, oil and basil and she generously basted the french loaf.

He was busy adding ingredients to and stirring a red sauce in a large, black and white, speckled pan, like those used for cooking turkeys.

"Whose army is joining us anyway?"

"Just us. But, with my large family, I never learned how to make smaller portions. So we'll eat what we want, and I'll freeze the rest in batches. The seasoning's better as it ages, anyway. Here . . . taste."

Lucas held the wooden spoon in one hand, and cupped the other underneath to prevent any spilling. She puckered to blow on the spoon, then tasted the delicacy.

"That's plain wonderful. Remind me to get the recipe. That really is good."

He bowed. "Well, thank you ma'am."

She opened several kitchen cabinets before inquiring, "Where's the salad bowl?"

"I have it chilling in the ice box. My mama always told me it keeps the lettuce crisp and fresh."

"Good idea."

In the crisper drawer she found the lettuce, tomatoes, onions, celery, radishes, mushrooms, and avocado, all pre-washed, peeled and ready for slicing. The small kitchen prompted them to accidently brush past each other several times while they worked at preparing dinner.

She completed the salad and her drink. "Time for another drink before dinner?"

"Sure do. The spaghetti water isn't boiling yet. So we have a few minutes."

Mel picked up their empty glasses and went to the bar to refill them both. When she turned, Lucas was sitting on the bar stool, smiling. He took his wine glass and clicked hers.

"Let's toast to more evenings like this. I like seeing you here, in an apron and all."

She bristled. "Is that as chauvinistic in Texas as it sounds in California?"

"Oops. No ma'am, it isn't. It's a very nice, warm, domestic side of you I haven't seen before. After all, the first quote, date, unquote we had, you pulled a gun and got me handcuffed."

They both broke out with the giggles. The kind of laughter that begins simple enough with polite chuckling, which progresses to an infectious tears running-down-the-cheeks type, until the coughing spasms start and you're totally out of control.

When they heard the water boiling over onto the stove, Lucas excused himself.

She held her drink, wandered through the living room and rounded the corner to the dining room table. Given his southern background, she half expected to see something in a red-and-white plaid and plastic covering the table. To her surprise the table cloth and napkins were a matching ivory. And adorning this, some Fitz and Floyd dinnerware she recognized, along with settings of a contemporary, flat silver service. She turned toward the kitchen and noticed a silver champagne stand against one wall with an iced bottle of Moet chilling beneath another ivory napkin.

"Mm . . . not too showy, but lovely."

"What?" he called out.

"Nothing," she muttered. "Can I help?"

"No. Everything's fine in here. What did you mean? Mm what?"

"You set a mighty fine table, for a cowboy."

"I must confess. I could take all the credit . . . but it was Patty. She picked out the linens and all and set the table. Patty also made me a grocery list and did my shopping."

"That's very nice of you two to go to this trouble for me."

He leaned toward her and touched her chin, then cupped it with one hand. Without invading her space, he planted a delicate kiss on her lips.

He released her chin and their foreheads touched, "Nice got nothing to do with it ma'am." With his index finger, he tapped her nose lightly.

A bit stunned, she stepped back and asked, "Ready?" Mel removed the apron and folded it on the kitchen counter.

"To eat? It's ready." He followed her into the dining room and held the chair for her.

Lucas tossed the salad and served portions of everything. He was a bit old fashioned and she was not sure if he would want to say grace before eating, or what. Mel waited for him to make the first move . . . and did not have long to wait.

He held his champagne glass and moved it toward hers. She grasped her glass and lightly touched it against his without comment.

"I'd like to make a toast to a warm, long-lasting relationship built on respect and friendship."

"I'll drink to that," she replied.

Dinner continued in the same warm tone . . . *or was that the wine?* She secretly wished the night would last forever. *God. I hope I'm not fluttering my eyelids like some beach bunny. I hate that.*

Sometime during dinner, she was not sure when, his stocking feet touched hers. Lucas slipped one foot under hers to raise her arch, slightly off the floor. With the other, he softly rubbed up and down her foot, beginning by separating her toes, one-at-a-time, then slowly moved up the foot to the ankle . . . no higher . . . just to the ankle. Like an explorer, carefully but thoroughly exploring each foot.

She broke into goose bumps.

"Are you cold?" he asked.

"I'm fine. Thank you," she answered, lowering her eyes to her plate.

*God. Now I'm sure I'm fluttering. Please stop that shaking.* No man she knew expressed such subtle tenderness and caring. She felt her vulnerability exposed and food dropped from her fork.

"I can cut the air-conditioning down, if you like?"

"No . . . really . . . I'm fine." She risked exposure by placing her hand on his.

They continued with some small talk about family and friends and careers. Later she would not be able to remember a word. But for now, it was heaven.

For a long time Lucas did not move his hand away. Then he lifted it, with hers lying on top. He brought their hands to his mouth, brushed his cheek against the back of her hand. Penetrating her eyes with his, he turned the hand over, closed his eyes and kissed the palm, leaving a bit of wetness lingering behind.

*Am I going to climax right here at the dinner table? This guy's got the corner on foreplay.*

Afraid that any smart-alec or cute retort would shock them back to reality, she remained quiet.

*I'm not ready for that to stop just yet.*

"More wine, Mel?"

"Huh?" She paused.

"More wine?"

"Huh, no. I've had plenty thanks. Some coffee, maybe?" She wiped her mouth and neatly folded the napkin beside her empty plate.

He pushed his chair back and leaned forward to pull hers out. She stood, gathered their dishes in several small stacks and moved them to the kitchen. He helped. In a few trips, they cleared the table, rinsed the dirty dishes and put them in the dishwasher. Their duties defined, Lucas attended the coffee maker. All this done in sensual silence.

"I usually put a little after-dinner liqueur in mine. Tia Maria? How about you?"

"That'll be fine," she replied.

He put both cups on a tray and left the room. She wiped her hands and the counter top and closed the washer door. She joined him in the living room where several large throw-pillows were propped against the back of the sofa, facing the bay. He had turned the air-conditioning down and opened the patio door so the sounds of evening filtered off the water into his condo.

Halyards banged against the aluminum masts. Boats slapped up and down in their berths. Noise from the docks dwindled as the sailors secured their boats for the night.

The music softly filled the background from within the warmth of his condo. She joined him on the floor and held her coffee cup with both hands.

"Smells good," she sipped. "Tastes good too."

She tried to avoid his eyes for the sun was setting as quickly as her defenses. Yet, she sensed his presence and his warmth. His shoulder brushed hers, as they both settled back . . . their elbows on the pillows.

They fell easily into a comfortable silence that became more intense as the moments passed. Then he spoke.

"Are we going to be the kind of friends who can hug? I need a hug . . . and I suspect you do, too."

Mel replied. "The night is young. Let's get that first awkward one out of the way."

## ∞28

The smell of coffee and cinnamon reached her nostrils before the sunlight met her eyelids.

"Good morning, Mel. Breakfast is ready."

She lay on her belly, with a pillow pushed against the bed's headboard.

"Huh?" she muttered.

*That isn't Rosa's voice.*

"Breakfast. You do eat breakfast . . . don't you?"

She rolled to one side and rubbed her eyes. "Oh my goodness . . . good morning, Lucas."

She covered her nakedness with a nearby sheet.

"Was it that bad?" he asked, setting the bed tray on the edge near her head. He lowered himself to the floor beside the bed and folded his lanky legs easily as he sat down tailor fashion.

Lucas scratched his head with one hand and pushed her coffee cup toward her, with the other.

"Huh?" Mel's head pounded like tom-toms, preparing for a war party.

"Maybe you could use some aspirin and juice?" He reached into his shirt pocket and withdrew some pills. She opened one fist, took them, and guzzled them with one big swallow. The other hand grasped the cover with all her might.

"Thanks," she said, plopping her head carefully back on the pillow, while holding her forehead, "I needed that."

"Last night? Or the aspirin?"

Blushing a bit, she responded, "Both . . . I think."

He bit into the roll and smiled at her. "I don't usually get such glowing reviews the morning after. Try to contain yourself."

She returned the smile. "I guess I'm a bit embarrassed."

"Mel," he said, sliding the tray onto the floor. He wore white jockey shorts and a wrinkled black-striped cowboy shirt with the top three snap-buttons open. Lucas slid under the top sheet, gently placing his left arm under her neck and lifting her toward him. His right elbow lightly brushed her breast as he rolled her body to one side. They lay facing each other with his arms around her.

Lucas traced his fingers across her temple and forehead, gently applying a light pressure. He kissed each spot as he passed. She could only reply, "That feels so good."

"You're welcome, Ma'am."

Her eyes were shut tight for fear of facing him. His touch was so soft and tender that she involuntarily quivered with chills. He pulled the sheet higher around her shoulders.

Her mind raced, trying to think of what to say next, and how to say it. She should not be panicking, but feared she was.

"Down boy," he whispered, adjusting himself.

She smiled, realizing that the pressure she felt around her pubic area was not a wadded swatch of sheet after all. She nestled and brushed her lips against his chest somewhere below the breastbone. He kissed her forehead.

"Breakfast is getting cold," he said.

"I think that's my line."

"Okay, you say it."

"Breakfast is getting cold."

He released her neck from his upper arm and gently laid her back on the bed. She leaned over for one more, short kiss to his belly, pushed away toward the opposite side of the bed and gathered her discarded blouse that had been lying in a heap on the floor.

She found a guest toothbrush, still wrapped in plastic, and a huge tube of toothpaste. Mel used them. She brushed her hair and picked at it with her hands, then washed last night's smeared mascara and stale makeup from her freshly glowing face. She smiled, buttoned her blouse and returned to the bedroom.

He returned with the bed tray. "The coffee got cold so I zapped it."

"Thank you." She selected a cup from the tray. "Are you always so generous? And so thoughtful?"

"Only to beautiful ladies who need hugs," he said lifting his mug to her.

They ate the cinnamon rolls, shyly glancing at each other and at the bay beyond the now-open, patio doors.

"I'm sorry the breakfast wasn't more generous. I wasn't expecting a sleep over."

"A sleep over? Is that what that was?" She grinned.

"Yep . . . that's what it was . . . all right." He put his mug and wadded napkin on the tray. She wiped her mouth and stacked her cup in his.

"A nice shower may help," he said. "There are fresh towels in the vanity below the sink."

He left the bedroom.

The caffeine jolted her courage. "Join me?" she called out.

"You sure know how to appeal to my finer senses, lady," he replied without a moment's hesitation.

Lucas pulled the balance of the snaps open and dropped the shirt to the floor. The jockey shorts bulged. He joined Mel in the shower, but not until after he pulled out several new packets of condoms from a vanity drawer and placed one on the sink counter.

\* \*
\*

They explored their bodies in hunger for each other . . . washed each other's hair and scrubbed their backs with louffa and liquid soap. His maleness rose again, until they lay on the furry bathroom rug . . . spent . . . exhausted . . . drained.

"WOW!" she exclaimed.

"Okay. That's the review I was hoping for." Lucas grinned and reached back to help her stand.

"Smarty britches." She rubbed her lower back.

"Don't get me wrong. For all my sensitivities I am a typical male with a normal, healthy ego system."

"Oh, I didn't doubt that. It's just that . . . oh . . . never mind."

"What?"

"Nothing. God, what time is it?"

They both stood naked in the bathroom. He looked over the front of his body, patting where his pockets would be and glancing at his bare wrist. "Can't help you there."

"Geez. I have several appointments this morning . . . big ones."

"Well, I'll get dressed and take you home," he said, disappearing around the door frame and out of view.

He called back to her. "It's nine o'clock. Need to make some calls?"

"No. I'm okay so long as we can leave soon."

They dressed in haste. Her clothes were wrinkled from their night on the floor.

"If you have things to do, can you call me a cab?" she suggested, brushing her damp hair.

"I dance with the one I brought, lady." He shook the car keys near her face. "I'm ready."

* *
*

Thank goodness this was Rosa's day off.

This saved Mel any unusual delay or explanations. She kissed Lucas goodbye and went upstairs, She changed clothes, grabbed her briefcase and was on the road in twenty minutes.

226

She paused at the one-hour photo shop long enough to pick up the blow-ups and sign her invoice.

After getting back on the highway, she called to check on Barry's schedule.

"Orange County Coroner's Office. How may I direct your call?"

"Hi Sally. It's me, Mel. Is Barry busy?"

"He's gone, Mel. Left you a message." She heard rustling of paper. "Here. It says 'meet me at Bernie's. Ten-thirty'."

"Thanks Sally."

"Come see us some time. Lunch with me, maybe."

"Sure thing . . . I'll call you . . . Bye."

At exactly ten-thirty, she pulled off Pacific Coast Highway onto the sand and gravel pot-holed area that Bernie laughingly called his customer parking lot.

The stifling heat held the air still and moist. Mel crossed the distance to the back door as quickly as possible, without breaking into a sweat. The screen door creaked and the ornate glass door knob wobbled in her grasp.

The dense air-conditioning noise prevented her from hearing her name, at first.

She scanned the small cafe and saw several cops at one table who acknowledged her with a nod. Barry called to her again and waved from a booth near the front door. Mel waved back and approached Barry, who stood to greet her.

Cookie passed her, gripping a coffee pot in one hand and a fruit plate in the other. "Hi Mel. Hungry?"

"Yeah. But I don't have a lot of time. How about one of those fruit plates and a diet something."

"On its way, hon," Cookie called over her shoulder as she poured coffee at a nearby table.

"You look positively glowing this morning, Mel."
Barry said hugging her and exchanging the traditional kiss
on the cheeks.

She blushed. "This must be a change for you, seeing a
live body, huh?"

Barry nodded gravely. "Most folks are a little gray by
the time I see them. Got a new fellow?"

"Aw, Barry," she said, scooting into the booth beside
him, "you're my only fellow."

"Is that a 'No?'"

"That's a 'None of Your Business,' love."

Cookie brought Mel's drink and salad. This broke the
mood and helped change the subject.

"Thanks, Cookie."

"Enjoy. More coffee, Barry?"

"Yeah. Looks like I'm here to work," he said,
fingering the photo envelope Mel placed in front of him.

"Serious time now . . . okay?"

"Okay. Can I look?"

"Sure. It's no surprise." She continued as he opened
the envelope, "It's the photos from Dad's crime scene."

His fingers paused in mid-air. "Are you supposed to
have these? Will I have to testify? Jesus . . . what have you
gotten into, Mel?"

"Yes, to the first. Maybe, to the second. X gave them
to me. To the last . . . Freedom of Information Act.
Remember it?"

Barry pulled the photos out and sorted them, facing
him, side-by-side across the table. "Okay, shoot."

"Check out the blow-ups of the footprints first. If I can
find the shoes on these . . . " She pointed with her spoon to

228

one mark and continued chewing her pineapple slice. She swallowed. "Could you ID the shoes to the person?"

"Probably . . . yes. I suppose I can, using that person's specific walking and wearing-down pattern. Maybe I could."

She pushed to the next picture with her spoon. "The bare feet would even be easier with corns and callouses, huh?"

"Yeah . . . huh . . . maybe." He shook his head and put one arm around the booth's back, holding the picture with the other. "Assuming you even think you *can* find one person in millions. And then . . . "

She interrupted him. "And then, I'm assuming these foot prints were left by the people who killed him and not by people who partied there days or even weeks before he died."

"Or prints left by the CSIs, Mel. I always thought . . . eh . . . assumed that the Crime Scene Investigators left these when photographing and IDing and doing their forensic work."

"Ever see a barefoot CSI?"

He picked through the pictures with his fingers. "Nope."

"Me neither." She took another bite. "Ever see a big toe this deformed?"

Barry put his eyeglasses on the table and brought the picture closer to his face. "Nope." He sipped his coffee and shuffled through all the pictures several more times.

Mel finished eating before she tested the waters again.

"Can you do some casts from these photos, since I believe none were done at the scene?"

He raised one eyebrow. "How can you assume that mounds weren't done? Do you have all of the file?"

It was her turn to be surprised. She glared at him saying, "I damn well better have all the file and there's not one damn word about a cast."

He laid his hand on hers and patted. "Maybe you don't know where to look on the reports, Mel. There are plasters . . . of the shoes . . . the tennis shoes . . . these."

"But, not the bare feet?"

"No. Those were thought to be feet of a surfer or a camper. And the casts are done as a matter of routine. Not for any real thoughts of homicide, you know."

"You still have 'em?"

"Somewhere. When a file is closed, they're put in boxes and stored away."

"Find 'em for me, will you?"

"When do you need 'em?"

"Just don't break the chain of evidence. You keep 'em where you can get to them. In the meantime, I'd like to see the casts, up close. So call me . . . whenever . . . okay?"

"Sure . . . now as to the bare feet. I can't do accurate casts from the photos. But I sure as hell can compare and swear to pictures *if* you ever find anyone who'll let you take pictures of their feet and that funny big toe."

He stared out the front window. Several of the cops called out a "goodbye" on their way out.

"Of course, Mel, this will only place someone, at some point in time in an area near where your dad died. It won't place the gun in their hands. And as you said . . . these marks could have been made days, even weeks before that. How are you going to prove anything?"

"Shit . . . I haven't even found the guy or guys, have I? I'll have to cross that bridge when I get there, Barry."

"You're assuming again, Mel, that this *was* a homicide."

"Thanks for your support, Barry."

He put his arm around her shoulder and drew her close to his side in a brief hug. "Aw, Mel. I loved T-Bone and I'm as mad as anybody that he's gone." He leaned over to whisper in her ear. "Don't you think we should leave the solving of crimes to the police department?"

"What's this WE shit?" She pushed him away.

Cookie came with the check which Barry grabbed. He glanced at it and laid a ten-dollar bill under the salt shaker, before Mel could reach her billfold.

"You in a hurry?" he asked, shuffling the photos back into one stack and putting them back inside the manilla envelope.

"Yeah . . . I'm meeting two nice old ladies and taking them on a tour of the police department today."

"What brought that on?"

"No reason . . . just trying to do my civic duty." She slid across the bench and stood. Barry did the same. Cookie returned with change. Barry dropped a couple of dollars on the table and sat the catsup bottle on them. They both said their goodbyes to Cookie and to Bernie, and Barry walked Mel to her car.

"Where'd you get this piece of shit?"

"This is a Jelly loaner. Darling isn't it?"

"You taking two ladies for a ride in this?"

"No, actually they had the same impression of this contraption and agreed to meet me there. Gotta go." She kissed him on the cheek. "Thanks for lunch and the information."

"I'll call you when I get those casts, Mel."

"Yeah . . . thanks."

With a clear warning, he added, "Be careful."

"What could go wrong . . . taking a tour of the police department?"

"You know what I mean. With whatever you're really doing, please be careful."

## ∞*29*

*I wonder what my chances are that the cop, I hope the ladies will identify, will be in the office today. God . . . He could be in the field or even off duty. What a long shot. Oh, well . . . hell.*

Mel drove into the visitors parking lot at the police department at exactly noon. When she entered the reception area the two ladies stood and waved vigorously at her. Mel put her best "visitor" face on.

Eleanor wore a gaudy, red-and-blue, cotton-print dress, two-inch, red high heels and earrings from which dangled two humongous red orbs. The balls clanged against each other as Eleanor approached Mel.

Not to be outdone, Miss Helen continued her polyester motif with bold, black-and-white, horizontal stripes which only broadened her beam by yards. Her blue hair boasted a large polka dotted black-and-white bow, her earrings were similar, black-and-white balls. On her feet . . . dingy, scuffed and torn white flats.

Mel gasped and choked. Their clashing scents overwhelmed her. One floral, like gardenias, and the other sour . . . like lavender and vinegar.

"My, aren't you ladies prompt. Good to see you Miss Eleanor, Miss Helen." She shook their eager sweaty palms. Miss Helen had a nervous twitch Mel had not noticed before.

*Maybe going to the police department does that to some people.*

"Hello Officer Walker." They both replied.

*Oops. Can't have the officer thing come out in public.* "Call me Mel . . . I feel like we're going to be such good friends," she said with emphasis on SUCH.

They gushed with excitement.

Could she pray for a better response?

The volunteer information officer sat beyond the counter.

*I hope he didn't overhear that "officer" thing.*

Larry did not acknowledge her approach. His civil-service-employee uniform bulged tightly across his middle-aged belly. With his neatly trimmed, gray hair and coke-bottle-thick eye glasses, Mel hoped the ladies might view Larry as husband material.

"Hi, Larry."

He glanced away from his book. "Hi, Mel. How can I help you?"

"I have two special friends who'd like a tour of the department today. This is Miss Eleanor and Miss Helen."

*With emphasis on the MISS.*

"Do you think Chief Murdoch would mind if I walked them through? It won't take too long ... and I'll do it myself."

She peered past Larry to the rest of the squad room where several officers were working at their desks.

He extended his best "public relations" smile to the ladies. They giggled. He did not turn a hair. "I don't think that'd be a problem." Larry buzzed them through the lock-out door.

The ladies tittered to themselves and grasped their handbags in death grips as they entered the large squad room.

Several officers worked around one particular area.

"Now, this department is known as 'Booking.' "

*The long shot is launched.*

Mel took them on a tour of the major, public-access places including fingerprinting, the jail and the communications room, which were all relatively quiet for a lunch hour. The ladies asked millions of questions and Mel did her best to answer the ones she knew, and faked the ones she did not.

"Chief Murdoch," Mel said, finding the chief. "I want you to meet these two Harbour residents."

"Hello, pretty ladies," he said, shaking their hands and nodding politely to them.

"I hope you don't mind, we're just completing a little tour of the department. They've never been here and were interested in seeing justice in action."

"Why, that's fine, Mel. I'm glad to see you doing some volunteer work like this. Put some of those old bad memories behind ... kinda' get on with your life ... so to speak."

The ladies' eyes widened.

"Why, Mel? What did he mean by that?" Miss Helen asked, as Mel whisked both of the ladies by their elbows over to the rogues gallery of all the officers, past and present.

"I'm, huh, recently divorced."

*Now that was quick, wasn't it? When you're good, you're good.*

"Oh my dear." Miss Eleanor patted Mel's arm reassuringly. "Although we're widows . . . we know how you feel. Those cads."

*Speaking of CADS, I am getting concerned. They've been here twenty minutes or so, and . . . nothing . . . maybe the lunch hour isn't the best idea after all.*

"So . . . this is our photo area of all our officers. Some of them have retired and others have died. See anybody you recognize here?"

Eleanor was the first to answer. "Why yes. This officer. Here . . . he's the one whose picture you showed us." She squinted and leaned toward the plaque beneath the bust pose. "Detective William Walker . . . yes . . . that's the man whose picture we saw."

Eleanor turned. Miss Helen nodded her agreement.

A black-booted patrolman entered the squad room from a nearby hall. He held a small, black notebook and several loose papers. Both women turned and smiled.

*Yes. This would be the stud, they really wanted to meet.*

"Oh, Bobby. Gotta minute?" Mel asked.

"Sure." He dropped the paperwork on a nearby desk and approached the ladies. The leather rubbed against itself as he walked. The noise caused by friction between holster and other equipment created an air of sensuality which could not be mistaken. Miss Eleanor's shoulders shook. Miss Helen stuttered a "Hello" when Mel introduced Bobby Escobar to them.

"Ladies, this is one of Harbour Pointe's finest officers. He does sort of double duty here. He's a motorcycle patrolman." She leaned over to whisper, ". . . *and* he's a member of our SWAT team."

Bobby looped his thumbs inside his belt and stood, legs wide apart, nodding to the women and acknowledging the introduction.

*God, they love this shit. Both of them.*

"So, let me see what else can I show you." Mel asked out loud, hoping for inspiration. She glanced around the room.

Bobby realized his job was done, nodded again and turned to leave. Mel watched those wonderful, tight buns surrounded by black leather as he and his sexy musk swaggered out of the squad room. She was not sure what the other two were staring at, but it was probably the same thing.

At that moment, the door to the evidence room opened and several officers, including X-Ray, the property clerk Agee, and the undercovers Daryl, Mikey and Whitey entered the room. A couple of them held manila file-folders. One chewed on a ballpoint pen and talked in hushed tones to one of the other patrolmen.

Miss Helen spoke first. "Well . . . hi  there. There's that nice man who came by for a brochure."

She walked around one desk to intercept the group of policemen.

Mel let her pass and watched in silence.

Miss Helen walked across the room to one of the policeman and asked him, "Hi . . . remember us? From the travel agency? I hope you had a nice trip."

"Lady . . . ," he replied, "I don't have a clue what you're talking about. I never saw you before."

He glanced beyond the travel agent and straight into Mel's eyes.

"Oh, Sir . . . I never forget a face. I'm sure it was you." She turned, seeking acknowledgement of her identification from her companion. Miss Eleanor nodded in agreement.

Mel had seen enough and interceded. "Okay, well . . . ladies, that about concludes our tour today. This has been fun, hasn't it?"

She looped her arms around both travel agents and walked them toward the front door. The officer groused something under his stale breath.

Mel did not want to know what he said.

All the way to their car the women tried to convince Mel that their memories were accurate and that the officer, despite his vehement denial was indeed, the officer who had come to their agency and taken a brochure or two, several months prior.

Mel nodded, smiled and continued to thank them, until she got them tucked safely inside their car and waved them on their way, promising to do this wonderful thing again, real soon.

Mel drove out of the parking lot, wondering if her life would ever be the same again. *Is my life safe? Are the ladies safe? It's drugs all right . . . it's also corruption . . . it just isn't Dad.*

Johnnie shuffled papers on the reception desk saying, "Just a minute," into the telephone, "I can't find a pen."

"Found one . . . shoot." He uncapped the cover with his teeth and said, "Okay . . . let me have that number again. Uh huh, got it. Well, Mel should be here any minute. I'll see she gets it. Yeah . . . right . . . okay . . . bye."

He went to the kitchen and poured a fresh mug of coffee, and grabbed some stale donuts that he stuck in the microwave. He heard the front door open and called out, "Is that you Mel?"

"Yep. Don't pay the ransom . . . it's me."

"Me, who got laid?" he said loudly. "Finally . . . "

She reached the threshold and leaned in. "What did you say?"

"Me, who got laid," he repeated.

"Oh . . . you too?" she said, sticking her tongue out at him.

"Smart ass . . . not me . . . you. He's called for you three times today, and it's not noon yet."

"Mm."

"So. Let me get you some coffee and tell me all about it."

"Forget it. I don't kiss and tell. Not like you, you sweet little queen."

"It's not the kissing I want to know about." He swatted her on the rear as she passed on the way to the kitchen counter.

"That's gross."

"It's also none of my business. Huh?"

"Correctamundo."

"Shoot." He snapped his fingers. "It was worth the try."

"What's in the micro?"

"Warm donuts. Want some?"

"Those donuts may be warm but they're at least a week old."

"But they go down better when they're warm and soft."

She poured her coffee, added cream and a packet of fake sugar and stirred. Johnnie placed several donuts on two paper plates and tore some paper towels off the roll. He sat them on the breakfast room table, then straddled the back of one chair. She paced back and forth and stared out the kitchen, bay-window.

Returning to the present, she asked, "Well, better get me current. Are we still in business?"

"Oh . . . yeah . . . sure. We got three new ones, mostly task assignments and I took 'em. One's a skip tracing on an attempted murder. We gotta find some witnesses who got themselves lost. And two others are routine stuff. Nothing I need help with right away."

"How's the apartment coming along? Got it painted yet?" She nodded at Johnnie's garage unit.

"I should be finished by this weekend. I found a new dream boat who's very butch with a paint brush. I ordered some blinds, new carpet, and a bottle of champagne. So I'll probably get moved in by the middle of next week . . . if no more new assignments come in."

She kicked at him playfully under the table. "Get serious now. How's the number game with the safe coming along?"

"Well, there's no good news. I've tried more combinations to open that safe than Carter has liver pills . . . *Nada* . . . nothing."

He motioned to his office. "I have a list of what doesn't work. It's somewhere on my desk. Gawd, is my work behind. Speaking of behind, how's your search for the Holy Grail? I mean that most lovingly. I mean, I can do all this work and I'm not complaining because the apartment is costing me a lot more than I thought it would. Besides, I could use the bucks. But I miss you lady."

"In other words you'd like for me to put all this nonsense away and get back to work huh?"

"You said it, Mel. I didn't." He leaned forward and patted her leg. "How's it going?"

She sipped her coffee and finished chewing a bite. Then, as if discussing hair-color with a best girlfriend, she said matter of factly, "Well. I know WHO did it. I just don't know why, yet."

"NO SHIT!" Johnnie vaulted to his feet and paced back and forth the length of the small area.

"Now, Mel. Maybe I'd better put all this investigation business on hold. Maybe hire a part-timer and help you. This is serious shit. I mean you can't simply accuse someone. You could get hurt. Geez, I'm not ready to lose you, too. I've lost enough loved ones and friends to AIDS and other shit. I'm not ready to let you get in trouble."

Still in a monotone voice and without looking directly at Johnnie, Mel added: "It's a cop."

"OH FUCK! Tell me it isn't X-Ray?" He pulled on his long ponytail and twisted it through his fingers.

"It isn't X-Ray," she responded flatly. "I don't think."

"Who is it?"

240

"If I told you, I'd put you in danger, too."

"You mean he . . . or they . . . know that you know?"

"Yep." She ran her tongue around her dry lips, stood and poured herself a drink of water.

"OH, FUCK!"

"Of course, I realize that since we both are good friends and work together, that this person might conclude that I would tell you. That alone could put you in jeopardy, regardless." She slammed the paper cup into the sink in one small wad.

"OH FUCK!"

"Get a grip! Well, there are one or two things that I hadn't worked out and this is an . . . unexpected one."

"So are you going to tell me?"

"Nope."

"It ain't that simple Mel. I'll have to start packing AND watching my back. I thought we agreed that we wouldn't take risks in our cases . . . in our work. But, this personal shit . . . well. I don't know. I'm getting too old for this."

"Don't whimper. Stop off at the gun range today and shoot a few hundred rounds. That'll help you feel better. You're a much better shot than me, anyway."

"Better shot's got nothing to do with it. I don't want to carry."

"Then don't." She left the room.

He followed. "It ain't that easy. Listen, why don't I get Chip to come in for a few days? He can handle these new ones easily enough. That'll give us a chance to double team and get this resolved."

"No Johnnie." She turned and gave him a big hug. "This is my deal. It's something I have to do alone. Thank you, though."

She sat on the edge of her desk-chair and pulled her Lady Beretta from the bottom drawer and checked the clip. She withdrew extra clips from a small gun-tote in the back of the drawer and put them in her bag.

Scotch-tape on one of the white butcher papers had lost its glue and one end hung loose. The one she had entitled *CADS.*

*Are you sending me a message, Dad?*

"Johnnie, listen. What you can do for me is keep working on the safe. Maybe something inside it would clear this up."

He sat in one of her overstuffed chairs against one wall. "In other words you don't have a fucking clue or have any plan on how to get this bastard yet."

"Right."

"Want some help on a plan?"

"I need a good answer."

"What's the question?"

"Can I trust ... X-Ray ... or is this a big internal conspiracy?"

"Oh, damn fine question, Sherlock."

\* \*
\*

Mel called X-Ray and chatted lightly for a few moments, concluding with, "Why don't you drop by at the end of the day, so we can visit?"

Mel shuffled through files on her desk and found a scratch pad and pen. She accidently touched the purse causing it to fall off the desk-edge, and its contents spilled across the floor.

On hands and knees, she picked up lipstick, used tissue and keys when she saw paper sticking out of the wallet. Mel sat on the carpet and pulled the paper out.

*The newspaper clipping: Two Officers Found Dead*
...

"I forgot all about David Frasier. How could I have forgotten him?" she asked. Mel got to her feet and re-taped the butcherpaper, adding the news article high above the center. Below, she drew a long vertical line, wrote *Dad* on one side and *David Frasier* on the other. "What do they have in common and where are the inconsistencies," she asked herself.

*Both detectives, long tenure, past drinkers, both single, grown children. And what I don't know . . . Harbour Pointe resident?* She put a question mark on Frasier's side. *Assets? Friends? Enemies?. Illnesses . . . heavy debt . . . depression . . . gambler? All questions for David's life.*

Her computer interrupted her thoughts.

"Big answers, I hope."

Earlier, Mel had entered the names of all police officers Miss Eleanor and Miss Helen approached, along with data she needed to verify about these individuals. The information network she belonged to usually had a slow response time, but not today.

She turned on the printer, dragged the mouse over the area marked *PRINT* and clicked on it. The laser monster spewed forth pages of material. Mel scanned it like ticker-tape on Dow Jones as the pages appeared.

"Bingo."

In the search column, Mel entered *David Frasier* and cross-referenced the name with real property, assets, civil and criminal activity, and banking information from both Orange, Los Angeles and Riverside counties.

Her face softened as she read each page. By the time the machine signaled completed delivery of some material, she faced over two dozen sheets of paper. She smiled like the proverbial Cheshire Cat.

"Mm. He makes thirty-six thousand a year at Harbour PD and has over two-hundred and fifty-thousand in clear, paid off assets. What a great little investor he is. I must know his secrets."

"Getting there," she said. "Easy, does it."

Mel made holes in the papers and put them under a brass fastener in her father's file. She tabbed the file, so they could be easily retrieved when she needed them later.

The computer beeped again and paper flowed through the printer. David Frasier's life in review.

"Gotcha! You bastard."

* *
*

"Hi. Anybody in the office?"

Mel quickly shut the folder and put it in a nearby filing cabinet, misfiling it on purpose, behind a tab marked Southern California Gas Company.

"I'm in here X . . . fix yourself a drink and join me." She checked the desk, making sure no loose notes or other incriminating material had been left behind. She stacked a few things in one corner of the desk and placed her telephone on top of them, when X-Ray entered.

"Hi. How're you doing?"

They hugged.

"You want a drink?"

"Not now. Maybe later." He plopped himself into a chair. "What's up?"

"What makes you think something's going on? You're always so suspicious."

"It's the cop in me. I'm always suspicious."

She shrugged, "I'm really trying, you know, to put this thing about Dad behind me."

He had been leaning back in the overstuffed chair with his legs crossed, but when she made that remark, his body jolted forward in the chair.

*I hate this deception shit.*

"That's good. That's very good, Mel. I'm glad you see the light, so-to-speak. You know . . . " he clasped his hands together over his knees, "we did everything we could. But the death was what it was . . . you know . . . eh . . . "

"Suicide, I can say it now."

"Good, oh, say . . . that calls for a celebration. Maybe dinner. So we can talk, like old times. I'd like to know what you're going to do with the rest of your life."

She drew back.

*Now for the "but" part of this fishing expedition.*

"But, as they say . . . I do need some closure. I can't understand how Dad could get involved in something so insidious and deadly as cocaine, you know."

"It's not that hard to understand, except knowing the person. That's the tough part for me. You know you can get cocaine anywhere . . . anytime. It's easy to get hooked, if you're weak."

"But Dad wasn't weak . . . was he? Or is that a part of him I didn't know about?"

"You know, that bothered me too. There are different kinds of junkies; poor and uneducated people we know more about, because they get caught so often. On TV cop-shows, we see those with their shirts off, tattooed and living in filth in some rat-hole. They use drugs to forget they've got nothing going for them . . . no reason to live or even be born. They have no past, no present and no future.

"But, the brighter ones . . . well . . . most intelligent and educated coke-heads are basically weak people with major character defects. And those defects eventually turn into their guts . . . and it kills 'em. I never saw, or even suspected, that kind of flaw in T-Bone."

"Me either." Mel turned away. "So tell me, they always say, 'we gave at the office.' How would he get drugs? At the office?"

X-Ray replied, "He didn't do drug detail, as a matter of routine, and wouldn't really have any reason to be around it. You know we have drugs there . . . and money too. So, there's access *and* opportunity."

"Okay, so let's play this scenario just for the hell of it. First, let's do a little Q and A here. How many kilos would a police department usually keep at any given time?" Mel asked.

"Well . . . in addition to what the undercovers have set aside for a buy . . . along with some flash money . . . we might have ten, twelve kilos."

"So, how do you get rid of the difference of over twelve kilos. Like, if you get a big haul of say, twenty kilos?"

"We have to keep it . . . along with the test results from the lab as to its purity and content . . . until the trial is over and time for appeal has past. We then purge the overflow."

"How's that done?"

"First, we take it to an incinerator near the Long Beach Terminal Island and it's burned there." He leaned back putting his arm across the back of the chair.

"What a high! Does everybody just sit around and inhale?"

Laughing to break the tension he responded, "No. Usually one of our guys hauls it to Long Beach and gives it to the folks at the burner. It's signed for and our guy returns to the station."

"After the burner what happens?" Mel asked.

"Well, at that stage it's now considered toxic waste and has to be disposed of. Years ago, all police departments dumped that type of waste, and all the weapons, on a barge and off-loaded it in a dump site in the Pacific. But now, with all the environmental issues and CAL-OSHA we have very strict rules to follow. The residue is usually taken to Riverside County and dumped into a regulation landfill."

"Are you guys satisfied with the checks and balances on that disposal?"

"Satisfied? I don't know what you mean. That really isn't my territory. You know I'm not in charge . . . so I don't know how the signing off and stuff goes."

"It's not the signing off I'm thinking about."

"Whatcha mean?"

"I was wondering if the stuff could disappear," she leaned forward, conspiratorially and lowered her voice. "Just before the dope is destroyed, what's to prevent someone from cutting it . . . or even exchanging it . . . switching it entirely . . . for something like baby powder or baking soda? Anything like that?"

"WOW. What a concept. Like someone at the department might be skimming it off . . . or using it."

"Or selling it?"

"No, shit."

"Exactly. That's one way Dad could have gotten free dope and sold it . . . and got all the money you say he had. Dad couldn't have bought the dope unless he started out really small and graduated to the big time. But for FREE! See what I mean?"

"That's a damn good thought, Mel."

He stood and paced. Then stared at the floor and the ceiling.

She did not disturb his thoughts.

*Now, start trolling.*

"Interesting scenario, Mel. Wonder . . . if drug boosting's going on now that T-Bone's gone? That is . . . if it ever was?" Mel knew how cops' minds worked. If she kept quiet, his thoughts would carry him automatically into uncharted waters.

She sat in the swivel chair, her feet on the desk.

"Can I use the phone in the reception area?"

"Knock yourself out," she said, smiling in her heart.

Mel heard him dialing, but could not make out the conversation.

*The bait's on the hook . . . bobbing on the water. Now for the hard part . . . the waiting.*

In a few minutes he returned.

"You know your theory's very interesting."

She clasped her hands behind her head. "I thought so too, X-Ray. But it's only a theory you know. What with Dad gone . . . I was wondering . . . if that's one way he might have gotten involved in this mess. You know, I need to resolve the drug issue in my mind. I want some peace."

"Mel, you got me to thinking and I checked with Chief Murdoch. We have a delivery to the incinerator scheduled for Monday. I think it'd be a damn fine opportunity to test

248

your . . . so-called theory. You might have something there, you know. We've never NOT trusted our cops before. But, there could be something there."

"Oh, I doubt it. I mean you guys don't have problems the LAPD and other large metro areas have with personnel. I'm sure everything is kosher."

Mindlessly, Mel pushed papers and files from one stack to another.

"No . . . no . . . Mel. I think you have a hell of an idea and the Chief agrees. We'll meet tomorrow . . . finalize a plan."

*Bobbing a little . . . don't pluck it in . . . yet, easy now . . . don't press.* "You know the more I think about this drug conspiracy, X-Ray, the more I think it would be a total waste of man power and really . . . I'm sorry I even mentioned it."

"Quit saying that, Mel. You're really bright and it sure as shit ain't gonna hurt us to check this out . . . we'll use very little manpower, because the fewer folks who know about it, the cleaner the test will be. So . . . "

"Mum's the word, I got it." Mel motioned by zipping her mouth shut.

"Can I take a rain-check on dinner? I've got work to do."

"Sure with one caveat."

"What's that?"

"That you tell me how it turns out. Closure, you know. I'd like to know how Dad got the drugs . . . and this would seal it for me."

"Sure, Mel. I understand."

She stood. They embraced.

"You're so special to do this for me."

"While it's for you, it isn't entirely for you, Mel. If we've got some bad cops . . . well . . . it's probably well past-time to clean 'em out. Boy, that bothers me." X-Ray scratched his head.

"What . . . maybe having some bad cops?"

"Yeah."

"I took a big risk even discussing my theory with you, you know."

"Why'd you say that?"

They walked to the front door. holding hands.

"What if you were one of 'em?"

"Then you've put yourself in great jeopardy, haven't you?" He took one step away from her, dropped her hand and left without another word.

# ∞31

Lucas left on an emergency trip to Texas, creating a void in an otherwise long, lonely weekend . . . something about an oil well explosion and people hurt. Mel desperately wanted to call X-Ray and demand to be there when it all crashed. She wanted the satisfaction of seeing the bastard get caught . . . and had to know he was still dirty.

Bored and agitated, Mel spent some time in the sun, swam and slept. She also packed the rest of her bedroom office, so those boxes could be taken to the new business.

Jelly called. "Hey lady, how you doing? I'm still waiting on a few parts, but they should be here any day, and then we'll get this puppy painted . . . and it'll be ready to roll, no pun intended."

"Thanks. That's good news. I'm weary of the night-mobile," she told him.

* *
*

Sunday, the world tossed and tumbled. The earth shook several times during the day and well into the night. Mel needed no alarm the next morning. Her eyes popped open at five-thirty. Sensing that exercise might cure her overnight aches and pains, she put on sweats and tennis shoes and tucked her hair back with a barrette. Mel skipped down the wooden steps behind her home to the sand below.

She ran for thirty minutes in one direction and then turned; after she chased a stray dog one way, he chased her back the other, snapping at her heels. Mel lifted her knees higher and returned well ahead of her time schedule. She showered and washed and dried her hair. The natural curl created a perfect style for her face, giving her a soft and innocent appearance. *This will be the biggest and most important day of my life.*

She chose her wardrobe carefully, hoping that after the sting operation, she'd be making an appearance at the police department in mid-afternoon. Mel prayed the perpetrator had consistent stealing habits, and today would be no exception to his pattern.

Mel checked her appearance in the full-length closet mirror before leaving the house. She wore a white blouse with a green-and-blue scarf, navy slacks, pleated in front, and matching flats. She grabbed a blue blazer on her way out the back door.

Johnnie sat on the dining room floor with paper, pencil, and breakfast, working on the safe combination, when Mel arrived at the office.

"My, aren't we early?"

"Morning, Johnnie. This could be a happening day and I felt I should get an early start."

"Did you come up with a plan?"

"Yep."

"Can you share it with me?"

"You will probably find out soon enough ... hopefully today. Can you wait?"

"Okay ... suits me." He returned to the combination dial.

"How you doing with the safe?"

"Not even budging. Do you know any safe-crackers?"

"Hadn't thought of that." She snapped her fingers. "Of course, I hadn't thought the combination would be that hard to figure out."

"Me either ... I must have twenty hours in this project alone."

"Oh, Johnnie. I'm sorry." She bent sideways to her knees placing her hands on them. "I didn't mean to dump all of this on you."

"I didn't mean the hours in that way. I don't mind. Really ... I'm just as anxious to find out what's in there as you are."

"Want some more coffee?" She stood and dusted off her pants.

"Yeah, thanks," he replied and handed her his mug.

When Mel got to the kitchen, Johnnie asked, "Didn't you find it rather . . . uh . . . strange, that T-Bone never told you about installing the safe?"

"Yeah, I did as a matter of fact." She returned with their coffee. "There must have been a reason. One I immediately think of . . . is that he didn't kill himself. Otherwise, he would've left me the combination. With a suicide note, wouldn't he?"

"Didn't think of that."

"I have . . . several times."

"Is that another reason why you're so sure he was murdered?"

"Yeah, it's just one more . . . in a chain of events, I find aren't coincidental."

"I'm anxious to hear the entire story."

"Me, too. When I get it all sorted out."

"In the meantime, I thought of a few more numbers that I want to try on the safe today. Then I'll get settled down and get to work."

"Any appointments today?"

"Yeah, two . . . but they're both in Orange County. So I could get back here late afternoon in case, you know, something breaks that you think I would be dying to know about."

"Your hint is well taken. If my idea does hit, I'll leave you a note. I'll probably be at the police department. But I'll leave you a note for sure."

The phone interrupted their conversation.

"Walker Investigations. May I help you?"

"Hi, Mel."

"Hi, Lucas. Put out all your fires?"

"No. Actually I'm calling from Texas . . . Galveston. We came in for lunch and I need to get back to the derrick and the fire, but I wanted to see if I could catch you, first."

"You did."

"You sound kinda funny. Is everything okay?"

"Yeah, sure . . . well, I do sorta have a thing working here and hopefully it should come together later today. So I guess I'm a bit preoccupied. I do miss you, though."

"That's good to hear. I miss you, too."

Johnnie tapped the floor with his pencil and made kissing sounds with his lips. She threw a hand-full of paperclips at him. They clattered to the floor making a slight noise.

"Is someone else there? If you're busy I could call back a little later."

"Actually, Johnnie just came in and we have some things to talk about. I do have a business to run too, you know. Oh, I didn't mean to be short with you."

"That's okay. I'd rather visit when we can talk alone. I had a great . . . uh . . . night and . . . uh . . . morning with you. I'm not sure where this is going . . . I know you have other things on your mind right now, but I'd like you to give some thought to it."

*That's what I need. More things to worry about.*

"Me, too. And I will . . . I promise."

"I should have this inferno under control in a day or so and be home. Maybe I'm being too presumptuous about us. Should I even call you when I get back?"

"No . . . I mean yes. Don't get me wrong . . . really. I have a thousand things on my mind, and you're at least one of them. But I need a few days. Okay? I should have my business concluded in the next day or so."

"Great. I'll be calling you then, hon . . . take care."

"You too. Don't let it melt."

"Never."

"Bye."

"Bye, bye."

Johnnie mimicked, "Bye, bye ya'll."

She turned facing him. "Honestly, Johnnie. You're such a tease."

"It's because I love you lady, and I don't want anything, or anyone, to hurt you. Is this the real thing?"

"Who knows? It's too soon to tell. But it is . . . for now. I have so many other things going. I can't think about a relationship right now."

"Fair enough."

"Anyway, you have Cliff."

"Oh, that . . . that was just to get the painting done."

"What all . . . did he paint?"

"Ouch!" He stood placing his hands defiantly on his hips. "Now who's getting nosy?"

"Touche. But with AIDS and other icky illnesses out there I want you to be safe, too."

"Want to see my latest AIDS test results?"

"Yes, as a matter of fact. I would."

He tossed the paperclips onto the desk, pushed them to the edge with his hands, and dumped them into a box. He pulled out his billfold and withdrew something folded and handed it to Mel.

"New test report, huh? Only two weeks ago . . . negative, okay?"

Mel refolded the test paper and returned it to Johnnie, along with a kiss on the cheek.

"I worry about you, too," she said.

"Thank you. I'm glad somebody does."

"When's your first appointment?"

"I'll be leaving in ten minutes or so and hope the traffic has cleared."

Mel walked into her office and checked the mail that had accumulated for several days. She needed something to keep her busy for a few hours.

She heard water running. "I'll do those dishes later," she called out.

"It's done . . . and I'm out the door. Good luck." He leaned into her office, knocked on the door frame, and shot her an imaginary gun.

"Thank you, Johnnie. Be careful . . . see you later."

"Bye, bye, ya'll," he teased.

"Bye, Silly."

* *
*

Mel passed the day writing checks on long over-due bills. She was grateful for the computer accounting program that printed checks out, which she then placed in neat little, pre-stamped window-envelopes.

*This fishing is hard work.*

The phone rang several times, startling her each time. One was Cliff looking for Johnnie. Then two calls from solicitors and one new assignment.

"I'm ready to put all this behind me and get back to work. I love the investigation and undercover stuff. Phase three is ready. Where are you, X-Ray?" Mel called out.

She typed an acknowledgement letter to one company, telling them Johnnie Blake would be their investigator.

The phone rang.

*It's two o'clock. Make this . . . the call.*

"Walker Investigations. Mel Walker speaking."

"Mel. We got the bastard . . . you'll never guess who it was!"

"Agee," she quietly responded. "Gotcha."

∞*32*

After a long pause, X-Ray said, "I hate it when you do that. How'd you know?"

"Did you pull a full-out sting operation? I want to hear all about it."

"I want to know how you knew it was Agee, first. So get your ass down here . . . NOW. You've got some questions to answer yourself, Missy."

"I love it when you talk butch. I'm on the way."

She hummed *Michael, Row the Boat Ashore,* freshened her lipstick, and combed her hair.

*When I see Agee face-to-face, I want to look my best.*
* *
*

Mel pulled into Harbour Pointe Police parking lot, left her car and entered the building. With the shift changing, several officers acknowledged her and she stopped to visit with one.

"Mel, get your butt in here."

"Chief's calling for me," she said, excusing herself from one officer.

Mel hastened her step, and followed Chief Murdoch without comment. In the Chief's office, X-Ray leaned against a filing cabinet and cleaned his fingernails with a pen knife. X-Ray did not acknowledge Mel.

"Can we leave the door open? It's cold in here," she said.

Chief Murdoch shut the door, went around his desk and dropped into his well-worn captain's chair.

"Sit down," he ordered.

"Is somebody mad at me . . . here?" She eased into the chair as directed.

"Tell us how you know . . . about Agee's drug dealing?"

"No . . . I don't think so."

The two men leaned forward in disbelief. They both shouted, "What do you mean you won't tell us?"

"Mel, you don't have a choice here," Murdoch said.

She hesitated, "I didn't mean I wouldn't tell you. I meant the answer to be, that I wouldn't have a problem telling you."

*Boy, when those fish are caught . . . they sure do wiggle.*

X-Ray sat in an adjacent chair holding his notepad and pen, ready for information. Chief Murdoch leaned back with both elbows on the arms of the chair with his fingers spread, tips touching.

"Of course. There is one tiny catch," she said.

"What the hell are you talking about? You've got nothing to trade here, Mel. You wouldn't want us to hold you for questioning would you? Maybe you knew exactly what T-Bone was involved in . . . maybe you inherited the business. You did get the money didn't you?" Chief Murdoch was unrelenting in his questioning.

It would have continued. But X-Ray interceded, holding his palm out to the Chief. "Now Chief, Mel wouldn't obstruct justice. I'm sure she'll tell us everything she knows."

"In due course," she answered.

Murdoch remained quiet. X-Ray spoke. "So what's this tiny catch?"

"I know you have someone questioning him."

"Daryl and Whitey . . . so what?"

"I want to ask him a few questions of my own."

"You what? What for?" X twisted his body in the chair and faced Mel with a puzzled expression on his face. He gripped the chair arm, his knuckles white.

"There is no negotiation here. No way I could allow this." Murdoch spoke.

"Of course, you could be in the other room listening in. We might even find out some things none of us know, right now."

"Has this got something to do with T-Bone's death?" Murdoch asked.

"Yes, I believe it has everything to do with Dad's death," Mel replied.

X-Ray asked, "Got any real problem with that, Chief?"

"This is highly irregular . . . having a non-police person question a suspect. What kind of shit is this?"

Mel pressed further trying to support her position. "But, if you keep Daryl and Whitey in the room, you haven't relinquished your authority. I believe they'll catch on, as the questioning develops. You might be surprised at what we could learn."

"First, before we can agree to that . . . I wanta know what you know about Agee. How'd you guess it was him?"

"I didn't guess, I knew. Listen, if you'll give me a few minutes with him . . . stay on the other side of the mirror, and I believe you won't be disappointed."

"What've we got to lose?"

"Famous last words . . . okay," Murdoch cautioned. "But, if we don't hear what we expect, we'll hold you for further questioning . . . got it?"

"Got it." Mel answered.

They all stood and followed Mel from the small office. X-Ray walked to the interrogation rooms. Mel stood aside, X-Ray knocked once, and Daryl came out.

"Mel's been granted permission to talk with Agee, but you and Whitey stay in the room with her at all times. Keep the recorder going and follow her lead," X-Ray explained.

"I'll be with the Chief on the other side of the mirror."

X-Ray opened the door. Mel entered with Daryl close behind her. With four bodies in the room, it felt like the inside of a toaster oven. The thin, stale air and the heat from the fluorescent light bore down on a small, brown, wooden table. Agee sat in a metal and wooden chair with his back against one wall. His elbows rested on the table. He played with a broken paper clip. A plastic cup, with the dregs of previously hot coffee, sat in the middle of the table. There were two more chairs in the room, but little else.

Mel spoke first.

"I'm not sure how much time I have in here with you Agee, so I'll get right to the point . . . why'd you kill my Dad?"

She heard a chair hit the floor in an adjoining room. Both officers' jaws dropped open, but they turned without giving their surprise away.

"I didn't kill nobody."

"Yes . . . you did . . . and I can prove it."

"Try it."

"You went to a travel agency and got a brochure." Mel said.

"So I killed him with paper, huh?"

"No . . . you planted the travel brochure . . . and the AA information in Dad's home. Just like you planted the cocaine residue on the coffee table. To frame him for your shit."

"How would I get in his home?"

"Getting to Dad's ring of keys would be no problem for someone who worked here. Dad always left them on the desktop at home and he did the same thing here . . . old habits are hard to break, you know. You stole Dad's keys. Made a wax imprint and returned them. You duplicated them from the wax mold. I don't know where, yet. But, it won't take too much police work to find out where. There aren't that many places between your home and the station. And you're not exactly a brain surgeon."

"You don't know what the fuck you're talking about, lady."

"When I picked up his belongings here, I found wax residue on Dad's house keys. Next . . . I want to know how you got him out to the bluff?"

"Get this dumb broad outta here. I don't have to listen to this crap."

"No, but we love bedtime stories. Tell us how he did that?" Whitey chided.

"You suspected Dad was getting close. You set a plan in motion to meet at the bluff. I don't think you did this alone. But he came . . . and you and your friends knocked him out, got his gun, stuck it in his mouth, and pulled the trigger . . . killing him."

"Bullshit . . . GET HER OUTTA HERE I SAID!"

"She stays," Daryl spoke. "Go on Mel . . . then what?"

"I can't find Dad's black book. I believe, and this area's a little gray, that he suspected you of cutting the cocaine and he may have been doing some undercover work himself. Then he got a little too close. Feel free to stop me when you're ready to confess."

"Bullshit. You'll never prove any of that crap. T-Bone was deep in this. Why, he was the ring leader." He leaned the chair back on two legs, balancing against the wall.

Whitey and Daryl both moved but Mel beat them into Agee's face. Mel put her own face so close, she detected his garlic breath. She jabbed her index-finger repeatedly against the bridge of his nose, right between his eyes, "Don't even think of pulling that shit on me, you asshole. Dad was white as snow and you know it."

As Mel turned to go back around the table, her right foot hooked the back leg of Agee's chair and pulled it. Agee's chair fell and his head hit the wall and the floor on the way down. Neither officer moved.

"Mel, you've been seeing too many movies." Daryl said matter-of-factly, while he checked the shine on his own shoes.

"I know."

Agee crawled to the edge of the table, stood, straightened up the chair and sat again, muttering something about police brutality.

"What about police brutality? We're sitting in a chair clear across the room. How about you, Whitey?"

"Me, too. I never moved, never touched him."

Agee rubbed the back of his head.

Mel opened her briefcase and removed a file folder. "Look what I found."

The officers leaned in to peek over her shoulder.

"See, Agee? I have these print-outs. You'd be surprised what kind of tracks we Americans leave. Lots of lovely paper-trails."

"I don't know what you're talking about."

"How about this for starters. You make thirty-six thousand a year here, huh?"

"So what?"

"How come you own a thirty-one foot Eliminator boat, free-and-clear?"

The two officers whistled.

"How much that cost . . . Mel? 'Bout fifty?" Whitey wanted to know.

"Naw," Mel said. "Agee paid eighty-five thousand CASH for his."

"My uncle died," Agee said.

"BUZZ. Wrong answer! Don't try to lie to the paper-gods, Agee. I checked the National Registry on inheritances. No such luck."

"And besides . . . I'm a good saver."

"Maybe you are . . . let's see . . . what kind of car do you drive to the office?"

"My old Toyota. It's a ten-year-old model and it's paid for. WOW, so sue me."

"Yeah, but what about that brand-new Cadillac you have in the garage at home? Fifty-five thousand for that, I believe."

Whitey scanned the sheet over her shoulder.

"Cash?" Daryl asked.

"Looks like," Whitey replied.

"I traded in several old cars and an old boat . . . got some money together . . . bought it."

"Is that how you bought that cabin in Big Bear?"

"A cabin in Big Bear?" the officers queried. Daryl stood and joined Whitey as they advanced on Agee.

"You guys stay away from me! I'll scream brutality. Don't touch me."

She scanned several papers and selected a new one. "And then there's some gambling losses in Vegas."

*Bluffing is good.*

"Yeah." His fingers splayed across the table, tapping it over and over. He added, "Yeah, I forgot. That's where I got some of my money too . . . you win some . . . you lose some. I was lucky. That ain't against the law."

It was a hit she could not ignore. "Not reporting it, *is*." She leaned over and showed him. "The IRS says you reported only your ordinary salary for the past ten years," Mel said.

"And, of course, not reporting income from legal, as well as illegal sources, could get you in a lot of trouble with the IRS too . . . not to mention this murder rap." Whitey added.

She handed Daryl a page. He said, "It's my turn. Talk more about the income? What about the rental units you have?"

"Rental units?" Whitey's eyes widened with anger. "Why you asshole . . . you'll burn for all this shit . . . really burn."

"Has this been going on a long time, Mel?" Whitey inquired.

"Ten years at least. I can go back in the records history further. But, I have enough to tie him into drug dealing for ten years . . . with what I have here, today."

"We got you dead-bang, guy. Assets . . . murder . . . money. Wow. What a nice haul," Whitey said.

Mel continued. "Agee, let's discuss this little line-item. It appears that some of those assets were purchased at a great discount or given to you by a big corporation. Ever heard of Stanford Acquisition?"

"Nope." Agee answered.

"Try harder."

Whitey asked, "You don't want to go down alone. Do you?"

*Silence.*

They waited.

Then he answered, "Okay—Okay . . . so let's say . . . we could maybe make a deal. I won't go down by myself . . . you know. First now . . . I didn't kill T-Bone and I'm not gonna burn for it. You might get me for the dealing, you know, about the drug skimming. But no murder rap."

"Oh, Agee. Just giving up a couple of druggies ain't enough, big guy. We want it all . . . right now. We ain't dealing and you're not in a good position to negotiate."

"No deal then. You ain't getting shit from me!" Agee crossed his arms across his chest and stared at the ashtray.

The officers walked to the door and opened it. That startled Mel.

She did not want to leave. Not now. *Let's keep the pressure on. He hasn't asked for a lawyer yet. Guys, don't fold now.*

Whitey motioned for her to leave. She reluctantly did as she was told.

Mel, Whitey, and Daryl walked through the squad room and X-Ray and Chief Murdoch followed. The large room bustled with activity, men talked and phones rang. But the solemn procession ignored it all.

Once inside Chief Murdoch office, they closed the door. Mel gave her papers to X-Ray. He scanned them and handed them to Chief Murdoch. She sat on a bench while Whitey and Daryl read them more closely.

X-Ray spoke first. "Okay, what are our choices here?"

"Can you deal?" Mel wanted to know.

"Well . . . yes and no." Murdoch answered. "We don't really have the authority to deal. That shit you see in the movies is just that . . . shit. On the asset forfeiture, we can make an election not to file on his assets . . . i.e., let him keep 'em."

"We can also write a letter to the DA and request a plea for leniency in return for his cooperation," X-Ray said.

Whitey added. "And we can let him out on OR and put a wire on him."

"That OR. Is that 'own recognizance'?" Mel asked.

"Yeah."

"But, guys. I don't want the next druggie in line in the foodchain. I want the guys who killed my dad."

They turned to Mel. "You mean you don't have any proof it was Agee?"

266

"Nice bluff, huh? I have no proof. None whatsoever. In fact, I believe there were at least one or two others in this with him. Not in the dealing, but in the killing."

"Okay it's your turn . . . give it up Mel," X-Ray said.

She opened her briefcase and pulled out the larger pictures of the crime scene.

"Barry has a set of his very own. If we can get a search warrant of Agee's house and if we can match his feet," she selected another photo and pointed, "or any of his shoes to these . . . we can place him at the scene."

"Aren't these CSI feet?" X-Ray asked.

"Do they conduct their investigations in bare feet?" Mel asked.

"No," Chief Murdoch replied, looking more carefully at the picture. "Mm."

He handed the photo to X-Ray who reviewed it, then handed it to Whitey and Daryl.

"Do they conduct their investigations in tennis shoes?" Mel asked.

"No," Chief Murdoch replied.

"At least two people were there. One wore tennies and the other was barefoot." Mel said.

"Even if we can get a search warrant for him and his home, this doesn't put the weapon in his hand," X-Ray said.

"That's true. I'm still working on that." Mel said.

"Well, I like the twist we've got on him so far. He's sweating bullets right now. We have forty-eight hours before we have to give notice to attach his assets. So we move now. Make him believe we'll try for straight possession. Maybe he could do one year county-time with three years probation, and when he's done about nine months of that sentence, he can go sailing away on his boat. Far, far, away. Free and clear." X-Ray sighed.

"But he's gotta wear a wire and . . . he's gotta give us the dopers and the murderers. AND . . . if he was there at the scene, he gets Murder Two, on top of the drug time." Chief Murdoch said.

"So. if he wasn't in on the murder, he has nothing to lose." Daryl said.

"That makes my bluff work, doesn't it?" Mel asked.

"Yeah. That makes it work. And I like it," Murdoch replied, smiling for the first time since Mel entered his office.

## ∞33

Ten minutes later with the plan finalized, Whitey and Daryl returned to the interrogation room. Mel joined X-Ray and Chief Murdoch behind the mirrored wall in the adjacent room.

Sweat glistened on Agee's face, around the collar of his shirt and under his arms. Mel hoped the officers would notice this and use it to their advantage.

Whitey spoke first, outlining the proposed deal. "But you'll have to deliver three-for-one. You know the routine . . . we want the top drug-dog . . . AND the guys who helped you murder T-Bone."

"I'm telling you guys. I never killed nobody."

"Would you be willing to give us permission to search your home?"

"Sure, that ain't no problem. What else?"

"Can we take a photograph of your bare feet?"

"My feet?" He pulled off his shoes and socks.

"God . . . Agee!" Whitey said, backing away. "Don't you ever take a bath? The fumes are melting my contacts."

Daryl held the camera and his breath and snapped two pictures.

"I don't know what that's all about, but that's no big deal."

"Thanks," Whitey answered. "Sign this permission slip for us to search your home . . . 'eh . . . homes . . . boat . . . and any storage areas."

"Sure." He read the warrant and scribbled his name. His hands shook. "I'm not sure what you want with my shoes because, guys, as I told you, I didn't have anything to do with the murder. I swear . . . I just do drugs. I swear."

"Whoever killed T-Bone left their foot prints in the sand at the crime scene."

"No shit?" Agee exclaimed loudly. "Well that'll clear me. Take all the friggin' pictures and shoes you want as evidence. Because," he emphasized, "I wasn't there. I didn't do it."

"Who did?"

"Ramirez."

The bombshell hit both rooms. Both Whitey and Daryl stared at the mirror. And, on the other side, Mel and Chief Murdoch stared open-mouthed at Xavier Ramirez. No one was more shocked than X- Ray.

"Ramirez!" Whitey and Daryl exclaimed.

Agee laughed so hard he got the hiccups. "You silly bastards NOT OUR RAMIREZ! It's the snitches . . . Ramirez."

In the next room Mel gripped X-Ray's arm and whispered expectantly, "That's what the date book meant."

Chief Murdoch said, "What date book?"

"I found Dad's calendar, and on the afternoon on the day he died, his entry said, 'Meet Ramirez'."

"God . . . Mel," X-Ray said. "That's right. I remember Johnnie found the calendar in the black trash bag."

"I thought, naturally enough, that Dad was making reference to X- Ray. Obviously the entry meant the CIs, not you." Mel said.

X-Ray left Mel and the Chief behind in the witness room and burst into the interrogation room. "So guys, how're we doing?"

His sense of naivete about the newly discovered information caused Mel to smile.

Agee spun in his chair and hiccupped. "You assholes . . . don't kid me. You heard it all . . . you was on the mirror side."

"Not me, man. I was . . . uh . . . doing some reports."

Daryl decided to repeat the deal and pass it by Agee once more. Mel knew a pattern of consistency would be important right now.

"We told Agee we couldn't cut no big, you know . . . really big deal without a three-fer. Like he's gotta give us three giant goodies and we'd pass on the asset forfeiture and seek maybe . . . Murder Two, where he has some chance of parole in this lifetime."

Agee, who had been facing Daryl, turned and slammed both palms on the small table.

"So gimme three, Agee . . . We need three. You know the rules. It's three-for-one."

"I can promise you this: I-personally-did-NOT-do it . . . you know, kill T-Bone. I got no beef against him."

"He wasn't close to you on the drug thing?"

"If he was, he never once let me know. I swear."

"Was he onto your big coke deals, cutting it and all?" Whitey asked, propping one leg on one of the empty chairs.

"If he was, I don't know that, either. He never let on he was checking us. Guys, you gotta believe me. I didn't kill him." Agee pulled at his greasy hair, twisting it through his equally grimy fingers.

X-Ray turned toward the door, sighed deeply and shook his head. "Oh, man . . . That's too bad . . . I need three. Two perps ain't enough."

"Wait a minute! Wait a minute!" Agee's hands opened to the air, as he pleaded to be heard.

"I can't give 'em to you. Let's work this out. Aw, come on guys." He implored everyone in the room, one-at-a-time, to understand his position. He begged with his eyes and pounded the desk with his fists, as heads shook with a unified resounding, "No."

X-Ray had one hand on the doorknob, but paused and turned. "There could be a way. Will you wear a wire and set a meet? We need the guy . . . guys above them. That is," he added, "unless you already know the dudes."

"I wish I did, guys. I'd sure as hell give 'em up now." Agee's elbows rested on the table. His hands held his shaking head. "I'll give you a full statement on my drug dealing and cutting it. But the Ramirez brothers were my direct sources. What didn't go into my nose, went straight to them." He shook his head. "Okay, Okay. I'll do it. I'll wear a wire . . . anything."

Whitey asked. "How far from the top dog are we?"

"I think . . . " Agee wiped his chapped lips with his hands and cleared his throat, his voice cracked, "That the Ramirez' brothers report direct to the *Man*."

Daryl interjected shouting, "Don't fuckin' lie to us, man."

"I'm not lying to you, guys. This is a huge operation. But I'm pretty sure Mr. Big is the next link in the chain."

"Make me believe you," X-Ray said.

"Gimmie a wire . . . I'll do it . . . I'll do it. Today, tomorrow . . . whenever." Agee's anxious voice wavered.

X-Ray said, "Well, a wire is a good start. Why don't you take the rest of the week off on vacation? I'll clear it with the Chief. We'll put you in a safe-house in Orange County, so if we're dealing with another dirty cop . . . " X-Ray gritted his teeth and the sentence hung in the air, unfinished.

Taking a deep breath, X-Ray warned further. "Two more things. One, I don't want any word of this to leave this room. Two, I want the wire done in twenty-four hours. I'm tired of this crap. I'm ready to get back to real police work."

He walked back and poked his index finger hard against Agee's shirt, then jerked him to his feet by the shirt front. They were face to face, nose to nose.

"Don't fuck with me, you cocksucking four-eyed piece of shit. You got twenty-four hours to turn this trick or you'll be a clear case of suicide and . . . I'll do it myself." He ground his teeth with the last words.

He released his hold on Agee's shirt and Agee floated to the floor in a cold, dead faint.

"What a pig," X-Ray said. He slammed the door behind him.

* *
*

Mel spent the next few minutes with X-Ray, Whitey and Daryl. "Thank you, guys, for all your efforts. Honestly," she told them, "I didn't think Agee would wear a wire."

*I would kill to know their plan. This is the part where the police tell me to go home and let them do the work they have to do. I hate this crap . . . this condescending crap.*

At least Mel knew the most important part of the police plan. She had less than twenty-four hours to pull an end run on them.

After some quick hugs all around with reassurances that, "We'll call you . . . don't call us," Mel left the police department and returned to her office and the computer.

"Ah, I have something the police can only dream of . . . my wonderful little machine," she muttered to herself as her fingers tapped the keys and more data filled the screen.

The department had a computer, but it belched out information in slow motion on a dated dot-matrix printer. They pulled things like NCIC matches, fingerprints, photos and the FBI and Interpol connections. But, they don't have an open exchange of data or cooperation, except between FAXes and telephones, with other law-enforcement groups, and certainly not the Pentium hot bed of Freedom-of-Information that she could punch out in a matter of minutes.

She hummed, remembering on one occasion that X-Ray referred an Orange County Deputy Sheriff to her. He was holding a soon-to-be-stale warrant and could not find the perp he had been trying to locate for months.

She had responded, "Stanley, can you hold . . . or shall I call you back?"

Stanley called her a smart alec, but expressed great sincerity regarding some future *quid-pro-quo* event for locating this particular suspect.

Mel found the perp in twenty minutes through an unlisted phone number. He was living with his girl friend in a Bethesda, Maryland, apartment that was rented in yet another party's name.

Stanley expressed his thanks, then said, "I'm teletyping my warrant to the Bethesda Police Department right now."

Today, she entered five names into her information highway pipeline. She also placed a call to Stanley for a return on her "*quo*."

"Orange County Sheriff's Department. How may I direct your call?"

"I need Stanley . . . in auto theft, I believe," she said.

"Auto Theft Division, Stanley Talbert."

"Hi, Stanley . . . Mel Walker here. Remember me?"

"Ah, yes, the computer queen. How're you doing?"

"Fine. Listen, I need a little help from you. Think you can help?"

"I'll try. Watcha need?"

She gave him the five names, "Xavier Ramirez . . . Daryl, Whitey, Agee, and Chief Murdoch."

"Let me get the spellings from you. I want to make sure I have it correct. Although I must admit, I can't promise the prompt turnaround time you're so famous for."

"So long as you get it in less than twenty-four hours, that's all I'm asking," she said.

"That, I can do. A high priority item, I assume."

"You assume correctly."

Returning to the PC, she found the information pouring in faster than the laser printer could spew out. She added more paper to the tray and went to the kitchen for some hot tea.

A ream of paper and an hour later, the computer curser blinked silently, awaiting further instructions.

In the meantime, Mel made a separate file for each of the five suspects and tabbed all the paper under a brad closure.

"What am I looking for? What is the connection here?" she asked herself. "There should be something different. More than normal, an oddity, a motive . . . a method or a means. Anybody on the short-list tied to the Ramirez' brothers?" She paced the length of the room.

There seemed to be no end and no clear answer to the tedious work.

"Maybe an outline would help . . . shit. Maybe a good stiff drink will help."

Johnnie came in to drop off some dictation and get his telephone messages. He ducked his head into her doorway and said, "Remember our training . . . 'When in doubt, think it out.' And, 'Do it smart, make a chart.' "

"Ah, butcher-paper time again," she answered. His idea seemed the best to her. "At least it's a place to go next."

She unrolled paper and laid a long horizontal piece on the floor. With a black-marker she entered a coded numeric number to track with the alphabet.

"So, dear friend X-Ray, you just became Suspect number twenty-four."

X, the twenty-fourth letter in the alphabet, appeared to be a fairly simple code, but suited her purpose fine for the time being.

It also protected her work, which could be easily observed by any of the suspects. She put thumbtacks on each end and nailed the paper across another wall of her conference room.

"If they knew, I could be in big danger."

She heard Johnnie from his office. "Shit . . . Mel, you could be killed."

The comparisons evolved. She added other people to the list . . . those who knew Dad . . . had business with him . . . with her. "Mm. Four out of eight are registered Republicans in the last election. Well, remember, this is Orange County."

She heard Johnnie laugh in the distance.

"Five of the eight file income-tax returns. Four of the six own property. Some things overlap. Others don't."

Johnnie entered the room, finishing off a sandwich. "Mm. Need any independent ideas?"

"You're right. I could be in big danger, so right now . . . the less you know, the better off you are."

"While that might sound logical to you, considering our special relationship, they might think you filled me in on everything already."

"I've thought of that. Why don't you and Cliff, or whoever it is this week, go to Palm Springs for the weekend? I should have this all resolved by next week."

"Are you sure you don't need some help? I carry a gun too, you know."

"Naw. Really. I'm just doing some heavyweight computer comparisons and X will be by later today. We'll formulate a plan together. I couldn't be in better hands than X-Ray's, now could I?"

"Yeah. I guess you're right. I do have a couple of appointments near Hemet. So I could coordinate it with the desert and take . . . what's his name . . . I guess." His head dropped to his chest.

"Now, don't get your feelings hurt. You'll be back in time for the big finale next Monday. I'm sure nothing will happen until then."

"Promise?" He hugged her.

"Would I lie to you?" She kissed him on the cheek and returned the hug.

"Well!" He turned and she swatted him on the butt as he scooted out the door. "I'll be back late Sunday afternoon. So save the cherry-topping for me, will you?"

"You got it, big guy." And under her breath, "The sundae will be melted by then."

She was glad he would be out of the area when the fireworks blew the top off the police department.

One name came up, time-after-time. "Who is this Stanford Acquisition Corporation?" She noticed more connections than she had seen earlier. Some interesting patterns ... "Mm, a real estate company ... mortgage company ... maybe a holding company. Whoever owns it, is funding at least one cop that I know of. Wonder who the Registered Agent is?"

She returned to the computer keyboard and entered her code, checked the log for the correct numbers to request the Department of Corporations data and punched them in.

The computer screen blinked. "The information will be returned to you within thirty minutes."

*Seems soon enough.*

She tapped a pencil on the side of the desk, keeping in rhythm with music only she could hear.

A thud of letters dropping through the mail-slot in the door disrupted her thoughts.

The blank screen prompted Mel to push back her chair and leave the room, thinking *a watched pot never boils.*

Mel grabbed a Coke from the refrigerator and opened it. She stopped by the conference table and glanced over the list Johnnie had left her.

"Bless his heart," she said, checking over the three pages of carefully outlined numbers, none of which opened the safe. "He's really worked on this project." She laid the list on the table, downed a slug of her cold drink and walked toward the mail clustered inside the door.

The phone rang.

She put the can on the desk and picked up the phone. "Walker Investigations. Mel Walker speaking. Can I help you?"

"Sure."

The hair on the back of her neck tingled, causing a slight shiver through her shoulder. Mel turned on her telephone recorder making sure she would have some evidence to play back later.

"I'm glad you called. I wasn't sure how to reach you two guys."

"Yo? Why'd you wanna talk with us?"

"Well, I've been shot at, run off the road, threatened over some shit like ... as I recall from one of our last conversation you want the coke, the cash and the book, right?"

"Yeah. You ready to give it up?"

"Yeah, I am, as a matter of fact. Actually, I just located the aforementioned items."

"What?"

Mel rolled her eyes.

"I couldn't find 'em till now, you stupid bastard."

"But now you have 'em?"

"Yeah."

"All of them?"

"I don't know if it's all or not."

"How're we gonna know?"

"I suggest a good, safe place to meet and you can see for yourself."

"What place would that be?"

"It sure won't be a cliff and a sandy area with boulders near Scotchman's Cove. I'm not as naive as Dad."

She heard a slight chuckle and the speaker covered the microphone to muffle his discussion with someone else.

"By the way, is this Lozano or Alfie Ramirez? I like to know who I'm speaking with."

"Lozano," he replied, hesitantly.

"Fine. I see we can work this deal out like adults. That's a good sign."

"Yo. So, if you ain't as stupid as Walker, when are we going to meet?"

"Tonight, would be good . . . right after dark. Maybe about six o'clock?"

"Yo, lady. That's fine. Where?"

"My turf. Bernie's."

"Whoa. Dat's where all the cops go, lady. We ain't stupid either."

"What better place than the parking lot at Bernie's? I'll feel safe 'cause it's a public place and . . . you can get the stuff I have and split. I'm not inviting you to dinner, asshole."

He covered the telephone receiver once more. She pressed to hear the conversation but could not make it out.

"Okay. But, we're packin' and if this is a double cross we're gonna off-you . . . right then and there. Cops, or no cops."

"Would I be that stupid? I'll be the one holding the evidence. That could get me arrested too, you know."

"Okay, six o'clock then. Be on time."

"With bells on."

"What?"

"Forget it, asshole. You wouldn't understand."

The computer beckoned. She hastened her pace, positioned herself in front of the monitor and checked the computer for paper. The screen filled with data. She scanned the monitor with her finger.

"There it is, no shit, the agent for service of process. Well . . . I'll be damned."

The printer hum signalled ready and the papers flowed through one-at-a-time. She grabbed the first one and went to the wall charts, entering some data below one suspect.

She stood back and looked long and hard at the facts entered. She plopped down and chewed on the colored marker. The more she chewed, the madder she got. Mel bounced out of her chair and went to the butcher paper. Starting with one end, using the marker, she joined that suspect's name crossed to the other line of suspects, connecting her number one suspect, to suspect number seven.

She threw the empty can across the room screaming, "Traitor. You damn traitor," she screamed.

## ∞35

Mel located one of her father's briefcases and stuffed it with paper and one of his armored vests, which had to be folded over so the case-top would lock. The brown leather had cracked in hundreds of places over time. It had a musty smell . . . but it would do.

She remembered to grab the small grocery sack with the black hood from the first assault on her, from the bottom of her desk drawer. She might need it later.

\* \*
\*

She arrived at Bernie's shortly before six o'clock, but remained in her car and slouched down in the driver's seat so that arriving patrons would not recognize her. Several cars entered the parking lot and screeched to a halt, half-blocking several marked parking stalls.

Daryl and Whitey exited one of the department's undercover cars and joined other officers, making small talk as they entered the rear door at Bernie's. The screen door slammed shut behind them.

She was glad to have the old junker to drive. The cops would have recognized her own car.

The setting sun cast shadows which gave her courage more of an edge. She pushed the cranky front door open, but remained in the driver's seat. She hugged the briefcase with both arms as if cradling something near and dear to her.

At five-forty-five, a dark-blue, late-seventies Pontiac rolled into the driveway. She saw the shadows of two heads and prayed they were alone. Gang members generally travel in larger numbers. They need an applauding crowd and are very proud of their conquests and their random revenge attacks on the innocent public.

*I have no intention of becoming another of Orange County's rising statistics of drive-bys. Not today, anyway.*

The car lights went out immediately, then blinked back on. She tapped her brake lights and made sure the ignition key was in position. She got out of the car, held the briefcase across her chest, and walked toward the darkened vehicle. Both front doors of the car opened and two men stepped out.

She focused her attention toward the driver, the taller, thinner of the two. "*Flaco?*"

"*Si,*" the skinny one answered.

"Are you Lozano?"

"*Si.* You have something for me?"

"Yeah, I do." She moved her right hand to the warm cozy place between her bosom and the suitcase. She grabbed the wood-wrapped, steel butt of her Beretta and withdrew it. She called to them, but not loud enough to draw company from within the cafe.

"First, we've got a few things to clear up."

Her action was quick, but Alfie stooped to a crouching position, pulled a gun from under his shirt and fired wildly at her.

The bullet flew by her head, which she protected by raising the armored briefcase. She aimed high and to the right, returning fire and dropped Alfie with one shot. Blood spurted against the car's hood as Alfie fell to the ground, holding his chest.

"Goddamn bitch shot me . . . Lozano, kill the bitch, *mano.*"

Lozano raised both arms, palms open, to Mel and screamed, "Don't shoot, I ain't carryin'! Oh, man! You shot my brother."

Lozano knelt and touched his brother, then, let his arms fall to his side, one of them out of Mel's view.

She hollered back, "Don't move asshole! Back away from him." She needed to get Alfie's gun, which lay somewhere near the moaning, writhing body.

The back screen-door of the cafe swung open and cops with guns drawn, filled the small opening between two parked cars.

Whitey and Daryl moved toward Mel. One gun covered her and the others covered Lozano and Alfie.

"Okay," Whitey shouted. "What's going on here? Let's drop the gun, Mel."

Daryl moved toward Lozano, motioning for him to step away from his fallen brother.

"All of you! Stay back!" She waved the gun back and forth between the cops and Lozano.

Lozano moved back, his hands raised above his head, until he reached the rear of a nearby car.

"No way, Mel. We can't have you shooting private citizens. Let's have it. We don't want anyone else to get hurt."

"Bullshit, you guys. What we have here are two cop killers. And they're all mine."

"It's not a 'mine' and 'yours' kind of thing, Mel. Let us do our job." Whitey said.

"I tried that. Now, we'll do it my way."

She advanced on Lozano and fired a shot over his head, missing him by ten feet. The bullet slammed into a billboard.

"Yo, Man. Make her stop. Make her stop." Lozano cried out.

"Geez, Mel." Whitey lowered his gun. "I thought you was a better shot than that."

Daryl got the hint and lowered his as well, adding, "That one was a little high. Aim a little lower, to the left, I think. That'd be just about right . . . huh, Whitey?"

"Yeah."

"Yo guys. We gotta right to be protected. You can't let the bitch shoot us. We got rights."

"Just like the rights you gave my Dad?"

"We didn't kill Walker. I swear."

She fired again, striking a wooden fence behind the car. Lozano jumped and fell to his knees, his hands now in the air. "You know the arrest routine," Mel shouted to him.

Lozano crossed his legs behind him and put both palms together, locking fingers behind his head.

"Why'd you mug me in the cemetery?"

"We was looking for Walker's book and stuff."

"Look, I got no gun. You can't let her kill us like this . . . in cold blood."

"As I recall . . . that's exactly how Walker got it."

"Yeah, in cold blood." Whitey replied.

The circle of four got no closer. Mel moved in and kicked Alfie's gun clear of his body. Whitey protected the crime scene by standing over the gun.

"You killed my Dad and you know it! And now I know it. And now you'll tell these nice officers exactly how you did it . . . won't you?"

"Yo bitch, I'm telling you. Like we didn't burn nobody. Not Walker. Nobody."

She fired again.

Lozano bent over and flinched.

Daryl spoke. "Aw, Mel. I've been at the gun range with you lotsa times. You can sure as hell shoot straighter than that."

"Oh geez." Lozano dropped his shaking head.

"What would you say if I told you I had clear evidence you did?"

"You can't prove nothing, bitch."

"Well, let's try this scenario on for size. My Dad had an appointment with you the night he was killed. Your names were on his calendar."

"That ain't shit."

She shot again. This time the bullet whizzed closer to his right ear. "Shut up, asshole."

The two undercovers chuckled and motioned to the other officers who had joined the stand-off. Those cops re-holstered their weapons and stood next to the cafe, witnessing events.

"So, you assholes got him to meet you . . . on some pretext, at the cliff and somehow, probably with a chop to the neck or a stun gun, you knocked him out long enough to get his gun from his holster. You then put his right hand around the gun, after cleaning your prints from it. Then you put it in his mouth and pulled the trigger. That's how you got gun powder on his hands."

"You can't prove none of that, bitch."

"Oh, I probably can. I have the bare footprints of one of you, and the tennis shoe prints from the other. One of you has a deformed big toe. I believe they will match you both, nicely. And one of you must be bandaged somewhere from a gunshot wound, from when you were shooting at me from the bluffs near my home."

Lozano's eyebrows closed tighter as he squeezed his eyes and grimaced. He pleaded with Whitey and Daryl. "Can we deal? We need a deal."

"Sure," Whitey answered, "we can deal. We won't let Mel kill you, if you give it up."

"That's a deal? What kinda fuckin' deal is that?" Lozano cried out.

"Sounds fair to me," Daryl answered.

"Shit, that ain't no fucking deal."

Daryl added. "Oh, we could sweeten it a bit. Like . . . if you give up who hired you. You two did the contract. But you two don't have the balls to burn Walker . . . not for nothing."

Mel's gun remained poised at Lozano as she moved into a closer position and pointed at his heart.

"Time to shit, or get off the pot, *flaco*," she whispered.

"Okay, Okay, let's deal. We can deal. What do we do?"

Mel needed confirmation. "Let's see if my story so far works for us."

"Yeah, yeah . . . that works," Lozano answered. He gritted his teeth and swallowed hard.

"And," she wanted more, "you did shoot at me from the cliffs one night. I know my friend must have winged one of you. Which one got the bullet?"

"Yo, yeah. That was me." Lozano, his hands still in the air, pointed at the front of his shirt with one hand. "We done that."

"What about the breaking into my home and hurting Rosa? Who hit her?" Mel asked.

"Yeah, Alfie, he did that one." Lozano replied.

"You ran me off the road last week too," she said confidently.

"No, you can't stick us with that. We wasn't anywhere near you that night," Lozano pleaded.

Mel conceded, "Okay, not that one for now. But I know you guys were doing some big-time drugs with Agee as one partner. I would guess you guys had the scam neatly worked out. Agee would take the cocaine destined for the incinerator and drive off in the van, like he was routinely destroying it. But, you guys would meet along the way and exchange it for some nothing shit. You then stole the coke, big volumes I suspect . . . about twelve or fifteen kilos at a time."

Lozano nodded with each sentence. Mel inhaled again.

"You were running drugs for someone with brains, money and influence. Like someone who could go your bail, give you some property to live in, so you could cut it and store it safely. Somebody like Stanford Acquisition Mortgage Company. Somebody to get you wheels, like this car. Someone like Jeffrey Williams, Attorney at Law."

## ∞*36*

Both Whitey and Daryl stood wide-eyed, staring between Lozano's nodding head and Mel's well-aimed gun.

"Yeah," Lozano answered. "Yo ... I'm glad that's over."

"Oh, it isn't over, Lozano." Whitey walked over with his handcuffs. "Not nearly over ... yet."

\* \*
\*

Mel and Johnnie drove along Pacific Coast Highway toward the police department, making small talk.

"Jelly did a great job repairing the car huh?" Johnnie asked.

"Yeah."

"I knew you wanted to be there at Jeffrey's office when they arrested him."

"You bet your ass I did." Mel's eyes never left the road. Her anger boiled at the crushing traffic which barred her route toward her goal.

"I think, at least from what X-Ray told me that the cops were afraid you'd come in like a commando . . . and shoot him."

"They're probably right."

"Well, at least you didn't kill Alfie. That was a nice shoulder shot."

"I could have killed them both, like *that*." She snapped her fingers.

"With no remorse?" He quit smiling.

"None whatsoever."

"Well, at least we can be there when they bring JW in."

"Jeffrey Williams . . . his big, fancy Wilshire office, silk suits and his view of the Hollywood Hills."

"We still have a trial ahead of us, Mel. But at least all the confessions clicked. What are they going to do, if anything is said about you firing the gun?"

"I don't know . . . guess I'll find out soon enough."

"Is your CWP license current?"

"My California Weapon Permit? I think so."

"Well . . . here we are," Johnnie said.

The parking lot buzzed with patrol cars. She made two sweeps through and finally parked in her father's old spot, now formally used by the daily squad leader.

Mel presented herself to the desk-clerk who buzzed her and Johnnie past the reception area. As they entered the squad room, Mel noticed the air-conditioning was not working. She could hardly catch a breath. The air hung sticky, noisy and thick.

Johnnie tugged at his shirt-collar.

One uniform motioned them, without a word, toward Chief Murdoch's office. Mel nodded.

The empty office greeted them. "We must be early," Johnnie said.

"That's okay. It's important that I see the expression on JW's face when they bring him in."

"I know."

They sat without talking further while the department buzzed with activity beyond the doors. Ten minutes passed when the hum suddenly rose, causing Mel to stop pacing, walk to the blinds and peek through.

"They're bringing him in now," she said. Without waiting for Johnnie or any further instructions from the cops, she burst into the room and ran toward the attorney.

Jeffrey had dressed in his finest suit on this day of his arrest, the dark-blue, silk one with the small lapels and closed back flaps. He wore a red-and-blue striped tie over a woven Egyptian, white-on-white, cotton shirt.

"Mel," he pleaded, "they have this all wrong. I'd never have Bill killed. You know me."

"Yeah, I know you, you traitor." She slapped him across the face as Whitey and Daryl, the two arresting officers, intercepted her next move.

"At least she doesn't have her gun," Whitey replied.

"Can we talk about this. I'm sure there's been a great misunderstanding. I'm a respected member of the Bar."

"There ain't no such thing," Whitey mocked. "There's respected people and then there's lawyers. The two are not compatible." He moved the foursome toward an interrogation room.

At the room they paused. Chief Murdoch, X-Ray and Johnnie joined them. Chief Murdoch gave the orders. "Mel you can't go in there this time. Come on with me. X . . . you and Whitey and Daryl conduct the interview."

They guided the handcuffed attorney inside the room and closed the door behind them. Chief Murdoch motioned Mel and Johnnie to join him in the adjoining room behind the reflection mirrors. They followed as instructed, without another word, and sat facing the mirror.

"I apologize, Mr. Lawyer. But our air-conditioning seems to be on the blink today . . . so it's a little close in here and the quicker we're done here, the faster we can get you into a cooler place."

X-Ray offered his explanation as Jeffrey sat in the chair recently occupied by Agee. They removed the handcuffs.

"Want a cigarette?" Whitey asked.

"No."

Whitey tapped the end of the package, removing one for himself.

"Since the air is out, please don't add to the pollution," JW said.

Whitey lit one anyway, drawing a long drag and filling the stale air with smoke.

X-Ray led the questioning. "You know we wouldn't have brought you in today without some pretty good cause, don't you?"

"You might think you do, but you're mistaken. I didn't kill Bill. And I didn't order any contract on him. I loved him."

"Well, this is how this case stands. You can confess now and save us, and the state, a lot of paper work. Or, you can stay in here until you're ready to tell us why you had him killed."

"We have several confessions, you know." Daryl tightened the noose.

Jeffrey loosened his tie and unbuttoned the top button of his shirt. "I'm sure I don't know what they, whoever they are, confessed to. Because I don't know anything, about any murder."

"We can agree, then . . . it was a murder, not a suicide?" X-Ray wanted the comment made.

"Well, uh . . . I'm merely repeating what you said. That you think I hired some people to kill . . . somebody. So that would be a murder wouldn't it?"

The exchange went on for hours. First, X-Ray would leave the room and then return to relieve Whitey and Daryl. Mel stayed glued to the reflection mirror, becoming increasingly angry as time passed.

Chief Murdoch left to take an urgent call. When he returned he dropped some papers in Mel's lap.

"You might as well go home, Mel. We may be here all night and beyond. But these," he gestured, "should clear a few loose ends for you."

She read the material. He interrupted. "Remember, we had two deaths labeled suicides that month?"

"Yeah. Dad and Detective David Frasier. I remember."

"Well, according to Lozano and Alfie's confessions, Jeffrey hired them to kill a bad cop who had skimmed some coke off the top and cheated Jeffrey on some of his deals."

"Yeah?" she answered, somewhat puzzled.

"Well, the boys have identified T-Bone as the one they killed."

"Yeah? I still don't get it. Who did Agee ID as the bad cop; Dad or Frasier?"

"Agee identified Frasier."

She held the papers in one hand and turned to the mirror.

"So Frasier's death really *was* a suicide? He knew he'd be caught or killed sooner or later for skimming drugs from JW. Can I tell JW? I need to be the one to tell him." She pleaded.

"Sure, what have we got to lose?" Chief Murdoch stepped aside.

Mel knocked on the interrogation room door and X-Ray admitted her, a baffled look on his face.

"I carry news . . . hot off the presses, guys."

"Okay," they responded, stepping back to admit her into the already cramped quarters. Her lungs briefly contained the only fresh air around.

Mel squared her shoulders and walked straight toward the side of the table. Her eyes, already inflamed from the close air in the room, were red with anger. She brushed her hair back and battled her rising temper as she leaned over to whisper, but loud enough for everyone in the room to hear.

"Tell me about Stanford Acquisition Mortgage Corporation?" she asked.

"I never heard of it, Mel," JW replied.

"Don't you know you can't hide from my trusty computer, JW? You are Stanford. *You* used a corporate-veil to hide assets from drug sales. I should have realized you were a coke head. You displayed too many signs that I overlooked until now. You also provided Agee, Lozano and Alfie with funds, houses, cars, boats and other goodies from that company."

"Mel, I wouldn't get involved in drugs and . . . I certainly wouldn't associate with those scum bags. You must believe me."

"I remember your nose bothering you both at Patty's Christmas party and again when I met you in the office. You also scratch yourself a lot. I suspect the police can do a search warrant and find you are holding, selling, and using narcotics."

"Honestly, Mel, you don't know what you're talking about." He stared at Mel through cold, emotionless eyes.

*Time for the big guns,* Mel thought.

"The confessions are in. JW. Two cops died. Can we agree on that?"

"Yeah, so what?" JW replied.

"Detective David Frasier and Detective William 'T-Bone' Walker. Dad . . . the good cop and Frasier . . . the bad cop. You put a hit out on Frasier. The Ramirez' brothers killed Dad. They killed the wrong cop. Frasier really was a suicide. You're only as sick as your secret . . . set it free, J.W."

She turned and left the room, joining Johnnie along the way through the great room which was now filled with painful sounds from the interrogation room. Sounds of an animal caught in a trap.

# *Epilogue*

A small band of people gathered in the new offices of "Walker Investigations" to celebrate the death-penalty verdict and a late Christmas.

Earlier Johnnie and his friends had strung lights across the eaves and lined up more lights along the walkway. Inside, a large Christmas tree trimmed with twinkling lights, ornaments and old fashioned popcorn-and-cranberry garlands filled the reception area. Music from the stereo proclaimed this a radiant holiday season. Champagne and Mexican food flowed freely, with Rosa working hard to please the guests.

Well after midnight, the crowd dwindled to Johnnie, Mel, X-Ray, Lucas, and Rosa.

"I have one more gift for you, X-Ray." Mel said.

"You didn't have to do anything special. What is it?"

"Open it."

Inside a gaily-wrapped box, a brown grocery bag lay inside white tissue paper.

"You've been carrying that sack around for days. What's in it?" Johnnie asked.

X-Ray unfolded it and laughed as he withdrew a home-made black hood with a venetian-blind cord strung through the edges.

"That's your personal 'humnet'," Mel said. You have to keep the hood till you solve your next crime."

X-Ray told everyone about the 'humnet,' then stuck his tongue out at Mel.

"Speaking of a 'hummer' day, did you ever get the safe open?" X- Ray asked.

"No, but we've been working on it," Mel replied.

"Me too." Johnnie said.

"You too, sweetie. But you're much too drunk to work on anything else tonight. Need some help?" Mel asked.

"No, thank you." Johnnie answered indignantly."I can fall upstairs by myself." He staggered through the kitchen spelling C-R-A-P.

Mel snapped her fingers. "Johnnie, that's it."

"That's what?" X-Ray demanded, also a bit intoxicated.

"The combination! It was there all along." She dropped to her knees and pulled back the rug covering the safe opening. Mel spelled out C-A-D-S, while turning the combination lock. First to the right, then left, right and left again.

Nothing.

Mel spun the tumbler again. This time she started with a turn to the left. When she stopped there was an audible click.

"Shit." Lucas hiccuped.

Mel pulled the safe-door open and peered into the well. On top of a stack of papers was an envelope addressed to her. She easily fell into the Lotus position and called to Johnnie, "Come back here. I got it open."

Johnnie came tripping back into the room, "You got what opened? What's all the excitement about?"

She opened the envelope and read out loud for all to hear:

*Dear Mel,*
*So you finally found the safe and opened it. I*
*must be dead. Hopefully, I've lived to a ripe old*

*age and you're happily married again, retired and resting on a beach in Hawaii somewhere. I never liked Taylor, you know. What an asshole.*

*Now, if I died under mysterious circumstances, I was killed by or at the direction of Jeffrey Williams. Another asshole attorney in our lives. It's a long story involving bad cops and the Ramirez brothers and cocaine. I'm just about to wrap it up and turn everybody in. See envelope C for my evidence and notes. I could not leave it in the safe-deposit box in case Williams got to it first.*

*About the large sums of money being deposited to my bank accounts. It isn't graft or anything like that. I wanted to tell you, but I just couldn't. I could not even tell the guys at the department. They'd just laugh at me for wanting to keep working. I won the lottery! I won one million-six-hundred-thousand dollars. It's paid annually for twenty years. I get eighty thousand dollars, less twenty-eight percent, which the government takes as taxes, for a net to me of fifty-seven-thousand dollars. Can you believe, I used Carole's and my birth-dates?*

*I would have told you about the lottery ticket and paid back what I owed you, but you were going through that messy divorce and I did not want to jeopardize your ability to keep the house and car. I worried that if you had a lot of money, that you would not come out of the divorce as well financially, so I kept it from you too. Then your business started doing better, and well, I thought I'd save it for you. For a rainy day.*

*I don't need much to live on. The house is free and clear and I use a police car. I really appreciate you being there for us financially when Carole was so sick. And now it's pay back time. I hope this will be a nice nest-egg for your future. I love you honey. Take care of yourself . . . and be happy."*

*Love, Dad*

They stood in a small circle hugging each other and crying as Mel finished reading the letter.

Then X-Ray laughed.

"Now he tells us," he said.

## About the Author

Joyce Spizer, a Texan, Oregonian, Californian is described in *International Who's Who of Professionals 1996*, as "married to Harold ... enjoys writing, golf, travel and charity work." Considered the "Hart-to-Hart" of investigators in Southern California, Joyce and Harold have a large portfolio of prominent cases including such stars as Frank Sinatra, Joan Rivers, Rosanne Barr, Juliet Prowse, Michael Jackson, and most recently the death of gansta rapper, Biggie Smalls.

An animal lover, Joyce is looking for the perfect Bichon Frise to replace her beloved Max who lived to age fourteen. "Max was the perfect critic. He loved all my stories."

When asked about her writing future, the author replied, "I won't quit writing until my brain's empty. And right now it's full of stories of intrigue, death and dismemberment, betrayal and government cover-ups, which will all be fictionalized to protect both the innocent ... and the guilty." Stay tuned ...

# DEADLY DREAMS
## by Gerald A. Schiller

*It was happening again . . . the mist . . . struggling to find her way. Then . . . the images . . . grotesque, distorted figures under plastic sheeting, and white-coated, masked figures moving toward her . . .*

When Denise Burton's recurring nightmares suddenly begin to take shape in reality, she is forced to begin a search . . . a search to discover the truth behind these horrific dreams.

The search will lead her into a series of dangerous encounters . . . in a desert ghost-town, within the restricted laboratories of Marikem, the chemical company where she works, with a brutal drug dealer and with a lover who is not what he seems.

A riveting thriller.

ISBN 1-881164-81-0
$9.95

A thriller of fear and retaliation, *Gary Phillips,* **author of Perdition, USA;** . . . promising gambits .. a *Twilight Zone* appetizer, **Kirkus Reviews;** . . . a brisk, dialogue-driven story of nasty goings-on and cover-ups in the labs of a giant chemical works with a perky, attractive, imperiled heroine, *Charles Champlin* **[Los Angeles Times].**

# TWISTED

## CAHROUL CRAMER

As the Chief of Homicide, the newly
promoted Lieutenant Turner Fleece was
expected to act as a supervisor and not as
an investigator. But when an up and
coming recording artist and her lover are
brutally murdered in the woman's San
Francisco home, the thrill of the hunt is
more than Fleece can resist. He is
seductively led through a maze of deceit
and corruption. And at the very moment
when it seems he has untangled the
mystery, he realizes it has only become
more twisted.

SBN 1-886411-82-9
LCCN: 97-42995
$9.95

# Murder in Amsterdam
## Baantjer

The two very first "DeKok" stories for the first time in a single volume, containing *DeKok and the Sunday Strangler* and *DeKok and the Corpse on Christmas Eve.*

First American edition of these European
Best-Sellers in a single volume.
### Second Printing

From critical reviews of **Murder in Amsterdam**:

If there could be another Maigret-like police detective, he might well be Detective-Inspector DeKok of the Amsterdam police. Similarities to Simenon abound in any critical judgement of Baantjer's work (*Bruce Cassiday*, **International Association of Crime Writers**); The two novellas make an irresistible case for the popularity of the Dutch author. DeKok's maverick personality certainly makes him a compassionate judge of other outsiders and an astute analyst of antisocial behavior (*Marilyn Stasio*, **The New York Times Book Review**); Both stories are very easy to take (**Kirkus Reviews**); Inspector DeKok is part Columbo, part Clouseau, part genius, and part imp. Baantjer has managed to create a figure hapless and honorable, bozoesque and brilliant, but most importantly, a body for whom the reader finds compassion (*Steven Rosen*, **West Coast Review of Books**); Readers of this book will understand why the author is so popular in Holland. His DeKok is a complex, fascinating individual (*Ray Browne*, **CLUES: A Journal of Detection**); This first translation of Baantjer's work into English supports the mystery writer's reputation in his native Holland as a Dutch Conan Doyle. His knowledge of esoterica rivals that of Holmes, but Baantjer wisely uses such trivia infrequently, his main interests clearly being detective work, characterization and moral complexity (**Publishers Weekly**).

ISBN: 1-881164-00-4
LCCN: 96-36722
$9.95

# *DeKok and Murder in Ecstasy*
## Baantjer

The driver is killed, shot down, during the assault on an armored truck. An especially cowardly act, according to eye witenesses. The robber made a special effort to turn back and fire two bullets through the head of the victim. Within an hour after the event, DeKok is already in the middle of the investigation. Is it a coincidence that the transport was carrying an unusually large amount, this time? DeKok, like most policemen, does not believe in coincidences. He fears that the affair is less simple than it appears. He *knows* that the hunt for the murderer is just the beginning and the driver is not going to be the only victim in this macabre dance for more than $3 million. He looks at Vledder, his assistant, who is composing the text of the All-Points-Bulletin: "You know, Dick," he says sadly, "money . . . money is an invention of the devil. Some are possessed by it."

*Also a major motion picture, directed by Hans Scheepmaker.*

ISBN: 1-881164-16-0
LCCN: 97-42994
$9.95

*Also From InterContinental Publishing:*

# VENGEANCE: Prelude to Saddam's War
## by Bob Mendes

Shocking revelations concerning his past move Michel Moreels, a Belgian industrial agent and consultant, to go to work for the Israeli Mossad. His assignment is to infiltrate a clandestine arms project designed to transform Iraq into a major international military power. Together with his girlfriend, Anna Steiner, he travels to Baghdad and succeeds in winning the trust of Colonel Saddiq Qazzaz, an officer of the *Mukhabarat*, the dreaded Iraqi Secret Police. At the risk of his own life and that of Anna, he penetrates the network of the illegal international arms trade, traditionally based in Brussels and the French-speaking part of Belgium. He meets American scientist Gerald Bull, a ballistic expert. Gradually it becomes clear to Michel that neither Bull, nor Anna, are what they appear to be. The more he learns about international secret services and the people who are determined to manipulate him, the more his Iraqi mission takes on a personal character: one of Vengeance!

A "faction-thriller" based on actual events in Iraq and Western Europe.
A Bertelsmann (Europe) Book Club Selection.
First American edition of this European Best-Seller.

## ISBN 1-881164-71-3  ($9.95)

Bob Mendes is the winner of the (1993) "Gouden Strop" (Golden Noose). The "Golden Noose" is an annual award given to the best thriller or crime/spy novel published in the Dutch language. "An intelligent and convincing intrigue in fast tempo; in writing *Vengeance*, Bob Mendes has produced a thriller of international allure." **(From the Jury's report for the Golden Noose, 1993)** . . . Compelling and well-documented—Believable—a tremendously exciting thriller—a powerful visual ability—compelling, tension–filled and extremely well written—rivetting action and finely detailed characters—smooth transition from fact to fiction and back again . . . **(a sampling of Dutch and Flemish reviews).**

# ALSO FROM INTERCONTINENTAL PUBLISHING:

**TENERIFE!** (ISBN 1-881164-51-9 / $7.95) by Elsinck: A swiftly paced, hard-hitting story. Not for the squeamish. But nevertheless, a compelling read, written in the short take technique of a hard-sell TV commercial with whole scenes viewed in one- and two-second shots, and no pauses to catch the breath (*Bruce Cassiday*, **International Association of Crime Writers**); A fascinating work combining suspense and the study of a troubled mind to tell a story that compels the reader to continue reading (*Mac Rutherford*, **Lucky Books**); This first effort by Elsinck gives testimony to the popularity of his subsequent books. This contemporary thriller pulls no punches. A nail-biter, full of European suspense (**The Book Reader**).*

**MURDER BY FAX** (ISBN 1-881164-52-7 / $7.95) by Elsinck: Elsinck has created a technical tour-de-force. This high-tech version of the epistolary novel succeeds as the faxed messages quickly prove capable of providing plot, clues and characterization (**Publishers Weekly**); This novel by Dutch author Elsinck is so interestingly written it might be read for its creative style alone. It is sharp and concise and one easily becomes involved enough to read it in one sitting. MURDER BY FAX cannot help but have its American readers fall under the spell of this highly original author (*Paulette Kozick*, **West Coast Review of Books**); This clever and breezy thriller is a fun exercise. Elsinck's spirit of inventiveness keeps you guessing up to the satisfying end (*Timothy Hunter*, [Cleveland] **Plain Dealer**); The use of modern technology is nothing new, but Dutch writer Elsinck takes it one step further (*Peter Handel*, **San Francisco Chronicle**).

**CONFESSION OF A HIRED KILLER** (ISBN 1-881164-53-5 / $8.95) by Elsinck: Elsinck saves a nice surprise, despite its wild farrago of murder and assorted intrigue (**Kirkus Reviews**); Reading Elsinck is like peeling an onion. Once you have pulled away one layer, you'll find an even more intriguing scenario. (*Paulette Kozick*, **Rapport**) Elsinck remains a valuable asset to the thriller genre. He is original, writes in a lively style and researches his material with painstaking care (*de Volkskrant*, **Amsterdam**).

---

* Contains graphic descriptions of explicit sex and violence.